To

Tim Wynne-Jones

The Pepper Trader

With best wishes,

Geoff Bennett

GEOFFREY BENNETT

THE
PEPPER
TRADER

*True Tales of the German East Asia Squadron
and the Man who Cast them in Stone*

illustrated by Karel Doruyter

EQUINOX
PUBLISHING
JAKARTA SINGAPORE

PT EQUINOX PUBLISHING INDONESIA
Menara Gracia 6/F
Jl. HR Rasuna Said Kav C-17
Jakarta 12940

www.EquinoxPublishing.com

Text © 2006 Geoffrey Bennett
Illustrations ©2006 Karel Doruyter

ISBN 979-3780-26-6

The Pepper Trader is published with the kind support of

 Embassy of the
Federal Republic of Germany
Jakarta

Printed in Indonesia.

To Dr. Robby Ko

A distinguished Indonesian doctor, naturalist, speleologist and educator –
an enthusiastic historian who introduced me to Artja

And to my three friends, mentors and storytellers

Nanno Nommensen   *Pater Adolf Heuken*   *Alex Papadimitriou*

And in memory of Adja

THE INDONESIAN LANGUAGE

The modern Indonesian, Javanese and Sundanese alphabets are pronounced much the same as in English, with the following exceptions:

c or *tj* like *ch* (during the Dutch era the letter *c* was spelled *tj*)
dj in old names is pronounced like *j*
g is always hard as in *g*arden
i like *ee*
sy like *sh*
u like *oo*
y as in English except in *Y*ogyakarta, pronounced *J*og*j*akarta

All letters are enunciated, including the final letter *e*.

For example:

cuti like *chootee*
Arca (or *Artja*) like *Archa*
Gede like *G'day*
Puncak like *Poonchak*

Ci is the Sundanese prefix for river and is prononounced *chee*. Many villages in West Java are named after a nearby river.

With the exception of *Artja*, *Adja* and *Po Tjong*, all Indonesian words, names and places are given the modern "post Dutch era" spelling.

GLOSSARY

aduh	–	an exclamation	*kretek*	–	clove cigarette
amok	–	berserk	*kris*	–	sacred dagger
bahasa	–	language	*mandi*	–	washroom
batu	–	stone	*nasi goreng*	–	fried rice
belum	–	not yet	*orang*	–	person
dalang	–	puppet-master	*Pak*	–	sir or Mr.
dukun	–	healer, soothsayer	*pikul*	–	bundle
gamelan	–	Javanese orchestra	*pulau*	–	island
garuda	–	mythical bird	*raja*	–	king
golok	–	heavy knife	*tidak*	–	no
gunung	–	mountain	*toko*	–	shop
hutan	–	forest	*tuan*	–	sir or Mr.
jaga	–	watchman	*waringin*	–	type of Ficus
kampung	–	village	*warung*	–	stall
kemboja	–	type of Plumeria	*wayang*	–	shadow puppet
kraton	–	palace			

ISLAM is used by Indonesian Muslims as an acronym for the five daily prayers

I – *isyah* (evening)
S – *subuh* (dawn)
L – *lohor* (noon)
A – *asyar* (mid afternoon)
M – *maghrib* (late afternoon)

TABLE OF CONTENTS

PART 4
ARTJA

ILLUSTRATIONS

PART 3 - THE GERMAN EAST ASIA SQUADRON

PART 4 - ARTJA

PASSAGES

FOREWORD

"Why were U-boat sailors buried on a mountain in Java?" When Robby Ko first showed me the German graveyard in the hills beyond Jakarta, I asked him the same question that others have since asked me. Robby didn't really know. He was more interested in the huge fig trees that tower above the crosses. I looked for an answer in the words engraved on a tall white pillar in the centre of the grove. But the memorial was dedicated to German sailors in Asia who had died during the first world war, not the second. I read the inscriptions on the headstones more carefully and realized that most of the U-boat men had died in late 1945, several months after the Germans and the Japanese had surrendered. I was intrigued and confused. I had no idea what the German Navy was doing in Asia in either war. Nor could I imagine the motive for such a desperate U-boat mission – sailing underwater in cramped and dangerous conditions, surviving for months in hostile seas only to die on land in Java.

Robby had little patience with the narrow strictures of historical research. He contented himself with different but interesting theories of

German history and focused more on the mystical aspects of this graveyard in the clouds. He loved the sacred trees, the old stones, the Hindu saga, the secretive Baduy tribe and, above all, the legend of Artja Domas. In his good-humoured and irrepressible way he showed me the secrets buried beneath the surface.

A journey can be as rewarding as the destination, and so I embarked on my own voyage of discovery. Two mysteries led me on – the fate of the German sailors in Asia and the legend of Artja Domas. I found no tidy answers, instead hundreds of obscure documents, unreliable websites and books in foreign languages. Along the way I met and corresponded with memorable people, older men in particular, of various ethnic backgrounds, all of whom were keen to tell me their stories. When I thought I had learned enough I wrote a pamphlet and passed it around the Jakarta community. The dense prose served mainly to confuse readers, to disseminate factual errors and to illustrate the bewildering divide between Javanese mythology and the German Navy.

This problem resolved itself through the fortuitous intervention of my sister-in-law, Gretel Harmston. On a trip to Germany she met Jörg Helfferich, the great-nephew of Emil Helfferich – the man who in 1926 had dedicated the monument in the graveyard. She explained my quest and he allowed me to borrow his uncle's privately published memoirs. Later on he filled in many personal details. It soon became clear that Emil Helfferich was an integral part of the saga, indeed he was the key piece in the puzzle. He lived in both Java and Germany. His long life encompassed a dramatic business career, two world wars and the transition from Dutch colonial rule to Indonesian independence. He was a keen observer of native culture, a good storyteller, a romantic poet, and the devoted companion of a remarkable lady.

I decided to write a book and to use Helfferich's biography as the underlying structure. If I imagined the story as a wheel – with the German graveyard at the hub and with tales emanating like spokes from the centre – then Helfferich's life was the rim which held everything together.

The book took on a satisfying circular shape, connecting Emil Helfferich to the German Navy and the legends of Java. Several years passed as I collected a seemingly endless supply of relevant facts and long-forgotten stories. It soon became clear that the "unicycle" could no longer support the weight of a single book. Two wheels were in order.

Helfferich's life and the course of history offered an elegant solution. I split the saga in two at the year 1928. *The Pepper Trader* describes Helfferich's first fifty years, a turbulent but generally happy life in the Dutch East Indies. It includes the history of the German East Asia Squadron during World War I, resolves the riddle of the monument, and ends with Helfferich's return to Germany in 1928. The second book covers his later years in Germany during the rise and fall of the Third Reich, a time in which he cast his lot with the Nazis and faced an ethical quandary. It revolves around the vast epic of Axis submarines in Asia and answers the question posed at the outset, "Why were German sailors buried on a mountain in Java?"

I have introduced three characters in the first book whose stories do not actually appear until the second. These are Alex Papadimitriou, the Greek-German-Japanese sailor who "did not surrender;" Nanno Nommensen, the Dutch soldier whose great-grandfather was the legendary "Missionary to the Bataks" and whose father died in one of the greatest but little-known tragedies of World War II; and finally, Mohamad Syarib, a *haj* pilgrim and a humble farmer of German-Sundanese descent.

Woven into the fabric of this very real historical drama are the myths, legends and Hindu prehistory of Java and Sumatra. On a visit to her earthly abode in the Queen's Harbour, I beseeched the Goddess of the South Sea to guide us on this voyage through the mystical past. The journey ends in the second book on the bank of the Last River in the Forbidden Forest, where I watched Baduy tribesmen build a bamboo bridge to their hidden sanctuary, Artja Domas.

All the places, descriptions, historical events and people in this book are genuine. The war stories have been carefully researched and are as accurate as the many, but sometimes contradictory, sources allow. In a similar vein I have portrayed the life of Emil Helfferich as honestly as possible. Memoirs can be self-serving of course, and so I have looked between the lines to form my own interpretation of his motives and actions. Since he left few records of his conversations I have been sparing in the use of dialogue. For those moments when I wanted to hear him speak, I have tried to project his true feelings and character. I have added little to his stories of the people he met, with two exceptions. His climbing guide on Gunung Gede may not have been as loquacious as I portrayed him and old Captain Kamdami may not have troubled to tell him the whole story of Tunku Tiga. On one other occasion I imagined that Helfferich purchased a book of Shelley's poems on a visit to Bombay. Knowing that he was fluent in English, a fan of Rudyard Kipling, and a prolific poet himself, I felt confident that he had a wide-ranging interest in English poetry.

Having said that, I would also claim that a slavish adherence to the bare facts goes against the grain of Indonesian culture. Any visitor to Indonesia soon discovers the blurred line between fact and fiction. Just try to ask directions or to get information. Even a well-educated person like Dr. Ko firmly believes that "history is ten percent fact, ninety percent fiction." Initially I scoffed at his percentages but gradually came to realize, in Indonesia at least, that he was indeed close to the "truth." This disregard for the facts is exasperating to most newcomers but there is a certain charm to the friendly dissemblers of Java. Unpleasant realities are consigned to the "memory hole" and replaced with myths that are more palatable, such as the fate of the stone soldiers, the predictions of the sea goddess and the tale of how the Dutch came to Java. Myths are obviously fictional but other stories from the Hindu era, such as the origin of the Baduy tribe, tend to straddle the line. A dearth of written accounts has led to a variety of plausible theories.

In such a climate of cheerful inventiveness, I have modified and rearranged the pieces of my own personal odyssey to suit the linear framework of the main story. Again with only minor exceptions all the modern people, places and events are real, but I have altered the sequence in which they occurred. The main exceptions are the Baduy elder, Yakmin, who is a blend of Baduy tribesmen I have read about and met; the woman in the green sarong, whom I wish I had met; and the late but very real *Pak* Adja. Although he was custodian of the graveyard and could hear voices in the trees, I am quite certain that he could not recite the whole Ramayana. May he rest in peace.

These exceptions aside, I have tried to write an honest account of this strange voyage through the Indonesian archipelago and beyond. Around campfires in Java years ago, Boy Scouts would ask me, "Was that really a true story?" I always replied, "Of course!"

PART 1

A GERMAN GRAVEYARD IN JAVA

ONE

PUPPET-MASTER

Graves and a Tree at Artja

At midnight a man lit a torch outside his hut and walked up a dirt path to the monument among the old trees. A woman chased the shifting light beneath his slippered feet. High overhead the volcano's black ragged edge sliced through a veil of stars in a moonless sky. As they approached the grove the flame of the torch illuminated the dim surreal shapes of four ancient fig trees, their dark limbs twisted like grey serpents in a ghostly embrace. Lizards darted in the shadows and cicadas buzzed in the trees.

In the centre of the grove stood a white pillar, its domed crown barely visible in the flickering light. The man whispered the words as he passed the torch back and forth over the familiar inscriptions. The pale yellow flame gleamed in his thick glasses and tinted his grey beard. Shadow and light danced across the faces of Buddha and Ganesha, stone idols brooding beneath the trees on the dusky edge.

He laid the sputtering torch on the gravel bed and gently grasped the woman's hand. They sat down to rest on the steps in front of the pillar and stared at the distant Java Sea. The old year faded into the new as they gazed into the starlit sky and an uncertain future. Later in this New Year of 1928 they would sail away from the East Indies forever. So much had happened since the turn of the century: so much love and anguish, great fortunes won and lost. So many people had come and gone.

❦

Seven decades later the man and the woman had long since passed away. I was standing in the same grove of trees at the invitation of an old friend, Robby Ko. Earlier that morning we had set out for a walk from his house and had looked up to the vast volcanic bulk of Gunung Pangrango. Its green fluted ridges beckoned to us in the sunshine. Robby had asked, "Would you like to see the German Navy graveyard?" Of course, I replied. Dutch would have been interesting but German was highly unusual. Why would German sailors be buried on a mountain in Java?

"It's on this side of the mountain, above the town of Cikopo – on the edge of the tea plantation," he said, "They call it Artja, the Place of Statues."

Dr. Robby Ko is a highly regarded skin specialist in Indonesia. He graduated in medicine from the University of Indonesia near the end of the Sukarno era, just before "the year of living dangerously." The government has presented him with awards for his writings and for his achievements in the field of ecotourism. In his rambling home on the Puncak highway above Bogor he teaches young Indonesians about their natural environment. An expert cave explorer as well, he shows them how to rappel off the roof of his house – alongside a massive stained glass window of a man in a cave. With Robby you never know what to expect.

"Look at those bushes over there. That's quinine, *kina* in Indonesian. In Latin it's *Cinchona*. The bark cures malaria. Dr. Franz Junghuhn stole some plants from the Peruvians over a century ago and planted them here in Java. By the time the Japanese invaded, the East Indies supplied most of the world's production. That's why the Americans developed chloroquine, a synthetic substitute."

I looked at Robby doubtfully. He seemed so confident and he had a theory for everything. I once argued with him when he told me that history was ten percent fact and ninety percent fiction. His dark eyes were shining as they often did, his surprisingly youthful features rumpled in a playful smile. He walked over to one of the three huge fig trees that surrounded the graveyard.

"These are figs, of course, but what kind? There are hundreds of different *Ficus*." He reached up and plucked a leaf from a low-lying branch. "If you tear the leaf in half it exudes a milky sap – like this." A drop of sticky latex fell to the ground. "I think it must be *Ficus elastica* or something similar. The villagers call them *waringin* or *karet kebo*. *Karet* means rubber, you know. In the old days – before the automobile – the Dutch made a kind of rubber from this tree. But it wasn't good enough for tires. Then someone discovered that *Hevea brasiliensis* produced a better grade of latex. Sir Henry Wickham stole rubber seeds from Brazil in 1876 and brought them to Kew Gardens in England…and from there to Singapore. That kicked off the big rubber boom of the early twentieth century. Rubber plantations popped up everywhere."

I felt sorry for those unfortunate South Americans. First the Spanish took their gold, then the Germans their quinine and the British their rubber. I enjoyed listening to Robby's stories, whether ninety percent fiction or not. He told them in a gentle but eager voice, somewhat high-pitched, with a fluid and cultured English accent part way between London and Singapore. He spoke no Mandarin, despite his Indonesian-Chinese ancestry, but he was most comfortable in the Dutch language of his childhood as well as the various languages of Java. I followed his gaze up the trunk of the tree to the uppermost branches, where a serpent-eagle was picking at a lifeless snake. The bird had settled in the tallest of three fig trees that neatly delineated three of the four corners of the small graveyard. The tree was at least eight metres in diameter, a nightmarish tangle of muscular roots and stems. Gnarled, sinewy, grey arms twisted, grasped and squeezed each other in a dismal *danse macabre*. Dark crevices lurked between the stems, secret passageways to a deep, gloomy and primitive world. How long had these fantastic trees kept their silent vigil? Five hundred years? A thousand? Who had planted them and why?

Robby knew. "There used to be a fourth tree in that empty corner. It blew down in a wind storm about fifteen years ago. Interesting, isn't it? Four huge trees at the points of a square…no other trees like this anywhere near…on a high mountain ridge overlooking the ocean. In the old days they called it Artja Domas. 'Artja' means statue in Sanskrit. Many Indonesian words come from Sanskrit, of course. 'Domas' is old Javanese for the number eight hundred. Ergo the 'Place of Eight Hundred Statues.' I am certain this was a graveyard for Hindu royalty. They buried their kings and queens here a thousand years ago." Robby turned to face me. He looked quite serious. "The Germans desecrated this graveyard by clearing the land and burying their own dead on top of Hindu kings. They brought a curse upon themselves. That's why they lost the wars."

A curse? It seemed a rather improbable leap from cause to effect, from crime to punishment. In fact, at first glance, this whole graveyard seemed quite improbable. I set aside Robby's intriguing theories for the moment, pulled out a notepad and began to record distances, times and the more mundane details of our hike. My plan was to write a guidebook and to make maps of my favourite trails. As a Boy Scout leader in Jakarta, I needed paths to explore and places to camp. These beautiful mountain ridges would be ideal.

Among his many interests, Robby was a promoter of ecotourism and a keen supporter of my mapping project. He left me alone with my notepad and wandered farther up the hillside to look for flowers. I turned my attention to the cemetery among the trees. A dirt path led from the road to an iron gate set in a hedge. When I passed through the gate my boots crunched on white gravel. A plaque proclaimed that this *Friedhof* was the property of the German Embassy. The cemetery was not large, just twenty metres across the top and thirty metres deep. A low fence framed the upper end with round black stones set in white plaster. The effect was strangely reptilian, like the scales on a snake's belly. At the lower end on my left lay a freshly clipped lawn with a pair of concrete benches and a shade tree. To the right a central path led up a series of shallow steps between a pair of flagpoles. On either side of the steps lay the graves of ten German sailors, four on one side and six on the other.

A sturdy Iron Cross marked each man's grave. The distinctive emblem hearkened back to the medieval Teutonic Order, founded in Palestine during the Crusades. In later centuries the Iron Cross came to represent the traditional German award for courage and leadership in battle. Fashioned in concrete and set on a solid white plinth, each white cross stood almost a metre high, massive and permanent. In the centre of each, at the intersection of the four arms, a square black plaque described starkly in words and dates the bare facts of a young man's life.

Fragrant pink blooms of *kemboja* trees arched gracefully over each headstone. The dainty ornamentals, a type of *Plumeria*, had been planted on top of the graves in accordance with local Muslim custom. I stepped slowly up the central path. Straight ahead on the highest terrace loomed a tall white pillar.

Helfferich's Monument

I stopped in front of the unusual monument. It was three metres high, four-sided with five main levels tapering to a miniature onion dome on the peak, vaguely oriental like a mosque or perhaps a Buddhist stupa. It reminded me in an odd way of the ninth century temple of Borobudur, the outstanding Buddhist monument of central Java. A plaque on the second level declared:

DEM TAPFEREN
DEUTSCH-OSTASIATISCHEN
GESCHWADER
1914

Another plaque on the base announced simply:

ERRICHTET
VON
EMIL UND THEODOR HELFFERICH
1926

This statue had evidently been erected in 1926 by two German brothers, Emil and Theodor Helfferich, to the memory of sailors who had died in 1914 while serving in the German East Asia Squadron. But what was the German Navy doing in East Asia and who were the *Tapferen*, the "brave ones?" How and where did they die? Who were these German brothers and why did they build a naval cenotaph among these magnificent trees? Perched incongruously on the flank of a Javanese volcano, this curious pillar was a foreign object, the exotic flotsam of an alien culture, a white enigma.

I noticed a mismatched pair of statuettes, one on each side of the memorial. On the right a white Buddha sat serenely in the lotus position, eyes cast demurely downward in an image of peace and tranquil humility. It blended harmoniously with the pillar's Buddhist style and the gentle ambience of the graveyard.

The piece on the left was entirely different. An elephant squatted on a bed of skulls. Skulls adorned its ears and grinned from the crown. A battle-axe poised menacingly in its uppermost hand. Eyes bulged from a sloping forehead. This apparition portrayed the vengeful Ganesha, the Hindu god of knowledge, son of Siva the destroyer, the lord of beasts. From where I stood the elephant was framed against the twisted trunk of a fig tree. A recent coat of white paint had not quite obliterated the green fungus mouldering in the skulls' cavernous eye sockets. It seemed an unlikely ornament for a cemetery, this fanciful god of knowledge. What has knowledge to do with skulls and axes and a warlike elephant? Learning leads to enlightenment. But it can be dangerous to know too little. Perhaps, upon further reflection, Ganesha was not out of place in a war cemetery at all.

Ganesha

I turned my back on the grim idol and stepped down to the next level. Moving across the line of Iron Crosses I read the brief German inscriptions, engraved in white letters on a black background:

ObLt H. Haake, *U-196*	1914–30 Nov 1944
Lt Wilhelm Jens	7 Nov 1907–12 Oct 1945
KptLt Herman Tangermann	11 Oct 1910–23 Aug 1945
ObLt Friedrich Steinfeld, Kdt *U-195*	15 Dec 1914–30 Nov 1945
Schiffszimmermann Eduard Onnen	14 Dec 1906–15 April 1945
Lt W. Martens	– Oct 1945
ObGefr Willi Petschow	31 Dec 1912–28 Sep 1945
ObLt Willi Schlummer	– 12 Oct 1945

and two graves marked *Unbekannt,* unknown.

Something did not make sense. These graves had nothing to do with the monument. These sailors were not the "brave" men of the German East Asia Squadron of 1914. They were still young boys in Germany when the Helfferich brothers dedicated their memorial. At least two of them served in the notorious World War II U-boats of the German "wolfpack." One of them, the thirty-year-old Steinfeld, had been the captain of *U-195*. What madness had brought them to Java in submarines, so far away from home?

The dates were curious too. Only Haake and Onnen died during the war. The rest met their untimely fate in the months following the Japanese surrender. If the war was over, why did they die? When the time comes, sailors usually die at sea. Why were they buried here on the slope of Gunung Pangrango – sixty kilometres from port and one thousand metres above sea level, among these old trees, beneath a monument to an earlier war?

I tried to picture these men embarking from blockaded ports in Germany and squeezing into submarines for a hazardous voyage around the world. They lived and died in a place their parents would never see. The two Willi's probably had jolly faces to match their names. My mind wandered down memory lane as I stood on the gravel path between the rows of crosses. The youngest men were born around the same time as my father, Bob, and his younger brother, Tom. Like these German sailors, Tom never came home either – missing presumed dead, shot down over the Mediterranean in early 1942. Bob soldiered on through Italy and Holland while his parents mourned and worried at home. He survived the war but the Canadian government gave his mother a Silver Cross for the loss of a son in battle. She wore it on her lapel every year on Remembrance Day.

A procession of women interrupted my daydream. They chatted to each other as they walked down from the plantation. Some carried tea leaves in cloth bags around their waists; others balanced baskets of vegetables on their heads. Their bare feet padded silently down the dirt path through the quinine. They were mostly wrinkled middle-aged Sundanese women; but one, in a green sarong, was much younger and prettier than the others. She glanced in my direction then turned away.

A pair of feet rustled on the gravel path behind me. I turned to see an elfin little man with a straw broom. His eyes twinkled and he opened his mouth in a wide toothy grin. Yellow-stained teeth protruded from his gums at odd angles. He had big ears and puffy eyes but his thin grey hair was carefully brushed. He wore sandals, clean patched trousers and a blue short-sleeved shirt which hung loosely on his emaciated frame. A *golok*, a heavy knife, dangled from a scabbard on his waist.

His leathery cheeks creased in a friendly way as he asked, "Do you have a cigarette, *Pak*?" He pronounced the Indonesian words carefully.

I kept a couple of cigarette packages in my bag for just such occasions: Marlboros for the feisty young *ojeks*, the motorbikers who took me places, and a more traditional brand of clove cigarettes, *kreteks*, for the older men. He gratefully accepted a few *kreteks*, lit one and took a long satisfied puff. I waited for the inevitable second question.

"*Dari mana, Pak*? Where do you come from?" he asked, right on cue.

I explained that I was Canadian and that I had lived in Jakarta for a long time. I gave him my name. He responded by telling me that he lived in a nearby hut with his wife, Imas. He tended this graveyard for the German Embassy and his name was Adja. He was the *jaga* of Artja – the groundskeeper of the Place of Statues. His command of Indonesian and his careful enunciation surprised me. Like most country people, he spoke *Bahasa Indonesia* as a second language, preferring to slip into one of hundreds of regional languages and dialects. Adja rightly guessed that I would be lost in his native Sundanese and so we conversed in the national language.

A rooster crowed and a goat bleated from the direction of his hut. The burning cloves in his cigarette popped and crackled as the sweetly scented smoke drifted my way. Adja told me that he had just finished whitewashing all the monuments and the headstones. The workers from the embassy had brought him new brushes and cans of white paint. They told him to spruce up the graveyard for the annual ceremony in a few weeks' time. I realized that it was autumn already, the season of remembrance, and that the leaves in Canada must be turning colour. In Indonesia it was easy to lose track of the northern seasons. Here the leaves fell from trees every day. Daylight lasted twelve hours year-round. The temperature was constant and a dry "summer" alternated with a wet monsoon "winter." Adja looked ruefully at the dry leaves drifting down from the graceful *kemboja* trees and the gigantic *waringin*. He poked the stubby *kretek* between his lips, grabbed the broom in both hands and began to sweep in a rhythmical and methodical manner, almost as if he were dancing. I watched him for a moment then resumed my own leisurely ramble through the crosses.

After scribbling for a short while I caught sight of Robby striding back down the path. He was carrying a bunch of white lilies in his left hand.

Hairy brown bulbs dangled from the base of the green stems. "Look what I found," he called. "Amaryllis lilies…*Amaryllis belladonna*…a 'beautiful lady' but an alien species – and deadly – the bulb can kill you! The Germans must have planted them. They were all over the place," he continued, a little out of breath. "I walked up to Artja Manik, where the plantation supervisor used to live in a small cottage. It's in ruins now. There's a large tree growing in the old *mandi*, the wash-basin. And these lilies are everywhere. It must have been a garden once. I'll take them home and plant them in a border."

I admired his fine bouquet and asked about Artja Manik.

"You must see it some time. I talked to a chap who was pulling out old tea bushes. He told me how to find the cottage. It's by the trail that leads to the summit of Pangrango. The forest is protected now, all overgrown. It was a *punden* in the old days, you know, a sanctuary. *Manik* means 'beads' or 'sparkling.' The beaded statues, maybe? Statues in water? He said there was a freshwater spring but I couldn't find it – or the gate, built from two *lingga*…sacred stones. In the old days birds avoided the *punden* because, if they flew over it, they would die instantly and plummet to the ground!" He announced this last fact with satisfaction and waved his arms dramatically.

As if she had been listening, the eagle suddenly leaped from her perch in the high branches. With slow powerful wingbeats she headed up the mountain. I looked at Robby quizzically and wondered if he would tell me that the bird was really a magic *garuda* – the mount of Vishnu – a mythical winged creature with bulging eyes and a nasty beak. But Robby was staring instead at Adja, who was still sweeping in a far corner of the graveyard. He called over to him as if to an old friend. The wizened man turned to face the doctor and they spoke for a few minutes in Sundanese. I folded my notebook, shared a drink of water with Robby and then we got up to leave. Adja stopped sweeping and lit another *kretek* as we walked away. He nodded his head and smiled. "*Sampai jumpa lagi*," I said, "See you again soon."

As we tramped back down the stone road to the village, I told Robby that Adja and I had introduced ourselves. I remarked on his surprisingly good language.

"He was a *dalang*, you know, a puppet-master," said Robby. "When he was younger, of course. He can recite the whole Ramayana. Ask him sometime. He knows a lot, too much maybe. He says he can hear voices in the trees."

I glanced sideways at Robby but he seemed unaware of any irony. So old Adja was a puppet-master. That would explain the careful diction and his fluid motions. I could imagine him squatting behind the lit screen, making shadow puppets dance to the sound of the *gamelan*, keeping village audiences entranced for hours. All night long he had sung and talked in old Javanese, bringing to life Arjuna, Semar and all the other wily characters of the Ramayana. He told black magic tales of warriors and Hindu princesses, elves and fairies, *garuda* birds and golden snails.

"Windmills!" said Robby.

"Pardon?" I swivelled my head to see where he was pointing.

"You can hear them, can't you?" Indeed, each blade hummed a reedy tune, a gentle reassuring whistle. "The sound soothes the souls of farmers in the fields. It can be lonely sometimes, among the endless rows of cassava, at the edge of the mountain wilderness." Robby laughed and swept his arms sideways with a majestic flourish. The lilies wobbled in his left hand.

I thought of the voices in the trees, the invisible spirits of Adja's life. In the dusky light of late afternoon, the *waringin* trees would cast long chaotic shadows across the primly whitewashed stones. The trees reared up in testament to a primitive origin, to the pagan underworld which floated just below the green surface. The shadows would creep across Ganesha and Buddha, icons of two great Asian religions, opposing each other across the white pillar much like the ancient temples of Hindu Prambanan and Buddhist Borobudur, silent below the smouldering peak of Gunung Merapi. Militaristic Christian crosses lay in the shade of *kemboja* trees, planted in accord with Islamic tradition and Sundanese notions of the afterlife. It was indeed a strange place, a peculiar hodgepodge of religious symbols. A seemingly peaceful coexistence concealed epic struggles, like plants and animals in an ancient wilderness.

"*Datura!*"

"What?"

"*Datura*. Moonflower… a nightshade. Look at this beautiful flower, huge, like a white trumpet. Absolutely poisonous. It can kill you. Don't allow your Boy Scouts to eat it!"

I clapped Robby on the shoulder and laughed. "Well, I'll just have to tell them not to cook any flowers – or amaryllis bulbs." We picked our way through huge cobblestones and listened to the windmills, gently turning.

TWO

THE SERPENT-EAGLE

Gede and Pangrango

We first met in the German graveyard, the serpent-eagle and I, and we often crossed paths in the months to come. She lived high on the north slope of Gunung Pangrango, a huge volcano, dormant through long centuries since it last exploded into ash and molten rock. She haunted a primeval forest, a mountain solitude unchanged since the time of Hindu princesses.

Throughout the long tropical night she perched among the highest branches of a tall tree. Beneath her nocturnal roost beat the silent heart of restless green life. Roots, trunks, leaves and vines crept upward in a slow desperate struggle for food and light. Night creatures lurked below her in the darkness: wild dogs and black leopards; pythons, pangolins and black spitting cobras. They slithered and scuttled, padded and crawled in the musty humus among giant trees. Deeper still pulsed the magma chamber of the slumbering volcano. Its life-force squeezed through black basalt and burst into sulphurous craters, cascades of hot water and pools of bubbling mud.

With dawn's approach she peered through the canopy of leaves. Distant peaks cut the luminous eastern horizon. The rising sun coloured the sky blue, then livid pink. A damp mist lingered in the valley and shrouded the mountain forest, blurring its outline in a shifting grey veil. Cold beads of water dripped from the fronds of tree ferns, from the thorny vines of rattan and from the leaves of immense, bizarrely twisted fig trees. The forest was quiet but for the croaking of frogs and the slow staccato patter of dripping water on dead leaves.

The serpent-eagle unclasped strong yellow talons, stretched and curled again as she gripped the stout branch. She shook a droplet of water from the tip of her hooked beak, ruffled her crest and smoothed the long feathers of her wings. Hard yellow eyes searched the murky depths where flocks of hungry foragers hunted their sluggish prey. Soft whistles marked their passing, joined by the rising clamor of other birds and the rustle of leaves in the morning breeze. A gentle breath of wind fanned the warm lower slopes and brought with it a foreign sound, the vague rumble of distant humanity.

A ray of light pierced the gloom and illuminated the eagle's yellow eye. Silver spots glittered in her chestnut breast. She spread her wings, dropped from her perch and swooped ghostlike over the trees.

On some fine mornings, when the sky is clear and the wind is right, she catches a rising thermal and soars upward to the summit of Gunung Pangrango. She circles higher and higher until the forest resembles an immense green hide, a living cloak that softens the muscular contours of the deep-rooted volcanoes. The humid valley breeze and the monsoon wind from the sea coalesce each day into clouds draping the three thousand-metre mountain. By mid-afternoon the billows darken into thundering anvils of driving rain. But the morning view is unsurpassed in all directions. From her home on the north slope near Artja she wheels around the summit, scanning her domain to the east, south, west and back again to the north. The serpent-eagle's unfathomable eyes, in their black primordial depths, survey the fertile landscape, distant peaks and hazy shimmering seas. Against the flaming disc of the rising sun lie a long line of jagged summits....

> Volcanoes form the backbone of Java: Gunung Tangkuban Pra-hu, the "Upside-down Boat," lies high and dry above the city of Bandung. Gunung Merapi, the "Fire Mountain," broods steep-ly and dangerously over Yogyakarta and the shattered temples of Borobudur and Prambanan. Boulders tumble off unstable cliffs into smouldering gullies. Milky-grey braided streams pick their way through the indifferent waste and ferry rich particles of clay to the fertile valleys below. The smoky cones and blasted tips of other giants stretch away to the shining horizon. This is the ethnic heartland of the Javanese, where the Sultan still holds court and where shadow puppets bob and weave to the music of *gamelan* gongs, retelling old Hindu tales of the Ra-mayana.

A high saddle separates Gunung Pangrango from her younger sibling to the south. Pangrango, the taller of the two peaks, is graced by a green mantle of trees and a perfectly shaped cone. Gunung Gede, the "Giant Mountain," looks quite different. Its barren summit is flanked by steep columns of basalt. An exposed, yellow, hissing crater hints at the roiling forces beneath. Far to the south, beyond the twin summits, green waves of paddies and plantations ripple down to the foaming shoreline of the Indian Ocean....

> Two rocky points and a brown crescent of sand frame Pelabuhan Ratu, the "Queen's Harbour," where red and blue sailboats sup-ply a thriving fish market. Rumbling surf batters the sandy shore in an everlasting rhythm and retreats with a surly hiss. Beyond the curling waves the restless Indian Ocean rolls unimpeded to the leaden horizon, to the grand curve of the earth's surface and the icy Antarctic shore. At the lip of the harbour the sea floor plunges steeply into a dark and dismal trench, seven thousand metres deep. The earth groans as monumental forces thrust black

oceanic rock beneath the mountains of Java. Squeezed at great
depth by unimaginable pressure, the rock melts, rises and erupts
in spasmodic bursts from volcanoes. The watery abyss hides living
wonders. Hammerhead sharks patrol the murky coast. Strange
toothy fish, wide-eyed and festooned with lights, flicker dimly
above the skeletons of a thousand ships. This is the realm of *Nyai*
Roro Kidul, the Queen of the Southern Ocean, a raven-haired
siren in an emerald sarong who plucks her victims from the swirling rips and the spume of perilous seas.

Across a wide valley to the west looms the serrated ridge of another active
volcano, Gunung Salak….

On its crumbling summit rest the bones of a *wali*, a high priest,
carried there centuries ago on the bare sweating shoulders of
young men as they stumbled upward through the mud and tangled vegetation. The modern city of Bogor bustles on its northern
flank – the leafy town once called Buitenzorg, the whimsical "No
Worries" of the Dutch era. Buried beneath the elegant colonial
architecture lie the ruins of Pakuan, the royal Hindu seat of the
Sundanese Pajajaran kingdom, archrivals of the Javanese and
stubborn fifteenth-century foes of the new Muslim converts. Beyond Gunung Salak the attenuated hills drop down to a remote
corner of West Java. Strange creatures inhabit the western valleys,
chief among them the reclusive and gentle Java rhinoceros. The
highlands protect another mysterious and endangered species,
the relict Baduy tribe – cloistered, inbred and magical – the last
glowing ember of old Sunda. Beyond the last hill lie the Sunda
Strait and the distant mountains of Sumatra. Grey surf pounds
the reef-lined shore. In the centre of the strait a young volcano
belches smoke and fire from its treacherous crater. Its cataclysmic
upheaval in 1883 spread ash around the world and extinguished
the lives of thousands. This precocious child of Krakatau grows
by six metres a year.

A brown smudge to the north betrays the presence of Indonesia's largest metropolis, an impossibly crowded city, home to millions upon teeming millions....

> Jakarta broods sullenly on the muddy edge of the shallow Java Sea. Little remains of its colourful past when Sunda Kelapa was the maritime gateway of the Pajajaran Empire. Six hundred years ago Chinese junks anchored in the harbour while their captains bartered with Hindu royalty. In 1526 the Muslim warrior Fatahillah sacked the port and won a "complete victory" – *jayakarta* – over allied Hindu and Portuguese forces. Less than a century later, in 1619, the Dutch in their turn destroyed Jayakarta and established Batavia in its stead. For most of the next 323 years Batavia lay at the heart of the sprawling empire of the Dutch East Indies until Japanese conquerors defeated the Dutch and renamed the city Jakarta. Today the romance and the colonial charm have almost vanished. The city is an improbable patchwork of stylish suburbs and traditional *kampungs*; helicopter pads and red-tiled roofs; mosques, cathedrals and alien Russian monuments; crowded freeways and narrow lanes. Generals in black limousines jockey for space with bicycles, pony carts, motorcycles, trucks, wildly careening buses and trains filled to overflowing. Lepers beg in the streets; children pick through trash heaps; refuse-choked canals fester beneath gleaming new high-rises. And through it all, above the dirt, the din, the poverty and the corruption, shines the patient and cheerful face of modern Indonesia.

But an eagle, even a serpent-eagle, cares little for superb vistas, the works of man and the panoramic sweep of history. In her ancient, unsentimental, avian mind she feels only the daily struggle to survive. There is little to eat on a windswept ridge. Buffeted by the freshening breeze, she soars back down the mountain. Her keen eyes search for prey in the forest canopy on the north slope, where the morning sun throws wrinkled gullies and ridges into sharp relief. She picks out the human imprint of roads, red roofs and the silver and jade mosaic of flooded terraces. Sinewy men urge water buffaloes through the sticky mud of rice paddies. Women bend from the waist to plant new shoots while children wiggle lines of white flags to frighten away hungry birds. Stubby blue buses putter from one small *kampung* to another, threading mountain roads edged with mangoes, bananas and the slender notched trunks of coconut palms. Tea bushes drape the higher elevations in gently undulating waves of darker green, surging upward to the shadowy jungle. Small rafts of women drift through the tea and pick the fresh leaves. Their woven sunhats float like mushrooms on a verdant sea.

Beneath the green surface hides a lurking menace, safely distant from the chatter and the shuffling feet. A clutch of eggs stirs in a leafy nest. A female king cobra, the largest venomous serpent in the world – a tea-picker's nightmare – eyes her hatchlings with care as the bird swoops overhead.

The serpent-eagle dips lower, skims the treetops and scatters small birds in panic. The early morning hour rouses her senses and whets her appetite. On a nearby ridge the canopies of three giant fig trees rear above the plantation. The eagle flies rapidly toward the grove and spots her prey. For an instant she hovers, then drops into the branches and seizes a small green snake in her talons. With one deft snap of her yellow beak she kills the wriggling creature. A rasping satisfied shriek rings across the ridge. The bough sways unsteadily beneath her as she lowers her wings.

Crested Serpent-Eagle

I watched the bird on that first morning from the base of the monument. I could imagine her leafy home in the forest, her flight around the mountain, unbounded vistas of Java and a link to a mysterious past. And I thought of her ruthless but focused instinct for survival. The terse inscriptions on the cenotaph and graves hinted at another kind of struggle, no less ruthless, a mortal mystery set in stone. Many years had passed since 1926, when Emil and Theodor Helfferich built this memorial to brave men who died in "the war to end all wars." In front of the pillar beside me, as if in mockery, lay the human traces of another colossal battle – an apocalyptic conflict even worse than the Great War – a nightmare that the two brothers could never have imagined.

THREE

A DAY OF REMEMBRANCE

Volkstrauertag at the German Graveyard

For weeks I collected stories. The more I learned about the graveyard the more gripping it became. Others fell under the spell, too, and urged me on. Swiss and Dutch friends helped me with translations. Robby sent me faxes with pictures and arrows like Treasure Island. With literary flourish and extravagant fonts he admonished me to be careful:

"… I am not **that** superstitious, neither am I too fond of novels about the <u>mysterious world</u>, or <u>life beyond</u>, but as an Asian, and Indonesian, **I still keep an open mind** to '<u>unexplainable phenomena</u>,' trying to probe into some 'possible' clues, which frequently cannot be grasped by the '<u>logical mind</u>'…I just wonder why these Germans underwent such a <u>melodrama</u>. It is as if they were always on the <u>wrong place at the wrong time</u>. They were <u>*not*</u> *heroically* fighting for a cause. It was not a <u>saga</u>. On the contrary,

they were _compelled_ to accept their fate, which was always a sad
one…I personally consider it NOT TACTFUL, if you bring it to
the open, since that will probably hurt German Pride…we have
still to **respect** the Germans working so hard, but dying so fate-
fully, unfortunately and meaninglessly…"

With more presumption than good sense, I hastily printed a pamphlet on
the history of the graveyard and passed it around the Jakarta expatriate
community. I asked and received permission to attend the upcoming ceremony at Artja – _Volkstrauertag_. On a Sunday in mid-November, several
days after other nationalities observe Remembrance Day, Germans gather
to remember their own war dead.

In the pre-dawn hours of a Sunday morning, I drove along the Jagorawi toll road toward Bogor and turned left onto the Puncak highway. At
this time of day the roads were mercifully clear of traffic. Within a few
hours cars would be backed up for miles. Peanut sellers and water vendors
would be hawking their wares all along the line of idled vehicles. Near
Cikopo I turned steeply uphill toward the little village of Pasir Muncang
where I parked the car. A few boys appeared from nowhere. I promised to
tip them if the hub caps were still on the car when I returned.

I had no wish to risk the car on the narrow cobblestone road. The
early morning walk, about two kilometres uphill, would be pleasant anyway. Women both young and old stood on the doorsteps of small white
houses. I said good morning and they asked me where I was going, where
was I from. Was I an "_orang jerman_?" Children scampered on the road in
front, enjoying a day off school. A chorus of "Hello meester" greeted me
at every turn. Roosters crowed and goats bleated from cramped wooden
pens. Barefoot labourers staggered down the road with heavy netbags slung
in pairs from poles across their shoulders: _pikuls_ of firewood, red peppers,
orange carrots and purple eggplants. Men and women planted and hoed in
the paddy fields behind the houses. In the glancing light of early morning,
rice shoots glowed electric green and the newly flooded terraces sparkled
like mirrors. Coconut palms and bananas lined the edge of the levees. On
the hills above, the tips of cinnamon trees flushed pink. Bamboo windmills turned and hummed in the freshening breeze.

The road climbed steadily. Beyond the last house the potholed asphalt yielded to rough grey cobbles through which I gingerly picked my way. The valley of the Cisukabirus River dropped away sharply on my left. When the road finally levelled off I passed between two tall fig trees that met at their tops in a natural arch. They seemed to form an old gateway. On a slight rise to the right, a grove of spindly quinine bushes shone brightly in the sun, the spiky blades tipped with red, like daggers. Ahead of me the road veered to the left, toward the trees and headstones of the German cemetery at Artja. I could hear the sound of sweeping.

Adja was dressed in his best clothes, a rumpled white shirt and grey trousers, cinched halfway up his scrawny chest with a piece of cord. His unruly grey hair was slicked down. I said hello and complimented him on the spotless cemetery and the bright white stones. He smiled and accepted a cigarette. The smile faded as he exhaled a cloud of blue smoke. He scanned the graveyard in a distracted manner, a little tense. I looked around too, wondering what to say next, until the distant whine of a diesel engine broke the awkward silence. I heard the grinding of gears and saw the cab of a truck lurching up the stone road.

A Kijang pickup truck bumped to a stop a few metres from the cemetery path. Four young men stared out the cab windows. Several others uncoiled themselves from a pile of folding chairs in the back. One by one they dropped to the ground, stretched, looked around, lit cigarettes and waited for someone else to start working.

Adja hid the broom behind one of the *waringin* trees. He stubbed the *kretek* on the trunk and wedged it safely in the bark for later use. Then he strode in his sandals toward the truck, tucked in his shirt and smoothed back his hair. In his baggy patched trousers he stood as tall as possible and greeted the young men solemnly with all the authority of his many years. He waved in the general direction of the lawn. The driver bestirred himself and spoke to the others. The youngest one dragged chairs from the truck. Metal screeched on metal as they clattered to the ground. Each man hoisted a few chairs to his shoulders but paused first to inhale a deep puff of smoke and to stuff the cigarette between pursed lips. In loose shirts and flip-flops they hauled their burden down the path to the grass where Adja arranged the chairs in tidy rows.

Attracted by the rattle and clamor of the truck, a few curious villagers trudged up the road and gathered in the shade of the trees. Their numbers swelled as others turned up in twos and threes: mothers with children, youths and old men. Adja was still fussing with the chairs when the first cars arrived. German children flew out the car doors, followed more stiffly by their parents. An officer and two soldiers in grey uniforms tied German and Indonesian flags to halyards on the two poles. With Adja's help they placed a paper *Volkstrauertag* program on each seat. One of the soldiers pulled out a silver bugle and played a few tentative notes. German women in plain cotton dresses instructed their drivers to lift trays of food out of car trunks. Sandwiches, cookies, *Sachertorte*, coffee urns and jugs of lemonade appeared on the tables. The children hung around the edges, ferrying small platters and earning a treat for their efforts. Others scurried among the gravestones and played tag in the trees.

Sweating and red-faced, a group of hikers puffed their way up the road, their walking sticks tapping a steady tattoo on the stones. Like German-speaking folk everywhere, they took pleasure in a brisk *Spaziergang*, a Sunday walk in the hills. Striding along, arms swinging, they paused to wipe their brows with handkerchiefs and to exchange hearty greetings with the passengers in cars headed uphill. Amid the parade a black Mercedes toiled noiselessly upward. The car rocked on the cobbles, passed the village children, the chickens and the goats in their pens, and parted the hikers who turned to wave. At the top of the hill, the driver and an aide leaped out nimbly and opened doors for the German ambassador and his wife.

Suitably dressed in a somber black suit, the ambassador greeted his expatriate flock with earnest cheerfulness. Bespectacled and silver-haired, he wandered amiably through the crowd, shaking hands and exchanging morning pleasantries. His tall young wife promenaded beside him, in her own way as spectacular as he was discreet. Long blond hair cascaded dramatically down the back of a silk leopard skin pantsuit. In gold lamé high heels she picked her way daintily through the uneven grass, teetering on the cusp of high fashion. The women at the food tables nudged each other and whispered cautionary hisses to their mesmerized husbands.

Beside the parked cars, drivers gathered into congenial knots of chatting men. Some squatted on their heels, others leaned on the hoods as they laughed and enjoyed a leisurely smoke. A subtle air of big-city superiority glinted in their eyes. Barefoot boys squirmed closer, eager to listen to stories of exotic Jakarta and to hear fanciful descriptions of these foreigners, the *orang jerman*.

Beneath the old trees, beyond the fence at a discreet distance from the crowd of white faces, inscrutable dark eyes watched in silence. I could see wrinkled cheeks and missing teeth, grizzled men in round black hats, old women with scarves wrapped loosely round their hair, scruffy barefoot children holding hands and babies snuggled against the breasts of young mothers. Beside me I saw blue eyes and blond hair, beards and eyeglasses, uncomfortable neckties, shoes and high heels. The contrast was intriguing: the two nationalities, the mix of young and old, the different faces, gestures and language. The two groups stood apart but mingled politely at the edges. They both belonged here but for different reasons. The Germans had come to honour their war dead, men who might have been their fathers or grandfathers. The villagers had lived there forever and had buried their own dead in these hills. They relished a glimpse of the wider world and they welcomed foreigners with courtesy and shy curiosity. Perhaps a few of the older ones remembered dimly a shared moment in wartime or on the plantation. Half a century later they were now, in the popular phrase, "*tuan rumah,*" masters of their own house. But old attitudes die hard. On this Sunday in November, in the waning years of the tumultuous twentieth century, each group still felt reluctant to embrace the other. Under a veneer of tolerance, tension lingered in the air, a sense of alienation.

Pak Haji Mohamad Syarib

In the distance I spotted an elderly man walking up the road. He looked wrinkled and thin but he stood erect and he walked with dignity. He proudly wore the white skullcap of a *haj* pilgrim and a fine batik shirt in a *garuda* motif, a mythical bird in brilliant white, blue and gold. As he drew closer and recognized his village friends, he smiled and his brown cheeks creased into well worn furrows, like the muddy fields in which he spent his days. Crow's feet spread from the corners of dark laughing eyes. He acknowledged each respectful greeting with an affable wave of his right hand. When he saw Adja under a tree he walked up to him with hands outstretched. Adja bowed his head and pressed his palms together in a *sembah*, a sign of respect. The pilgrim clasped Adja's hands between his and then the two men turned to watch the ceremony.

Two Christian ministers, one Lutheran and one Catholic, donned their vestments and white surplices. Men, women and children ambled over to the chairs and leafed through the programs. The ambassador and his wife, the dark suit and the leopard skin, sat prominently in front. Beside each flagpole a German soldier stood rigidly at attention. The pure notes of a bugle reverberated through the grove and silenced both the congregation and the surrounding crowd. The flags ran up the poles and the soldiers saluted. Heads bowed in solemn prayer.

> *"Wir haben uns heute hier versammelt – auf dem Soldatenfriedhof.*
> *Wir gedenken am heutigen Totensonntag aller verstorbenen Gefal-*
> *lenen und unserer lieben Verstorbenen. Viele sind in jungen Jahren*
> *gestorben..."*

"Today we have gathered here together – at the soldiers' cemetery. We remember today, on this Remembrance Sunday, all soldiers killed in action and our own beloved deceased. Many died at a young age..."

> *"Gott, guter Vater, wir beten um den Frieden für unsere Welt.*
> *Lass uns mitarbeiten an der Überwindung von Vorurteil und*
> *Spaltung und uns für Mitmenschlichkeit und Versöhnung ein-*
> *setzen..."*

"God, heavenly Father, we pray for peace in our world. Let us work together to overcome prejudice and disharmony, to reconcile our differences and to build a community of man…"

> *"Vater unser im Himmel.*
> *Geheiligt werde dein Name…*

"Our Father, who art in heaven.
Hallowed be thy name…

> *…Und vergib uns unsere Schuld,*
> *Wie auch wir vergeben unseren Schuldigern…*

…And forgive us our trespasses,
As we forgive those who trespass against us…

> *…Denn dein ist das Reich und die Kraft*
> *Und die Herrlichkeit in Ewigkeit. Amen."*

…For thine is the kingdom, the power and the glory
Forever and ever. Amen."

My eyes wandered from the reverently bowed heads to the two ministers in white, the soldiers in grey, the ten crosses and the cenotaph, from Ganesha and Buddha to the massive trees arching over the formal scene. Adja hovered in the shadows. His slight figure, with his bony arms and baggy trousers, blended almost invisibly into the twisted grey stems of the tree. The pilgrim stood beside him, his dusky face seemingly lost in quiet contemplation. Adja told me later that the man's name was Mohamad Syarib and that his father had been a German plantation worker, perhaps not unlike the grandfathers of the pink-cheeked men in the chairs. I wonder now how he must have felt as he stood outside the fence watching his alien cousins. Anger and envy? Probably not. Regret or forgiveness? No, more likely he was just curious. And what would they feel for him – if they only knew?

I felt pleasantly drowsy from the effects of the early morning departure, the walk in the fresh mountain air, the bird songs in the trees and
the resonant cadence of the German priests. As I looked over to Adja and
Mohamad I glimpsed a young woman in a green sarong wandering behind them. She cut a striking figure with her long dark hair. I thought
she looked like the woman who had walked down the mountain with the
tea-pickers a few weeks earlier. She faded into the crowd and disappeared,
perhaps just a figment of my sleepy imagination.

A soldier stood to attention and placed the silver bugle to his lips. He
played the old, slow, haunting melody "*Ich hatt' einen Kameraden…*I had
a comrade…" A few older men hummed the tune or mumbled the words.
The last note floated in the quiet air amid the rustling of leaves.

With a creaking of seats the congregation rose to sing the closing
hymn. From my seat at one end, I noticed for the first time three distinctive men in the centre. One of them was quite tall with slightly rounded
shoulders. A thicket of white hair clung to a high forehead. Bushy white
eyebrows perched on wire-rimmed glasses. He looked like a learned profes-
sor or perhaps a distinguished theologian. Beside him stood a shorter man,
sturdily built, his short-cropped grey hair contrasting with swarthy features and dark eyes. The third was of medium height, robust and muscular,
his feet planted firmly on the ground in the manner of an old soldier. A
thick white mustache twitched on his tanned face. These men stood apart
in the crowd of earnest, mostly younger, faces. Like "the three wise men"
they radiated a knowledge of distant times and places.

After a final benediction the service concluded. Small groups moved
in various directions. Some took photos by the monument while others
headed for the refreshments. Children sprawled on wicker mats or lined
up for sandwiches. The ambassador's wife cut the *Sachertorte* into little
pieces and handed them to hungry bystanders.

The German military attaché, a dashing colonel in grey uniform, cornered
me as I wolfed down a piece of cake. He had read my pamphlet and wondered if I would be willing to make a short speech. "In German?" I gagged.
He reassured me that everyone understood English. Within moments I
was licking my fingers and wondering what to say as he passed me the

microphone. He introduced me as a Canadian who knew some interesting German history.

I have never experienced anything more bizarre. Surrounded by the monuments of a German war cemetery, shaded by trees from a Hindu past, poised on the slope of a volcano in Java, I struggled to think of something appropriate to say. Behind me stood Indonesian villagers; in front of me, German families. Robby's admonition came to mind. I imagined the ghosts of my Canadian forbears looking down upon the scene: my father, a war veteran; my uncle, shot down over the Mediterranean; and all the old men with poppies and medals on their chests.

So I just told stories. I talked about the Helfferich saga, *Graf* Spee and the German East Asia Squadron, the men in the submarines and what happened to them after the war. Everyone wanted to know about the U-boats. I described the dramatic moment in May, 1945, when the German sailors in Java had to surrender to the Japanese Navy. In conclusion I hinted at a mysterious past before the Germans, before the Dutch era, before the Muslims even. What little I knew, I condensed even more.

After brief and polite applause, everyone resumed eating, drinking and mingling. A few people came up to chat. One asked, in good humour, why it was that Germans didn't know their own history, why it was that a Canadian had to explain it to them. I shrugged and suggested that a "neutral" Canadian was uniquely positioned to tell the story. I remembered Robby's warning to be tactful and left the rest unsaid. For Germans the wars still bled like open wounds.

The three distinguished gentlemen had been standing to one side. Now they came forward to talk to me. One of them, the shorter one with the swarthy features, introduced himself.

"Mr. Bennett, my name is Alex Papadimitriou. I enjoyed your talk but I just want to tell you one thing. I was a German sailor in Surabaya in May, 1945 – and I did not surrender!"

FOUR

QUEEN OF THE SOUTHERN OCEAN

"She left her palace beneath the waves..."

I had to know more about the man who had not surrendered. His eyes crinkled with avuncular good humour as he fielded my questions. Alex Papadimitriou was a naturalized Indonesian, born on a Sumatran plantation between the wars to a Greek father and a German-Japanese mother. After a lifetime in the tropics, his swarthy Mediterranean features could pass for Indonesian. During the war he served as an interpreter in both the German and the Japanese navies. He knew the ships and the submarines that these long dead sailors had served on. Why had he not surrendered along with the others? Ah…that was a long story, he said.

His two companions introduced themselves in turn. The sturdy man with the bushy white moustache was Nanno Nommensen, the son of an officer in the former KNIL, the Royal Dutch Indies Army, and the great-grandson of Ingwer Ludwig Nommensen, the man who brought Christianity to the Bataks of Sumatra. Nanno was born to a Dutch-Javanese mother in Batavia in 1937. In addition to his native language he spoke fluent German, English and Indonesian. As a retired Marine colonel his job in Indonesia was to maintain the graves of 25,000 Dutch soldiers and civilians who died during World War II and the Indonesian revolution which followed. I asked him why he had come to the German ceremony. "You could say that I have a professional interest in graveyards," he replied, "…and I come in memory of my father."

The third gentleman, the tall one with the glasses and the tousled white hair, introduced himself as *Pater* Adolf Heuken. Call me "Romo," he said, as the Indonesians do. He was a Jesuit priest from Germany and a long-time resident of the genteel suburb of Menteng in Jakarta. As I came to know him better over the ensuing year, I marveled at his breadth of knowledge. He was a particularly erudite member of the Society of Jesus, an order famous for its love of learning. From a small desk in his book-lined study he wrote an encyclopedia of the twentieth century Catholic Church, a German-Indonesian dictionary and a popular book on the historical sites of Jakarta. He was also a publisher, a tour guide and a mentor to young Indonesian Christians. Like many others, *Pater* Heuken attended the ceremony to renew a commitment, to comprehend the unthinkable and somehow to address a tragic history.

A photographer called us all over to the cenotaph for a group picture. As we milled about the white pillar, *Pater* Heuken pointed to the inscription at its base and remarked that he had some books by Emil Helfferich that might interest me. After the photo he and I stood among the statuary while he reminisced, as if Helfferich were an old friend….

> On an October Sunday in 1926, as Germans struggled with pain, pride and guilt in the aftermath of a senseless war, Emil Helfferich rallied his battered expatriate community in Batavia with this monument to German naval heroes. In a white jacket and starkly contrasting black pants, the bearded and bespectacled 48-year-old businessman stood beside the Buddha and delivered a rousing speech. He spoke to the cadets and officers of the training

ship *Hamburg*, the first German naval vessel to visit Batavia since
the beginning of the Great War.

We imagined the echoes of Helfferich's speech, like voices whispering in
the leaves of the old trees. The priest felt a kinship to these two brothers
who, like him, had spent so many years in the Far East. Emil especially
intrigued him. *Pater* Heuken described an eager young man in a new white
suit, leaning over a steamship railing and sailing into the glow of an eastern dawn at the turn of the century. In 1899 and again in 1926 the future
must have looked rosy, with no hint of the horrors to come. He was a poet,
a sensitive man, and he must have found in this beautiful glade a fitting
site for a memorial. Did he know what lay beneath?

Grey clouds and a distant rumble of thunder brought us back to the
present. *Pater* Heuken's gaze drifted sideways to the fanciful Ganesha. The
Jesuit priest grinned good-naturedly at the elephant which loves knowledge. The leaves rustled insistently beneath the darkening sky as another
peal of thunder rumbled around the mountain. A mechanical clatter intruded on the hubbub of conversation. The young men reappeared and
removed the chairs, tossing them into the back of the Kijang truck. Adja
hurried over to supervise them. A soldier lowered the flags. Car doors
opened and shut. Waving farewell to the thinning crowd, the ambassador
and his wife stepped elegantly into the black Mercedes. The car purred
slowly back down the mountain. The remaining men and women folded
the tables and packed the dishes and cutlery. Small ragged children darted
into the crowd and picked up the leftovers. One by one, hikers and cars
turned down the road and disappeared out of sight.

I had already planned to stay behind and chat with Adja. My three
new acquaintances, Alex, Nanno and "Romo," picked up their walking
sticks and waved goodbye. I promised *Pater* Heuken that I would drop by
his house to borrow the Helfferich books. Nanno strode briskly down the
road ahead of them and turned around. "Hurry or you'll be caught in the
rain!" he shouted.

Mohamad and Adja bantered on the concrete benches at the foot of
the graveyard. They were telling each other stories, legs crossed, cigarettes
dangling from their lips one moment and waving about in their hands the

next. I walked over to where they were sitting. Adja introduced me to the *haj* pilgrim as a "Canadian from Jakarta" and we shook hands. After a minute or two of pleasantries Mohamad tossed away the stub of his cigarette, making sure it landed beyond Adja's neatly manicured lawn. With a certain dignified courtliness he stood up to leave. Resplendent in his batik shirt and white cap, he flashed us a wide toothy smile as he headed down the road.

Adja motioned for me to sit down beside him on the other bench. He looked tired but more relaxed now that his duties were over. His broom lay on the ground at his side and the *kretek* I had given him dangled loosely from his fingertips. He smelled of stale smoke and sweat. I asked him about the pilgrim. Adja cleared his throat and spit expertly into the distance. He told me that *Pak* Mohamad Syarib had indeed been to Mecca on the *haj*, one of the few people in the village to have undertaken the long and expensive journey. His father was a German who worked for Helfferich on the tea plantation, probably just a few years before they built the monument. Adja pronounced the man's name as "Binderop." He returned to Germany when Mohamad was just a baby and left the boy's Sundanese mother to bring him up on her own. *Pak* Syarib had become a successful farmer and had built a fine gazebo on a hill overlooking his rice paddies.

Thunder rolled again in the distance. A group of tea-pickers trotted down the road to the village. They moved at a brisk pace to reach home before the oncoming storm. I caught a glimpse of a younger woman among them, wearing a green sarong. I pointed her out to Adja and mentioned that I thought I had seen her walking behind him during the ceremony.

Adja looked at me curiously and said nothing. He took a deep drag on his cigarette so that the cloves snapped and glowed. There was a twinkle in his eye, a bit of mischief. I knew that he was going to pull my leg. Most Indonesians like nothing better than a good joke, particularly at the expense of a naïve *orang putih*, a white man. "The goddess wears a green sarong," he said finally. "You saw the sea goddess."

I went along with the game. "So tell me about her. Did she come for the souls of the sailors?"

Adja looked at me in mock horror. "You mustn't make fun of the Queen of the Southern Ocean – *Nyai* Roro Kidul." He rolled the r's and let her name slide sonorously off his tongue. "She plucks men from the ocean to be her soldiers and women to be her servants. She sends storms when she is angry and she causes the rice to grow." The puppet-master warmed to his subject. "*Ratu* Kidul was a princess of the Pajajaran Empire, a beautiful woman whose father banished her from the court when she refused to accept an arranged marriage. He placed a curse upon her. Scabies disfigured her face and she smelled like fish. She wandered down to the south coast at Karang Hawu and dreamed that she would be cured if she jumped into the ocean. And so it happened. Now she lives in a splendid palace on the floor of the sea. She will become mortal again on the Day of Judgement. Her spirits inhabit caves along the south coast of Java – like the cave at Karang Tretes, east of the river Upak. Only sultans, kings and princes have the courage to enter that cave, where the goddess grants revelations to her favourites – like Senopati." His eyes stared dreamily into space as he conjured up a hero of ancient Java. He stood up slowly and began to move his skinny arms and legs to the rhythm of the Ramayana.

"Senopati founded the Mataram kingdom. Enemies surrounded him in his early years. To soothe his restless soul, he fished with a cast-net in the river Samas. One day some fishermen caught a huge fish, an *olor*, and offered it to Senopati. He took pity on the creature and ordered the men to set it free. Later on, when he was swimming in the river, the *olor* approached and offered to carry him on its back. And so he rode down the river until he reached the southern coast. Feeling tired and lonely, Senopati prayed to God. All at once a storm arose. It whipped the sea, smashed waves against the rocks and broke the trees. When the winds settled down, many fish lay dead on the beach, so powerful was his prayer.

"*Nyai* Roro Kidul felt the turbulence of the waters. She left her palace beneath the waves to find the source of all this restless movement. On the shore she spied a tall man absorbed in prayer to God. She said, 'He must be the one for whom God stirs up my ocean,' and she read his mind. She left the waves and walked toward Senopati. The goddess bent over his feet and joined the palms of her hands in a *sembah*, a sign of respect. 'Prince, banish from your heart those thoughts of sorrow which disturb my sea. Allay your wild wishes so that the winds may cease to be unruly. Make your mind serene so that the broken bodies may be restored. Have mercy, for it is my task to protect the seas. Your prayer to God has been heard. You will rule Java and so will your descendants after you. You will also rule the spirits, the jinns and the fairies, and they will help you against your enemies. You will be the father of Java.'

"When Senopati heard these words he felt great joy. The waves subsided; the trees rose up again and stood on their roots. The fish came back to life and dived into the ocean. The goddess smiled and flashed her eyes, dark green flecked with gold like the hills of Pajajaran. She walked into the sea and beckoned him to follow. He strode through the surf and felt as comfortable in the water as if on land. She moved so gracefully that Senopati instantly fell in love. She led him to her palace in the ocean, through a gate of pearls, past walls of silver and across floors of rubies. She bid him rest on a golden divan, where fairies and sea nymphs brought them food and refreshment.

"Senopati, deeply in love, pressed his body against *Ratu* Kidul. He feared that he could not make love to her because he was a mere mortal. She encouraged him with smiles until he was emboldened to ask, 'I should like to see your bedroom Ni-Mas, golden girl.' She took him by the hand and together they floated down to her bedchamber.

"'Ni-Mas, this must be heaven. It is beautiful – like you. I do not want to go back to Mataram. Will you marry me?'

"'It is better to be a queen than to be married,' she answered. 'I do not wish to take orders from anyone.'

"'Ni-Mas, can you cure me of my love for you?'

"'Prince, I am no *dukun*. You have all the women you desire in your own land.'

"'Ni-Mas, it is only you I want.'

"She encouraged him further until he took her in his arms and laid her down on her bed. They made love for three days and three nights, caressing each other endlessly. She taught him how to command the spirits, the jinns and the fairies, how to call them from afar. On the fourth day she asked him to depart.

"'If you should ever need me,' said the Queen of the Southern Ocean, 'stand straight with your feet together and your arms crossed on your breast. Look up toward the southern sky. Soon I shall arrive with my armies of sea spirits, all fully armed. Now you must go back to your own country.' Broken-hearted, Senopati walked back over the waves. He stepped onto Java's shore and turned around to face the ocean. But she was gone."

Pak Adja

The old puppet-master bowed from the waist. I was impressed. "Senopati – he was real, wasn't he?" There was a street in Jakarta named after him.

"Of course," Adja replied, "He was buried in 1601. You can see his tomb in Kota Gede, on the outskirts of Yogyakarta. He was the grandfather of the famous Sultan Agung. The goddess is real too. She visits a special room in the hotel that Sukarno built near Pelabuhan Ratu. Our sultans still consult her on important matters. Even *Pak* Suharto has meditated in her cave. Did you know that she appeared before Sultan Hamengkubuwono the Ninth six months before the Japanese army arrived? She warned him that the Japanese would replace the Dutch. She also told him when the Japanese would surrender and she predicted our national revolution."

He would have continued but it was time for me to leave. The air smelled damp and a chill wind blew through the trees. Leaves swirled noisily across the graveyard. Adja walked over to a nearby banana plant and deftly sliced off a leaf with his *golok*. He passed me the large droopy frond just as the first rain drops started to fall. I thanked him for the "umbrella" and for the entertaining story.

"It's all real, what I tell you. Be careful. Don't visit this graveyard by yourself late at night and don't wear green when you swim in the ocean." Then he smiled enigmatically and chanted in a high thin voice:

"Kinadjriha dĕdĕmit sadaja
         tan ana purun
Miwah yen kekesahan jim setan
         tan ana wani
Aneng wona sato galak pan lumadjar."

"That's Javanese, *Pak*. I don't know what it means." I said.

Adja translated the words for me from the language of central Java, of the shadow puppets and the Sultan:

"Be feared all the spirits,
         none can oppose them.
When the devils take wing,
         none shall dare to oppose them.
In the forests savage beasts do run.

"Those are the last lines of the *Sĕrat Sakondar*, the story of Java," Adja replied proudly. Large rain drops spattered on the gravel path. Tree boughs heaved in the gusts and the twisted grey trunks creaked in the fury of the wind. Adja grabbed his broom and scurried back to his hut.

Feeling a little silly with a banana leaf on my head, I watched the inscrutable old *dalang*, now the *jaga* of Artja, as he disappeared from view. Then I turned and marched briskly out of the graveyard, down the stone road to the village. Far below me the tea-pickers padded downhill on the soles of bare feet. The woman in the green sarong guided us all home. I felt strangely light-headed, as if I were embarked on a voyage through the olden days.

The rain engulfed me. The storm roared down the mountain in a grey wave. My feet splashed through puddles and slipped over the cobbles. Mud spattered my legs. I stopped abruptly by the bamboo windmills. The wind tugged at the flapping banana leaf and flung droplets of spray into my blinking eyes. The blades spun madly in the howling gale. They wailed and moaned like devils on the wing, "savage beasts" groaning in anguish. My skin crawled. Shivering, I turned my back to the horrible noise and jogged all the way down.

Soaking wet but determined, the boys squatted by the car. They pointed to the four intact hubcaps and stretched out their palms. I paid them and drove home.

FIVE

A VOYAGE DIVINE AND STRANGE

"...and now we are embarked..."

...not a sound
Was heard; one horrible repose did keep
The forests and the floods, and all around
Darkness more dread than night was poured upon the ground.

Hark! 'tis the rushing of a wind that sweeps
Earth and the ocean. See! the lightnings yawn
Deluging Heaven with fire, and the lashed deeps
Glitter and boil beneath: it rages on,
One mighty stream, whirlwind and waves upthrown,
Lightning, and hail, and darkness eddying by...

...while through the sky
The pallid semicircle of the moon
Passed on, in slow and moving majesty;
Its upper horn arrayed in mists...

...the hue
Of the white moon, amid that heaven so blue,
Suddenly stained with shadow did appear;
A speck, a cloud, a shape, approaching grew,
Like a great ship in the sun's sinking sphere
Beheld afar at sea, and swift it came anear...

A course precipitous, of dizzy speed,
Suspending thought and breath; a monstrous sight!
For in the air do I behold indeed
An Eagle and a Serpent wreathed in fight...

The Eagle, hovering, wheeled to left and right,
And hung with lingering wings over the flood,
And startled with its yells the wide air's solitude.

A shaft of light upon its wings descended,
And every golden feather gleamed therein –
Feather and scale, inextricably blended.
The Serpent's mailed and many-coloured skin
Shone through the plumes its coils were twined within...

And casting back its eager head, with beak
And talon unremittingly assailed
The wreathèd Serpent, who did ever seek
Upon his enemy's heart a mortal wound to wreak...

Floated the shattered plumes; bright scales did leap,
Where'er the Eagle's talons made their way,
Like sparks into the darkness; – as they sweep,
Blood stains the snowy foam of the tumultuous deep...

...the vast bird would shake
The strength of his unconquerable wings
As in despair, and with his sinewy neck,
Dissolve in sudden shock those linkèd rings,
Then soar – as swift as smoke from a volcano springs...

It had endured, when lifeless, stark, and rent,
Hung high that mighty Serpent, and at last
Fell to the sea, while o'er the continent,
With clang of wings and scream the Eagle passed,
Heavily borne away on the exhausted blast...

"...there was a Woman, beautiful as morning..."

There was a Woman, beautiful as morning,
Sitting beneath the rocks, upon the sand
Of the waste sea – fair as one flower adorning
An icy wilderness – each delicate hand
Lay crossed upon her bosom, and the band
Of her dark hair had fall'n, and so she sate
Looking upon the waves...
It seemed that this fair Shape had looked upon
That unimaginable fight...

...but she rose, and on the gale
Loosening her star-bright robe and shadowy hair
Poured forth her voice; the caverns of the vale
That opened to the ocean, caught it there,
And filled with silver sounds the overflowing air.

She spake in language whose strange melody
Might not belong to earth...

Then on the sands the Woman sate again,
And wept and clasped her hands, and all between,
Renewed the unintelligible strain
Of her melodious voice and eloquent mien;
And she unveiled her bosom, and the green
And glancing shadows of the sea did play
O'er its marmoreal depth...

Then she arose, and smiled on me with eyes
Serene yet sorrowing, like that planet fair,
While yet the daylight lingereth in the skies...

And said: 'To grieve is wise, but the despair
Was weak and vain which led thee here from sleep:
This shalt thou know, and more, if thou dost dare
With me and with this Serpent, o'er the deep,
A voyage divine and strange, companionship to keep.'

A boat of rare device, which had no sail
But its own curvèd prow of thin moonstone,
Wrought like a web of texture fine and frail,
To catch those gentlest winds which are not known
To breathe, but by the steady speed alone
With which it cleaves the sparkling sea; and now
We are embarked — the mountains hang and frown
Over the starry deep that gleams below,
A vast and dim expanse, as o'er the waves we go.

And as we sailed, a strange and awful tale
That Woman told, like such mysterious dream...
'Speak not to me, but hear! Much shalt thou learn,
Much must remain unthought, and more untold,

In the dark Future's ever-flowing urn:
Know then, that from the depth of ages old,
Two Powers o'er mortal things dominion hold
Ruling the world with a divided lot,
Immortal, all-pervading, manifold…

'Such is this conflict – when mankind doth strive
With its oppressors in a strife of blood…
The Snake and Eagle meet – the world's foundations tremble!

'List, stranger, list, mine is an human form,
Like that thou wearest – touch me – shrink not now!
My hand thou feel'st is not a ghost's, but warm
With human blood. – 'Twas many years ago,
Since first my thirsting soul aspired to know
The secrets of this wondrous world…
'Woe could not be mine own, since far from men
I dwelt, a free and happy orphan child,
By the sea-shore, in a deep mountain-glen;
And near the waves, and through the forests wild,
I roamed, to storm and darkness reconciled…

'A dying poet gave me books, and blessed
With wild but holy talk the sweet unrest
In which I watched him as he died away…

'Thus the dark tale which history doth unfold
I knew, but not, methinks, as others know,
For they weep not; and Wisdom had unrolled
The clouds which hide the gulf of mortal woe…'

Excerpts from "The Revolt of Islam, Canto I"
by Percy Bysshe Shelley, 1817

PART 2
EMIL HELFFERICH

SIX

THE RHINE AND THE ELBE

Hamburg's Port on the Elbe, 1895

Thunderstorms lashed Jakarta in November, the beginning of the winter monsoon. Sheets of driving rain and huge pools of water brought traffic to a standstill. Roads became rivers. Motorcycles massed under the protection of bridges. People ran for shelter, their heads covered with newspapers and purses. A relentless cascade of rain and lightning pummelled the city.

After an hour the curtain lifted, the downpour drizzled to an end and the clouds slowly drifted apart. Between the towering masses blue patches opened, through which fingers of late afternoon sunshine probed the wet earth. Grey gloom and shadows briefly vanished in the golden moment before sunset. Sunlight glistened on dripping leaves and reflected brightly from puddles on flooded roads and lawns. Flaming red petals of *flamboyan* trees swirled in the water and gaudily flecked the green grass. Traffic moved again fitfully as bleating columns of cars sloshed through the wide tree-shaded avenues of Menteng. Every taxi was full. In vain I waved at the passing cars.

A three-wheeled *bajaj* puttered noisily down the street. It weaved between cars and gingerly furrowed the deep puddles. A black vinyl roof and cheap plastic windows capped a battered and boxy orange frame. Two wobbly headlamps stared froglike from the front panel of this glorified motorcycle. The driver gripped the handlebars tightly and peered through the cracked windshield. A greasy red bandana covered his forehead. In desperation I flagged him down. I squeezed into the cramped compartment and agreed to a fee befitting an *orang putih* stranded in the rain. We drove off as fast as the tiny wheels could take us.

Past stately embassies and colonial mansions we crawled, past iron gates and high garden walls topped with broken glass and barbed wire, past magnificent umbrella-shaped rain trees. From the tiny cab in the back, through a taped and torn plastic window, I strained to read the distant house numbers.

"*Disini*! Here!" I cried. The *bajaj* lurched to a sudden halt in front of a rambling colonial-style home. A tall tree overhung the driveway, its branches festooned with huge leaves of epiphyte ferns and *Philodendron* vines. I paid the scruffy driver from a wad of red Rupiah notes then rang the bell beside a metal gate. A *jaga* answered and led me through the garden, down a narrow corridor to an entrance at the side of the house. He insisted I should enter while he went around to the front to call the priest.

I removed my shoes and crossed the threshold into a small study. Though not as large as I had imagined, the room had a tall ceiling and a window overlooking the back garden. Bookshelves lined the walls and a small desk sat at an angle in one corner. The room had a warm brown wooden feeling, old-fashioned and welcoming. After a short while *Pater* Heuken entered through an inside door.

He was comfortably dressed in slippers and a short-sleeved shirt and he stooped slightly to pass under the lintel. His tousled white hair and his friendly smile reminded me of a tall elf, full of energy and sprightly good humour. He slipped easily into a chair behind his desk and motioned for me to take a seat in front. As he peered through wire-rimmed bifocals at the books on his desk, I saw for a moment the learned Jesuit priest, reflective and serious. Outside the window, in the gathering dusk, the shadows of trees lengthened and moved imperceptibly.

We talked of many things, as the old saying goes, of sea goddesses and sailors and submarines, of Hindu empires and the modern world. At one point he stood up to call the cook, who returned later with coffee and two plates of fried rice. Our discussion turned to the graveyard's mysterious beginnings and its multifaceted history.

"You should start with Helfferich," he announced firmly. "Emil – not Theodor. Theodor was his sickly younger brother. Emil's life spanned almost a hundred years – through two world wars and many ups and downs. He was a mirror of his times and a witness to the greatest events of the century." In his methodical manner the Jesuit priest showed me photos of Helfferich and expounded on his life. He cleared his throat and leaned forward on his elbows, pressing his palms and fingertips together. I remembered the *sembah,* the sign of respect that Adja gave to Mohamad and the sea goddess to Senopati.

Helfferich was a dynamic person, the priest continued, a man bursting with energy and vitality. I could see from the photos that young Emil possessed the innocent good looks of a choir boy – slender, with smooth cheeks, a high forehead and dark wavy hair. A firm jaw and a steady gaze hinted at the man he would become. He had a good nose for business though he began very humbly as a trader in Sumatra. As the years went by he matured into a successful and influential businessman both in the Indies and in Germany, where he directed several large companies. His hairline receded as his waistline expanded. A thick bushy beard – a *Rauschebart* – matched the image of elder statesman. But he was neither a simple merchant nor a heartless tycoon. Behind the thick spectacles his eyes looked vulnerable and serious. A romantic dreamer and a sentimental poet, he searched for a woman who would love him and look after him. He was sensitive to indigenous people in an era when many white men treated natives with contempt. Beneath a logical mind and a courageous heart lay a soft spot and a belly that made most of his decisions. He tried to make his parents proud, to be a good man who helped others and did no harm.

The human urge to be respected drove him on – to be popular and to be remembered as a "pillar of the community."

His later life was full of sadness and he lost much of what he loved. Despite his liberal leanings he was an ardent German patriot and he admired the military. The Third Reich presented him with an ethical quandary. He tried and failed to prevent terrible things. After the war the British jailed him briefly and investigated his Nazi connections.

Pater Heuken interrupted his soliloquy and stood up from his desk. He walked over to the bookshelves. "Helfferich left behind several books and at least three monuments – to sailors and other victims of war – and to his *Lebensgefährtin.*"

"*Lebensgefährtin?*" I asked in bewilderment.

The white-haired priest squinted through his glasses at some tomes on the upper shelf. "She was the love of his life, his constant companion – *die Lebensgefährtin*, as he called her – 'the one who travels life's road with me.' A strange name when you think about it, not as cozy as 'wife' or 'sweetheart.'"

He wiggled his glasses up and down to read the titles. "Here it is – *Ein Leben – A Life.*" He pulled the book down and passed it over to me. "It has good pictures too. A book must have good pictures. Look at the front cover – there is a drawing of his monument at Artja. Here is another one, a little book with a long name, *Südostasiatische Geschichten – Southeast Asian Stories*, and another short one, *Erlebtes – Experiences*. They are all in German so that will give you good exercise. I can also lend you a *Wörterbuch* if you like." He hummed a little tune as he pulled out Langenscheidt's official German-Indonesian dictionary, the one he had written himself.

I declined the rather esoteric dictionary but gratefully accepted the other three books. They were all privately published, old and out of print. I opened *Ein Leben* and thumbed through the pictures, stopping at a 1903 portrait of Helfferich's *Lebensgefährtin*. The woman in the painting wore a flowing full-length kimono and a white camellia over her left ear. Her left hand rested on her hip in a manner both graceful and bold. Sadness tinged her defiant eyes.

I heard a gurgling sound. The priest poured two glasses of schnapps from a crystal decanter. He passed one glass over to me and raised his own in a toast.

"You must write a book. I don't know how you will do it but you must tell the story. I drink to the success of your project. As Helfferich would say – *Santé*." We downed the schnapps in one gulp.

Pater Heuken escorted me to the sidewalk in front of his home. He rousted the *jaga* out of his comfortable *kursi malas*, the "lazy chair," and asked him to hail a taxi for me. I didn't want a long ride home in a *bajaj*. Cicadas buzzed and whined in the tall trees of Menteng as I stepped into the cab and waved goodbye. The three books were tucked safely under my arm. Late that night I read the first page in the life of Emil Helfferich.

❦

The young boy stood scared and exhausted before the door of his house. His shoes were dusty and the night was dark. Summoning his courage, he burst through the door and shouted to his worried parents:

"I have seen the Rhine!"

Early that morning ten-year-old Emil and his friend Christian had hatched a secret plan to walk from their homes in Neustadt to the fabled river, twenty-five kilometres away. With a one-mark coin to last them the day, they set off at a jaunty pace into the rising sun. For the first time in their lives they splashed their feet in the Rhine and scrambled aboard the bridge of an empty ship. They spent the coin on a sausage and bread and plodded the weary road back home. He survived that youthful adventure – and the loving wrath of his parents. Unknown to the boys, firemen and forest rangers had been combing the Haardt hills for hours.

On fine summer days he played with Christian and other friends in those same hills, topped by ruined castles. They were Indians one day, Visigoths the next, and their battle cry was "*Titibum!*" For the rest of his life Emil could feel the dent in his skull where an overenthused rival had beaten him with a club. He was skinny and small, but courageous, and blessed with a knack for leadership and a zest for life.

Emil Helfferich was born on January 17, 1878, on a cold winter's day in Neustadt an der Haardt. The town nestles among rolling green fields of grapes, wedged between the high Pfälzerwald to the north and the Vosges Mountains of Alsace to the south. It was founded in the Middle Ages by the Count Palatine of the Rhine. By the late nineteenth century it had endured a bewildering succession of French and German armies, overlords, kings and emperors. Soldiers vied to control the west bank of the old river while priests of two Christian religions struggled for the hearts and souls of its people. The village was fortunate to avoid the excesses of these great upheavals and the ugliness of the industrial revolution, much as the busy *autobahn* bypasses it today. Renamed Neustadt an der Weinstrasse in a modern marketing ploy, "The New Town on the Wine Road" still retains a picturesque medieval character.

The little boy was the fifth of seven children born to Augusta and Friedrich, the prosperous owner of a weaving mill that manufactured fine cotton and woolen tricots. Their home was busy, happy and unremarkable. All the children were born within a year or two of each other. Karl, the eldest, would become the most famous scion of the family. After Karl came Emilie, the only girl, then Philipp, August and Emil. Emil was five and a half years younger than his eldest brother. Theodor was born when Emil was two and Wilhelm, the baby, when he was four.

Summer passed and with it the endless sunny days of adventures and play-fights in the hills. During the long school year and the dreary winter months Emil dreamed of warm faraway places. A Japanese parasol hung over his desk at home and a map of the world faced him as he studied. When he opened his clothes closet a stuffed seagull peeked out from beneath the shirts. If he closed his eyes and squinted hard he could hear its keening call above the roar of distant surf.

Young Emil excelled at his studies, except for mathematics, and found pleasure in writing from an early age. His style tended to be passionate, sentimental and immoderate. Yearning for the romance of foreign travel, the precocious fifteen-year-old once poured his soul into a 36-page essay on the Far East. The teacher laboured through the effusive prose and publicly accused him of plagiarism. Emil stoutly maintained his innocence. The essay, he claimed, was merely the product of a young and unfettered imagination. That same year he wrote a five-act play entitled "Mohammed" of which he was very proud. "Mecca is taken!" shouted the prophet in the opening stanza of Act I, formerly Act II. His eldest brother had insisted he delete the first act as too sensual. Karl also struck out an explicit verse in which Mohammed expressed his fervent love for a woman named Saphie. Emil grudgingly accepted the dictates of his unsentimental, prudish older brother but the original version lived on in the family archive.

In a leap of romantic faith Emil thought he could empathize with the founder of Islam. In a similar fantasy of his imagination, the fictional Saphie symbolized his first love. Her real name was Maria and she came from the Black Forest in Baden. From a discreet distance Emil admired her graceful figure, her marvelous greyish-blue eyes and her exotic complexion – honey-brown like a Malay. She squinted endearingly when she laughed. Emil was only twelve when he first fell in love with the older girl but he never spoke to her until the year he wrote "Mohammed." He felt a mystical bond. Her family name was Daur, an uncommon surname but one which had already appeared once in his family tree. When Friedrich Helfferich had searched the record to find a name for his newborn fifth child, he discovered an Emil Helfferich in the eighteenth century. This earlier Emil had married a woman named Maria Daur. When Emil learned of this genealogical curiosity, he was convinced that his life and Maria's were intertwined by destiny. He found excuses to walk beneath her window and he considered himself lucky when he saw her face behind the glass. Gradually he worked up the nerve to drop off gifts of flowers, chocolates and oranges. One evening at the end of the final school term, Emil and some friends stood outside her door and sang a sentimental song. This was as close as the shy young teenager could come to introducing himself. He loved her in the abstract.

He spotted her on the street soon afterward, heading toward the train station. "When are you leaving?" he stammered in surprise. His face flushed. These were the first words he had ever spoken to her. Now she would finally reveal her secret passion for him.

"At a quarter past one," she flatly replied. She walked on and disappeared around the corner, never to see him again. Emil stood rooted to the ground, his first love gone forever and his dream of destiny shattered.

Emil had just finished his six years in the *Realschule*. He looked at the map on the wall and the seagull in his closet and thought about running away to join the new German Navy. That's what you did if your heart was broken. Unfortunately he had started to wear glasses and his eyesight wasn't good enough. Soon a more realistic plan took shape in his mind. On a Sunday morning he walked over to the mill where his father sat in an empty office, catching up on the week's paperwork. Emil knocked on the door, entered and stood apprehensively before the massive desk.

"*Vater*, I know what I want to do," he announced, "I'm going to be a businessman – an overseas businessman." Emil's great-grandfather had been a merchant in foreign trade. Business, world commerce and a passion for politics resonated through the Helfferich family down the long generations. His father smiled proudly and shook his hand.

Friedrich sent his son to Switzerland for a year to learn French and English, languages that would be useful in foreign countries. Emil spent the last three months in Cointrin, living in a country house with a retired teacher and his aged Russian mother. In a nearby house lived the Golay family. *Madame* was a lovely, charming woman of the world and *Monsieur* Golay owned a jewelry store in Geneva. They had three daughters, one of whom stole Emil's sensitive heart. Jeanne was dark-skinned like Maria but with large doe-like eyes, clever and well read. This time he introduced himself without hesitation. They played croquet, enjoyed outings on the lake and shared their innermost thoughts. Within weeks their relationship blossomed.

"Emil," she asked, as they floated in a boat along the shore of Lake Geneva on a lazy summer afternoon, "do you like me?"

Emil stopped rowing and let the oars drift in the water. He blushed and furrowed his young brow in thought. "Yes, of course, Jeanne...I like you very much." His mind raced with passionate eloquence, like the characters in his play, but his tongue felt thick and clumsy.

"Pretend we could do whatever we wanted, Emil. What would make you really happy? What's the most romantic thing you can think of?"

A gull flew overhead. Emil watched it and paused, his hands lightly gripping the oars. "Travel, Jeanne...for me I think the most romantic thing would be to travel." He warmed to the thought and gazed over the rippling water. "I would love to sail on a ship to the far side of the world, to live in a thatched hut and work with natives in the jungle, to build something with my own hands – a business my father would be proud of. At night I would write poems in my little hut...with my true love beside me," he added quickly as he pulled hard again on the oars. "And what about you, Jeanne, what would you like?"

She smiled sadly at the thought of a hut in the jungle and looked away to where the oar blades made little whirlpools in the water. "Oh, I don't know, Emil... I think this is quite perfect here." She turned around again and asked, "Would you write me a poem some day?"

"I will write hundreds," he replied and they laughed as the warm sun shone down on their heads. The water rippled and gurgled in the wake of the boat.

Young love was interrupted when Emil returned to Neustadt and contemplated his uncertain future. His parents persuaded him to go to Hamburg. A cousin lived there, someone who could help him get started. On a sunny autumn morning in 1895, Emil hugged his parents goodbye and boarded the train to the famous city. Behind him lay his childhood; before him stretched the unknown. A lump formed in his throat as he waved at the receding figures on the platform. The lonely romantic had an inkling that his life had changed forever, that a grand adventure awaited.

Seventeen-year-old Emil arrived in Hamburg in October, 1895. After a hesitant start he signed a three-year contract as an apprentice clerk with the firm of Jürgen Peters, Importer and Exporter of Wines and Spirits. The dark musty office, squeezed into the cramped Catharinenstrasse near the docks, did not quite measure up to his rosy dream of foreign trade. Bluntly warned that his handwriting was poor, he spent the first few agonizing weeks learning how to write in a flowing script. Answering the telephone was his primary responsibility and his greatest fear. The telephone was a recent invention and older callers, in particular, yelled at him through the handset. Few could understand his slow, lilting, *Pfälzer* dialect.

For relief from the office he strolled through the winter drizzle down the wet cobbled streets to the harbour. There he could talk to sailors, ship chandlers and captains, men who had sailed around the world. Ever since the time of Napoleon the merchants of Hamburg had plied their foreign trade from this port on the Elbe. They faced a world already divided among the great European powers. Lacking the support of a nation-state, German businessmen nevertheless carved out small but lucrative niches for themselves in Africa, the West Indies, South America, Asia and the islands of the Pacific. Emil ambled along the piers amid stacks of wooden crates bound for overseas, their exotic destinations stencilled on the sides in black paint. Tall three-masted schooners, elegant symbols of a dying era, vied for dock space with modern coal-fired steamships. An odour of hemp, tar and coal dust suffused the damp grey air. On occasion he spent a few *Pfennige* for a tour of the harbour, so that he could stand in the bow and relive his clandestine adventure with Christian on the Rhine. Ships' bells and foghorns sounded across the river and real seagulls cried overhead.

Every day as he walked to the gloomy office on 17 Catharinenstrasse, he passed beneath the gabled roof of Number 37. This was the Hamburg headquarters of Arnold Otto Meyer, owner of Behn Meyer, a successful import-export firm which had recently celebrated its golden jubilee in Singapore. In the decades to come old Meyer would have reason to treasure young Helfferich – and to reproach him.

Each evening Emil returned to the rented room in his cousin's house on Schürbeckerstrasse. He played with the young children and sang nursery rhymes with the housemaid. Her name was Martha, a pert sixteen-year-old Hamburg girl in a black dress and a white cap. She teased and tempted him in a way that Jeanne had never dared. One evening, after the children were safely put to bed, they lay down on the sofa and lost themselves in love for one passionate hour. It was a blissful new pleasure for Emil but he soon put the hasty encounter out of mind. Half a century later, in the aftermath of World War II, a tiny grey grandmother would pay a surprise visit to his home on the Elbe. She was the mother-in-law of his chimney sweep. Emil recognized the saucy gleam in her eye and invited Martha inside. The lonely childless man sang nursery-room songs with the former housemaid and reminisced about the old days, in a happier time before the wars.

Although Martha had awakened a new appetite within Emil, he pursued a more platonic relationship with a very different woman who lived one floor above him. She was a delicate, slender lady, so thin as to be almost translucent. Early each morning she sang down to him in a soft silvery voice, "O my sweet Oscar!" They called each other pet names and he never did remember her real name. They snuggled together on winter coach rides. On hot summer days they drifted around the lake in a boat, his head nestled in her meagre lap. But she suffered from a chronic lung disease and slowly wasted away. One bleak day she left Hamburg for her home in northern Germany and died soon after, leaving Emil at a loss once again for companionship.

"*Gelt, Emil, bleibst brav*! Remember, Emil, be good!" These had been the parting words of his mother on the train platform. Tellingly, these were also the first words Helfferich later chose to print in his memoirs. At Christmas he received his first wage – 100 Marks in ten gold pieces. His own money now jingled in his pocket. One evening his cousins invited him down to St. Pauli and the notorious Reeperbahn. Emil had demurely circled the perimeter in a carriage once – with his girlfriend in the daytime – but he had never before ventured into those extravagant, sinful streets at night. With a thrill of excitement he plunged into the unknown.

What first struck him was the noise: tipsy carousers laughing and shouting, touts barking from doorways, voices singing lustily inside. Sailors on leave jostled good-naturedly with dandies in top hats. Emil and his cousins elbowed their way into the Kaisersäle where the admission was free. Everyone was singing. Beer steins swayed to the beat and a cloud of smoke hung over the revellers. They shouted to hear each other above the din. Mirrors lined the walls on three sides to give the illusion of space. Chairs were crammed right up to the tiny stage where, one by one, the dancing girls flounced across, kicking their legs high to show off frilly pink undergarments. Each girl sang her maudlin piece in a voice made low and husky from too much smoke and beer. The patrons belted out the chorus. Hawkers weaved through the tables selling bouquets of violets, which they later retrieved from the stage and resold. Sometimes the dancers leaped off the platform, all leggy and busty, and cuddled up to the men in the front row. Emil was mesmerized by the dresses and the smell of hair and perfume. He returned again and again to St. Pauli.

Polkas and waltzes reverberated in the dance halls. Restaurants served huge meals. Conversations lasted all night in cafés. Snake charmers, magicians, jugglers, dogs, horses and monkeys played in the variety shows. At the Favorite-Hammonia club Emil once performed on stage as a woman in a parody of a play by Schiller. Two sponges served for breasts; his "baby" was a pillow strapped to his belly. Another time he played Leda with her amorous swan. Wild orgies in the brothels of Altona inevitably followed these performances. For the rest of his life Emil never saw anything like it anywhere else in the world.

The red-light district of Altona lay out in the open, unlike the strait-laced quiet streets of Hamburg where the business of sin was conducted discreetly behind green shutters. Brothel after brothel lined the streets. Women lounged barebreasted in brightly lit windows and called down to lusty passers-by. After the loss of his ethereal girlfriend Emil visited more than a few brothels, searching for love and never finding it. He seemed to prefer lively conversation with cheerful motherly types to pleasures of an earthier sort. His favourite was a tall high-spirited blonde named Stefani but the most memorable woman was *Tante* Buhr. She owned the largest and most expensive bawdy house in the city. Here one could sit at white-lacquered dinner tables and enjoy good food and drink and witty inter-course of a more social kind. Those who so wished could pass through the velvet curtain to the inner sanctum. Emil preferred to join *Tante* Buhr at the table where she sat fanning herself, resolute and corpulent, as she par-ried clever remarks from her guests. She called Emil "*Djung*, young one." When she died a decade later, her funeral resembled that of a head of state. Wreaths adorned the stairs of the church and hundreds of admirers fol-lowed her bier. *Sic transit gloria mundi.*

As the three years with Jürgen Peters rolled by, Emil rapidly learned the basics of business. Unhappy with clerical work, he longed for some-thing more exciting. He joined a literature group with some friends, bicy-cled through the countryside, rowed competitively and immersed himself in the night life of St. Pauli. When his contract expired in 1898 he joined the army.

Founded by Bismarck, the Iron Chancellor, the fledgling nation-state of Germany obliged its young men to serve in the military for one year as "*Einjährige*." Following in the footsteps of his three older brothers, Emil tried to sign up with the Field Artillery. There was a unit in Bahrenfeld near Hamburg. But upon his arrival at the barracks the army summarily rejected him. "A weak body," proclaimed the medical officer. Emil was flabbergasted. Perhaps it was just his weak eyesight, he thought. He stood forlornly outside the barrack gate, uncertain whether to turn left or right. As he picked up his bag and started to walk away, an imposing military man strode down the sidewalk toward him. Emil greeted him politely. The man noticed his suitcase and stopped to talk.

"I see you're leaving the barracks. Have you just signed up?" the officer inquired. Emil ruefully described his rejection. The major sized him up and spoke to him in a friendly way, "Would you definitely like to join the artillery?"

"Yes, of course," Emil replied spiritedly, "and right here in Bahrenfeld!" The major, who happened to be the commandant, took him under his wing and marched him back into the barracks. Ten minutes later Emil Helfferich had joined the 10th Battery of the 24th Holstein Field Artillery Regiment.

Emil enjoyed army life to the full, right to the very end of the year. He willingly submitted to eight harsh weeks of recruit training and enthusiastically learned to ride a horse. They seemed to learn more about the cavalry than the artillery. Through the pastoral Holstein countryside they rode, summer and winter, sometimes bareback, sometimes with hangovers. His eyesight failed him only once, when his horse stumbled into a barbed wire fence, but he quickly recovered from his injuries. A strong military spirit infused him and his fellow *Einjährige*. They loved the discipline and felt a patriotic duty to their newly unified country. The adventure contrasted sharply with their comfortable bourgeois upbringing. They played at soldiering, wore swords and old-fashioned uniforms. No one got hurt. A gallant era was ending – a time before trenches, poison gas, submarines, aircraft, world wars and the mad slaughter of soldiers and civilians.

In April 1899 the commandant promoted him to Lance Corporal, one of only three among twenty-five. No longer did he have to walk into town in his peculiar recruit's uniform: the violet-blue breeches and the shiny black riding boots. Now he could wear civilian clothes and take longer passes. His love life improved as a result. One snowy night, while Emil stood guard in front of the barracks, bundled in his greatcoat and holding his rifle at the ready, a grey form loomed out of the blizzard. Käthe, his favourite girlfriend, had walked all the way from home to see him, to hug the gentle young soldier who wrote poems and dreamed of warm far-away places. She had a beautiful figure and long dark hair, a soft voice and friendly grey eyes. After a brief word with a sympathetic sergeant, Emil smuggled her into a deserted artillery shed. Among the cannon barrels and wooden wheels, in a nest of greatcoats and woolly scarves, he forgot all about the army and the snow falling outside. Decades later Käthe would surprise Emil once again. She, a silver-haired grandmother like Martha, appeared on his doorstep amid the bleakness of postwar Germany. He, a white-bearded old man with tears in his eyes, held her hand as they talked about a time long past.

The road from Bahrenfeld to Hamburg led through St. Pauli. Emil and his pals frequented the dance halls and cafés as much as ever – a ceaseless pursuit of male bonding and female affection. Returning home alone by train one dark night, he was startled when a statuesque woman boarded the half-empty carriage and took a seat near the front. The woman was his friend, Stefani, the blonde call girl from the red-light district. When the train rolled to a stop in Bahrenfeld she stood up to leave. Emil followed at a safe distance and shadowed her through dimly lit streets. She stopped and knocked on a door. It opened a crack. In stunned silence Emil recognized the face of his lieutenant, his favourite riding companion. Several days later, Lance Corporal Helfferich and Lieutenant von Welzien rode together by the Elbe on a fresh spring morning. Emil was itching to speak but what should he say? Finally he blurted, "*Herr Oberleutnant*, you and I share the same girlfriend – Stefani!" The lieutenant spun around in his saddle, eyed Emil warily and then burst into laughter. "So you know her too? A famous girl!" Emil laughed with relief. The good friends spurred their mounts and galloped away.

Helfferich loved the military life: the horses, the guns, the discipline of field maneuvers, the excitement and the romance. Were it not for his poor eyesight he might have stayed in the army. In 1914 he might have commanded a regiment on the western front, where his youthful zeal and patriotic ardour would have died along with his comrades. By good fortune his fate lay elsewhere.

Emil Helfferich in the German Army 1899

During his stint in the army he made several good friends but none so lifelong as his fellow recruit, Georg Rademacher. Georg was sensitive and slight, a sheltered boy who gave no hint of the dynamic and successful businessman he would become. He was intelligent, well read and he shared with Emil the same love of adventure. Together they made plans to quit the military and to follow their star overseas. When their tour of duty ended, Emil and Georg knocked on doors in downtown Hamburg and soon found jobs with two firms in the Malacca Straits of Southeast Asia. Full of excitement and anticipation, Emil visited his parents in Neustadt and told them of his plans.

"When will we see you again, Emil?" his mother asked.

He couldn't say. With mixed feelings he left them once more on the train platform. The grey hair, the brave faces and the sad eyes faded into the distance.

The train chugged and whistled and took Emil south to Geneva to visit Jeanne Golay. All through his apprentice years and then later during his army service he had written her faithfully. Despite the cabarets of St. Pauli, the pleasures of Altona and the spirited Stefani – despite his fling with Martha and his pursuit of Käthe – he worshipped Jeanne as his guardian angel on an island of purity.

They played croquet as before, drifted around the lake in the little boat and chatted happily in three different languages. Emil brimmed with enthusiasm. He had mastered his business apprenticeship and had enjoyed all of the pleasures and none of the pain of a brief military career. Now he looked forward to a rich and exciting future. He felt a little sorry for Jeanne's quiet uneventful life at home.

"I'm sailing to Penang in a few days. I'm going to do what I've always wanted."

She gazed into his determined eyes. He was twenty-one now, no longer the callow sixteen-year-old she had known. Tall and robust, he projected an aura of youthful self-confidence. Perhaps he would change his mind after a couple of years in the tropics. "I'll miss you, Emil."

"I'll miss you, too, Jeanne. You're my angel." Should he ask her to join him? A tempting thought but, no, it was too soon. "Promise you'll write me?"

"Of course, Emil. I'll write you once a month. Don't stay away long."

The days shortened and the first autumn leaves scudded before the freshening wind. Emil boarded a train to Genoa and met Georg at the station in Italy. In high spirits they transferred their trunks to a Dutch steamer, *Prinz Heinrich*. The ship's horn sounded, the ropes were cast off and southward they sailed on the first leg of their life adventure.

Standing in the bow, the two friends gazed at the foaming waves, watched the wheeling birds and breathed deeply the salt tang in the air. They rolled past Corsica and Sicily, through the narrow Strait of Messina into the empty expanse of the eastern Mediterranean, through the Suez Canal and the Red Sea, past the sandy, barren, shimmering coast of Arabia and on into the vast Indian Ocean. With mounting anticipation they skirted Ceylon and the northern tip of Sumatra.

At dawn on November 21, 1899, Emil and Georg leaned excitedly over the forward deck railing. Their destination shimmered on the eastern horizon – the port of Penang in the Straits Settlements, a thriving British toehold on the long sinuous Malayan peninsula. A reddish glow gleamed behind the low-lying coast. A few lights winked from warehouses in the harbour. Small fishing vessels converged on the docks; sturdy brown-skinned men pulled down the sails and called to each other in Malay. Emil had imagined this scene as a young boy and now here he stood, looking handsome in his new white tropical suit, his heart filled with hope and wonder as he and his best friend exulted in the dawn of their new lives and fortunes.

Something felt odd. He glanced down at his white suit. A deep blue stain spread malignantly from the left breast pocket. He gasped in horror and yanked out the offending fountain pen. It was a new invention of the time and a parting remembrance from his family. Ink stained his fingers. Cursing profusely, he emptied the leaky pen over the side and shook the ink vigorously from his hand. A gold ring fell off the end of his finger and disappeared into the ocean. It, too, was a gift from his parents. Emil stared in shock at the receding bow wave, empty pen in hand, his small gold band lost for eternity. A queasy wave churned in his belly and black thoughts crowded his mind. Georg smiled in sympathy and planted a firm hand on his friend's shoulder. *Prinz Heinrich* dropped anchor in the bay.

SEVEN

SUMATRA PEPPER TRADER

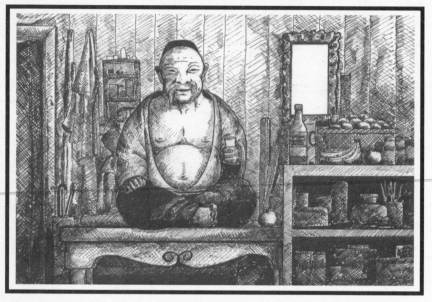

Po Tjong

Emil Helfferich sweated profusely from the heat and from the embarrassment. If *Herr* Adolf Friederichs, his new boss, noticed that Emil greeted him in a most unusual way, with his left hand over a stained breast pocket, he was too polite to comment. This earnest apprentice was just what he needed in Penang – an honest hard-working young man from the old country, a clerk who would count the ingots of tin and pay the bills of his busy trading emporium on the west coast of Malaya.

Georg Rademacher took a placement with a different firm. The jobs were much to their liking: buying, selling and haggling; treks to distant ports, mines and remote mountain outposts; new faces, new languages and above all a hazy, languid, humid land utterly unlike the German countryside of their recent youth. Emil absorbed this new world into his soul. He wrote poems about his exotic surroundings and began to dream about the next adventure.

One day, more than a year later, he travelled to the east coast of Sumatra to buy tobacco. Dutch, German and Swiss planters cultivated the leaf to produce the highly valued wrapper for cigars. On the way to a plantation he stopped in a forest clearing where men had set fires to make way for crops. Smoke cast a pall on the scene and the stench was acrid. Fire crackled through the charred underbrush; the canopies of huge trees burst into flame; a cascade of ash and sparks rained all around. Emil dismounted from his horse and marvelled at the awesome inferno – an overwhelming and spellbinding force of destruction. As he resumed his journey he pondered his life in sleepy Penang: the easy routine, a pleasant boss and a comfortable career stretching far into the misty future. He contrasted that with the primeval jungle around him, the wilderness and the solitude, the raw power and the potential.

Between the years 1895 and 1901 the price of tin doubled and the price of pepper quadrupled. Emil heard the siren call of high prices and easy money. Soon after his return to Penang he offered his apologies to *Herr* Friederichs and terminated his contract. He packed his trunks, said goodbye to Georg and boarded a steamship to Lampung on the southwest coast of Sumatra. In May, 1901, the winter monsoon was just ending. Emil was twenty-three and had been employed a mere one and a half years. Now he was completely on his own – no friends, no boss, no plans, no money. How would he earn a living?

Kuala Lumpur and Singapore passed out of sight on the port side. Coconut palms and low mangrove swamps rimmed both shores as the vessel threaded the narrow passage between Sumatra and the island of Bangka. After rounding the southernmost tip of Sumatra the steamer plowed through the choppy swells and swift currents of the Sunda Strait, where the Indian Ocean spills into the Java Sea. A line of volcanic peaks loomed in the remote interior. The grey-green coast of Java slumbered in the distant eastern haze.

Emil steadied his legs in the breeze on the port bow as the steamer chugged southward. The white tropical suit lay safely stowed in a trunk below. He gazed at a distant, ragged group of islands that commanded the centre of the strait – the barren hollow shell of Krakatau. Eighteen years earlier, on August 27, 1883, Krakatau had erupted with a blast that was heard in Australia and felt around the world. Clouds of ash turned day into night; hurricane-force winds howled from the west; tremors knocked men and women off their feet. One violent explosion after another left people gasping for air and shattered windows and street lamps as far away as Batavia. In the eerie noonday darkness, at the height of the maelstrom, a series of massive waves stormed ashore and snuffed out the lives of 36,000 helpless inhabitants. Water funnelled into the narrow bay at Teluk Betung, rising to the incredible height of forty metres as it obliterated every last vestige of the town. Only the lofty estate of the Dutch resident survived. Muddy water lapped the stone steps – and then the surly wave withdrew.

The remains of Krakatau disappeared astern as the vessel turned to the northwest on the last leg of her journey. In the heat of the day the boat steamed into the placid bay of Teluk Betung, the rebuilt provincial capital and the largest town in Lampung. The sun blazed directly overhead and hardly a soul stirred. Emil strode resolutely down the gangplank. Bare-chested porters carried his luggage up the road to a hotel frequented by Europeans. After lunch and a refreshing cold-water *mandi* he stood in the shade of the front veranda and debated his next move. Two white men fanned themselves in lounge chairs by the entrance. Emil introduced himself and politely inquired after their business in Teluk Betung. After a long pause one replied warily, "We're waiting for news." Neither of them looked up nor spoke any further; they just resumed their quiet vigil. Not knowing what else to say, the puzzled young German excused himself and descended the steps to the street.

Through hot dusty lanes he made his way uphill to the home of the Dutch resident. Curious eyes stared from the darkness of doors and shuttered windows. Some were survivors, the ones who, eighteen years earlier, ran, swam, or clung to trees on the highest ground as the filthy waters roiled around them. Others were opportunists who moved in from the countryside to rebuild a shattered village. They stared indifferently at the young white man, striding purposefully upward in the glare of the sun. He would probably fail or disappear, or else turn to drink or go mad, as all the others had.

Emil wiped the sweat off his brow and climbed higher through the dust and the afternoon heat. Debris from the brutal wave lurked half-buried at the edge of young orchards. A rusty old mooring buoy lay surrounded by a field of peppers. Scars high on the largest trees bore mute witness to the catastrophe. Far beyond the plantations, in the mouldy jungle a few kilometres from the coast, the skeleton of the Dutch naval vessel *Berouw* rested where the fickle wave had dropped her. The crew of twenty-eight had perished when the first wave smashed the paddle-wheeler into the beach. The second wave picked her up again and tossed her deep into the forest. *Berouw* means "remorse." Dark windows glared at the human scavengers who picked her clean. Vines crept across the deck and monkeys hid in the cabins.

From the top of the hill the mansion commanded a fine view of the bay and the distant Sunda Strait. At Emil's knock a servant opened the door and ushered him in. The Dutch resident, Wijmalen, rose listlessly from behind his desk and greeted the newcomer with caution. Emil paid his compliments and introduced himself.

"My name is Helfferich. I am a German citizen. I have worked for a year and a half with *Herr* Friederichs of Penang and now I wish to start a business in Lampung." He described his background and waited politely for a reply.

The Dutchman scrutinized the young man's eager face and the intelligent, determined eyes. Finally he spoke, "Why would an obviously well-educated young man such as yourself, from a good family in Germany, wish to throw it all away and come to live here in such a godforsaken place? Tell me, honestly, did something go wrong for you back home? A family quarrel? A woman, perhaps?"

Taken aback, Emil blurted a naïve and unconvincing reply about "opportunity" and "potential." The Dutchman grunted, turned away and walked over to the sideboard where he poured two shots of *genever* gin. He passed one to his guest, cleared his throat, then spoke as if making a toast, "Well, *Herr* Helfferich, I can only hope that your efforts will succeed where those of most others have failed. This is no place for weaklings. You have seen Krakatau. Lives hang by a hair. The tropics grind you down: the heat, the rain, the jungle, wild animals, swamp fever, feckless natives, swindlers, thieves, dreamers and deadbeats...the temptations of easy money, young women, and, of course, the bottle." He stared regretfully into his glass, paused for a moment, then raised it high and looked his guest squarely in the eye. "*Santé, mijnheer, santé.*"

Somewhat chastened, Emil returned to the sanctuary of his hotel room and considered his options. He thought of the men in the lounge chairs and felt a bit queasy. His life had unwittingly begun to imitate art. Unknown to him, a Polish-born writer living in faraway England had just published a book entitled *Lord Jim*. Joseph Conrad described Jim as an idealistic young sailor who was "one of us...romantic." Among his crewmates aboard *Patna*, a pilgrim ship bound for the *haj,* Jim saw "the soft spot, the place of decay, the determination to lounge safely through existence." Jim had a soft spot too. Under pressure from his frightened mates, who told him the ship was sinking, he abandoned the pilgrims and jumped to save his own life. He fled to the jungles of Sumatra to search for a new life as a pepper trader among the natives of fictional Patusan. "Submit yourself to the destructive element," counselled Stein, the wealthy butterfly collector. Be courageous; plunge into the unknown; seize the opportunity. On the voyage to Patusan, Jim, like Emil, saw

> "the sea with its labouring waves for ever rising, sinking and vanishing to rise again – the very image of struggling mankind – and faced the immovable forests rooted deep in the soil, soaring towards the sunshine, everlasting in the shadowy might of their tradition, like life itself. And his opportunity sat veiled by his side like an Eastern bride."

More than thirty years would pass before Emil "sailed on *Patna*" himself – before he and many others would sense their own soft spots and "jump." In the meantime the romantic young German submitted himself to the jungle and seized his opportunity. He became a pepper trader among the natives of Teluk Betung, among the immovable forests by the shore of the labouring sea. As Joseph Conrad enthused, "...pepper seemed to burn like a flame of love in the breast.... Where they wouldn't go for pepper!... the bizarre obstinacy of that desire made them defy death in a thousand shapes; the unknown seas; the loathsome and strange diseases; wounds, captivity, hunger, pestilence and despair. It made them great! By heavens! It made them heroic...."

In Lampung the pepper harvest approached. An air of brooding somnolence hung over the town. The natives rested under thatched roofs and waited. Each day at noon Helfferich dined at the hotel and greeted the two comatose men in lounge chairs. Pepper had yet to make heroes of the men of Lampung.

Within a few weeks he rented office space in the home of a retired Dutch official and busily set to work making plans and writing letters. A light sea breeze wafted through shaded windows. High ceilings tempered the dreadful heat. He worked in his shirtsleeves, often late into the night, stopping only for meals and for short invigorating walks into the surrounding jungle. The clouds at sunset and the long dark nights entranced him.

Down the hall from his office an open doorway beckoned. In the darkened room beyond lay a large bed draped in a hazy gauze of mosquito netting. Each day just after lunch, the young brown-skinned wife of his elderly landlord padded barefoot down the hallway past his office. She glanced demurely at Emil then vanished into the bedroom. Leaving the door ajar, she undressed slowly, swept back the netting and draped herself languidly over the cotton bedsheet. Emil could barely stand it. Passion gnawed at his common sense. He chewed his pencil to a stub and remembered his guardian angel, Jeanne, and his first love, the dusky Maria.

The news of another lovely Maria had swept through the European community a few days earlier. She was the beautiful daughter of a Dutch planter named Bosman and his native wife. Blessed with a remarkable face and considerable physical charms she was, unfortunately, not particularly clever. At considerable expense the father sent the shy young woman to a finishing school in Brussels. Upon her return to Lampung it was sadly evident that she had learned only how to say *oui* and *non*. To the other planters this was of no great concern. Her arms and hips swayed rhythmically when she walked. The eighteen-year-old beauty dazzled them with her soft voice, her golden skin and her dark brown eyes.

Bosman's plantation fell on hard times. Whether this was due to poor management, bad luck, or a desire to spare no expense for his treasured child, Emil never found out. The money simply disappeared and the whole operation was placed under the auctioneer's hammer. Heavy equipment, tools, furniture, even dishes, all sold for trifling sums. But there was one item which gripped the buyers' imagination. A large four-poster bed, upon which the lovely maiden had slept, attracted a bevy of ardent bidders. Maria watched in a daze as the bidding war spiralled out of sight. To the envy of his lascivious friends, an otherwise upright and sober Dutchman purchased the bed for the incredible sum of 2,000 guilders, the price of a modest house.

There was suddenly no room left for Maria in Bosman's broken home. Meekly accepting her fate, the charm school beauty married a junior official and moved to the interior. She passed her days staring out the window of a thatched hut on the edge of the jungle. One soft night she strolled through the garden as the moon's pale rays illuminated her innocent face. Cicadas and crickets trilled loudly in her ears. Gibbons hooted from their evening roost. She never heard the silent tread of the tiger behind her. In one horrible bound the beast leaped upon her back and smashed her to the ground. Grasping her lovely neck in its terrible jaws, the tiger dragged her limp form into the shadow of the night.

Emil winced at the thought of this beautiful young woman, killed in such a macabre way, a pawn of forces over which she had no control. He looked down the hallway to the open door that beckoned so invitingly. Summoning all his willpower, he rose from his desk and found a new place to work.

In a short time he bought his first house for 1,800 guilders, somewhat less than the cost of Maria's bed. The house was relatively cheap owing to its unfortunate location between the coast and a vast swamp. The house swarmed with mosquitoes. Malaria struck him early on, a feverish scourge that tormented him sporadically for the next sixteen years. However the house lay conveniently close to the docks and the business centre. It served as both office and living quarters and it came with a young Chinese manservant to cook meals and clean house. For the next two years Helfferich was the only European businessman in Teluk Betung. The others worked in the government bureaucracy, toiled as planters in the rough back country or idled their lives away in the pursuit of empty dreams. At first the Chinese traders and the indigenous Malays treated him with cautious reserve, if not actual contempt. He struggled to learn both Dutch and Malay. During his first year he watched in dejection as the other traders ostentatiously counted their rolls of paper money and their silver bars from Batavia. He was the white man with empty pockets. There was no one to turn to, no one from whom to seek advice or companionship.

His initial capital was very modest. There was no bank in Lampung and the Dutch bankers in Batavia would give no cash advances. The boats travelled to Batavia every fourteen days, which meant that a month passed before any money arrived. It seemed to Helfferich as if he were floating on a tiny raft in a perilous sea, with his flimsy lifeline – a line of credit – tied to a distant bank in Hamburg.

By dint of hard work, but also through a sense of fairness, his rare sensitivity and a genuine friendly interest in the native culture, Helfferich gradually gained the trust of the local inhabitants. From England he imported manufactured goods, wine from Hamburg, sardines from France, singlets from Barcelona and tobacco from Holland. He started a small business making sarongs and began to sell produce from the forest and the plantations. Out of frustration with the slow pace of commerce, he became a *de facto* banker and began to arrange financing for local businesses. The plantations were all fairly new and most of them were poor. Sometimes the coffee crop would fail, or the tobacco became woody, or the machines ground to a halt for lack of spare parts. Helfferich helped the planters through these rough patches, not knowing whether he would ever see his money again. He learned accounting at the edge of the wilderness.

In his second year he had amassed sufficient capital and credibility to pursue his original plan of trading in pepper. He gained an advantage over other pepper merchants in that he exported directly to the customer rather than going through middlemen in Batavia. During the pepper harvest he often stayed up late when the sacks were ready to load, waiting for a ship to come in. He sat at a wooden table in the godown – a Malay *gudang* or warehouse – drinking red wine and bantering with the merchants and planters. Under the table a boy swatted mosquitoes off their legs.

One of these pioneer planters was a Swiss named Hermann von Mechel. A large red-faced man in his mid-forties, with beefy hands and scraggly eyebrows, he lived by himself in a thatched hut on stilts at the edge of the forest. Rats scuttled across his snoring body at night and tigers roamed beneath the floorboards. He ate little but smoked and drank a great deal. Three enormous Australian horses were his special pride. On market days he rode them joyfully to the godowns in Teluk Betung, swigging whisky from a jug and singing bawdy songs.

Drunkenness among the planters was a frequent problem and Helfferich was wary of von Mechel in particular. He was as crafty as he was violent. Local officials and merchants wilted in his presence. A young clerk named von Hüttenbach rode to his hut in the bush one day to seek payment on a long overdue bill. Von Mechel grandly welcomed him and treated him to a sumptuous meal that included preserves and champagne from von Hüttenbach's own warehouse. Eventually the nervous clerk summoned the courage to inquire about the account in arrears. Von Mechel clapped him on the shoulder with one meaty fist and bellowed, "I have no money, young fellow – but you can have my utmost respect!"

Helfferich himself was no stranger to this "respect," in fact he recognized the hidden virtue in von Mechel and financed the old drunkard's wedding. The story began when von Mechel took a trip to Dresden in Germany. One evening the homesick planter stumbled tipsily down a dreary back alley and staggered into a rundown night club. Most of the tables were empty. The singer was a diminutive woman with an elderly brittle voice, but in his addled ears he heard the song of an angel. He invited her to his table where she introduced herself grandly as *Signorina* Castelli. Within hours they were engaged to be married.

Upon his return to Lampung he told no one of his affair and he soon forgot his hasty promise. But there came a fateful day when he received a telegram from Suez. She was on her way! Rumours swirled around Teluk Betung, especially among the women. Was the crusty old lecher – a filthy bachelor and a notorious misogynist – really getting married?

His financial woes were at their most calamitous. Cap in hand and flat broke, he asked Helfferich, the ersatz banker, to loan him money for the wedding. How could he refuse? Emil secretly admired the rough-and-tumble survivor, the tough guy with the heart of gold. He imported champagne, gifts and other foodstuffs with his customary zeal and he asked the wife of a German planter to meet the bride in Batavia. On the day of the wedding a local official stood in a long white frock above the unlikely pair. Stiff and starched in an ill-fitting woollen suit, the groom towered above his tiny companion. Beads of sweat dripped from his ragged eyebrows and trickled down the jowly furrows of his rubicund cheeks. He glanced sideways at the pale veiled face of his tenacious bride. Her charm and beauty had long since crumbled under the ebb and flow of a destitute life. But she stood in triumph beside her man. With an air of grand solemnity the official addressed *Signorina* Castelli: "You are the castle by the sea, the rock against which the waves break. This is the loyalty that the woman promises to the man." Tears welled in von Mechel's bloodshot eyes and joined the streams of perspiration on his contented face. That night the guests enjoyed a feast of venison from the forest and toasted the end of the old planter's bachelor days. Emil twirled his champagne glass and smiled. He had rescued a good man, a loyal and loving man, from oblivion.

The pianist at the wedding was a Mrs. Wood. Emil knew that she was the right person to wheedle lilting tunes out of a reluctant old piano. She lived with her husband in a wooden shack in Tanjung Karang, in a form of social limbo between the Chinese camp and the European neighbourhood. Although the house consisted of little else but four walls and two sleeping platforms, a brown upright piano enjoyed pride of place in the centre. On top of the piano stood a large bottle of whisky.

The grey-haired Mr. Wood was quiet but friendly in a philosophical way. At first glance the even-tempered Scotsman looked like the type to shrug off adversity, the sort of man who could defy the odds. He had come overseas to install some machinery at a plantation. Unfortunately the business went bankrupt and he lost his job. Undeterred he decided to try his hand at prospecting. After all, he said, Sumatra was a land rich in minerals for the taking. One day he called on Helfferich in the strictest confidence, barely containing himself. He had just discovered a huge coal seam under the beach! All he needed was some risk capital. Emil gave him cautious encouragement and then made some discreet inquiries. A few days later a native brought him the unwelcome news that the "seam" was actually a heap of coal from the paddle-wheeler *Berouw,* dumped ashore by the colossal wave. "Mining is a risky business," opined Mr. Wood. In vain he combed the hills. Their savings dwindled then disappeared altogether.

Mr. and Mrs. Wood turned to whisky for comfort. The worse their situation became, the more they drank to forget. Emil would sometimes drop in for an afternoon visit on his way back to the harbour from the outlying plantations. He always sensed a welcoming air and a whiff of alcohol, although they never offered him a drink. The whisky bottle stayed put on the piano lid. Mrs. Wood was a superb pianist. She loved to play romantic music for her dashing young visitor: Mendelssohn's "Song Without Words," Beethoven's "Moonlight Sonata," and Chopin's "Nocturnes." Emil could not fail to be moved. As a young boy at home he would sit enthralled when his eldest brother, Karl, played Beethoven. He marvelled at the beautiful soaring melodies that she coaxed from the piano with her stubby fingers, fat and festooned with rings. With a sense of foreboding he glanced at her massive face, at the dark pouches below watery blue eyes, staring serenely into space. The Woods were romantic dreamers, life's losers, and he was at a loss to help them.

One day they finally had to sell the piano and the house. They moved into a squalid hotel room down by the docks and Mrs. Wood died soon thereafter. She had to be buried that afternoon but no one had made any arrangements. Her husband lay on his back in bed, passed out, the body of his wife in the other. The frantic hotel owner sent word to Helfferich, who soon turned up with a friend and a simple wooden casket. Lifting the heavy woman by her arms and legs, they grunted and struggled to wedge her inside. As they nailed the coffin lid shut, Mr. Wood sprang bolt upright with a piercing howl. Just as swiftly he dropped back down. Emil stood rooted to the floor in shock, hammer and nails hanging limply in his hands.

Four soldiers from the detachment in Benteng arrived to carry the casket. They hoisted it to their shoulders and trudged outside into the pouring rain. Water streamed down the faces of the struggling men as their feet slipped in the fresh red mud. Helfferich and his friend, the only mourners, followed behind with shoulders hunched and eyes downcast. Sheets of rain lashed their faces and thunder boomed in the heavens. After ten minutes of hard slogging they reached the cemetery high on the hill. Normally the view swept grandly down to the bay but today there was nothing to see but grey sky and the ghostly bones of *kemboja* trees. Although a grave had been freshly dug it was already one third full of water. With considerable effort they lowered the casket and forced it to the bottom. It splashed and gurgled and bobbed and glugged as one of the soldiers stood on top and shoved it down with his boots. Moonlight Sonata, Nocturnes, Songs Without Words.... They tossed spadefuls of mud onto the coffin until the grave was full. They folded their hands, removed their caps in the pouring rain and bowed their bare heads in prayer. Mr. Wood died three days later *in delirium tremens*.

Emil ruminated on the fate of the Woods as he sat at the table in a pepper godown, waiting with his friends for a ship to come in. He looked around at the jovial faces of the planters and traders. They too had their "soft spots," their foibles and temptations. None of them were saints. Neither were they strangers to drink and foolishness. At times they were opportunistic and conniving but with a hard streak at the core. None of them chose to "lounge safely through existence." They faced misfortune with backbone, simple wisdom and a sly sense of humour. "Helfferich!" one of them called, "Tell us a story!"

One of the merchants in Teluk Betung was a wealthy Chinese man named Po Tjong. In the marketplace he owned a *toko*, a small shop in which he lived with his family. He also owned a large godown by the harbour. He was a canny businessman who dealt in the produce of the land: pepper, rattan, resin, rubber and coffee. He never speculated.

Emil took pleasure in visiting the jolly old man in his little *toko*. From a distance Po Tjong resembled a squat temple idol, sitting on a round table with his short legs tucked beneath him. A roll of fat spilled over the top of his shiny black pants. Like two gentle hills his bare hairless chest drooped below sloping shoulders. Friendly wrinkles lined his face and mischievous eyes twinkled under thin white eyebrows. A wispy moustache framed his open, laughing mouth and a long strand of white hair protruded from a black mole on his chin. A black silk cap graced the back of his bald head.

Po Tjong loved brandy and bitters but his wife saw the devil in his drinking. A window slammed shut whenever Emil drew near. Po Tjong welcomed him grandly, as if they had not met for a year. While they talked shop and gossiped, the crafty old man quietly offered him a drink. If Emil didn't refuse he bellowed to the boy that *Tuan* wanted a drink. Two large glasses appeared and Po Tjong beamed happily as he cradled one in both hands. Then came a second and a third glass of brandy, followed by bitters. He became loud and loquacious. He padded off to his safe and returned with his treasured rhinoceros horn, showing it off and fondling it tenderly. He thanked the young man profusely for his visit and asked him to return anytime, especially when he was thirsty. Emil smiled as he walked away. The window reopened and shrill accusations poured out. "What could I do?" her husband lamented, "*Tuan* asked for a drink. I had to join him." And so this little play would act itself out each time, throughout the course of his agreeable life.

Po Tjong was an honourable businessman. He took no greater share than any other efficient Chinese merchant. He took care never to harm anyone and no one ever harmed him. Money was his religion: profit was virtue whereas loss was a sin. However there came a day when he found himself caught between loss and dishonour.

The pepper harvest was in full swing. All week long the caravans arrived from the north and the west, the wagons laden with sacks of dried peppercorns. Water buffaloes pulled the groaning carts, heaving and clanking the whole night long. By the light of day, brown coolies in red loincloths urged the long line of beasts forward. Farmers in dirty white turbans sat beside drivers in sarongs. Chinese clerks in flapping blue pants greeted them at the docks.

The air was thick with the pungent odour of black pepper. It had been a rich harvest and prices were high. Extra steamers were hired to transport the cargo. In the godowns bulging sacks of pepper were stacked high to the rafters. Po Tjong's godown was one of the first to be filled. In the evening he nodded thankfully as he latched the heavy padlock to the crossbar. Slowly he shuffled back to his *toko*, half an hour away. It had been a good day and yet he was not quite happy. A year such as this came only rarely. He wanted even more pepper at even cheaper prices. With these troubling thoughts he drifted off to sleep.

The night was dark and thick clouds covered the moon. Only the odd doorlight pierced the gloom. One could see and hear nothing. The guards dozed in their watch posts. Around midnight a hand rapped gently on Po Tjong's back door. After several quiet knocks a worried voice called from inside, "Who is it?"

"Would Po Tjong like to buy some pepper?" whispered the visitor. The old man poked his head out the door. A weak light shone from within but the caller's face was invisible. They spoke a few words and made a few hand signs. Sack after sack of Sumatra's finest pepper emerged from the dark on the backs of thieves. Po Tjong's lips moved silently as he counted them. When the count reached thirty the leader of the band handed him a note. Money changed hands and the men vanished into the shadows. Alone again, Po Tjong rubbed his hands in delight. He disapproved of black market deals – but at 600 guilders, what a price! Thirty sacks of pepper for twenty guilders each when the going rate was thirty. He could sleep well after this purchase. And so he did.

Very early the next morning another caller appeared at the door. This time the knocking was loud and insistent. "Po Tjong! Po Tjong! Something terrible has happened! Po Tjong! Someone broke into the godown last night! They took thirty sacks of pepper!" The merchant opened his sleepy eyes. It was no dream. The coolie's cries mingled with the scolding of his wife and fuelled his silent fury.

He slouched on top of the round table in his *toko* like a broken man. It was all very clear. Last night he had bought his own pepper, thirty sacks in all. He had lost 600 guilders and there was nothing he could do about it. Po Tjong, the wise and the good, was trapped between loss of money and loss of face.

Emil arrived at the *toko* around noon, already knowing everything. Po Tjong's son-in-law, a lazy wastrel disdained by the old man, had eavesdropped on the transaction and rushed to tell him the story. The merchant sat immobile on the table with his arms and legs folded. He didn't look up. Emil walked in anyway and sat down. In a moment the friendly wrinkles returned, the eyes sparkled and he laughed. "Good day, *Tuan*! Would you like something to drink?" Out came the brandy and bitters. Between glasses, Emil told him what he had learned about the break-in. Soon Po Tjong was ranting and railing against thieves, untrustworthy coolies and corrupt policemen. When Emil asked him if he had made a report and whether he would be pursuing the matter, the old man shook his head and laughed bitterly. "No, *Tuan*. Nothing will come of it. The police will never catch the rogues. They are much too cunning. Too difficult, too much bother. Better to rise above it. Sometimes you win, sometimes you lose!" Then he raised his glass of bitters in both hands, nodded slyly at his guest and offered a toast: "*Santé, Tuan, santé!*"

Around the table in the godown, the planters guffawed at the familiar story as they swatted mosquitoes and swigged their wine. "*Santé,* Po Tjong!" they cried.

Within two years of his arrival in Teluk Betung, Helfferich's import-export business was booming. He lured his good friend, Georg Rademacher, away from a comfortable job in Penang to work with him in Sumatra. Together with another German friend, Albert Paulmann, the three partners soon transformed the fledgling company into the largest pepper exporter in Lampung.

Batavia, the capital and largest city in the vast Dutch colony, beckoned to them like a siren on the north coast of Java. But before they could set up an office in the city they needed more credit and the support of a bank in Hamburg. Helfferich would have to make a business trip to Germany. With mounting excitement he packed his bags and made plans for his first visit home in four years. He would see his beloved parents again and Jeanne, of course. He had written her every month and received letters in reply. After four years without female companionship he looked eagerly around his empty bedroom. Perhaps she would return with him.

His partners wished him good luck and Godspeed. In March, 1903, he bid farewell to the Dutch resident, the planters, the traders, Po Tjong and the rest, and then boarded the mail packet *Sri Tadjau* to Batavia.

Sri Tadjau was just a shallow-draft river steamer with an odd name: "The Earthen Vase Princess." An old Malay captain named Kamdami piloted her with the help of a dozen crewmen, all of whom set out on their fortnightly voyage across the Sunda Strait with some trepidation. Emil watched curiously as the old skipper threw a banana and a plate of rice onto the windswept sea. Kamdami sensed his passenger's inquisitive stare.

"This food will keep the spirits happy, *Tuan*. The sea goddess too." He gestured with his thumb at three craggy islands, the angular edges of Krakatau's submarine crater. "That used to be a pointed mountain. I remember when it exploded. The sea boiled and the air was black. Now those three islands are all that is left – and a strange red rock, like a needle, that rises from the depths. It is the trident of Tunku Tiga, the farmer who fought the evil spirits."

"Tunku Tiga?"

Kamdami nodded to his mate in the wheelhouse. The man smiled and raised his hand in reply. The skipper, his face furrowed and hardened from a lifetime in the wind and the sun, leaned back on the deck railing and told his tale.

In the olden days the Sunda Strait was busy with the traffic of many countries. The kingdom of Tulangbawang on Sumatra grew rich from trade. But one day the king heard rumours that pirates were attacking ships and killing the crews. Worried that his country would be ruined, he ordered his army and a fleet of five magnificent battleships to destroy the pirates.

To their horror they found no pirates but supernatural monsters and giants. Thousands of swordfish, crabs and huge squids grappled with the ships and killed every last man. The king had sent his young men on a desperate and hopeless mission. Now the monsters were angry and they sank more ships than ever.

In the countryside at that time lived a hard-working, kind-hearted old farmer called Tunku Tiga. He worried about the giants terrorizing his country. Night after night, week after week, he sat under a tree in the forest and meditated, waiting for inspiration.

Late one night he opened his eyes and saw, to his surprise, a very old man standing beside him, dressed all in white. "Why did you call me?" asked the man in white.

The farmer explained that he wished to rid the sea of evil spirits. The man uprooted the tree beneath which the farmer had been sitting. He tore off the uppermost branch and fashioned a spear with three points – a trident – and gave it to Tunku Tiga. "With this magic weapon you can defeat your enemies. When you have finished, plunge the shaft into the bottom of the sea, sit on the points and meditate until we meet again." Then he vanished.

With his trident in hand, Tunku Tiga strode confidently to the king's palace. The king laughed at the farmer's story and gave him only a small sailboat. The brave old man sailed off by himself to do battle with the monsters of Sunda Strait.

A column of white smoke towered over the middle of the strait. Behind the smoke a huge and terrifying crocodile reared up to attack him. The spry old farmer jumped away from its scaly tail and wicked claws. With one sharp blow of his magic trident he killed the horrible creature. The crocodile roared in pain then disappeared in a cloud of ash.

A storm arose the next day. Huge waves pounded the boat and the wind ripped at the sails. Tunku Tiga lost control. The mast broke with a snap and the sails tore to shreds. A mountainous wave picked up the boat and tossed him overboard. As he struggled to hold his trident and stay afloat he heard a blood-curdling cry above the wind. A monstrous shape leaped out of the ocean, a creature with sharp teeth and burning red eyes. They fought for hours. With superhuman strength the farmer jumped out of the water and jabbed his trident again and again at the beast. With one mighty heave he plunged the three points deep between its flaming red eyes. The monster wailed and collapsed in agony. It, too, vanished in a cloud of ash.

The little farmer had rid the sea of evil spirits. Of course he owed his success to faith and the power of prayer. Remembering his promise to the man in white, he pushed the handle of the trident down into the depths of the ocean. It grew longer and longer until it stuck in the mud at the bottom of the sea. Tunku Tiga sat upon the three points and perched precariously over the waves. He folded his arms and legs, closed his eyes and began to meditate.

For what seemed like a hundred years he sat on the trident and continued to pray. Finally the old man in white appeared before him and said, "Come with me." His body has never been found. He just disappeared. All that remains are the three points of the trident.

Kamdami grinned with satisfaction, as if the sea goddess, evil spirits, misfortune and epic struggles were just a normal part of life on the coast. "So, *Tuan*, that's why we offer gifts – and why we pray."

The two men gazed at the distant remnants of Krakatau, where the grim pillar called "Bosun's Rock" lurked hidden among the waves. Emil tried to picture the scene of devastation twenty years earlier, the very real horror of that grey cloud of ash, the plume of glowing rock and the monstrous black wave.

Sri Tadjau chugged across the Sunda Strait without incident and passed the new Anyer lighthouse on Java's northwestern tip. They steamed along the north coast of Java, past the notorious island of Onrust, where the Dutch quarantined returning pilgrims from the *haj*. Then they turned to starboard into Pasar Ikan, the bustling fish market in Batavia's old port.

No sooner had he arrived in Batavia than Emil suffered a relapse of malaria. Since the city could be miserably hot for a weak and feverish patient, a doctor recommended a period of convalescence in the cool mountain resort at Sindanglaya. He sent Emil by horse carriage south to Buitenzorg, then east around the foothills of Gunung Pangrango, high over the rutted Puncak Pass and down the far side to the mountain hotel. Within a few days the fresh air reinvigorated him. As he lay in a lounge chair on the veranda he worried that he would miss his sailing date to Europe and his reunion with Jeanne. He gazed upward to the green summits of Gede and Pangrango and a crazy plan formed in his restless mind.

At five o'clock the next morning he crept through the darkened corridors of the hotel and met two Sundanese guides in the garden. On quiet feet they wove their way upward through sleeping *kampungs*, stooped beneath low-hanging eaves, balanced on the edges of rice terraces and stepped gingerly through rows of fresh vegetables. Ducks and chickens squawked at the intrusion. Roosters crowed. Men and women emerged from their homes and wrapped themselves in blankets to ward off the dawn chill. From the roof of a tiny mosque a muezzin called the Muslim faithful to *subuh*, the morning prayer: "*Allahu akhbar!* God is great!"

As they climbed higher and the sun rose at their backs Emil revelled in the sights and sounds of a tropical dawn. Pots of bougainvillea lined the lane along which they walked. Blooms of orange, red and violet burned in the golden sunshine. Above him the mountain lay silhouetted against a clear blue sky. The ancient forest, like a rumpled green hide, rose a vertical mile to the two summits. To his right the cone-shaped peak of Pangrango brooded silently; to his left a column of smoke drifted heavenward from the high rocky cliffs of Gunung Gede. The mountain had erupted spectacularly in 1840, when flames over 200 metres high flashed out of the crater. Showers of rock and ash blanketed the upper slopes.

Ahead of them lay the Cibodas Gardens, a mountain reserve inspired by Sir Stamford Raffles's renowned Botanical Gardens in Buitenzorg. The trees and plants were just twenty years old, having been planted by Dutch botanists around the time of the Krakatau explosion. Beyond the garden gate the primeval forest towered overhead, seemingly impenetrable. Gibbons and leaf monkeys hooted and crashed through the high canopy. The jungle throbbed with the morning songs of birds, whistling and calling to each other after the long night. The small band of climbers caught flashes of scarlet and yellow – minivets, scimitar-babblers, barbets and bulbuls. A serpent-eagle soared overhead.

Emil's guides were a middle-aged man from the village and his young son. The man had lived on the eastern slope of the mountain for his entire life. The birds and animals were old spiritual friends. Little escaped his attention as they toiled their way up the stony root-choked trail to the summit. He chatted amiably with Emil in Malay, touched the trees, picked fruit and flowers and searched the leafy branches and forest floor for the more elusive creatures.

Low down on the trail, the guide approached a wicked-looking rattan and sliced off one of the scaly round fruits with his *golok*. He cracked it open and showed Emil the red crystalline resin inside. "Dragon's blood, *Tuan,* from the devil's bush."

Hundreds of years ago Arab merchants traded this "blood" with India and Europe. They used it to make varnishes and to treat stomach problems. The Arabs told their gullible European customers that this was the blood lost by dragons while fighting elephants.

He cut a long spiny cane and whipped it around his head with a fearful crack. Rattan canes are used to make baskets and furniture but the man described a more devilish use from the old days. Before a thief broke into a house, he removed his clothes and smeared himself with oil. That made him very difficult to catch. But one swipe around the legs with a rattan cane and he would crash to the ground.

The trail steepened. Cobblestones gave way to roots and boulders. The guide and his son stopped beside a huge tree to allow Emil to catch his breath. "*Rasamala* tree, *Tuan. Rasamala* is the old Sanskrit word for dung." Emil stared uncomprehendingly at this giant of the forest, over sixty metres high and one metre in diameter. The man explained that, thousands of years ago, the Egyptians embalmed their dead with tree resin from the Mediterranean. They called it lion's dung and the Arab traders obliged by naming it *rasamala.* Later on, in the days when Hindu kings ruled Sunda, the Arabs discovered that this tree was a cheaper and better source of the resin. He patted the massive trunk. "And so they called it the 'dung' tree."

Halfway up the mountain they stopped at the edge of a hot waterfall. Steam enveloped the small group and billowed around the tops of giant tree-ferns. Water dripped from every leaf. Scalding water and slippery green algae covered the rocks underfoot. The trail led across a shaky ledge from one side of the waterfall to the other. Emil looked down to where the water tumbled steeply into the mist. Soaking wet, he grasped the hot slimy rocks with his hands and stumbled across the ledge. After safely reaching the far side he turned around to look at the tree-ferns. Clad in bark resembling snakeskin, with feathery fronds drooping overhead and young fiddleheads curling upward, these strange trees had changed little in three hundred million years. They were older than dinosaurs.

His guide picked a round green fruit from the path. "This fig comes from a *waringin* tree, *Tuan.* But no good to eat," he continued. A tiny female wasp burrows a tunnel into the centre of each fig and lays her eggs inside. Little flowers actually bloom inside this unusual fruit. The male wasps never come out. They mate and die while the females dig their way out and carry pollen to other figs. Each species of fig has its own kind of wasp. Birds and monkeys eat the figs and excrete the seeds on tree branches. The seeds germinate and send roots down to the ground. Eventually the roots wrap themselves around the trunk and strangle their host to death. Thus figs and wasps and animals survive. "Only the tree loses, *Tuan*. Inside the *waringin* is the ghost of a dead tree."

His lungs heaving, Emil wondered if perhaps he had offered to pay too much. Despite the chatter he was glad for the rest. He had been walking uphill for almost four hours and he felt weak from the malaria. The summit was still far away. His clothes were drenched and his feet were sore. His heart pounded in the thinning air as he hauled himself higher. The man stepped confidently upward in bare feet, intent on the surrounding forest. The boy seemed detached from the natural world. He grinned at the white man's exertions.

Stopping abruptly, the guide reached for his *golok* and hacked away at a large clump of ferns beside the path. He was obviously looking for something. "This plant is called *kembang berdoa* by the Bugis people." Emil nodded wearily and bent over with his hands on his knees. He knew of the Bugis, the renowned seafarers and pirates from Celebes. They had a lusty, violent reputation. When he arrived in Batavia's harbour aboard *Sri Tadjau* he had seen their beautiful schooners at Pasar Ikan, perhaps a hundred of them, vividly painted, with elegant upswept bows and billowing sails, one of the largest sailing fleets in the world. Barefoot crewmen hauled their cargo one piece at a time across a wobbly gangplank. Spotting Emil's white face, a woman on deck had lifted her skirt and whistled.

"*Berdoa* means praying," the man continued as he chopped through the thick clump. The fronds of the plant stretch outward then curl at the tip toward heaven, like sails or praying hands. When the plant is young it grows on a branch but takes nothing from the tree. Leaves and other bits collect in the middle, trapping water and food for ants and other animals. "*Aduh*! Here's one." The man pulled a giant blue earthworm out of the middle. "The singing worm, *Tuan*! This worm whistles late at night from the middle of his 'boat,' calling to his lady."

Upward they climbed. Lianas trailed from every bough; mosses and ferns draped the larger branches; trees choked in the quiet embrace of strangler figs. Thorny rattans ambushed the unwary and huge *jamuju* and *rasamala* trees bullied their way to the top. Enormous black-and-yellow orb spiders straddled their webs with long hooked legs. Spines, poisons, large leaves, insects and excrement formed weapons in the arsenal of survival. Plants and animals vied for space in a slow, silent struggle, an illusion of peace.

The grade decreased slightly as they approached the saddle between the two summits. The trees diminished in size. Turning left toward the barren crest of Gunung Gede they confronted a steep cliff band of crumbling basalt. Emil tackled the wall hand over hand, labouring heavily. Beyond lay an endless dreary gully of loose dry rock. He thought back to his two years in Teluk Betung, to all the hard work and trouble and further back like a mirage, to the day he and Christian walked home from the Rhine one step at a time.

The man and his son were calling to him. Emil looked up numbly from his trance. The scrubby trees gave way to a bare ridge which fell off steeply to the crater on his left. Alpine shrubs carpeted the gentle sunny slopes on the right. The trail to the summit beckoned; the sun was dazzling, the sky blue. He could see his guides waving and he could hear their voices. With beating heart, renewed energy and an enormous sense of achievement, he trudged the last few steps to the top of Gunung Gede.

Pangrango – "veiled like an Eastern bride"

The sun shone directly overhead at the apex of a hazy blue dome. The wind ruffled his hair and felt surprisingly cool on his cheek. He took a deep breath of fresh air and scanned the horizon around him. To the east the dark purple cones of Malabar and Tangkuban Prahu loomed above Bandung, their bases shrouded in mist. To the west a line of peaks zigzagged from the ragged maw of Gunung Salak near Buitenzorg, down to the mountain refuge of the reclusive Baduy tribe and then far beyond to the remote hazy tip of Java at Ujung Kulon. A long indistinct line shimmered in the south: the restless, brooding, blue Indian Ocean, eternal abode of the goddess, *Nyai* Roro Kidul. Turning northward, Emil cast his eyes upon the forested peak of Pangrango. A broad six-hundred-metre-deep saddle separated the two summits. Two fearsomely sharp ridges plunged down its western slope, jagged arms wrapped around a hidden valley. Clouds rose and parted on the flanks of the mysterious mountain, where his opportunity lay "veiled like an Eastern bride," where, in the misty future, green fields of tea would make his fortune and where, among the ancient trees, a memorial would bear his name.

Emil smelled the sweet odour of incense and turned to see the guide and his son squatting beside a small fire. "It is for *Raja* Bukit, *Tuan*, whose spirit dwells on this mountain. Holy men are buried on these summits. And also for *Nyai* Roro Kidul, the sea goddess, who once lived on this mountain and who causes the rice to grow." A wisp of scented smoke curled away on the breeze. Emil stared into the awful crater below him, at the sulphurous hissing plume of steam, and smiled as he recalled the morning call to prayer – the fervent appeal to *Allah,* the one God. Apparently there might be more than one God. Then he lay down and slept on the warm rocks in the cool fresh air of a perfect day.

An hour later the stiff-kneed party bestirred themselves and meandered back down the ridge. Over the cliff band, to the right at the saddle, across the steaming waterfall, through the tall mossy forest, they twisted down the cobbled and rooted path, slipping and grunting, dropping endlessly to the valley below. Clouds gathered, turned grey and darkened the path. The first drops spattered on leaves. Within a minute the rain gushed down in torrents and drenched their clothes. A stream gurgled in the path; pebbles tumbled downhill. The man slashed a banana plant with his *golok* and passed one of the huge leaves to Emil. "*Payung hutan, Tuan!*" he shouted amid the din of pounding rain – a "jungle umbrella."

By sunset the rain tapered off and they reached the hotel. Emil thanked his guides and paid them generously. Wet, filthy and bedraggled, he wobbled through the front door, greeted the astonished doctor and told him where he had been. The other patients could scarcely believe that this young man, so recently stricken with fever, had spent the last twelve hours climbing up and down the giant peak. The next morning, shaking his head in both wonder and disapproval, the doctor released Emil and allowed him to travel home. Within a week he boarded a steamship to Europe.

EIGHT

A SHIPBOARD ROMANCE

Moonset off Ceylon

The ship plowed through the waves of the Mediterranean, bound for Marseille. Emil Helfferich paced the deck in growing excitement. On this bright spring day in 1903 he had much to feel glad about. He had overcome malaria, climbed the Giant Mountain and dodged the evil spirits of Krakatau. Helfferich and his two partners were the most prosperous pepper traders in South Sumatra. In a few weeks he would face the bankers in Hamburg and negotiate an expanded line of credit. And he would finally go home to his parents. After four years overseas the young man missed his mother badly and he yearned to tell his father all about his successes and his dreams for the future. Best of all he would soon be in the arms of his girlfriend, Jeanne. He imagined a romantic reunion on the shore of Lake Geneva. With luck he might even propose to her.

Emil had sent a short but ardent telegram to Geneva to let Jeanne know that he was on his way home. He had reason to be concerned. Although she had written to him faithfully for the first three years, there had been no mail from her for the past twelve months. Perhaps she was travelling and the letters had gone astray. After several impatient weeks at sea, he arrived in Marseille and strode up to the desk of the shipping agent. His heart pounded as he asked for his messages. The man gave him a note from Jeanne and he tore it open. "Come home quickly. I'm alone in the house and we can talk. Jeanne." What joy! The words sang in his ears and love soared in his heart. On the train to Geneva he stared in a happy daze at the passing countryside, now abloom with spring flowers. In his mind he composed passionate poems and rehearsed his heartfelt proposal.

Several hours later he stood by the window of her room overlooking Lake Geneva. He fingered the curtains and stared at the lights of the bridge. Tears welled in his eyes and a lump formed in his throat. What could he say? All his plans and poems had flown out the window and vanished into the lake. The lights shimmered in the dark water. Jeanne stood behind him and laid her head on his shoulder.

She had tried to spare his feelings but there was no easy way to say *adieu.* The worst of it was that he didn't know why. Was there another man in her life? No, she firmly replied. She offered no other hints. He remembered she had said, "Don't be long." For him the four years had flown by quickly but for her, waiting in her quiet home, maybe it seemed like forever. Or perhaps, he guessed, it was something he had written. How would she feel, sitting by this window with one of his letters in hand, reading about life at the edge of the jungle? In his boyish enthusiasm he might have been too passionate, too dramatic. In effusive prose he had described the heat and humidity, the rain streaming in torrents, mosquitoes, malaria, an alien language and culture, drunkards and failures, hard-bitten men and their suffering wives, and even his simple wooden hut. He should have described more of the romance and less of the adventure. Maybe she hoped that he would come to his senses, that he would purge this youthful passion from his system and return to a civilized life in Europe. Sumatra in 1903 was no place for her, a lady who enjoyed the comforts of a privileged home. If this was her dream, then she hoped in vain. His enthusiasm only grew with the passage of time.

The lovelorn Emil checked into the Hotel Baur on Lake Geneva and drowned his sorrows. He sat at a white table in the April sunshine as black thoughts coursed through his head. Jeanne had been his guardian angel... how could she be so cruel? Four years of work was ruined...his life was shattered...there was no point in living. The waiter filled his glass discreetly and kept a close eye on him, day after day for a week. He was too miserable even to write poems.

Gradually he pulled himself together. With a heavy heart he repacked his bags and boarded the train to Neustadt. Karl met him at the station and brought him home late at night. A candle flickered on the hall table. Emil carried the candlestick upstairs into the room where his parents were sleeping. He kissed his mother and she woke up with a start. They both began to cry. She had worried so much about him but now her prodigal son had finally come home. His father hugged him around the shoulders. The three of them sat on the edge of the bed, Emil between his two parents, with the dim light of the candle reflected in their faces.

They talked and talked for several days. His father wanted to hear about the new business and his mother wanted to learn about his life in Lampung and his poor state of health. She listened to his sorry tale of unrequited love. Emil's spirits soon recovered in the warmth of the old home. He picked himself up, focused once more on his mission and travelled on to Hamburg. As he rehearsed his presentation he worried that his weak arithmetic and self-taught accounting skills would be inadequate to impress a banker. But his fears were groundless. His successful record spoke for itself. With his natural enthusiasm, his ability to concentrate on a plan and with his intuitive grasp of people and the market, he quickly secured a substantial line of credit. His dream of a new enterprise in Batavia had come true.

To celebrate his success, Emil and his older brother August descended on the bars of St. Pauli. How could he resist? The cafés and dance halls were as lively as he remembered and his mood, for a while, improved dramatically. Wine, women and song masked the pain in his broken heart.

After visiting his old Hamburg friends, the whisky traders of Jürgen Peters, Emil returned to Neustadt for a few weeks of relaxation. Tension ebbed away but sadness welled up in waves. He wrote at least five melancholy poems of lost love. In his vulnerable state he fell for the first fair maiden he met. Gertrud's eyes, blond hair and laughter shone like the summer sky. Emil buried himself in her willing arms but he felt that something was missing. She was pure sunshine: no hidden depths, no romance, no intellectual excitement. When he gamely tried to express his love and affection, songs of sadness poured forth instead. Neither she nor Jeanne could be part of his new life in the Far East.

With the arrival of midsummer came the time for departure. He kissed Gertrud goodbye forever. Once more he bade his parents a cheerless farewell at the station. The train brought him south to Marseille where he spent the night alone in a hotel room and dreamed about the old days with Jeanne.

On August 7, 1903, Emil rode a horse carriage to the docks in Marseille and boarded the steamship *Australien* to Batavia. He checked into his single stateroom and wandered back outside. The people around him waved to their loved ones on the pier. As the ropes cast off and the boat moved ponderously out of the harbour, he felt none of the elation of his first cruise almost four years earlier. Although his business trip was successful, his love life was a shambles. Standing in his favourite spot at the bow he contemplated the long voyage ahead and a lonely bachelor life in the Dutch East Indies. At least he could expect a grand welcome from his partners.

At the first evening meal, passengers chose tables in a random fashion and scanned the room for congenial faces. Emil picked a vacant seat between two ladies and asked in French if it was taken. "*Non, monsieur,*" they replied and invited him to sit down. A pianist played the first stately bars of a Bach prelude. Emil ordered a bottle of wine and introduced himself affably to his two charming dinner partners. The woman on his right replied in fluent French and introduced herself as *Madame* Uhlenbeck. She evidently spoke Dutch as well but her grasp of German was limited. Emil's Dutch was more suited to the godowns of Lampung and so they conversed in French, the *lingua franca* of the dinner table.

Madame Uhlenbeck looked to be in her early thirties, about eight or nine years older than Emil. A white flower graced the dark curls above her left ear. She wore a flamboyant red blouse. Her voice, though clear and pleasant, had a confident ring that attracted attention. Conversation at the table centred naturally on her. In tune with the *crescendo* of voices the pianist warmed to his music. He slipped from the prelude to a subtle fugue, interweaving two melodies *un poco animato*.

At dinner the second night, Emil deliberately chose to sit beside *Madame* Uhlenbeck. He asked a few questions and she explained that she had spent the last three years painting in Paris. She spoke animatedly of the *artistes* she had met – the old Impressionist masters, Monet and Renoir and the young Henri Matisse, who had just begun to experiment with startling bursts of colour. Emil remembered the red blouse she had worn the night before. It reminded him of the flame trees, *flamboyan,* before the winter monsoon. He teased her gently, "So are you travelling to the Far East – like Gauguin in Tahiti – to paint the colourful natives?"

He hoped she would laugh but instead she looked sad. "No," she replied, "I wish that were so – but my father is very ill. I'm going home to look after him. Perhaps you have heard of him – General Ermeling in Buitenzorg. He used to command the KNIL, the Dutch army in the East Indies." She paused for a moment. "My name is actually Uhlenbeck-Ermeling."

Emil immediately regretted his little joke. "No, I'm sorry – I don't know him. I've been living in Teluk Betung for the last four years. It's a little out of the way." Up to that moment he had guessed that she was a Frenchwoman returning to Indochina but she was obviously Dutch – and married. He found it curious that she placed her maiden name last.

In her glamorous presence he felt rude and provincial. He was just a country boy from the *Pfälzer* hills, the former Lance Corporal Helfferich of the Bahrenfeld Artillery, now a pepper trader in the Sumatran bush. "I'm sorry for your husband, too," he added in what he hoped was a gracious recovery. "You may be away from Paris for a long time."

She lowered her wine glass and looked him coolly in the eye. Emil realized to his embarrassment that he had stumbled badly. "Unfortunately my husband died eight years ago on Java," she answered. "I've been earning a living as an artist ever since."

Emil mumbled another apology and fumbled quietly through the rest of his dinner. He listened absently as the pianist played the languid melancholy notes of a Chopin Nocturne. For a brief moment the music reminded him of the unfortunate Mrs. Wood. Excusing himself, he left the dining room and returned to his cabin.

The morning sun shone through his porthole window and awakened him early. He dressed in his clean white tropical suit, climbed the stairs to the upper deck and strode purposefully to the bow. A light wind blew from astern. Seagulls danced and soared in the breeze. *Australien* rolled gently in the swell and sailed into the sun through rippling waves.

Emil leaned on the railing, soaking up the warmth as he gazed into the dazzling blue sea. He looked older than his twenty-five years. Perhaps it was the high forehead or the sad eyes behind the spectacles. The wind ruffled his wavy hair and his white suit gleamed in the sun. Standing in the prow he looked like a dashing ship's officer, a romantic figure from an older era. Ladies in bustles strolled by with their escorts and exchanged polite greetings with the handsome man in the white suit. "Good morning...*goedemorgen...bonjour...*"

"*Guten Morgen, Herr* Helfferich," called a female voice. She sauntered up to him boldly.

Emil turned and smiled gallantly as he recognized his dinner partner. "*Bonjour madame. Comment ça va aujourd'hui?*" His belly churned as he recalled his *faux pas* of the previous evening. Would she forgive him?

"I'm well, thank you. What a perfect morning!" She joined him at the railing and watched the birds gliding over the wave crests.

"Yes, it is a fine day. We must be somewhere near Malta. I was just thinking of my first trip to the Far East. It was almost four years ago and I was wearing a white suit like this." Emil described his youthful excitement as *Prinz Heinrich* sailed into Penang. Then he laughed as he told her about the ink stain and the loss of his ring.

"Oh, no – you must have been so upset," she commiserated, even as she joined in his laughter.

"Yes, of course, but I was excited too. I wrote a verse about it later:

Ritt im Morgenschimmer
In die Welt hinein,

Nie konnt weh und schlimmer
Mir um's Herze sein.

I rode into the glow of the dawn,
Into the wider world,
And never again will grief enter my heart."

He felt a pang of guilt. He had actually written that particular poem in the aftermath of Jeanne's farewell.

She glanced sideways into his sad eyes. Coming from a Sumatra pepper trader this early morning poetic eloquence was a pleasant surprise. "That's lovely…was it really just about your stained suit?"

He smiled. "No, I suppose not…and the bit about grief was a little naïve. I'm sorry, by the way, about last night…about your father, I mean, and your late husband. It was thoughtless of me."

"That's all right," she sighed, "After all, how could you know? My father is sick, yes, but he's getting old…and a bit cranky too. And as for my husband – oh, he was certainly a wonderful man. His name was Karel…" She paused and blinked into the shining sea. "But, as I said, I've been on my own for eight years now."

Emil was relieved by her pardon. A hopeful feeling stirred within him. He stood up straighter and pointed melodramatically with one arm at the bright horizon:

"Und möcht' Dir ringsum weisen
Des Lebens Zauberpracht –
Und fühl's im tiefsten Herzen,
Dass ich Dich krank gemacht.

And I must show you the magic
Of life's splendour all around –
And I feel it deep in my heart,
That I made you so sad."

He grinned in a boyish way and she laughed at his exuberance. "Would you care to join me for breakfast, *madame?*"

"I would be delighted, Mr. 'Magic of Life's Splendour'…and, please," she whispered, "You can call me Dina."

Dina Uhlenbeck-Ermeling in 1903

The voyage passed in a happy blur of languorous promenades on deck and lively conversation at the table. Dina's German improved rapidly, as did Emil's Dutch, and they chatted fluently in both French and English. She enjoyed his description of a trader's life in Lampung. He in turn listened agreeably to stories of her childhood in Java and Holland. Her father was a crusty old soldier who had raised three sons and four daughters by three wives. Dina's mother came from Madura, an island off the northeast coast of Java, whose natives are renowned for their fierce independence.

She fascinated him. Her smooth brown face was extraordinary, not beautiful in the classic sense, but exotic and mysterious. She curled her thick black hair in luxurious waves. Slender eyebrows arched over dark eyes. Her nose was prominent, but refined, and her lips were small and delicate. A broad forehead and a firm chin enhanced her look of confidence. Her slender arms and hands gestured gracefully when she spoke. She seemed to float as she walked through the dining hall, her comely figure swishing elegantly among the tables.

Emil was falling in love. Had God deliberately laid a stone in his path only to remove another? What strange coincidence had brought the two of them together on the same ship? She had lost the man she loved most and now she stood alone in the world. He too had lost the love of another. Grief lurked in his heart and tore at his soul, write what he may in his poems. After the loss of Jeanne and the brief fling with Gertrud, Emil hesitated to rush into a new romantic entanglement. But he yearned for love and attention. Here was a woman who felt at home both in Europe and in Java, who was intelligent and multilingual, artistic and bold, charming and exotic. She was the embodiment of his youthful romantic dreams – Mohammed's Saphie, the lure of the orient, an "opportunity veiled like an Eastern bride." Wasn't Dina the woman he was searching for?

Time passed slowly on the ship. The more they talked, the more they drew together. Older couples smiled and nodded when they passed the young lovers on deck. One evening, as the ship rounded Ceylon in the middle of the Indian Ocean, Emil and Dina wandered outside after dinner. They stood arm in arm in the darkness of the aft deck and listened to piano melodies floating through the warm air. The wind was calm, the night soft and gentle. High overhead the Milky Way blazed a path through the sky and turned in a grand circle around the North Star, invisible below the curved horizon. The ship's phosphorescent wake trailed away to the west and met the new moon sinking into the sea.

Dina gazed at the glimmering, hypnotic trail in the water, in this moment of perfect peace. "Remember what you said in your poem… about 'the magic splendour of life…*Lebens Zauberpracht?*' Was there more?"

Emil looked into her dark eyes and realized that the pain of Jeanne's farewell had finally passed. He remembered the verse he had so recently composed in her honour. Gone now was the wistful melancholy that once gushed from his broken heart. He stroked the curls on her forehead and recited with sentimental fervour:

> *"Möcht' aus den schönsten Blumen*
> *Dir binden einen Kranz,*
> *Und ihn auf's Haupt Dir legen*
> *Um Deiner Stirne Glanz!*
> *Und möcht' recht heiter schauen*
> *Dein holdes Angesicht,*

Und Dir zum Herzen sprechen
Im lieblichsten Gedicht!

I will make thee a wreath from the loveliest blooms
Then this crown, on thy head will I place.
And then shall I gaze upon thy sweet face,
Love, I shall whisper to thee in poems."

She kissed him and rested her head on his shoulder. Emil held her tightly round the waist as they watched the crescent moon sink below the horizon. The twin cusps pointed heavenward in a gleaming smile, thin as an egg shell. The moon dipped into the ocean, touched the end of the shining sea trail and then vanished altogether.

With a sounding of horns and a bustle of stevedores, *Australien* arrived several days later in Batavia's harbour at Tanjung Priok. One of Dina's brothers came to pick her up and to drive her to their father's bedside in Buitenzorg. As Emil helped her step into the horse carriage she pressed her hand in his. *"Au revoir, mon ami."*

Emil watched her carriage disappear into the crowded street. *"Au revoir"* indeed. He wondered if he would ever see her again. Kamdami's crew picked up his trunks and transferred them to *Sri Tadjau*. On the following morning he sailed across the Sunda Strait to Teluk Betung.

NINE

HARMONIE IN BATAVIA

A ghost ship, a Bugis schooner, sailed across their bows

"Three fathoms!" hollered the man in the bow. He retrieved the lead and tossed it again. "*Stoperrr!* Drop anchor!"

The anchor chain rattled out of the hold as *Sri Tadjau* wheezed to a stop in the bay of Teluk Betung. Emil Helfferich stepped into a dinghy and waved to his two partners on shore. At the end of the wooden pier stood Georg Rademacher and Albert Paulmann, waiting to hear firsthand the good news from Hamburg.

"Is it true?" Georg yelled.

"Yes! Everything we asked for!" shouted Emil as the dinghy pulled up alongside the pier. The three men shook hands and slapped each other gleefully on the shoulders.

"Emil, you're not wearing your white suit," Georg laughed. "No pen, no ring?" He scanned the faces of the other passengers and asked more discreetly, "Where's Jeanne?"

Emil looked at his friend sadly. "We parted company. It's a long story. She won't be coming…but I met a wonderful lady on the ship," he added more cheerfully. "She lives in Buitenzorg." Georg rested his hand on Emil's shoulder as they walked slowly up the hill to the office, the little thatched hut beyond the docks.

The new line of credit from Europe allowed them to set up a firm in Java, "Helfferich & Rademacher," and to leave Paulmann in charge of the operation in Sumatra. Within a month of his return in September, 1903, Helfferich rented an office in Batavia on the east bank of the fetid Kali Besar, the so-called Grand Canal. The new office consisted of little more than a single room with plain white walls, a cheap desk and a closet. Despite the cramped quarters Helfferich soon built the pepper export business into a "going concern" and he began to trade in palm oil and other commodities. He forged a relationship with the venerable Singapore firm, Behn, Meyer & Company, the same company whose Hamburg office he had passed every day as a young apprentice. Behn Meyer was one of the oldest and biggest enterprises in Singapore, and would maintain a thriving business into the twenty-first century.

In Batavia's new suburb of "Well-Contented" Weltevreden, his rented home was more lavish, boasting a marble veranda and fine views of the tamarind trees surrounding Koningsplein, the magnificent city square later known as Medan Merdeka. He worked hard for six days a week and then relaxed on Sundays by exploring the surrounding countryside. Each evening in his spacious but lonely residence he dreamed of the lady who wore a red blouse and a white camellia. He imagined the crescent moon setting below the curve of the Indian Ocean. After several weeks he summoned the courage to send Dina a message, asking after the health of her father. He soon received a surprising and welcome invitation to spend the weekend at her family home.

Emil travelled an hour by train from the "Well-Contented" suburb to Buitenzorg, the city of "No Worries," where Dina picked him up in an open carriage. They sat arm-in-arm in the back seat, laughing and chatting as the horse clip-clopped along shady avenues to the grand home of General Ermeling. The old gentleman greeted Emil with gusto and verve on the front porch. Although he was hard of hearing he did not appear to be very sick. In fact he seemed rather spry for a 72-year-old who had recently summoned a daughter to his deathbed. Had he enjoyed a miraculous recovery? Or did the cranky old general just wish to keep his unconventional daughter under tighter control?

The house overlooked the Post Road and the Palace of the Governor-General. Dina ushered him into an airy room in the pavilion, complete with bed and bath, ironed pyjamas on the stool, a pair of wooden shoes, flowers on the table and white *melati* blooms in a crystal bowl. For a lonely and lovesick bachelor it was a welcome treat and a respite from the heat of Batavia. In the afternoon Emil and Dina visited the nearby Botanical Gardens, founded by Sir Stamford Raffles almost a century earlier during Britain's brief tenure over the Indies. Like Lilliputian lovers they strolled in the shade of enormous trees, along the edge of a lake covered in huge African lily pads and down a long, winding path to see *Rafflesia*, the world's largest flower. In the evening they sat close together on the veranda of her father's home and listened to the hum of cicadas as they talked long into the night.

After that first blissful weekend in Buitenzorg, Dina began to visit Emil at his home in Weltevreden. She left behind the prying eyes of her father in exchange for the curious stares of Emil's Sundanese servants. It was difficult for her to relax or to find real privacy. Dina – a widow, half-Dutch, half-Madurese – had no place to call home anymore, no painter's garret in Paris, no independent income. She was a genteel captive in her father's house and a sometime visitor to the home of an earnest young German businessman. She lived in two separate worlds and belonged to neither.

At Christmas time Dina joined Emil on a trip to Teluk Betung to spend the holiday with Georg and Albert. Dressed in a sarong, white jacket and turban, Captain Kamdami bowed from the waist and grandly welcomed them aboard *Sri Tadjau*. At the command "*Lepas tali*," the ropes were cast off and the boat moved away slowly from the old quay at Pasar Ikan. They left the fish market behind and steamed past a green shoreline of coconut palms and mangroves. The fleet of Bugis schooners lay to starboard, each vessel painted in gaudy colours, with the bow steeply upswept and the stern high off the water. The old captain maneuvered deftly through a swarm of bamboo fishing platforms then headed into the long lazy swells of the Java Sea. Standing by the deck rail, recalling the same magic moment four months earlier, the two lovers revelled in the tropical breeze and bright sunshine, the fresh salt air and the wide rolling expanse of ocean.

The boat sailed past lighthouses and the coral reefs of Pulau Seribu, the Thousand Islands. At St. Nicolaas Punt, Java's northernmost point, Kamdami and his crew prepared to recite the *lohor* prayer on deck in the hot noonday sun. First they washed their feet, faced westward to Mecca and kneeled on their mats. Pressing their hands together, they closed their eyes, bowed down low until their foreheads touched the deck and prayed to the one true God. Emil watched from a discreet distance. He remembered the burning incense on the summit of Gunung Gede and Kamdami's offering to the spirits of the sea.

After a dinner of curry and rice they reached the Sunda Strait and Sangiang Island, where high waves and a freshening wind buffeted the little river boat. The new Anyer lighthouse blinked in the darkness. The old one had been destroyed in 1883 by a six-hundred-ton lump of coral, tossed ashore like a coconut by the wave from Krakatau. Emil watched the light turning round and round in a steady hypnotic rhythm. A huge shape suddenly reared out of the gloom. A ghost ship raced across their bows and vanished as quickly as she appeared – a Bugis schooner with no lights, an ill omen at sea. The two lovers retired to their separate berths. Krakatau and Bosun's Rock passed invisibly in the night. After several hours of fitful sleep on the pitching boat, they sighted the mountains of Sumatra at dawn and steamed into the bay of Teluk Betung.

Georg and Albert came down to the dock to meet them. A crewman on *Sri Tadjau* swung the lead line and called out the depths. At three fathoms the steamer dropped anchor and the passengers rowed ashore in a dinghy. The two men eagerly greeted their partner's exotic new friend and showered her with attention. Stepping into two new horse buggies imported from Chicago, they drove into town in style. The men squeezed into the mosquito-infested hut while Dina stayed in more luxurious quarters at the home of a Dutch couple.

Not long after their arrival Paulmann asked bluntly, "How long are you staying?" Albert didn't like crowds and long visits, even at Christmas. Emil placated him with a box of cigars from Manila and a case of port wine from Hamburg. After Christmas dinner they toasted each other with the wine – to success in their new business venture, to good health, to friendship and to loved ones. Emil caught Dina's eye as they raised the glasses to their lips. *"Santé!"*

The three partners worked diligently over the next few years to build up their new business. In late 1905 Rademacher opened an office in Surabaya, the largest city in east Java and the largest market in the country, larger even than Batavia. Business boomed. They imported everything possible and in return exported copra from coconuts, resin from *damar* trees, rattan, kapok, peanuts, synthetic indigo and rice – all in addition to pepper, their main commodity. Owing to the peculiar nature of the pepper market, they had to buy and sell shipments in advance, in essence speculating on future prices. In 1906 they made handsome profits on revenue of 2½ million guilders by selling pepper forward at high prices in a falling market. They shipped about 6,000 tons overseas, almost two-thirds of the entire harvest of black pepper from Lampung and white pepper from Java. It would be the biggest annual profit in all their years in the Dutch East Indies. Helfferich & Rademacher were reputed to be the largest pepper exporters in the world. Thousands of sacks were shipped to New York, Genoa and Trieste, with the majority destined for Hamburg, to the same docks that Emil had wandered a decade earlier as an apprentice clerk. Emil imagined with satisfaction the huge mountains of pepper on the quay by the Elbe, his company logo stencilled on each sack, as seagulls wheeled and keened overhead in the cold grey sky of northern Europe.

Communication between Rademacher in Surabaya and Helfferich in Batavia was not easy. The two partners worked out a regular routine whereby they would each board a train at the same time and meet at Maos near the prison island of Nusa Kambangan, the halfway point between the two cities. The two trains arrived after sunset, crossed paths and returned just before sunrise the next morning. Helfferich travelled via Buitenzorg and Bandung, Rademacher via Yogyakarta. They never saw Maos except at night. Blackened by the greasy soot which seeped through the windows and doors of the trains, the two men sat facing each other across a bare wooden table in the deserted lobby of the Station Hotel. Maos lay in the middle of a sweltering fetid swamp not far from the south coast. Frogs croaked in the grass. Bats flew around the harsh acetylene light and sometimes fell onto their open ledgers. Mosquitoes bit their ankles. There was no young boy to swat them away – but at least the beer was cold. They talked and planned and drank all through the long hot tropical night until they left for home in the early morning.

As Emil's fortunes waxed, Dina's waned. Her affairs were not going well. She had interrupted her artistic career in Paris to care for her ailing father, now seemingly recovered. The feisty old man and the headstrong daughter bickered constantly. She found it increasingly difficult to live with him. In the end they disagreed profoundly over a family matter and parted in bitterness. Dina moved to central Java to live with her uncle's family. Torn between her dream of returning to Europe and her proud refusal to accept any support from her father, she resigned herself to the ascetic lifestyle of a struggling artist.

In Yogyakarta she lived and worked in a primitive hut beside her uncle's house, in a valley midway between the stone temples of Borobudur and Prambanan. The cemetery with her husband's modest grave lay not far away. To forget her worries she immersed herself in her painting. Her style grew moodier, with *chiaroscuro* contrasts more typical of Rembrandt than of the Impressionists or Matisse. Central Java was the homeland of the colour indigo, a deep dark blue that infused traditional batik design and darkened the appearance and character of the Javanese. Indigo seeped onto her canvas. Her masterpiece was "The Fortune-Teller," an eerily prescient work depicting a tense Javanese couple seated beside a traditional Chinese fortune-teller, reading cards by the dim light of an oil lamp. What misfortune worried the young couple? Poor health? No children? A vague sense of foreboding? She shipped the painting overseas to the jury of the Paris Salon but it arrived too late for the annual competition.

Emil and Dina wrote to each other often but saw each other only rarely. This changed in early 1906 when she finally tired of her austere existence. She longed to be a part of Emil's life amid the bustle of Batavia. To accommodate his rapidly growing company, he had just rented a large new office and, at the same time, had moved into a rambling house on a hill in Tanah Abang, the residence of a former Governor-General. With Dina's help he bought furniture at an auction and put the spacious mansion in order. She surveyed the happy scene, the bright hallways and a room which might serve as an art studio. Her future hung in the balance. On the one hand lay a poor and lonely life of defiant independence; on the other hand, a secure home filled with love and contentment. The scale tipped. She wrapped her arms around Emil's neck and kissed him on the lips. "Could you show me to my room?" she asked.

Emil was ecstatic, so happy in fact with Dina's constant love and companionship and with his successful business, that he stopped writing sentimental rhymes altogether. For the first time since he left his parents a decade earlier he felt truly at home. There were no children to share in the domestic bliss but pets and animals of many descriptions soon arrived to take their place: a long-haired Pomeranian spitz, "Tilly," which never strayed from Dina's side; a white terrier, "Muck," which Georg had brought back from a trip to Europe; "Lotti," her favourite terrier; "Schwabi," a greyhound from Australia; and "Rex," a leonine giant from Rio – a gift from a Danish captain. Two Sumatran deer, "Inka" the buck and "Inki" the doe, grazed on the lawn; "Bobby" the kangaroo, the gift of a Lloyd's captain from Melbourne, jumped and boxed like an athlete. There was even a young Sumatran bear, named "Atta Troll." Two ponies and a large Australian horse rounded out the incredible menagerie. They lived in the stable alongside an elegant phaeton carriage.

The carriage and driver were necessary, not only for business and social occasions, but to bring Emil home when he drank too much at the Harmonie Club. This was Batavia's best and oldest club, begun in 1810 by the Dutch Governor-General Daendels and finished in 1814 by Sir Stamford Raffles during the British interregnum. In 1985 the Indonesian Secretary of State demolished this symbol of colonial rule and built a parking lot over the ruins. Only the name lingers on but for almost one hundred and thirty years it was the centre of Dutch social life. Men from all nationalities were permitted to join although women, in the fashion of the time, could only attend Sunday concerts and balls. European newspapers were available in Dutch, English, French and German. The club also boasted a well-stocked library – and a bar.

In his early bachelor years Emil was an enthusiastic habitué of the Harmonie bar. He and his friends drank whisky sodas. He found it remarkable how, the more they drank, the more alert and clever they became. Late in the evening they shoved tables together and leaped over them, one after another. Some landed hard on the marble floor. Then they arranged a dozen chairs in a row and the game would be to slide a glass on the floor between the chair legs so that it arrived safely at the other end. Usually it shattered – to the hilarity of the spectators.

The height of whisky-fuelled entertainment was the *sado* race. The *sado* was a humble two-wheeled pony cart, dozens of which plied the wide Rijswijkstraat in front of the Harmonie Club. On the night of a race the drivers were paid to stand on the sidelines while tipsy European men took the reins in hand. The contest began on the bridge after midnight and ended at the club in a sprint, the like of which had rarely been seen since the heyday of the Roman Colosseum. The victor was carried on the shoulders of the exultant mob and feted with whisky sodas and ribald songs until the first light of dawn.

These wild club nights were a welcome release for young homeless bachelors. After an endless day spent in courteous, frustrating palaver with native merchants and government officials, they needed to let off steam. Emil enjoyed the drinking and the hijinks as much as anyone but Dina was now expecting him at home. She had no patience waiting late into the night for a drunken man to stagger in the door. Emil came to his senses. A happy domestic life suddenly seemed more important than the juvenile antics of a club evening. At the same time, his prestige and influence were rising in the business world. The Harmonie became for him less like a pub and more like an elegant setting in which to meet bankers, civil servants and other entrepreneurs.

Helfferich would never forget one particular club evening. In September, 1906, the winter monsoon was still two months away. The night was dry and calm, the gardens green and well lit, and a band played classical music as he talked with his friends. White men in tropical suits sat around the tables; native waiters in sarongs hovered in the background. Talk turned, as it did many evenings, to the complexities of working with the local Malay culture, of the slow pace and lack of ambition, of thievery and a lack of transparency. This was, of course, a one-sided discussion. A Dutchman joked, "You know what it means when they say '*belum*' – that they haven't done something yet? It's like the Spanish *mañana* – but without the Spanish sense of urgency." The table broke into uproarious laughter. An Englishman interrupted, "Wasn't it Kipling who called them the 'Malazy' race?"

Helfferich smiled uncomfortably. England's gifted poet – who would win a Nobel Prize the following year – was one of his literary heroes. In a children's story, "The Crab That Played with the Sea," Kipling had indeed described a "Malazy" fisherman who used the tides to catch fish. Despite accusations of racism, Kipling was sensitive to the plight of the native. Helfferich was fond of quoting the opening lines to his first volume of poetry:

> …The deaths ye died I have watched beside,
> And the lives ye led were mine.
>
> Was there aught I did not share
> In vigil or toil or ease, –
> One joy or woe that I did not know,
> Dear hearts across the seas?

He thought of the woman he loved, of the men and women he knew in Teluk Betung, of the long arduous hours spent in the fields or on boats, of the toil of feeding a family with one's bare hands. He noted, by comparison, the soft pink hands around the table. It might be true that a man in the field seemed to live in the present, without particular concern for the past or the future. Like the endless murmur of *gamelan* music, his life flowed onward peacefully, without ambition, without plan, trusting in fate. His traditions were ancient and "immovable," like Conrad's "forests rooted deep in the soil." He found solace and support within a large family. Modest and mild, strong and very proud, he faced the day's challenges with humour; he avoided conflict and embarrassment; and he deflected aggression with courtesy. "Yes" could mean "I hear you," not "I agree." He worked to a different rhythm than the European, a pace that a less astute observer might deem idle. A wise man found wellbeing by limiting his work only to that which was necessary – a lifestyle which, though Helfferich recognized its virtue, he could no more pursue than, in the words of Jesus, "a camel could go through the eye of a needle." Some of the indigenous poor felt more content and prosperous than did he or his wealthy European friends.

A grim-faced manager waded officiously through the tables. He clutched a telegram in his hand and called for silence. The laughter died away and a hush settled over the patrons as he announced terrible news from Bali.

Helfferich read the unabridged version later, in a book by a Dutch soldier named van Weede. The Dutch had only recently conquered the idyllic green island of Bali. The last and most easterly vestige of the ancient Hindu empire, the Balinese clung gently but stubbornly to the old ways. In 1906 the Dutch attacked in force, captured the whole island and killed 3,600 Balinese. Obstinate colonial ambition met with simmering resentment....

A motorcar, one of very few on Bali, ran out of gas one day in the hills above the capital of Denpasar. Its Dutch occupants searched vainly for fuel in a nearby village and returned to find that the car had been ransacked. They quickly pinned the blame on the *raja* of Badung and his followers. When heavy-handed attempts failed to recover the stolen goods, the Dutch sent in the army. Incensed by allegations of thievery, by the attempt to subvert his rule and by their loss of freedom, the *raja* told his people to fight to the death.

He assembled a small band of followers and led them down the mountain to Denpasar. As they drew closer to the Dutch garrison, a few faint-hearted souls drifted away and melted back into the hills. Two hundred and fifty men, women and children remained, with the *raja* and his princely son at the head of the column. They wore their most formal clothes: the women in white jackets with their hair worn loose and free; the men in red vests and black pants, dark hair carefully oiled and combed. Each man carried a gold-tipped spear or a *kris*, a large dagger. The sacred *kris* of the *raja* was inlaid with precious gemstones and surmounted by a golden figure. When he waved it high overhead, the sinuous blade gleamed in the sun.

The crowd marched steadily downhill to Puputan Square, down to the waiting soldiers. The young prince set one of his own temples on fire and whipped his people into a suicidal frenzy. They smashed everything inside. Onward they strode, wild-eyed, until they faced the grim line of Dutch infantry.

Through an interpreter the captain ordered the Balinese to halt. Still they kept coming. The crowd ignored further warnings and began to run toward them. At seventy paces they sprinted full tilt, *krisses* and lances levelled, hundreds of voices raised in blood-curdling unison. To hesitate was to die. The soldiers fired a salvo into the mob and the *raja* collapsed on the ground. Others pressed the attack and the Dutch fired back in self-defence. The soldiers watched in growing revulsion as the wounded stabbed their dying comrades. When the wounded themselves fell, others continued the bloody work. All seemed to lust for death. Women bared their breasts or backs to the blow. They stood in front of the soldiers, pointed at their hearts and begged to be shot. Some threw gold coins as payment for death. No man would shoot and so the women stabbed themselves. One old man frantically knifed the wounded to the left and to the right until he himself was shot by the horrified soldiers. An old woman continued his work until she too was killed.

The Dutch withdrew to a nearby hut when a second group of Balinese approached. At the head marched the *raja's* twelve-year-old half-brother, a boy who could barely hold his lance upright. When ordered to halt he hesitated briefly. His men thrust him forward but a hail of bullets cut him down. A grotesque pile of bodies lay in the middle of the courtyard. The *raja's* wives searched for their husband under the heap, then fell upon him and allowed themselves to be stabbed. The last of the wounded staggered over to the bleeding pile, where golden spear points glittered among the corpses. All but one Balinese died.

Only one Dutch soldier was killed. The others stared aghast at the incomprehensible carnage. Battle-hardened soldiers wept and vomited. What desperation, what point of honour had driven these men and women to mass suicide? Like the outnumbered Jews of Masada, they showed contempt for their overlords in the most extreme and bitter way. They chose death over surrender.

A Balinese kris

Helfferich stared blankly at the vase of flowers in the middle of the table. No one spoke. The band played "*Danse macabre*" by Saint-Saëns in honour of the fallen. Some guests excused themselves and walked out to the line of waiting carriages. He twirled an empty wine glass in his fingers and once more thought of the men and women in the forests, proud people who valued their freedom more than their lives. He remembered the fire in Sumatra, the great forests "everlasting in the shadowy might of their tradition," and the giant trees felled by European axes and saws. He heard the groaning, the splintering and the crashing.

Helfferich rode home in the back of the phaeton through the crowds and busy streets of Batavia at night. Nothing looked different. Everyone seemed oblivious to the distant massacre. He was deeply troubled but, in his optimistic way, he hoped that something good would come of this tragedy, that new life would spring up where the old had died. Surely, he thought, the Balinese would recover. Some day they would welcome the foreigners. Surely, he believed, his tea and pepper plantations would create useful work for the natives and add value to their land.

For the first time in many years he felt uncertain. He sensed an ill wind, a sea change in his affairs, as if in the gathering darkness a ghostly ship had sailed across his path. Like Lord Jim aboard the pilgrim ship *Patna*, he "seemed to gaze hungrily into the unattainable and did not see the shadow of the coming event."

TEN

THE CHINESE FORTUNE-TELLER

"More trouble will come your way."

Albert Paulmann was missing, nine days overdue on *Sri Tadjau*. He had just concluded a large pepper contract for the new harvest with *Haji* Andung, a merchant on the flat southeast coast of Lampung. Paulmann chartered *Sri Tadjau*, with Captain Kamdami and his crew, to sail to Labuan Maringgai with a cargo of coconuts from Teluk Betung and 40,000 guilders in heavy silver bars – almost a million dollars in modern currency. The trip there and back should have taken five days but now they had been gone for two weeks. Other boats searched the villages along the coast without success.

Helfferich paced up and down the quay at Tanjung Priok in Batavia. He spoke once again to the Dutch captain who had spotted the shallow-draft river steamer leaving Teluk Betung. She had been heading into bad weather and rolling heavily in the Sunda Strait. "*Nee*," the cheerless captain averred, "there is no hope of finding them alive, not after fourteen days." If the storm didn't sink them – or if pirates didn't find them – they would have died of thirst already.

With a heavy heart Helfferich returned to the Hotel des Indes, downed two glasses of port and then plodded home in the rapidly fading twilight. The veranda was dark and the house looked gloomy and foreboding. He walked through the door and called to Dina but she was still out.

Two cold white hands lunged at him from the darkness – Paulmann!

While he had been talking to the Dutch captain at Tanjung Priok, the crew of *Sri Tadjau* had arrived in the old harbour by Pasar Ikan. Paulmann had walked nonchalantly to Helfferich's empty house and waited for him to return.

It happened that, two weeks earlier, the storm had overwhelmed them and blown the hapless vessel into the open sea. When the clouds lifted, Kamdami looked around in dismay at the empty horizon. He could only navigate within sight of coastal landmarks. With his bearings lost and his brain muddled, he throttled back the engines and traced slow lonely circles in the middle of the Java Sea. Within several days they ran out of coal and food, then water. Drifting helplessly in the swells they broke open the cargo of coconuts and drank the milk. The sun beat down mercilessly on their heads. Kamdami faced Mecca and prayed to God. Then he dropped a coconut over the side in a plea to the sea goddess, the jinns and the spirits. After several more days of aimless drifting they spotted a native sailboat and waved fearfully to its occupants. Pirates infested the Java Sea. To their astonishment they encountered no pirates aboard the sailboat but *Haji* Andung instead, the pepper trader of Labuan Maringgai. *Sri Tadjau* had drifted almost to within sight of the coastal village. The sailboat towed the steamer at a snail's pace into the harbour where the crew and the remaining coconuts – and the silver bars – arrived safely at the dock. After allowing a few days to recover and refuel they steamed without further incident to Batavia.

Helfferich had taken similar trips in *Sri Tadjau* many times and had suffered a few near misses himself. On one occasion with Dina the boat ran into heavy weather and wallowed giddily in the foaming whitecaps. Dizzy with seasickness Emil leaned perilously over the railing. Dina, who was ill herself, spotted him just in time, wrapped a rope around both their waists and anchored herself to a bollard. Soaked to the bone they huddled in the scuppers as waves sloshed endlessly over their shivering bodies.

On another occasion the ship cast off from Teluk Betung at night with an empty hold. Riding high in a rising gale the riverboat bounced about like a tiny cork in the heaving swells. Thunder and lightning crashed down all around; huge combers washed over the bow; lighthouses and islands vanished behind dark sheets of driving rain. The gale sang in the stays like the windmills of Pajajaran, like sirens on a rocky reef. Abandoning the helm, Kamdami and his crew fled below to pray for divine help. Helfferich grabbed the wheel and turned it hard to starboard, forcing the boat to turn in circles. When the storm slackened, the captain returned anxiously to the bridge. By the pale light of the moon they spotted a white line of angry surf crashing onto the rocky island of Sebuki, dead ahead just three hundred metres away. They quickly dropped anchor and waited until dawn, unnerved by their narrow escape.

Paulmann seemed to be unmoved by his recent escapade. Over port and cigars after dinner Helfferich reminisced about *Sri Tadjau* and chatted with his taciturn partner. He was a loner, a very conservative and orderly person, and his carefully considered opinions were important to Helfferich. That night Paulmann warned him that the firm was overstretched, that they were expanding too fast and that their fortune was based on lucky speculation. Although Paulmann willingly submitted to his partner's judgment and leadership, he wasn't happy. They were heading into a storm.

The year 1907 began badly. In early January Emil and Dina packed their trunks for a long-awaited return voyage to Europe. Emil anticipated a grand welcome, not only from his parents but also from his bankers. Dina looked forward to the spiritual renewal of an artistic holiday in Paris. They asked Paulmann to come to Batavia to run the office and to mind the house in their absence. On the afternoon of his arrival he joined Emil for a drink at the club. While the two men were out, a burglar broke into the ground floor guest room and stole Paulmann's pocket watch. The servants wrung their hands in dismay, crying, "*Pencuri,* thief!" but left the fearless Dina to chase after him alone. Naked and smeared with oil the robber leaped over the fence. Dina cursed him in Javanese and described in loud and graphic detail what she would do to his miserable naked body if he ever returned. She wished she had a rattan whip, like the one brandished by Emil's guide on Gunung Gede.

The next morning Georg Rademacher telephoned with tragic news. In 1906 he had married his childhood sweetheart, Agnes Iser, at an English church in Singapore. Now, nine months later, their baby had just died in premature childbirth and his wife was gravely ill with typhoid. On January 10 he phoned again and announced in a flat voice that Agnes, too, had died. Mother and child were buried the next day, side by side in the same coffin. Georg was inconsolable. Heartbroken themselves, neither Dina nor Emil could offer support or attend the funeral – their ship was due to sail that afternoon. Emil blurted his condolences into the telephone and promised to see him when they returned. Paulmann drove the glum couple to Tanjung Priok and waved goodbye from the dock.

As they sailed through the Indian Ocean one week later, Emil marked his twenty-ninth birthday with a festive dinner. The celebration buoyed their spirits for a while and helped them temper the sadness. The dining room was stuffy with cigar smoke and the heavy equatorial heat. Emil suggested a walk in the fresh air, a romantic stroll under the stars. They left the dining room, linked arms and strolled onto the main deck.

"Emil! Look – the moon." The thin silver crescent of the new moon shone like a beacon ahead of the ship. The horns pointed heavenward as it sank majestically to the western horizon.

They breathed the bracing salt air streaming over the bow. Dina hugged him tightly round the waist and recalled a similar night under the same moon almost four years earlier. "Remember your poem about the "magic splendour of life?" she asked. He smiled wryly. "You were so passionate – I loved it." They stood in silence for a while, absorbed in their thoughts, listening to the rhythmic splash of waves against the hull, feeling the solitude at the centre of the grand vaulted dome of stars as if they were the only two people left on earth.

"Emil?" She stared at the moon and paused as he tensed imperceptibly. "You don't mind, do you, if we just go on like this forever?" she asked.

He knew what she meant. Despite his obvious willingness she had sidestepped the issue of marriage. He didn't know why but he had some guesses. She was feisty and independent. She had been married once before and still felt the loss. Georg's grief upset her badly. Sometimes she felt sad and depressed about the future. Maybe her father disapproved. An unwelcome thought flashed through his mind as he remembered his old girlfriend, Jeanne. She had recently written him to announce her marriage. The old wound had reopened as she described her happy new life. She, too, had been reluctant to commit herself. Perhaps *he* was the problem. He put so much of himself into his business – and the Harmonie Club.

"Is it me, Dina? All work and no play?"

"No, Emil, of course not. I love you…very much." She snuggled up closer. "Of course you work hard – but it's exciting. You're so clever and enthusiastic. And we do play…I just think it's more romantic this way. We don't have to get married – we can be lovers forever."

"Lovers forever…that's good. But we could get married and still be lovers. That sometimes happens, doesn't it?"

Dina smiled and looked away. She leaned on the railing and stared into the blackness of the sea. "Emil…I can't. I've been married once already. He died a year and a half later. I couldn't go through that a second time. It just doesn't seem right."

In his own mind Emil disagreed. He knew that Georg, for example, would want to remarry some day. But how could he argue with her? After twelve years of widowhood it seemed unlikely she would change her mind. The holy rite of marriage held no magic appeal for him anyway. His parents and siblings weren't religious. The Helfferich family went to church only for marriages and funerals. He felt no social pressure to sanctify their relationship even though it flouted the strict conventions of the time. In fact, he thought, it was rather exciting to walk arm in arm with a glamorous and confident lady in her late thirties, an exotic eastern flower, an *artiste* with the grand name of Uhlenbeck-Ermeling.

"So how shall I introduce you if you don't want to be called *Frau* Helfferich? A lady like you should have a magnificent title. How about… *die Lebensgefährtin*? The one who travels life's road with me, who shares in its 'magic splendour,' the love of my life. What do you think?"

"Oh! What a mouthful!" she laughed. "Call me whatever you like. At least that's better than what they called me in school."

"So what did they call you in school?"

"Well, you know that my parents divorced when I was little. Then Father sent me to school in Holland but it was lonely there. The other children called me '*Indo*' – half-breed. I remember as if it were yesterday." She thought about her upcoming visit with the Helfferich family. "How will your parents feel – or do you care?"

"I do care how they feel – but Mother is very sensible and my father loves pretty ladies of any colour," he said. "They prefer marriage, of course, but they don't really worry about what other people might think." He paused at the thought of his eldest brother. "I can't say the same about Karl. He's a bit hard sometimes, like a schoolyard bully. He has definite ideas about people and how we should all behave – marriage, children, making money and so on."

Dina gazed at the twin horns of the moon disappearing into the sea and thought again of Agnes and her baby. "I'm thirty-seven now, Emil. I'm too old to have children," she whispered, "And I wouldn't want our children to grow up as '*Indos*' in Germany anyway."

He kissed her on the forehead and followed her gaze to the vanishing moon. Emil loved children. "My *Lebensgefährtin*…it will be just the two of us then." The sound of band music and laughter drifted from the salon toward them. The doors opened as other couples waltzed around the deck. "May I have this dance?" he asked, bowing deeply.

Several weeks later they disembarked in Genoa after a subdued and un-eventful voyage. Despite the excitement of a triumphal return, Georg's loss weighed heavily on their hearts. They travelled to Paris by train where Dina met up with old friends. Emil continued alone to Neustadt for his first visit home in almost four years. Following a joyful reunion, his parents and siblings asked about the mysterious Dina. She would come later, he said, after her painting holiday and his business meetings. He boarded the train to Hamburg, the city that gave his career a start, and there he received the adulation due a conquering hero. Bank doors opened to the successful businessman, the famous young pepper trader of the Dutch East

Indies. To be popular and well respected was what he craved; it all seemed so easy.

He journeyed on to Holland where he watched Queen Wilhelmina and her new baby, Princess Juliana, drive by in a gilded carriage. From Amsterdam he sailed with his father to London for a short holiday. Each day the two tourists enjoyed lunch in a particular restaurant. His father carefully positioned his chair so that he could watch the comely young lady at the cash register. When they left for the last time, the greybeard squeezed the startled woman's hand and gave her a large tip. On the street outside the restaurant Emil laughed out loud at his blushing father. "You old rascal...that's where I get it from!"

Helfferich walked alone through London's unfamiliar streets. Gargoyles perched on the green roofs of old stone buildings. He opened a large wooden door and entered the office of Mr. Figgis, a well-known trader in pepper and other commodities. The wily curmudgeon had seen his fair share of ups and downs. He warned the young German that the pepper market could be brutal, that dealing in pepper was more of a gamble than an investment and that, after such a good year, he was due for a fall. Helfferich respected the wisdom and experience of old Mr. Figgis but he felt that he was different. He was confident in his own youthful abilities and in the strength of his partners. He had done well so far. If he worked hard and used his head how could he possibly fail?

The early spring days grew longer. The sun rose higher in the sky and hinted of tropical warmth. It was time to return. Dina left her friends in Paris and rejoined Emil in Neustadt, bringing with her "The Fortune-Teller," the painting that had arrived too late to the Paris Salon. She gingerly unpacked it from its wooden crate and presented it to Friedrich and Augusta. Their praise for her masterpiece was as effusive and genuine as their welcome for her, much to Emil's relief. But while his mother chatted with Dina in another room, he stared at the three figures in the sombre painting. An oil lamp illuminated the worried face of a Javanese wife, a woman not unlike Dina. Beneath a veneer of grace and confidence she betrayed the anguish of a former life and an anxious concern for the future.

Three days before his son's return journey to the Indies, Friedrich pulled Emil aside for a serious discussion. Would this be a lecture on marriage, Emil feared? No, his father only wanted to talk about Theodor, his younger brother.

Theodor had just turned twenty-seven. Eight years earlier, as Emil prepared to sail to Penang on his grand adventure, Theodor entered the Strasbourg military academy as a junior officer. Two months later he fell ill with pleurisy and had to quit the army. Chronic bronchitis had plagued him throughout his childhood and would frustrate all his future endeavours. During a long period of convalescence in the milder climate of southern Europe he taught himself banking methods. Later on his brother Karl helped him find a job with the Deutsche Bank in Berlin. It was Theodor's plan to join the German Overseas Bank and to move to Chile, where the dry climate would be good for his health. But a second bout of pleurisy put an end to his dream. He quit his job with the bank and spent a year recovering in the high Engadine of Switzerland.

Friedrich wondered if the hot Javanese climate might be good for Theodor and whether Emil would be willing to find him a job. Emil was not overwhelmed with enthusiasm. Theodor – sickly, introverted, conservative and critical – was his complete antithesis. Reluctantly Emil agreed to ask his brother if he would be interested in such a move, hoping perhaps that he would balk at the opportunity. But Theodor jumped at the invitation and packed his bags in a hurry. The three travellers were joined by Georg Rademacher's sister, Elli. She had agreed to live for a while in Surabaya to tend the house for her widowed brother and to keep him company. In April, as the first green buds appeared on the *Pfälzer* grape vines, Emil bade his parents a sentimental farewell and escorted Dina, Elli and Theodor on the long voyage to Java.

In his heart he was troubled but he kept his feelings to himself. He was not superstitious, he believed, at least no more so than the next person, but the recent spate of bad omens worried him: the loss of Georg's wife and child; Albert's narrow escape on *Sri Tadjau*; his own crises in the Java Sea; the need to look after his sickly brother; Dina's bouts of mild depression; even the vague unease caused by the troubles in Bali and his own role in the country's development. And why would Figgis predict he was due for a fall?

The four companions disembarked in Batavia in mid-May. Theodor, with his new and promising life in Java stretching before him, travelled on to Surabaya to stay with Georg and Elli. After a long overdue visit of condolence with Georg, Emil and Dina returned to a high-spirited welcome from all the pets. Emil went back to his office and immediately began to reanalyze the pepper trade. He sifted carefully through a stack of reports and newspapers. Last year, having correctly foreseen a bear market and slack prices, he had been wildly successful in his speculations. What position should he take this season? World pepper supplies were less than half those of previous years. Plantation owners were predicting that the harvest in Sumatra and Penang would fail, owing to a blight on the vines. Traders in Hamburg were optimistic about prices. There was a pleasing symmetry to the idea that a bull market would follow a bear. He tossed the papers into the basket. It was obvious, he concluded: there would be a bull market in pepper.

Pepper, more so than most commodities of the era, was prone to speculative manipulation: it was nonperishable and lasted for years in storage; harvests fluctuated dramatically; consumption was constant and unaffected by price. Pepper production was concentrated in Southeast Asia, particularly in the Dutch East Indies, and thus the market could be cornered. Great opportunities existed for profits but also for losses.

Helfferich wrote up new contracts with his suppliers and agreed to pay 25 guilders for a sack of pepper – a reasonable price given his anticipation of a bull market. Trading started off weakly but there was no cause for concern. Then the pepper blight cleared up and the harvest proved much better than expected. Prices fell further. So as not to endanger his position or prestige he had no choice but to buy pepper. A telegram from Behn Meyer in Singapore warned him to be careful but Helfferich remained steadfast. The market price dropped to 17 guilders even as he paid his suppliers 25 guilders. Unsold pepper was stacked high to the rafters. There was no turning back now. He had to grit his teeth and wait for the market to turn.

The market never recovered. A warning came from Hamburg that the world was plunging into economic crisis. Lloyd's left him in the lurch without enough ships, thus eliminating the American market. Local Chinese traders sensed trouble and reneged on their debts, forcing Helfferich to cut back on the sale of imported goods. Events unfolded in disastrous slow motion. At the worst moment of the crisis he held an unsold inventory of about 5,000 tons of pepper, optimistically valued at 2.1 million guilders. How could he possibly finance such an overhang? He tried in vain to send shipments to Europe but there were very few buyers. His Hamburg creditors sent angry telegrams; even the Java Bank cut him off.

One quiet Sunday morning in October, 1907, Emil lay in the *chaise longue* on the veranda of his home. A coded telegram from Hamburg dangled in his left hand. It was the end for him, the knockout blow. Dina sat on the end of the chair, her terrier Lotti curled in her lap as she squeezed his other hand. The two deer grazed peacefully on the lawn.

Emil moped around the house for a month, strangely paralyzed, unwilling to believe his misfortune and unable to do anything about it. One evening he sat on the veranda with Dina, watching the deer and the outlandish kangaroo. A skinny little man entered the garden and shuffled hesitantly up the steps. He was a Chinese fortune-teller. Emil waved him off but Dina called him back. He was dressed in a classical, almost exaggerated fashion, with a silk cap, a long braided pigtail, black pants and jacket and shiny, wide, black shoes. From his left shoulder hung a bamboo quiver filled with chopsticks; a small bird perched on the other shoulder. In his wrinkled hand he held a well-thumbed book. He bowed deeply, removed the quiver and offered the contents to his avian partner. The bird picked out one of the chopsticks. The fortune-teller gently retrieved the stick and read the Chinese characters on its side. Then he looked carefully at Emil and consulted a particular page in his book.

After a short while he announced in Malay, "*Tuan ada susah.* You are in trouble." Yes, for sure, thought Emil bitterly, tell me something I don't know. The bird picked a second chopstick and the man consulted his book again. "*Tuan dapat susah lagi.* More trouble will come your way." Emil could believe that too. The fortune-teller looked very worried but when he read the third stick his face brightened. "*Tahun baru cina susah habis.* By Chinese New Year your troubles will be over." Oh no, thought Emil, another four months of grief. The bird picked the fourth and last stick. Much relieved, the old man beamed broadly. His thin lips stretched grotesquely across his gums as he grandly intoned, "*Belakangan Tuan besar sekali*! Later you will become a great man!" Emil watched the little bird curiously as the man returned the sticks to the quiver. It cocked its head sideways, fixed him with a penetrating gaze and blinked.

During the next few months of turmoil, Dina was his pillar of strength, his castle rock. Despite her own worries she rescued him from despair and nursed him back to health. His partners and employees, though glum, remained loyal and uncritical. The banks treated him decently even as they suffered their own problems in the midst of the global economic crisis. Helfferich travelled to Singapore in January to meet with his creditors and with his partners at Behn Meyer. The reception was decidedly chilly. On February 4, 1908, they reached an agreement to liquidate the firm of Helfferich & Rademacher and to allow Behn, Meyer & Co to take over the assets. In return Behn Meyer agreed to retain Rademacher and Paulmann as managers in Surabaya and Teluk Betung, to retain Theodor as an assistant in Batavia and to keep all the other employees but Emil. He took the entire blame, he was unemployed and his dream lay irretrievably shattered.

Firecrackers exploded on Finlayson Green, just outside the Behn Meyer office. February 4 was the first day of the Chinese New Year. The fortune-teller was right so far. Although he was now a poor man, Emil could claim that he had no troubles left to concern him. He had survived and the tough decisions were all behind him. A friend at the Java Bank promised to help him in any new undertaking. He was still young and capable even though he felt old and washed up. In the middle of the debacle he had turned thirty. To Dina's dismay he spent more time drinking at the Harmonie Club. He watched helplessly as his former company sold off the surplus pepper. They took huge losses and depressed the market even further. Emil told his brother that they should have been patient – in one more year they might have at least broken even. He missed his old friend, Po Tjong. Over brandy and bitters they would have commiserated over their misfortunes and railed against such cruel twists of fate.

Amid all the upheaval of bankruptcy, Emil persuaded Theodor to join him at the Hotel Sindanglaya in the mountains south of Batavia. He wanted to forget his troubles and to recapture the magic of his first ascent of Gunung Gede. Emil also hoped to renew the bond with his brother, a cautious man so different from himself. But he accomplished none of this. After catching cold in the hills, Theodor fell gravely ill with pleurisy. He lay in a hospital bed in Surabaya for several months while Dina, Elli and Georg nursed him back to good health. Without their support he might have died. Although he never did climb Gunung Gede, he stayed healthy for many years. Thanks to Emil, he enjoyed a rewarding twelve-year career with Behn, Meyer & Co and eventually rose to the position of Director in Batavia.

In the meantime Emil and Dina had to vacate their first home and turn it over to the new manager. In a bizarre response to their master's misfortune, the dogs languished and died from a horrible infection. Dina wept as if she had lost her own children. She sent the kangaroo and the bear to a friend in Semarang, who shot the bear when it became too difficult to handle. The two deer survived and accompanied Emil and Dina to comfortable exile in Malabar near Bandung, where Dutch friends owned a tea plantation high in the hills. Emil soaked up the peaceful green surroundings, breathed the cool air and carefully observed the busy plantation routine. Theodor came to visit and, for the first time ever, Emil felt comforted by his presence. In the green shade of the garden they laughed at the irony: Theodor, healthy and employed, nursing his heartsick, jobless brother back to vigorous life. With each laugh the feelings of guilt and failure melted like the ice in his whisky soda.

Emil planned his next move. Friends and mountain air were good but there was only one sure way to rebuild his damaged reputation and self-esteem. He would have to return to Germany and start all over again. They packed for a long sojourn in Europe, not really knowing if they would ever come back. In July they boarded the ship. The horn sounded and the boat drifted away from the pier. They passed the breakwater and a line of gently waving palm trees. A surge of grief overwhelmed Emil as he gripped the railing tightly. What a contrast with his feelings at the same moment just over one year ago! On his last voyage, though he had mourned the loss of Georg's wife and child, he had felt no sense of personal failure. Joy and excitement had filled his heart, hubris even, the arrogant pride of a successful young man. Now his life lay again in apparent ruin. He remembered the long-ago anguish of Jeanne's farewell and his week of alcoholic oblivion on the shore of Lake Geneva. Five years had passed since then, he realized, five happy years with Dina. The loss of Jeanne had led him straight into the arms of his *Lebensgefährtin*. Perhaps, he mused, this tumble might be a good thing after all. He put his arm around Dina and stared at the coast of Java. The summit of Pangrango, his "veiled" opportunity, sank slowly below the grey horizon.

Before reaching India the ship weathered two violent storms. Water sloshed through the passageways and leaked into the cabins. As he clung to the sides of his bunk Emil wondered if he might be the ship's Jonah and whether there would be any end to his run of bad luck. He also wondered if the captain had tossed an offering overboard or had at least said his prayers. By luck or divine intervention they arrived safely in Bombay, where they paused on their voyage and toured the crowded city. Emil wandered into an English book store and browsed the dusty stacks of poetry. A new tome caught his eye: Hutchinson's recently published *Complete Poetical Works of Shelley*. It was printed in Bombay, bound in red morocco leather and stamped in gold letters. Emil checked the slim stash of rupees in his billfold and made an offer. After a few minutes of spirited bargaining the book was his.

The two wanderers drove deep into the hinterland, to the Western Ghats and the high Deccan plateau. For eight days they relaxed in a simple guesthouse, surrounded by fields of tawny grass where goats and cattle roamed at will. There were no other Europeans. Emil leafed through the pages of his new book and made notes in the margins. Shelley's major opus, "The Revolt of Islam," caught his eye. The romantic English poet presented, in his own words, "a succession of pictures illustrating the growth and progress of individual mind aspiring after excellence and devoted to the love of mankind...its impatience at all the oppressions which are done under the sun." Emil thought back to his heroic five-act play "Mohammed" and to his battles among the ruined castles of the Haardt hills.

Not far from the cottage lay the Ellora Caves, an ancient city in ruins. Emil and Dina wandered through empty temples, past solemn Buddhas and down into gloomy underground passages. Massive stone blocks, stacked in high walls and surmounted by brooding watchtowers, ringed the inner sanctum. Across a deep moat a stone bridge led to a massive wooden portal, still bristling with iron spikes to repel elephant-borne assaults. A giant cannon pointed mutely to the sky, a ramshead on its iron breech-block forged by a long-forgotten German artisan for his Mogul masters. At one time these walls had resounded with the bustle of many thousands: soldiers, pilgrims, priests and dancers; riders on horseback and mahouts on elephants; servants, eunuchs, a harem of women, and, above them all, a despotic king and his fawning court. Flowers and fruit once scented the air; secret chambers overflowed with gold, silver and gemstones. But the people and the treasure had all vanished. Only the stones remained. A hot summer breeze wafted through the silent ramparts and whispered over the ruins and the brown dessicated earth.

After returning to Bombay they boarded an Italian steamer and sailed across the Indian Ocean into the pale desolation of the Red Sea. In the midsummer stillness the ship's plume of smoke floated high in the white-hot sky. An awning over the deck offered scant refuge from the Arabian sun and the unbearable heat in the cabins. Lightly clad passengers lounged in deck chairs as they sipped ice water and fanned themselves in a desultory way. Emil flipped idly through the red morocco-bound book. He quoted passages to Dina, dozing in the *chaise longue* beside him.

"Shelley writes like you, Emil – sentimental, melodramatic, capitals and exclamation marks in every verse...."

He laughed. "Yes, but what passion!" He gazed at the parched coast-line, shimmering in the eastern haze. "Mecca is out there somewhere, beyond those hills. I wrote a play, once, about Mohammed...when I was fifteen. 'Mecca is taken!' That was the first line."

Dina squinted into the hazy distance then closed her eyes to the bright sun. "Was it full of passion and exclamations?" she asked.

"Of course. But Karl took out the romantic bits," he replied. He thought of his unsentimental eldest brother, the newly minted Director of the Deutsche Bank, and how furious he was over Emil's financial mismanagement. He was already distressed with Emil's choice of companion. Emil turned to a verse he had underlined in his red book:

"The toil which stole from thee so many an hour,
Is ended....

"Thoughts of great deeds were mine, dear Friend, when first
The clouds which wrap this world from youth did pass....

"Thou Friend, whose presence on my wintry heart
Fell, like bright Spring upon some herbless plain;
How beautiful and calm and free thou wert
In thy young wisdom, when the mortal chain
Of Custom thou didst burst and rend in twain,
And walked as free as light the clouds among....

"No more alone through the world's wilderness,
Although I trod the paths of high intent,
I journeyed now: no more companionless,
Where solitude is like despair, I went....

"Now has descended a serener hour,
And with inconstant fortune, friends return....

"Is it, that now my inexperienced fingers
But strike the prelude of a loftier strain?
Or, must the lyre on which my spirit lingers
Soon pause in silence, ne'er to sound again?"

He glanced up from his "prelude" into the half-closed eyes of his *Lebensgefährtin*. Shelley had written this dedication from "The Revolt of Islam" for his long-suffering wife, Mary, who at the time was writing her own masterpiece, a dark novel destined for much greater fame. Emil's mind wandered from Mary's Gothic "Frankenstein" to Dina's sombre "Fortune-Teller" to the old Chinese fortune-teller who said he would become a great man. How could his "great deeds" ever compare with those of the truly great? Helfferich & Rademacher had survived a mere four years, unlike the long-lived VOC, the grand old Dutch East India Company – or the massive temples of central Java, Borobudur and the "loftier" spires of Prambanan. He might just as implausibly compare his own rhyming verse with Shelley's monumental opus. And as great as they once were – the VOC, the temples, the caves at Ellora and "The Revolt of Islam" – all of them lay forgotten, neglected, or ruined.

Emil turned again to Shelley's peculiar tale of rebellion and Islam. In one hundred and twenty pages there is only one mention of Islam and nothing at all about Mecca, Mohammed, or even the desert. A woman guides a man on a voyage of discovery, fights a revolution as pure and exotic as the dawn of Islam and tries to save the world from evil. After gaining wisdom and understanding from the ancients, the young romantics are burned at the stake....

"I wandered through the wrecks of days departed
Far by the desolated shore....
Around me, broken tombs and columns riven
Looked vast in twilight, and the sorrowing gale
Waked in those ruins grey its everlasting wail!

"I knew not who had framed these wonders then,
Nor had I heard the story of their deeds;
But dwellings of a race of mightier men,
And monuments of less ungentle creeds
Tell their own tale to him who wisely heeds
The language which they speak; and now, to me
The moonlight making pale the blooming weeds,
The bright stars shining in the breathless sea,
Interpreted those scrolls of mortal mystery.

"Monuments...tell their own tale to him who wisely heeds the language which they speak...." Monuments like the enigmatic Buddhas, carved into grottoes in the Ghats and seated inside the stupas of Borobudur, or the elephant god Ganesha, lurking within the portals of Prambanan. What message might they whisper to the modern world?

He looked at Dina, now fast asleep beside him. One more verse and he would put the book down. He turned to "Ozymandias," a poem of the desert and a despotic Egyptian pharaoh, a man who built a kingdom to last forever....

"Look on my works, ye Mighty, and despair!"

I met a traveller from an antique land
Who said: Two vast and trunkless legs of stone
Stand in the desert.... Near them, on the sand,
Half sunk, a shattered visage lies, whose frown,
And wrinkled lip, and sneer of cold command,
Tell that its sculptor well those passions read
Which yet survive, stamped on these lifeless things,
The hand that mocked them, and the heart that fed:
And on the pedestal these words appear:
'My name is Ozymandias, king of kings:
Look on my works, ye Mighty, and despair!'
Nothing beside remains. Round the decay
Of that colossal wreck, boundless and bare
The lone and level sands stretch far away.

The elegant poem offered little in the way of consolation. "Nothing beside remains." Emil closed the book, leaned back in his chair and stared across the shining water to the distant coast and the land of Ozymandias. The lone and level sands stretched far away, boundless and bare.

ELEVEN

TEA AT CIKOPO

Pangrango, Artja and the South Cikopo Plantation

I'm sorry, *Herr* Helfferich, but *Herr* Witthoefft isn't in the office today." The secretary studiously avoided his eyes. "No, I don't know when he'll be back."

It was the same wherever he went. Nobody wanted to see him. He felt like the late Mr. Wood or like one of the old Helfferich & Rademacher shipping crates, sent back "empty returned." He and Dina bypassed his parents in Neustadt and travelled straight from Genoa to a Hamburg hotel. They avoided Berlin, too, where Karl Helfferich occupied a lofty corner office at the Deutsche Bank. Karl had always grumbled about Emil's relationship with Dina but his brother's financial collapse truly appalled him. Pride and self-respect prevented Emil from facing him. He would find a job first, he decided, before visiting Karl or anyone else in the family. They had enough money left for six months. In the meantime he wanted neither pity nor charity.

A few doors eventually cracked open at his persistent knocking. He talked, he argued and then he went back to the hotel and he thought some more. He needed to find a way to earn a decent living at overseas trade, to turn a good profit without risking too much. In October Helfferich finally got his first break. He worked out a deal with the venerable Arnold Otto Meyer to take over leadership of a global trading pool in pepper and co-pra. Meyer, the owner, and Witthoefft, the director, must have wondered if they were mad to hire him so soon after the catastrophe, especially as a pepper trader. Their company, Behn Meyer, was still reeling from the losses caused by the sale of Helfferich's huge warehouse inventory. But the forgiving Meyer was a good judge of character and not averse to risk. He gambled that his investment in the young man would be repaid many times over.

With a job in the offing and dignity restored, Emil and Dina returned to Neustadt in the late days of autumn, several months after their furtive arrival in Europe. His worried parents picked them up at the train station, where Dina saw the clear mix of love and concern on his mother's face. The first snows of winter fell. Christmas came, then the New Year, Emil's first celebration with the family in ten years. In early January, 1909, he and Dina left Neustadt and moved to a modest new home and a steady job in Hamburg.

On his thirty-first birthday Helfferich walked into the Behn Meyer office under the cold, grey, wintry sky of northern Europe. The dimly lit Catharinenstrasse looked even gloomier than he remembered. At first the other employees snubbed him, this aggressive young Icarus who dared to fly near the sun and who had lost his golden wings. He ignored the chilly atmosphere, both inside the office and out, and worked on his glob-al connections. He bought and sold copra – the dried white kernel of the coconut. Sending and receiving telegrams, collecting data and setting prices, Helfferich felt like an army general in firm control of a worldwide operation. Within months the business was thriving. He was vindicated, somewhat rehabilitated even, and he started to dream of greater things, of a triumphal return to Java.

For many years he had watched enviously as the big, solidly financed English and Dutch firms flexed their muscles in world markets. To compete successfully the smaller German firms would have to band together in syndicates and pool their efforts to finance a variety of products and industries. In mid 1909, with his credibility newly restored, he began to assemble a group of interested companies. Karl Helfferich, in his position as a director of the Deutsche Bank, was not enthusiastic. Emil worked on his aloof eldest brother for several months until finally he persuaded him to join too. On September 1 twelve companies formed the Straits and Sunda Syndicate under the leadership of Hamburg's Arnold Otto Meyer. The partners agreed to send Helfferich to Southeast Asia to search for investment opportunities in mining, industries and plantations, especially rubber, the hot new commodity used in automobile tires. He would report back with his recommendations within a few months, after which they would form an investment trust funded with ten million Marks. With a bit of luck he would manage a major overseas business, the goal of his dreams ever since the day he announced it to his father. Back in 1906, at the height of his success in pepper speculation, that goal had seemed within easy reach, only to be rudely snatched away.

After more than a year in Germany he relinquished his leadership of the pepper and copra pool to pursue this new opportunity with the Straits and Sunda Syndicate. In high spirits he boarded a steamship with Dina and sailed back to Batavia. Just before Christmas, 1909, they arrived to a jubilant welcome from Theodor, Georg and Albert, all of whom were still gainfully employed with Behn Meyer. The energetic Rademacher had even been appointed to the position of German Consul in Surabaya. Helfferich set to work immediately and toured Java from one end to the other. He read books on rubber and tea and diligently observed the local methods. At that time the Dutch were still producing latex from the fig tree *Ficus elastica* and were only just beginning to experiment with the rubber tree *Hevea brasiliensis*. In the seventies Henry Wickham had smuggled 70,000 seeds from Brazil to Kew Gardens. A few years later the British shipped 2,000 seedlings to Ceylon and in 1878 a mere 22 plants to Singapore and Perak. The trees grew well and formed the nucleus of the first rubber plantations in Malaya. With the invention of the motorcar the rubber industry expanded dramatically. As output from the overcut Amazonian forest dwindled, the supply from Southeast Asia struggled to match global demand.

But Helfferich, the chastened speculator, was leery of the "gold rush" atmosphere surrounding the rubber market. By March, 1910, he had learned enough and concluded that rubber looked risky but that tea plantations should return a healthy profit. Gathering up his handwritten notes and a typewriter, he left Batavia in a coastal steamer and boarded *Princess Alice* in Singapore, bound for Genoa.

At Albert's invitation Dina stayed in Teluk Betung during Emil's absence. She had no real home in Batavia and had no desire to live with her father in Buitenzorg. It was their first long separation in four years but money was still tight. Emil left her behind with mixed feelings, torn between the excitement of a new venture and the prospect of a lonely journey. He promised to conduct his business swiftly and to return within a few months.

Princess Alice was packed with businessmen and tourists enjoying the cooler spring travelling season. The Asian rubber boom was in full swing. Passengers partied, danced, gambled and drank until all hours. The good times tempted Emil but he disciplined himself to stay off the whisky and to work all day in his tiny cabin. Each morning he collected his notes, placed a bulky package on his bed and perched a typewriter on top.

The package contained a stone Buddha head, purchased from a Batavia hotel manager who was moving back home. The manager had removed the antique from the room of an impecunious artist who had died before paying his bill, leaving nothing of value but the mysterious Buddha. Emil stored the head safely in his cabin and used it as a platform on which to type his recommendations. Upon his arrival in Europe he gave the piece to his father. "Just what I always wanted," said the elderly gentleman. Decades later it graced Emil's wartime home in Hamburg where it served as a lucky talisman against Allied bombers.

In Hamburg and Antwerp, Helfferich delivered his report to the partners and recommended that they invest mainly in tea. A much lesser amount could go into rubber. He set the wheels in motion for the foundation of an investment trust, to which he gave the same name – the Straits and Sunda Syndicate. The two overseas directors were Helfferich and Philipp Adolf Friederichs, his first boss from the early days in Penang

– the man who had met him in 1899 when he stepped off *Prinz Heinrich* in an ink-stained jacket. The partners sent him back to Java with the authority to purchase and to build tea estates. For the first time in his career Emil felt as if he was truly going "home."

As soon as he returned he began to acquire tea plantations. The largest of these was Cikopo, on the north flank of Gunung Pangrango in West Java. A friend of his, Theodor Herrings, brought the property to his attention. Herrings, a freewheeling businessman known as the "King of Asahan," ran a vast enterprise in North Sumatra. Cikopo intrigued Helfferich, in part because the land lay on the slope of Pangrango – the mysterious mountain in the clouds, "veiled like an Eastern bride." In 1903, still weak with malaria, he had stared across the chasm from Gunung Gede to the forested peak.

The Cikopo property was 6,000 *bouws* in size, about 4,300 hectares. It stretched in a triangle from its highest tip at 2,400 metres elevation on Pangrango's northwest ridge down to the Puncak road at 800 metres. The wild upper reaches – South Cikopo – were undeveloped. The lower part – North Cikopo – consisted of 1,500 *bouws* of rice fields and *kampungs,* inhabited by 11,000 Sundanese. The soil was exceptionally fertile.

The Baumgarten family had owned the property for generations. Originally from Thüringen in the middle of Germany, the aptly named "tree garden" family had become thoroughly integrated into Dutch and Javanese life. South Cikopo was a so-called "Special Property," subject to rules which seemed almost feudal in origin. Helfferich weaved his way through the labyrinthine Buitenzorg bureaucracy and suffered through long and frustrating negotiations. His syndicate eventually gained title to the undeveloped southern property and leased the densely populated northern part.

Within several months workers cleared a small section of the South Cikopo plantation and planted tea bushes. In time they cultivated 1,300 *bouws* in tea and an additional 135 *bouws* in quinine. The higher slopes, covering more than half of the southern property, were left in a wilderness state. A short distance to the east, the French operated the Gunung Mas plantation, the "Golden Mountain" – a century later still in business as one of Indonesia's largest tea producers. A Dutch concern owned a smaller, higher plantation at Pasir Angin. Across the valley and somewhat separate from the rest, the British ran two plantations at Ciliwung and Megamendung. The Germans, French, Dutch and British formed a peaceful European map in tea – minus the taxes, sanctions and jealousies.

Helfferich built a tea factory in the picturesque valley of the Cisukabirus River by the village of Pasir Muncang, where oil from muncang trees was once used to light lamps. He chose a flat location on the west side of the stream, beside the immense spreading branches of a *saman*, a rain tree. The tranquil *kampung r*ang with the sounds of heavy construction: a shiny steel-girdered plant, powered by a modern, quiet, hundred-horsepower water turbine from Germany. The waxed tile floors gleamed beneath bright electric lights, dryers, rollers and machines for sorting and packing.

In a good month the plant could produce 100,000 pounds of dry tea. A gondola transported fresh tea leaves down from the hills where tough, sunburnt women in woven hats and sarongs picked the new green growth by hand. In the factory a workforce of more delicate hands sorted the leaves. To Helfferich's appreciative eye they looked like a flock of doves, pecking at the leaves and cooing as their eyes followed him shyly around the floor.

On a hill overlooking the east bank of the river Helfferich built a two-storey home for the plantation supervisor. Styled in the Dutch colonial fashion with a steep roof, high ceilings and shuttered windows, the spacious villa also served as a guest house. During an early visit to Cikopo, Emil escorted Dina from the villa to the factory a short distance away. They descended one hundred stone steps of a winding staircase, passed between a solid pair of gateposts and walked across the bridge to the bustling new factory. After talking to the young tea sorters Dina left Emil to his business and wandered outside. She strolled past tidy flower beds back to the bridge and leaned against the stone rail. The factory hummed in the background. Water gurgled down from the mountain, through rice paddies where buffaloes and barefooted men plodded through the rich mud. Above the fields the green fluted ridges of Pangrango rose to the hazy summit.

Emil soon joined her on the bridge and pointed up the valley to where the gondola wires stretched out of sight, high up the ridge to the fields of tea. "You see that hill up there on the right…with a grove of tall trees? We're going to build a little field house there, so that when the supervisor is up in the tea he doesn't have to come all the way back down to the villa. The villagers call it Artja."

"Artja?" Dina asked. "Are there statues?"

"Yes, in fact. The workers found a few blocks lying around here and there, underneath the old trees. Some of them do look like figures…a bit crude…but nobody seems to know much about them."

Emil took a deep breath of fresh mountain air and exhaled with satisfaction. The pain of the pepper debacle was fading from memory as new plantations sprouted under his hands. He and Dina had purchased a home in the stylish suburb of Weltevreden, not far from the house which Emil had rented in his early years. He imagined a day in the not-too-distant future when they could escape the heat and bustle of Batavia and spend weekends in the Artja hideaway. This felt like the happiest moment of his life, the fulfillment of his childhood dreams. His beloved *Lebensgefährtin* accompanied him on the rutted roads through this earthly paradise, at the dawn of a century still young and full of promise.

By the end of 1910 five plantations were under construction in Java and Sumatra. On October 14, 1911, the Straits and Sunda Syndicate Ltd was officially founded in Hamburg, with interests in at least twelve different enterprises. Two years later they had planted a total of 2,200 hectares in tea, 300 hectares in rubber and coffee, and they employed 57 Europeans and 6,800 native workers. Behn Meyer, a lead partner in the syndicate, enjoyed such a flush financial position that they could afford to finance their operations without help from the banks. In one instance, when the Deutsche Bank complained about an overdraft, *Herr* Witthoefft replied that the bills of exchange were drawn against shipments – and that if there was any further difficulty with the account he would have to close it.

In the rosy years before the war Helfferich travelled frequently. He scouted new prospects, checked on the old ones and reported back to the partners in Europe. Most exciting for him were excursions to remote corners of the archipelago. In Malacca he visited the thriving English plantations. The rubber boom roared like the Klondike gold rush, with hotels so full that Helfferich once had to sleep on a dining table with a tablecloth for a mosquito net. Like Lord Jim he paddled by native boat deep into the jungle, past riverbanks festooned with creepers and lined with crocodiles. At the rustic home of one plantation manager a humble outhouse perched over the river in the local fashion. The outhouse attracted fish which the cook served to his unwitting guests for dinner.

On another occasion he and Dina sailed by coastal steamer to the syndicate's Belimbing concession on the extreme southwestern tip of Sumatra. Emil and a few native workmen clambered into a boat, raised the sails and headed for the beach. Dina stood at the ship's railing and waved jauntily at her man, as thrilled as a boy in a pirate adventure. She watched them until they reached the shore, where bare brown backs and a white shirt hauled the boat above the tide line. Beyond the white sandy crescent, mangroves and forest stretched far into the hazy unknown. She stared at the receding figure. Bemusement gave way to a vague premonition – as when Conrad's Marlow waved farewell to Jim on the shore: "That white figure in the stillness of coast and sea seemed to stand at the heart of a vast enigma…a tiny white speck, that seemed to catch all the light left in a darkened world."

With goloks and axes the men slashed their way inland to a good viewpoint. Monkeys hooted in the forest; not a soul could be seen. At the end of the day, filthy and exhausted, they stumbled back down the root-choked trail to the beach. The weather had turned foul in the meantime and the ship had pulled away, far beyond the surf line. The shore party pushed the boat through the pounding surf and jumped in. The sails flapped uselessly in the gale and the small engine flooded. The helmsman hunkered in the stern and steered toward the ship while Helfferich and the others pulled hard on the oars. The bow hovered in the air above each curling breaker and crashed heavily into the trough on the other side. Spume washed over the boat and soaked the straining oarsmen. They paused for one extraordinary moment when an exhausted seabird landed on the head of the helmsman. Stroke by stroke they wallowed through the swells and clawed their way toward the rolling ship. At last they grabbed the rope ladder and clambered to safety. Collapsing on the deck in relief, Emil looked up at his beautiful saviour, her hair streaming in the wind. Dina offered him a welcoming hug and a stiff drink.

The countryside yielded its secrets only with grudging reluctance, even when inhabited. Off the west coast of Sumatra near Padang they anchored in the peaceful bay of a small island, Pulau Pini. The wanderers felt as if they had reached the farthest end of the world. But as they rowed ashore they were astonished to hear the unmistakable sound of clapping. The oarsmen laughed and pointed into the shallow water. The wrinkled gaping mouths of huge clams snapped shut as they drifted past. One lone native greeted them on the beach. When asked to describe the island's interior, he looked mystified and replied with sweeping gestures, "There is a mountain…and a swamp."

At least once a year Helfferich undertook the long journey to and from Europe for meetings with his partners. In 1911 – one year before the sinking of *Titanic* – he boarded the German ship *Seydlitz* in Penang, bound for Europe. Two days before reaching Ceylon, fire broke out among tobacco bales in the forward cargo hold. The crew sealed the hatches and pumped steam inside but smoke billowed from the ventilation shafts. Stewards evacuated passengers from the forward cabins as they reeled out the pumps and fire hoses. Dejected crewmen tossed overboard one thousand golden bales of North Sumatra tobacco. A light wind fanned the flames and dragged a heavy pall of smoke over the sea.

While a band played on deck the crew served soup to the anxious passengers and tried to reassure them. But the ship began listing to starboard as water filled the hold. The captain abruptly ordered each person to pack a small handbag and to prepare to abandon ship.

Helfferich waited on deck with his satchel. Would they have to lower the lifeboats? There was no way to send an SOS, no telegraph machine – at that time the new Marconi wireless was still confined to the American east coast. They rolled helplessly in the long powerful swell of the Indian Ocean.

Just before noon a speck appeared beneath a plume of smoke on the horizon. Out of the sea rose a warship with four funnels, the English cruiser *Diadem* on her way to Calcutta. Her lookout had reported an ugly cloud of smoke to the captain, who ordered a change of course at top speed to rescue the stricken ship.

Both ships lowered lifeboats into the darkening water as sharks cruised ominously in between. "Women and children first!" arose the gallant cry. Helfferich and the remaining passengers crossed safely in the second load but the crew remained aboard the crippled ship. That night the two vessels steamed in tandem to Ceylon as the bow of *Seydlitz* glowed red in the darkness. Upon reaching the coast the next morning, the captain ran *Seydlitz* aground. The crew quickly extinguished the fire and sent the cargo and baggage in a convoy to Colombo, where *Diadem* arrived soon after.

The German passengers had been well treated aboard His Majesty's Ship *Diadem*. The British officers vacated their rooms for the women while the sailors slept in hammocks beside the guns. The chief steward of *Seydlitz* issued chits to the passengers so that they could buy drinks for their rescuers. For two days Helfferich had a good opportunity to observe life in the Royal Navy. The friendliness of the officers impressed him, as did the games played by the sailors and the loose, amiable atmosphere on board, so unlike the strait-laced ships of the German Navy. Why, he thought, did it take a crisis at sea to bring people together? Was it so difficult to befriend someone who spoke a different language or someone who lived in another country? How could these men be his friends today, when these same men might be enemies tomorrow?

He leaned against a gun mount and pondered questions without answers. On the lower deck a Japanese judo master instructed a circle of English sailors. He thought back to all the friends, natives and strange characters he had met in the Far East – people like Po Tjong, von Mechel, the Woods, Kamdami, the Chinese fortune-teller and his guide on Gunung Gede. Men, women and their religions were the same at heart, he firmly believed. People try to survive, to muddle through each day as best they can, to put a roof over their heads and food on the table, to surround themselves with family and friends. But a malevolent primal instinct lurks within those hearts. Those same people find comfort by banding together in tribes and towns, valleys and countries. Waving flags and worshipping totems, they fear and envy and despise the folk of other tribes. Helfferich felt the lump on his head where a rival "Indian" had clubbed him years ago when they played among the old castles above Neustadt. Below him the sailors roared with laughter as they flipped each other on the deck. "God is on our side," they believed, even as German soldiers cried, "*Gott mit uns.*" Muslims recited, "*la ilaha illa Allah*, there is no god except God," while Americans proclaimed on their almighty dollar, "In God we trust."

German Artillery Piece 1914

In the spring of 1914 the drumbeats of war grew more compelling, an *ostinato* rhythm ever louder and faster. Despite the ominous predictions Emil and Dina returned to Europe for business and a holiday. After a long round of meetings Emil took the train to Neustadt to celebrate his father's birthday. On April 12, a beautiful spring day, Friedrich Helfferich strolled to an outdoor café with Philipp, August, Emil and Wilhelm. Surrounded by four of his children, as happy as a father could be, the old man gleefully ordered a bottle of sparkling wine. His face flushed red and he apologized for his rashness. He never thought he would drink wine with his sons on a Sunday morning in public. The boys allowed that he was old enough now to do as he pleased. They raised their glasses and drank his health: "*Santé, Vater!*"

The brothers chatted about Theodor, now securely employed and living a healthy life in Java, and their only sister, Emilie, who was helping Karl manage his bachelor household in Berlin. Their brilliant eldest brother, so severe and aloof, had never been very close to any of them. He had been the first Helfferich to join the artillery but a serious riding accident had ended his military career in 1893. It crushed his chest and damaged his lungs, necessitating, like Theodor's pleurisy, a long period of convalescence in a dry sunny climate. After spending a winter in Italy and the following summer in the Alps, he returned to those places throughout his life for rest and recuperation. Thwarted in his military ambitions, Karl earned a doctorate and lectured in history at the University of Berlin. His interest rapidly evolved toward economics and politics and gained him the attention of the German government. For five years he advised the German Foreign Office on colonial affairs and then, in 1906, he joined the Deutsche Bank. Almost immediately they posted him to Constantinople as Director of the Anatolian Railway, the bank's largest foreign project. There he developed the plan and the financing for the Baghdad railroad. Upon his return to Berlin the ambitious young man was promoted to Director of the Deutsche Bank where, among other duties, he now supervised Emil's work in the Straits and Sunda Syndicate.

"I hear that Karl is in the running for Secretary of the Treasury," said Emil.

"Yes," Philipp replied, "and if there is a war, he will be in the thick of it."

In a cheery café on such a sunny day, they found it hard to believe that grey clouds of war were descending on Europe. Father and sons ambled home, each immersed in his own thoughts. That same evening Emil hugged his mother and father goodbye and headed for the waiting carriage. Then he looked into the honest loving eyes of his father, dropped his suitcase and hugged the old man once more. A dreadful feeling gripped him, as if they would never see each other again.

Dina had been visiting friends elsewhere. They met up again and took the ferry to London, where the mood was as dark and sombre as the April showers that dampened the streets. Bowler hats and black umbrellas bobbed along the wet sidewalks. They cut their holiday short and retreated to the more pleasant ambience of springtime in Paris. To their dismay, jingoistic posters in shop windows pilloried the boorish German "Hansi." Dina suggested a visit to the Salon where the new paintings might revive their flagging spirits and where, she hoped, her own work might some day grace the elegant walls. The first offering that greeted them, in a place of honour as if to mock them, was entitled "*Le souvenir français.*" Against a pastoral backdrop of the hills of Alsace-Lorraine, the painting depicted a winsome French grandmother fastening a *tricolore* ribbon to the tunic of a chastened German soldier. The contentious Alsatian hills lay just south of Emil's homeland in the Pfalz. Sad and disappointed, they fled the Salon and boarded a train to Italy.

With mixed feelings of relief and foreboding they watched the port of Genoa vanish below the horizon. When the steamship entered the Suez Canal at Port Said, they left behind the Mediterranean Sea and the moral bleakness of Europe. A warm Middle Eastern breeze blew over the deck. In the sand dunes beyond the east bank Emil spied a line of camels, a military patrol perhaps, with colourful Koranic banners fluttering in the vanguard. On padded feet they floated silently in the shimmering haze, above the vast Sinai desert and the sands of Arabia. The shrill sound of a steam whistle intruded on the dream. Emil turned to see a locomotive, chugging and puffing along the tracks by the side of the canal. He thought of Karl and the Baghdad railroad. Somewhere far to the east, beyond the Sinai and Aqaba, his brother had financed a railway to shuttle Turkish troops from one end of their crumbling empire to the other. Within a year the same steel rails would bring home a singular band of German sailors, the last fighting men of the German East Asia Squadron.

Emil returned to the comfort of his cabin and to Dina's side. He sat down to write a long letter to his parents. War was coming; of that he was certain.

PART 3

THE GERMAN EAST ASIA SQUADRON

TWELVE

STONE SOLDIERS

Soldiers of Pajajaran

On a grey Saturday morning I drove into the mountains south of Jakarta. *Pater* Heuken had invited me to join him for the weekend at his cabin near the village of Cikopo. He had organized a Christian retreat for young people in his congregation. No, he said, I was not obliged to join in the services but he did have some more books to show me, books about the war.

An electric tension crackled in the humid Javanese air, an oppressive rumbling like thunderclouds before the monsoon. In early 1998 student demonstrators clashed with police and supporters of Suharto's corrupt regime. No one had been killed – yet – but feelings were running high. As a foreigner in a strange land I felt detached from this looming conflict. Overthrowing a government supported by rich businessmen and a huge army was, fortunately, none of my business. That was a job for Indonesians. The thought of escaping the chaos of revolution never occurred to me either, although the time would soon come when I and thousands of others would flee.

As I dodged the speeding buses on the Jagorawi toll road, such thoughts never entered my head. *Pater* Heuken was not expecting me until later in the day so I turned off the Puncak highway and drove high into the hills. A cloudy but rainless sky promised cool weather for a hike to the German graveyard. I parked the car, made a deal with the little hubcap-watchers and walked uphill amid a cheerful chorus of "Hello meester! Where are you going?" The forested hillside dropped away steeply beside me. In the valley a brown stream gurgled over rocks worn smooth with the passage of centuries. Bamboo pipes funnelled rivulets into sinuous terraces where men and women patiently tended the rice shoots and mended the intricate tracery of levees and paddies. Above their stooped shoulders bamboo windmills turned slowly and mutely in the morning calm. Golden orb spiders – impressively leggy giants – dangled by the hundreds from communal webs in the trees.

At the crest of the ridge I walked through the cemetery gate, along the gravel path and up the shallow steps to the cenotaph. The monument looked solid, timeless and reassuring. Immortalized on the face of the pillar, the *Tapferen*, the brave ones of the German East Asia Squadron, still endured long after they and their guns had fallen silent. The scene brought to mind John Keats's "Ode on a Grecian Urn" – a "foster-child of silence and slow time, sylvan historian...." Like the endless parade encircling the urn, these "fair youth, beneath the trees" would be "for ever young." Keats penned those lines soon after Shelley wrote "Ozymandias" and not long before both romantic poets met their own untimely ends, Keats in Rome and Shelley at sea.

In the corner of my eye I spied Adja stepping through the grass beneath the big trees. He approached me shyly and dipped his head in polite greeting. I offered him a cigarette and he gratefully accepted, grinning through gaps in his yellow teeth. As he lit the *kretek* I saw the blue veins in his hands, knotted like the trunks of the trees behind him. He held his ever-present broom in his left hand. I complimented him on the tidy state of the cemetery and talked about the last time we had met, about his story of the sea goddess and how I had run down the mountain in the pouring rain, following the woman in the green sarong while bamboo windmills wailed in the fields. The drama pleased him and he smiled at the recollection. Behind the impish face his eyes looked old and shrewd. We talked about other things and then I bluntly asked him about Artja Domas. I told him how, on my first visit to the graveyard, Dr. Robby Ko had mentioned the name and said that it meant "eight hundred statues" in Sanskrit and old Javanese. I looked around the tiny cemetery and the fields of quinine beyond. The only statues were the white pillar and the graves of ten sailors. Where were the eight hundred?

His eyes brightened again and a smile creased his face. He turned and walked down the steps away from the monuments, toward the lawn at the bottom of the graveyard. He pointed with his broom at one of the benches and motioned for me to sit down while he told a story. The old puppet-master remained standing, holding his broom as he waved his skinny arms for greater dramatic effect. His stick figure, with yellow teeth and big ears, looked tiny and comical beneath the gnarled limbs of the old fig trees. Like a shadow puppet in the *wayang,* he grinned and grimaced, popped his eyes, smacked his lips noisily, jumped in the grass, raised his broom in the air and died many horrible deaths as he recounted a tale of stone soldiers.

⚜

In the olden days Hindu kings ruled the whole island of Java. Half a millennium ago only one remained – *Raja* Siliwangi, who reigned over the Sundanese people in the Pajajaran empire of the west. His palace dominated the capital at Pakuan on the bank of the river which flows through the modern city of Bogor. Unfortunately for him, an aggressive new religion had arrived in the north Java ports of Banten and Sunda Kelapa. Islam, brought by Arab traders to Sumatra centuries earlier, had swept eastward into Java and found a place in the hearts of the poor farmers and fishermen along the coast.

In 1526 the Pajajaran kingdom lost its main port at Sunda Kelapa when Fatahillah stormed it with his Muslim warriors. Fatahillah was an Islamic fundamentalist from Aceh in northernmost Sumatra and a recent pilgrim to Mecca. He despised both the ancient Hindu infidels and their allies, the Portuguese, who had recently invaded Sumatra and occupied his home village. Despite a so-called friendship treaty with Pajajaran, including two pleas from the Sundanese *raja* for assistance, the Portuguese stepped aside when the Muslim army attacked the port. Fatahillah celebrated his "complete victory" by renaming the city "Jayakarta," a name which would serve for 92 years until the Dutch conquerors, in their turn, renamed it Batavia.

Two generations after Fatahillah's victory, in the town of Banten just west of Jayakarta, Sultan Hasanuddin and Pangeran Yusuf rallied their Muslim troops with cries of *Allahu akhbar*! God is great! They vowed to convert the last remaining unbelievers on Java and turned their attention to the palace at Pakuan, the Hindu heart of the beleaguered Pajajaran kingdom. The sultan wrote a letter to the *raja*, a descendant of the revered Siliwangi, and demanded that his entire folk convert to Islam or suffer drastic consequences. *Kyai* Santang, a respected Islamic scholar from Banten, carried the note to Pakuan. As a young man he had lived in Pajajaran and knew its people well. Under heavy guard he passed through the impressive archway of the palace, the majestically named Kraton Sri Bima Punta Narayana Madura Suradipati. The *raja* sat woodenly on his throne, listened to the unwelcome message and pondered the unpalatable options. Banten was far stronger than Pajajaran but religion meant more to the *raja* than mere mortal power. It would be impossible to renounce his devout Hindu beliefs. He solemnly refused the outrageous demand. *Kyai* Santang returned to Banten empty-handed while Pakuan prepared for a fearsome onslaught.

Two stalwart men commanded the *raja's* army: Morogol, the elder of the two, and his deputy, Wirakarta. But the young and ambitious subordinate was dissatisfied with his role and the insignificant duties allotted to him. He suspected that the *raja* doubted his loyalty. It was true that *Kyai* Santang of Banten was Wirakarta's cousin but should the king hold that against him? With preparations for the defence in full swing, he approached the king in private and pleaded for an honourable command. To his dismay the *raja* allowed him merely to guard the west gate of the palace, under the overall direction of Morogol.

The disappointed Wirakarta was now convinced of the *raja's* suspicions. Not knowing from whom to seek advice, he wrote a treacherous letter to his cousin in Banten. "How should one behave toward such a king?" he asked. *Kyai* Santang sent him a straightforward reply, "Betray your king and convert to Islam. You will be pardoned and protected by the Sultan of Banten."

In the fateful year 1578 the Muslim army descended on Pakuan. The two armies met in a terrible clash on the field outside the palace. Vastly outnumbered, the Hindu soldiers fought bitterly but in vain. Fearing the worst, Morogol advised the *raja* to leave the palace at once. The king, his family, his followers and eight hundred soldiers fled through a secret tunnel into the hills. Morogol remained in the throne room while his young deputy guarded the western entrance. Wirakarta listened with dread to the approaching tumult and watched in horror as battering rams pounded on the door. Moments later the screaming horde burst through the gate and cut him down without mercy.

To their astonishment the Muslim fighters found the palace empty. Their footsteps echoed in the vaulted hallways. *Kyai* Santang strode into the throne room. There stood Morogol, armed and ready to die a warrior's death. He was in no mood to retreat, nor would he reveal the hiding place of his king. From his long cloak Santang produced a wooden staff that he had carried on a pilgrimage to Mecca. With a grand flourish, he thrust the point into the ground and challenged Morogol to retrieve it. If he pulled it out, Morogol could retain his Hindu beliefs and walk away a free man. If, on the other hand, he could not dislodge the staff, he would have to concede defeat, convert to Islam and hand over the *raja*.

Morogol suspected a trick but he had nothing to lose. Even if he removed the staff, could he trust his captors to honour their promise? He grasped the stick disdainfully with one hand and gave it a sharp tug. The staff would not budge. He planted his feet firmly, held on tightly with two hands and he pulled with all his strength. Nothing happened. Confounded and humiliated, he looked into the smiling eyes of his captor.

Morogol surrendered. He asked permission to find his king and to persuade him to convert to Islam. Santang reluctantly agreed. Alone and unarmed, Morogol left the palace, walked unmolested through the Muslim perimeter and climbed into the hills on the north slope of Gunung Pangrango. After several hours of searching he found their secret hideout on the ridge under the old fig trees. He kneeled before his king and told him everything: the death of Wirakarta, the destruction of the army, the loss of the palace and the magic of *Kyai* Santang. The *raja* pondered the terrible events of the day and accepted the inevitability of his defeat. After long consideration he pronounced, "Nothing in life is eternal. Today Islam is ascendant and our way of life has been annihilated. Those of you who so wish may convert to Islam. The rest, come with me."

Then he turned his gaze heavenwards and beseeched the gods to take him home. In a flash of light and a puff of smoke the last Hindu king of Java disappeared before the stunned eyes of his people. His followers faced a difficult choice. One by one, then in larger and larger groups, they turned and trudged fearfully back down the mountain to an uncertain Islamic future. Surrounded by his eight hundred loyal troops, Morogol remained on the high blustery ridge. That night a thunderstorm lit the heavens and lashed the men with hailstones and torrents of rain. A cold wind whistled bleakly round the mountain. Voices whispered in the rustling leaves. The grey dawn crept silently over the ridge. Where once an army had stood, only eight hundred black stones remained – mute, steadfast and eternal.

Adja bowed low with a flourish of his arms and rose again solemnly. He held his broom like a magic staff. I clapped in appreciation and asked him where the stones were today – and the *kraton*. He sat down beside me and asked for a cigarette. I gave him the whole pack.

He told me that the Muslim invaders sacked the palace after taking the stone seat upon which the *rajas* had been crowned. The rubble lies hidden beneath the east bank of the Ciliwung River near Batu Tulis, a mysterious stone with Sanskrit inscriptions. Indonesia's founding father, Sukarno, built his own palace nearby. In more recent times a government minister tore up the ground beneath the old stone to look for gold.

After the battle *Kyai* Santang converted the heathen throughout south and west Java. Devout pilgrims still pay homage today at his grave in Godog, not far from Bandung. But some Hindu stalwarts refused to submit to Islam. We know them today as the Baduy tribe. They walked to the remote southwestern corner of Java, to the Kendeng hills where they live today in three secret villages on the edge of a forbidden forest.

The dates of the battles, the ruins of the *kraton*, the stone throne, the grave in Godog, the forlorn Baduy tribe – all of these were real. But where were the eight hundred stone soldiers?

"I'll show you," said Adja.

Leaves rustled in the uppermost branches of the tallest tree. The serpent-eagle had been resting there, unnoticed by either of us. Perhaps she was the same bird I had seen on my first visit. I had the unlikely but distinct impression that she was keeping an eye on me. As I watched, she rose from her perch and swooped away with powerful wingbeats, vanishing into the distant river valley. Adja stared impassively at the receding bird, and then he walked down the road to the village.

I took one last look at the cemetery and followed him in curiosity, wondering where he would lead me. With the stiff bow-legged gait of an old man he trotted downhill, surprisingly fast, his splayed toes curling around the cobbles. Just below the graveyard he stopped Two smaller fig trees arched over the path and a scrubby grove of quinine covered the slope with red-tipped leaves. He pointed to a ditch by the side of the road, thickly overgrown with weeds.

"That's where Suparman found the stones."

The name sounded odd, like "Superman" but with the accent on the middle syllable. Adja explained that his friend, Asep Suparman, had been a plantation supervisor for over thirty years. He retired in 1995 and was now living in a house in Pasir Muncang, next to the bridge over the river where Helfferich had built his tea factory. We were going to visit him. Down the stony road we trod, past the little white houses, the rice paddies, the spiders and the gently turning windmills. I had to focus on my feet so as not to slip on the large cobbles, as if I were stepping on stone heads.

Just before the village Adja veered off to the right into the middle of a soccer field. He led me to an Islamic elementary school, the Yayasan Islam Tarbiyatul Falah, a dilapidated old building perched on the edge of the bluff overhanging the river. The school was no bigger than a small house, built in the Dutch style with shuttered windows and a steep roof. Half the shutters and tiles were missing. Inside were two sparsely furnished classrooms, an office and a storeroom. The school was closed and the place looked haunted but Adja rattled the locked door anyway. Undeterred he walked around the outside to the storeroom window. He wiped off the grime, stood on his tiptoes and peeked inside.

"There they are!" he announced, stepping back to give me room. "The two stones that Suparman found. He calls the big one *batu gambang.*"

I cupped my hands to my eyes and peered into the dimly lit room. The black stones lay innocuously in a far corner, discarded and dusty. The larger one was about a metre long and two handspans in width. It looked vaguely like a xylophone, like the *gambang* instrument in a *gamelan* orchestra. Both were crudely hewn in a curved rectangular shape with no visible markings. They looked too heavy to lift.

"They used to sit outside, like gate posts, on the path in front of the school. But they frightened some of the children so the teachers moved them inside, out of sight."

"Were these the stone soldiers?" I asked.

Adja didn't hear me. He lit a *kretek* and squatted on the edge of the bluff in front of the school. I sat on the grass beside him as we gazed in silence at the sweeping vista up the river valley, past the trees of Artja to the hazy summit of Gunung Pangrango. Small brown figures tended the rice paddies far below us. The cloves crackled and snapped as Adja inhaled deeply and began to talk again. He told me that Suparman had a few smaller stones in his garden. The rest were hauled away a long time ago for building roads. Perhaps a few "soldiers" still remained, hidden underground like *batu gambang.* I felt a bit sorry for the old stones, whatever they were, ripped out of the ground, beaten down by trucks and bare feet, stashed away in gardens and old schoolhouses. I thought of the cobblestones upon which we had walked. Adja stared up the valley and finished his cigarette, flicking the butt over the edge. He stood up again and suggested that we drop in on Suparman.

We ambled down the path to the village and passed through a banana grove a short distance below the school. A big *waringin* tree towered overhead. Helfferich's two-storey villa used to stand nearby but some frightened villagers tore it down in the eighties. Like the little Islamic school it had fallen apart and looked haunted. The bananas were more useful anyway. A crumbling stone staircase, the last remnant of the old plantation, led from the banana grove down to the main road through Pasir Muncang. I imagined Helfferich and his *Lebensgefährtin* walking down this staircase to the tea factory not so long ago. The steps were fast disappearing beneath the weeds, like the stones of Artja Domas.

We found Suparman's modest home near the bridge over the river, at the end of a narrow alleyway just off the main road. A stout middle-aged man answered the knock. His hair was dark and oiled. His hands and face had a soft pudgy look from too many idle years behind an empty desk. Though retired he still wore the green uniform, clean and freshly ironed, of a plantation supervisor. The uniform gave him status and confirmed his tenuous link to officialdom. It fulfilled his need to belong to a family, to something big and important.

He looked mildly surprised at the strange visitation but he invited us to sit down and offered us two glasses of lukewarm coffee, thick and cloying. Adja engaged him in small talk and explained the purpose of our impromptu visit while I strained coffee grounds through my teeth. I heard the words "stone soldiers" and "*batu gambang*." With an unctuous smile Suparman turned to me and offered to tell his story.

His grandfather started work on the tea plantation in 1912, soon after Helfferich acquired it for the Straits and Sunda Syndicate. Before that time they grew only coffee and pepper. In the early days a cable car carried tea from the hills down to the factory by the river. In 1962, long after the Germans and Dutch had left, Suparman joined the still thriving plantation. He remembered walking through the factory and browsing the old photos from his grandfather's day. But on December 20, 1971, fire destroyed the sixty-year-old factory and everything inside including the irreplaceable photos. Suparman also watched as his neighbours razed the villa in 1987. Nothing remained from the German era but the stone staircase and a log book which he rescued from the burning factory. He showed me the slim volume but it contained little of interest other than the names of the old supervisors, Egloffstein and Schmidtmann. Egloffstein built the white field house at Artja, the one Helfferich had dreamed of, now long gone. Schmidtmann later built another cabin and a bathing pool at Artja Manik, the old sanctuary higher up on the mountain where Robby had found the lilies.

At the mention of "stone soldiers," he beamed proudly and pointed to his garden in the manner of a learned archeologist, a rescuer of antiquities. Half a dozen smooth boulders lurked behind a scruffy patch of vegetables. In 1984 he had found the stones in a ditch near Artja. He gave the two largest ones to the Islamic school and kept a few smaller ones for himself. His boss, Suratman, took eight more for his house in Bandung. He said he was lucky to find them because most of the stones had been plucked from Artja before the mid-sixties and used as cobbles on the plantation roads.

We stood up and walked over to the garden for a closer look. The stones were barely recognizable as carvings. Smooth and worn by the passage of time they were no more remarkable than river-washed boulders. Suparman put names to them, as one might search for shapes in the clouds. One stone looked like a misshapen pentagon; another vaguely resembled the legendary Hindu prince, Arjuna. I felt deflated. Where was the artistry that formed the soaring spires of Prambanan over a millennium ago? And the stupas of Borobudur? These relics of the Pajajaran empire were indeed mere cobbles.

Suparman picked up one of the larger stones and held it behind his back. He said, "*Pak* Adja told you about the soldiers. There is another legend. You saw *batu gambang*, how heavy it must be. Well, in the old days, if a woman was unable to bear children, she walked up to Artja and lifted a stone – a big stone, in the shape of a man – like this…" He squatted low to the floor with his hands under the block behind him and then he staggered to his feet, groaning under the imaginary strain. "If she succeeded, she either had a baby – or a hernia!" Adja laughed out loud.

I instinctively disliked Suparman, his soft belly and his oily manner. Moreover, I didn't like what he symbolized – an unwitting agent of destruction, one of millions eroding the country's heritage, piece by piece, as raindrops erode a mountain. They tore birds from the forest and fish from the reefs, chopped down trees, sliced off Buddha heads and paved roads with stone carvings. I had seen enough.

We offered polite thanks and farewells. I shook Suparman's sweaty palm and followed Adja back down the lane to the pavement. At the stone staircase we parted ways. I thanked him for the unusual tour and watched him climb bowlegged back up the hill. I wondered at the real story behind his stone soldiers. Then I walked down the road to the car.

❦

I arrived at *Pater* Heuken's rustic mountain cabin just in time for dinner. The others had driven up earlier in the day, the Jesuit priest and a dozen young Indonesians from his congregation. The recent upheaval in Jakarta had stirred them up. Rumours swirled around the city; army brigades massed on the outskirts; Suharto's iron-fisted rule hung in the balance. Some of them attended Trisakti University where students clashed with soldiers every day. Weeks later, on May 12, 1998, Indonesian troops would shoot and kill six unarmed protesters on the campus. President Suharto would be forced to resign on May 21. All this lay in the near future. The conversation at dinner ranged over the troubled state of Indonesia's government and the thorny issue of violent protest versus passive resistance. How could a few students topple a brutal regime?

Some of them advocated vigorous confrontation. They would wear red bandanas signifying blood and rebellion, wave red flags like the Communists in the sixties and make fiery speeches through megaphones. They would chant slogans and march down the main avenues of Jakarta to the lines of helmeted troops. If necessary they would throw stones and fight hand-to-hand. Others argued for a nonviolent approach – white banners, candles, songs of reconciliation, huge but peaceful rallies – a massive democratic groundswell, irresistible like the tides of the ocean. The two points of view mirrored the stark red and white bands of the Indonesian flag, the natural split down the middle of the Indonesian psyche. Years earlier, when Sukarno declared Indonesia's independence and chose a flag for the new republic, he tore the blue strip off the base of the Dutch flag. When asked what the remaining red and white colours represented, he replied half in jest, "Blood and semen!"

The bowls of *nasi goreng* disappeared and the brave talk sputtered to an inconclusive end. A young woman reached out with her hands to her friends on either side. We linked hands around the table and bowed heads as she offered a prayer for reconciliation and forgiveness. The priest closed with a benediction and offered hope that God would ensure a peaceful resolution in a land where harmony and consensus are treasured above all else.

Amid the clatter of dishes I returned to the table with two cans of local Bintang beer. In the sitting room two young men sprawled on the floor, humming songs from the sixties and picking tunes of protest from the strings of their old guitars. *Pater* Heuken returned from the loft with some books and dropped them on the table in front of me. We popped the tabs on the cans, wrinkled our noses at the whiff of formaldehyde and took a swig of the insipid brew. *Santé*!

The books covered the Great War and the German East Asia Squadron. *Pater* Heuken pulled one from the pile and flipped through the pages. He reeled off names of old battles and vanished ships: Coronel and the Falklands, the gallant *Emden*, "Swan of the East," and the elegant *Ayesha*. "So many young men," he mused, more to himself than to me. He paused over a photograph of the cruiser *Dresden* under fire. "I don't think old Helfferich would have been impressed by *Dresden*. To sail away or to turn and fight…to flee or not to flee, that is the question, *ja*?" He chuckled at his little joke and took another sip of beer. "Anyway, read these and you will see why Helfferich built his monument. Tell me what you think." He reached for another book, opened it to the first page and grinned with delight. "This is a good place to start. Read about the German squadron and Tsingtao beer. It's much better than Bintang, wouldn't you say?"

I leaned over the table and started to read. The two guitarists strummed a passable version of a Bob Dylan tune. The familiar lyrics ran through my head:

> "Yes, 'n' how many deaths will it take till he knows
> That too many people have died?
> The answer, my friend, is blowin' in the wind.
> The answer is blowin' in the wind…"

To the Brave Men of the German East Asia Squadron

I remembered the Vietnam era and thought about these young Indonesians squaring off against their own army, about Adja's stone soldiers and the displaced Baduy tribe, about the long-ago massacre in Bali and the sailors of 1914 who refused to surrender. And what was it that Alex Papadimitriou had said to me at the German *Volkstrauertag*? "I did not surrender!"

The guitar strings thrummed. A more primeval sound seeped through the thin cabin walls: the sighing of the wind and the harsh whine of cicadas trilling among the ferns on the forest floor. Through the black windows, beyond the woods and across the valley, Gunung Pangrango lay wreathed in darkness, brooding invisibly above the white pillar of Artja.

THIRTEEN

THE BATTLE OF CORONEL

HMS Good Hope, Glasgow, Monmouth and Otranto

In the early part of the twentieth century, Tsingtao boasted one of the finest harbours in the world and the best beer in China. Tsingtao was the capital city of the German colony of Kiaochow on the Shandang peninsula. Halfway between Beijing and Shanghai, this huge point of land juts deep into the Yellow Sea toward Korea. In 1897 Germany acquired the port in a race with other European powers for a foothold on the coast of China. Britain was negotiating for control of Hong Kong. Portugal controlled Macao. France and Holland ruled a huge slice of Southeast Asia. To trade and compete with these traditional seafaring nations, Germany sought to expand her own network of ports and colonies and to curry favour with China.

Germany's 1871 unification had impressed China's leadership. One of the oldest countries in the world invited representatives from one of the youngest to modernize the Chinese armed forces along Prussian military lines. The curious relationship prospered for several years. The Chinese hoped to fend off future aggressors, European as well as Asian, and the Germans opened the door on a whole new world of opportunity. Ships of the new German Navy left their base in Kiel, sailed around the globe and docked in Chinese ports.

After two years in the Far East, one of these splendid sailing vessels, the corvette *Elisabeth*, cast off from Singapore and tacked home through the tricky currents and winds of the Sunda Strait. In the middle of the strait on May 20, 1883, a loud explosion startled Captain Hollmann and his crew. A magnificent white cloud billowed eleven thousand metres into the sky. Within hours, a ghostly blanket of sticky ash coated the sails, rigging and decks. The men of *Elisabeth* were the first Europeans to witness the initial eruption of Krakatau, three months before the final cataclysm in August.

Relations between China and Germany deteriorated not long after that memorable event. The Germans proved themselves no different from other Europeans, bent on a self-serving policy of colonization. In a short space of time the young nation-state acquired substantial overseas interests in Africa, Mexico and the Pacific: the far-flung islands of the Carolines, the Marshalls, Kaiser Wilhelmsland, Samoa, New Guinea and the Bismarck Archipelago. The annexation of Tsingtao anchored the outer rim of this vast but tenuous web.

Even Franz Heinrich Witthoefft, the staid and sober director of Behn Meyer, joined in this *fin-de-siècle* rush of colonial enthusiasm. He signed a contract with the Sultan of Kedah to turn the idyllic island and harbour of Langkawi (near Phuket) into a German Protectorate. The King of Siam repudiated the contract before the British had time to react. Undeterred, Witthoefft shocked his British friends even further when he purchased eleven British coastal steamers for Norddeutscher Lloyd. The *Singapore Free Press* wrote, "Nobody can criticize our German friends… But it is nevertheless disturbing for British interests to watch the almost incredible development of German trade and German shipping in this part of the world." One English steamer captain allegedly lowered the

Union Jack, kissed it, folded it – and then raised his middle finger to the German flag.

Mindful of their exposed position among their "friends," the directors of Behn Meyer in 1897 petitioned Admiral Tirpitz for permission to establish a German Association in Singapore. The association would provide "a means to further our business interests where forceful persuasion is required." One of its additional objectives would be "enlarging the navy." In August 1900 the German community celebrated their new association with the opening of the Teutonia Club, an imposing building which lives on today as the stylish Goodwood Park Hotel.

In that same year, *Graf* Waldersee passed through Singapore with a contingent of German troops. They were part of a multinational force sailing to China to crush the Boxer Rebellion. The coastal steamers – the former British ships – gave them a grand sendoff from the harbour with flags flying. The significance of the event was not lost on the British. Witthoefft began to have second thoughts about a rapid expansion of German trade. He sensed the sad truth behind the Chinese saying, "Beware should your wishes come true."

To protect distant German possessions and business interests required a stronger naval presence. Kaiser Wilhelm II was determined to build a navy to challenge England's supremacy over the world's oceans. A grandson of Queen Victoria, he had visited the docks at Portsmouth as a boy and was indelibly impressed by the pomp and glory of Britannia's Royal Navy. Through adept political manoeuvring and with the help of Admiral Tirpitz, he seized direct control of the German Navy. This touched off a jealous and escalating spiral of shipbuilding competition between the two countries. By the time Queen Victoria died, German warships were a common sight in the Far East.

The German Navy in Asia needed a port and Tsingtao was one of the best. A modern city of brick and stone rapidly arose, its architecture more reminiscent of the Baltic than of the Yellow Sea. Streets were paved, power stations erected and trenches dug for underground plumbing. A new brewery, that quintessentially German establishment, produced thousands of litres of Tsingtao beer under the watchful eyes of traditional German brewmasters. In later years Tsingtao beer weathered two world wars, various rebellions and a Chinese revolution to become modern China's leading beer export and the main Chinese brew sold worldwide. The label even survived the postwar conversion to Pinyin spelling of its home town Qingdao. It could be argued that Tsingtao beer has been one of Germany's most enduring contributions to Asia.

The port of Tsingtao became the home of Germany's fleet in the Pacific, the *Deutsch-Ostasiatische Kreuzergeschwader*, the German East Asia Cruiser Squadron. By the summer of 1914 the fleet consisted of two heavy cruisers, *Scharnhorst* and *Gneisenau*, and three light or unarmoured cruisers, *Emden*, *Leipzig* and *Nürnberg*, named after cities in Germany. Sporting a peacetime coat of white paint, *Emden* achieved early fame as "The Swan of the East." Her distinctive colouration hinted at the uniqueness of her captain and her future career as a lone raider.

Several other vessels rounded out the squadron: two armed merchant cruisers, *Cormoran* and *Prinz Eitel Friedrich*, the latter a former luxury liner; the gunboats *Jaguar, Luchs, Tiger* and *Iltis*; the smaller river gunboats *Tsingtau, Vaterland, Otter*; and the torpedo boat *S-90*. The peacetime purpose of the cruisers and gunboats alike was to show the German flag and to put down rebellions in the various possessions, not only in German colonies but in other European outposts as well.

Summer duty for the sailors in Tsingtao was an unaccustomed pleasure: warm weather, sporting events, parties, good beer, pretty girls and a life of colonial luxury. Even better, in Tsingtao it was the Chinese workers who carried the sacks of coal aboard the ships, not the sailors as was the custom in Europe.

Coal supply was a major strategic problem for the Germans and would eventually contribute to the demise of the East Asia Squadron. The elegant *Elisabeth* and her sister ships had long since relinquished their combat role to ironclad coal-fired warships. In the brief interval between canvas and oil, naval vessels devoured the humble but precious resource at a voracious rate. *Scharnhorst* and *Gneisenau*, the heaviest ships, each carried 2,000 tons of coal. At the most economical speed of 10 knots they consumed half a ton of coal per mile and used up their fuel supply in less than three weeks. At action speed of 20 knots they burned more than twice as much. All the cruisers, large and small, had to coal every five days when travelling at high speed. Their only secure source in all of Asia and the Pacific Ocean was Tsingtao, where trains brought the coal down to the coast from the mines in Shandang. Coal could also be purchased in Japan but this source became less and less reliable as Japan tilted toward an alliance with England and France. None of the German islands of the Pacific possessed any coal resources. With their many bases and colonies surrounding the Pacific and Indian Oceans, the British Navy could strangle the squadron simply by denying it coal.

A network of leased ocean-going colliers partially compensated for this disadvantage. The warships and colliers travelled far and wide, fanning out from the squadron's home base in Tsingtao to distant harbours in its vast sphere of influence. Of all the ports of call none was more popular than Batavia, the largest city of the Dutch East Indies. When the northern latitudes suffered through the gales of winter, Batavia provided a welcome tropical refuge. Every year on January 27, the Kaiser's birthday, the German community turned out *en masse* to welcome the grand ships of his navy.

The tradition began in 1905 with the first visit to Batavia by a German warship, *Bussard*. The visit of *Bismarck* in January, 1906, was the beginning of a long relationship between Emil Helfferich and the German fleet. With the exotic and capable Dina now by his side, he entertained the ship's officers and the commander, Admiral Breusing, in his new home in Tanah Abang. Later on he escorted them to the Harmonie Club for a rowdy evening of drinking and pony races. More than a decade earlier Helfferich had tried to enlist in the navy but his poor eyesight let him down. Now his hearing was failing, too, although he could still gain vicarious pleasure by listening to the swashbuckling stories. His year in the artillery allowed him to talk knowledgeably about guns. Clutching a whisky soda, Helfferich nodded approvingly as the young officers described the rigorous drills and boasted of their marksmanship at 10,000 yards.

Emil's younger brother, Theodor, also fell under the navy's romantic spell. Thwarted in his own military ambitions by lung disease, he volunteered his services to the German Naval *Etappe* as a *Vertrauensmann*, an intermediary between the navy and the Dutch administration. When he moved from Surabaya to Batavia in 1912, the navy appointed him chief *Vertrauensmann* for the Dutch East Indies. They gave him the code book and kept him informed of their movements. From that time on, in his own quiet and methodical way, Theodor monitored the comings and goings of all warships throughout the archipelago and passed this information along to the German Navy.

Emil took pride in his younger brother and admired his impressive title and his access to privileged military and political intelligence. He was proud also of his best friend and former partner, Georg Rademacher, who filled the prestigious position of German Consul in Surabaya. Helfferich never aspired to an official post himself. He displayed his fervent patriotism for the fatherland in other more sociable ways.

In addition to his more serious duties, Theodor helped Emil prepare the venues and plan the festivities surrounding the Kaiser's birthday. In January, 1913, the big armoured cruiser *Gneisenau* docked with much fanfare at Tanjung Priok. They laid on a lavish party at the Semplak estate near Buitenzorg, one of the new plantations operated by the Straits and Sunda Syndicate. Three hundred and fifty officers and sailors, all splendidly uniformed in tropical whites, attended the gala. A year later the Helfferich brothers entertained in similar style the men of the flagship *Scharnhorst* and the famous Admiral *Graf* Spee himself.

Vice-Admiral Graf Maximilian von Spee

In 1912 Rear-Admiral (later Vice-Admiral) *Graf* Maximilian von Spee had taken command of the German East Asia Squadron. Born in Copenhagen in 1861, he grew up in his father's castle at Heitorf on the Rhine near

Düsseldorf. In 1889 he married and in time became the father of five sons. Two of them were now lieutenants serving proudly under his command: Otto on *Nürnberg* and Heinrich on *Gneisenau*. The tall, dashing, broad-shouldered admiral possessed the manners of an aristocrat and the sharp blue eyes of a seasoned hunter. At times those angry eyes could flash like lightning on a grey sea. *Graf* Spee's keen intelligence, aggressive fighting spirit, strength of will and willingness to take risks made him a dangerous adversary. In the two years following his appointment he drilled his crews relentlessly.

The naval commanders of various nationalities in the Far East worked together in a spirit of wary cooperation. In the early days of the ill-starred summer of 1914, Vice-Admiral Sir Thomas Jerram, commander of the British China Squadron, sailed to Tsingtao in his flagship, *Minotaur*. There he enjoyed the hospitality of *Graf* Spee in the German admiral's wardroom while the men competed at sports and partied late into the night. When the British left on June 12, Jerram's last words to his counterpart were, "Live well and goodbye until we meet again." It would be their last meeting. Sixteen days later a Bosnian Serb teenager assassinated Archduke Ferdinand and his wife in Sarajevo. He touched off a chain of events which would pit the two navies and the rest of the world in mortal combat.

During the anxious month of July, von Spee expected war to break out at any moment. He ordered his squadron offshore for more training. *Emden* cruised the seas around Korea and Japan. *Leipzig* exchanged places with *Nürnberg* off the west coast of Mexico, where ships of several nations protected their perceived interests during the interminable Mexican Revolution. One of the gunboats sailed south to the Pearl River, upstream of Hong Kong. Under the admiral's command the rest of the squadron steamed far to the southeast to Ponape, a remote atoll in the Caroline Islands east of the Philippines. There they practiced their gunnery and the more mundane, but crucial, task of taking on coal at sea.

More concerned than ever about his tenuous coal supply, von Spee ordered the charter of every collier on the China coast. When one of these dirty little boats chugged into the blue waters of Ponape, the officers in charge of the operation changed into old uniforms and the men stripped down to shorts and singlets. To avoid the coal dust, the remaining senior officers fled to other ships or ashore. Almost every man aboard had a job to do. In wartime there would be no civilians or coolies to do the work. The crew laid canvas sacking over the decks for protection, hung tarpaulins and covered up doorways and hatches. They muzzled the guns and pointed them upward to keep out the soot. The awkward exercise had to begin and end in the bright light of day, leaving the ships almost defenceless.

Sailors in small dinghies hauled ropes over to the collier and winched the two vessels closer together. In the collier's hold they shovelled coal into thousands of 100 kg bags and slung them ten at a time into cargo nets. Donkey engines rattled and clanked as they hoisted the nets and swung them over the water to the bunker slides of the warship. Men unhooked the bags from the swinging nets, taking care neither to fall overboard nor to break any fingers. They unloaded the sacks into wheelbarrows and hustled across the deck to open chutes where they tipped the coal into bunkers. The work was dirty, hard and exhausting.

Stokers descended on ladders into the filthy holds to level up the pile. They wore goggles and headlamps, tied sponges to their faces and covered their heads with towels. The upper bunkers were about ten by five metres in size, with sloping floors to funnel coal into the lower bunkers. Lumps of coal thundered down the chutes and raised clouds of dust, reducing visibility to less than two metres. Stokers could hear, but not see, the other men working beside them. They shovelled the pile under constant threat of burial and the lurking fear of black lung disease – coughing, choking and sweating in the stifling heat and darkness.

Every two hours the stokers changed shifts to wash and drink. Black as miners, they snatched hurried meals when they could. Coal dust covered the deck to a depth of several inches. Everything on board tasted, smelled and felt like coal. A fine layer of black dust seeped into cabins and settled on white uniforms.

Throughout the ordeal a band played military airs from a safe vantage point and the sailors sang along. The operation required one full day to complete, after which they thoroughly scrubbed and hosed down the ship – and themselves. Excess sacks of coal remained on deck. Whenever they dumped these sacks into the bunkers the crew had to rinse the decks and bulkheads all over again. No sooner was the ship clean than the whole process had to be repeated – every five to fourteen days, depending on speed.

In the strange calm before the looming conflict, while the squadron took on coal and drilled the gun crews, the von Spee family found time to row ashore to the nearby island of Oroluk. There the three Germans collected tropical plants and animals in the grand English tradition of Cook, Wallace and Darwin. More solemnly, in this remote, forlorn and forgotten outpost of the German empire, they paid their respects at graves of Germans killed in a native uprising in 1910.

Every day they listened to the worsening news from Europe. The range of wireless communication in 1914 was normally limited to a few hundred miles. Messages to and from distant ships and islands followed a tortuous path via underwater cables and wireless. Often these messages went astray, were garbled or intercepted. Nevertheless all the ships of the squadron learned on the decisive day, August 1, that Germany had declared war on Russia.

On the next day von Spee took his two sons ashore on Ponape one last time. They walked with other Sunday worshippers to the Roman Catholic church where, one by one, they entered the confessional and prayed for forgiveness, "...*wie auch wir vergeben unseren Schuldigern.*" After returning to his flagship, *Graf* Spee read the messages from his captains and quickly made plans to rendezvous in Pagan, an island in the Marianas between Guam and Iwo Jima.

Among the messages, the admiral read with particular delight that *Emden's* enterprising Captain von Müller had already captured the squadron's first merchant prize of the war, a Russian steamer. He was now escorting the outraged and incredulous crew to internment in Tsingtao.

Von Spee ordered his gunboats to return immediately to Tsingtao where they were to meet up with *Emden*. On August 2 the order reached one of the small boats high on the Pearl River in China, where Captain von Moller was enjoying a pleasant day of hunting with his friend, the commander of the British gunboat *Teal*. Von Moller had failed to appreciate what might happen in the wake of Germany's declaration of war against Russia. Late at night, after drinks and dinner with the British, the German gunboat slipped away. The tardy departure would prove costly. Events unravelled rather too quickly for the unfortunate Germans. On August 3 Germany declared war on France. One day later on August 4, as von Moller descended the Pearl estuary and approached Hong Kong, Britain declared war on Germany. Trapped between the garrison and *Teal*, suddenly realizing they would be unable to run the British gauntlet, the crew abandoned ship and split into several small groups. The dauntless von Moller and five of his men headed overland from China to Germany.

War against Russia, France and Britain meant that much of Asia was turned against Germany. Although Japan had not yet declared her intentions, she possessed the largest navy in the Pacific and was unlikely to sympathize with Germany. Australia, New Zealand, India and the French Pacific fleet would fight with England. America was officially neutral although she too leaned strongly toward the British. The Dutch, mindful of their exposed position both in Asia and in Europe, were strictly neutral and threatened to intern any warship that overstayed a 24-hour layover.

Von Spee's squadron of five main fighting ships looked suddenly quite lonely in the vastness of the hostile Pacific. Since they would find it difficult to punch through the British blockade, they were ordered to carry on "cruiser warfare" against enemy merchant vessels, to confiscate or destroy contraband in neutral vessels, to raid enemy coastlines, to bombard military bases, to destroy cable and wireless stations and to engage enemy forces to reduce the pressure on the Home Fleet. Communication was forecast to be difficult; therefore each captain was instructed to make his own decisions. In a quiet moment of introspection von Spee wrote, "I am quite homeless. I cannot reach Germany. We possess no other secure harbour. I must plough the seas of the world doing as much mischief as I can, until my ammunition is exhausted, or a foe far superior in power succeeds in catching me."

Among the panicky German residents of Tsingtao rumours flew that Japan was preparing to invade. The combined British and Japanese forces heavily outnumbered the German East Asia Squadron. If caught in the harbour the squadron would be annihilated. Von Spee made the difficult decision to abandon Tsingtao. *Emden* and the two auxiliary cruisers escaped just before the British Navy arrived. They headed for the open ocean, bound for a rendezvous in Pagan. On August 23 Japan declared war on Germany. Two months later they descended upon the scuttled gunboats and the lightly defended harbour of Tsingtao.

⁂

In those early days of August, 1914, the German East Asia Squadron touched the lives of sailors in a vast and peaceable land far from Tsingtao. Canada's naval tradition stretched back a mere four years and the fledgling Canadian Naval Service had barely grown since its inception. Two antiquated British cruisers, *Rainbow* and *Niobe*, had been purchased from the Royal Navy, thus inaugurating a dubious tradition that continues to the present day. Though nominally under the control of Canada's Parliament, both ships received their tactical orders from the British Admiralty. *Rainbow*, by far the smaller of the two warships, guarded Esquimalt on the west coast. Four thousand four hundred kilometres to the east, *Niobe* served as a training vessel for cadets in Halifax.

On Sunday, August 2, 1914, as Admiral *Graf* von Spee worshipped with his two sons on Ponape, as Captain von Müller of *Emden* captured a Russian steamer and as Captain von Moller slipped quietly back down the Pearl River, Midshipman Malcolm Cann joined the crew of *Niobe*. He already knew this boat. Exactly three years earlier, as a fifteen-year-old naval cadet, he had been sailing on *Niobe* went it ran aground in a fog off Cape Sable. The wireless operator transmitted an SOS – one of the earliest instances of wireless being used in an emergency. A British warship, *HMS Cornwall*, gallantly sailed to the rescue and promptly ran aground herself. It fell to Nova Scotia fishermen to rescue the men and cadets from the stricken *Niobe*. Badly damaged, Canada's largest warship limped back to Halifax and remained in port until the outbreak of war. The debacle ended in the first court martial of a Canadian naval officer.

Cann must have been disappointed with his 1914 posting to *Niobe* and must have watched with envy as Rear-Admiral Sir Christopher Cradock steamed into Halifax harbour in command of *HMS Suffolk* and other fine ships of His Majesty's Navy. His disappointment lasted only a few days. The Admiralty ordered Cann and six fellow Canadian "snotties" to join *Suffolk*'s crew. The handsome eighteen-year-olds bid farewell to the dazzled young ladies of Halifax, marched up the gangplank with their sea-bags and proudly turned aft to salute the British ensign. On August 15 they sailed away from Nova Scotia to seek out the enemy. Two days later Admiral Cradock transferred his flag to the armoured cruiser *HMS Good Hope*. He found room on board for his dog but only four of the Canadian midshipmen. The seven classmates of the first graduating class of the Royal Naval College of Canada drew lots for the honour. The lucky winners – Victor Hatheway, Arthur Silver, William Palmer and Malcolm Cann – were destined to meet the German East Asia Squadron in battle.

While Cann was still stewing aboard *Niobe*, the tiny Pacific half of Canada's navy had received a very disturbing order: "*Rainbow* should proceed south at once in order to get in touch with [*Leipzig*] and generally guard the trade routes north of the equator." Commander Walter Hose contemplated his impossible task. He had no real ammunition. The railroad refused to ship modern high explosive shells across Canada and so the resourceful captain had filled old shell casings with gunpowder. Even with proper ammunition, *Rainbow*'s antiquated six-inch guns were no match for *Leipzig*. The German cruiser was also much faster and her crew was superbly trained. In stark contrast, Commander Hose had been forced to recruit local naval enthusiasts who had never even served in the reserves. Vastly outgunned, much slower and manned by amateurs, *Rainbow* sailed away from Esquimalt in the early morning hours of the fateful fourth of August, 1914. Half a world away, Britain declared war on Germany.

A day later Hose received the welcome news that the high explosive shells had finally arrived in Vancouver. But no sooner had he turned about than he received a countermanding order: "*Leipzig* reported 4 August off Magdalena Bay [in Mexico] steering north. Do your utmost to protect *Algerine* and *Shearwater*, steering north from San Diego. Remember Nelson and the British Navy. All Canada is watching." *Algerine* and *Shearwater* were two small and aging Royal Navy sloops, fleeing to safety in Canada. Hose had no choice but to obey the preposterous order. The defenceless *Rainbow* turned south to engage the enemy.

On August 6, *Rainbow* arrived in San Francisco and took on fifty tons of coal. Hose had ordered a much larger quantity but the Americans refused, citing wartime regulations now in effect. Warships from combatant countries were permitted to buy only enough coal from neutral countries to enable them to reach the next friendly port. They could not return to the same country for a period of three months. *Rainbow* sailed back out to sea and patrolled the waters off San Francisco.

For four days the lookouts peered anxiously through their binoculars for any sign of the two sloops – and for the dreaded three-funnelled silhouette of *Leipzig*. Other ships came and went but there was no sign of the British or the Germans. Down to the last few tons of coal, Hose had to abandon his mission and sail back to Esquimalt. *Leipzig* steamed into San Francisco harbour on August 12, barely a day after *Rainbow's* departure. Thanks to American rules of neutrality *Rainbow* had narrowly averted catastrophe. Several days later, the two British sloops arrived safely in Canada.

⌘

The grey silhouettes of half a dozen German warships floated incongruously off the palm-ringed shore of Pagan. Motor launches ferried the eager and expectant captains to the admiral's flagship. On August 13, surrounded by his senior officers, von Spee laid out their options and enjoined them to debate.

Flush with the honour of striking the first blow, Captain von Müller of *Emden* seized the initiative. He had no interest in wandering around the empty Pacific. Instead he persuaded the admiral to allow him to raid ships in the Indian Ocean, so as to disrupt British trade on the vital routes to India, China and Australia. He would take with him one or two colliers and live off the coal of his prizes. Owing to the coal supply problem it was not possible for more than one cruiser to survive in this fashion. *Emden*, a lone raider, would have to cut herself off completely from the rest of the squadron and from any hope of support. Von Spee admired this audacious but doomed plan. Indeed, the light cruiser could wreak havoc out of all proportion to her size, but how long could she survive?

The remaining captains agreed that the best strategy for the rest of the squadron was to harry English shipping along the South American coastline. They would be farther away from the strong British and Japanese naval presence in the western Pacific. Good hiding places lay among the remote and convoluted inlets of the uncharted southwest coast. Interpreting the rules of neutrality in a more flexible way, the Latin countries were more willing than the Dutch or the Americans to resupply German ships. They could get coal both from South America and from colliers chartered by Germany. Von Spee decided to make a break for Chile, where the government was openly pro-German. The squadron could leave its prizes in Valparaiso and take on coal in Chilean ports.

On August 13 the squadron steamed out of Pagan. *Emden* signalled one last time then turned southward to embark on her grand adventure. The two armed merchant cruisers, *Cormoran* and *Prinz Eitel Friedrich*, sailed off to the Coral Sea to raid Australian shipping. *Scharnhorst*, *Gneisenau* and *Nürnberg* began a long circuitous route to Chile, attacking remote allied outposts along the way. No one else in the world knew the whereabouts or the intentions of the German East Asia Squadron. Von Spee was unaware of the conclusion reached by his own General Staff in Berlin: "It may be assumed that the Cruiser Squadron is in East Asiatic waters. Japan's impending entry into the war makes its position hopeless. It is impossible to judge whether the squadron will be able to choose against which enemy it will deal its dying blows. We are ignorant of the Commander-in-Chief's coal supplies and, judging from his oft repeated utterances, it may be taken for granted that he will attempt to bring the enemy to action. Whether he engages the British or the Japanese must depend on their relative situations and any interference on our part might be disastrous. The Commander-in-Chief must have complete liberty of action. If he succeeds in beating the British before the Japanese have time to come in, we should regard it as a great achievement. In view of the above it is better to send him no instructions."

To the British and their allies, von Spee and his ships had sailed off the face of the earth. According to Winston Churchill, the First Lord of the Admiralty, "He had no lack of objectives. He had only to hide and to strike. The vastness of the Pacific and its multitude of islands offered him their shelter and, once he had vanished, who should say where he would reappear. So long as he lived, all the Allies' enterprises lay under the shadow of a serious potential danger. We could not be strong enough every day everywhere to meet him."

Leipzig had left Mexican waters several days earlier and headed for the United States to negotiate the leasing of several colliers. Captain Haun was unaware that two British sloops, *Algerine* and *Shearwater*, were fleeing northward ahead of him and that the dauntless *Rainbow* was steaming south to intercept him. He missed all three ships and a chance for glory.

Good luck continued to elude the Germans from the moment of their arrival in San Francisco. The Americans would not allow them to dock for longer than 24 hours, to set up supply bases, nor to stockpile any coal. Accordingly, the US government confiscated 2,000 tons of recently arrived coal as war materiel then ordered *Leipzig* to move to another pier to take on American coal. The coal company filled the bunkers half full then stopped and demanded cash, refusing to take German credit. The consul frantically toured the city of San Francisco and collected banknotes from bewildered German residents. Then the US Navy weighed in with a decision to refuse Captain Haun's request to leave prizes in American ports. Any such prizes would be interned, nor could the Germans unload any coal from their prizes. US Customs then complained that suitcases of personal belongings, which had been delivered to the consul for safekeeping, had entered without inspection. Newspapers alleged that the suitcases contained secret documents and thus violated American neutrality.

A bear presented an even more awkward problem. The ship's mascot, a brown bear symbolizing the city of Leipzig, had accompanied the crew in peacetime. However a ship at war was no place for a bear. The captain decided to send it ashore but US Customs refused point blank to admit the animal. Undaunted, Haun persuaded the harried German consul to take the bear into his own home. The consul's shocked wife soon convinced the local zoo to adopt the unfortunate beast.

Leipzig departed in haste in the middle of the night. As they left the inner harbour a drunken American pilot ran *Leipzig* into an English sailing ship when he mistook her running lights for a marker buoy. Leaving the pilot to deal with the accident, Captain Haun headed for the open ocean. Though relieved to be leaving San Francisco, he was disappointed that American sympathies lay with the British. The Germans would not be allowed to use American ports to solve their coal supply problems.

Cut off from home, *Graf* Spee was now entirely dependent on his own resources. In drawing up his plans he had to consider what the situation might be in almost every part of the world. By dividing his forces, keeping their locations and intentions secret and maintaining radio silence as much as possible, his squadron threatened the British and their allies throughout the boundless Pacific and Indian Oceans. However by mid-September the Allies had occupied most of the German colonies in the southwest Pacific: German New Guinea, Kaiser Wilhelmsland, Samoa and the Bismarck Archipelago. The Japanese seized the Carolines and the Marshall Islands. The British destroyed the German wireless station at Yap. *Graf* Spee realized it was impossible to retake and hold the captured German possessions.

His three warships meandered eastward through the Pacific Ocean and wreaked havoc in a gentlemanly fashion. The admiral and his sons took time off for nature walks on Christmas Island. On Fanning Island, *Nürnberg* destroyed the British wireless station, cut the Australia-to-Canada cable and took some gold sovereigns from the safe. As they approached Bora Bora in Tahiti, *Scharnhorst* and *Gneisenau* lowered their flags and painted out their names. A dozen natives in a handsome war canoe paddled out to meet them. A French policeman stood up unsteadily from the centre thwart and clambered aboard. Oblivious to the details of the German uniforms, the Frenchman assumed the vessels were British. Von Spee was delighted. Carelessly he asked, "What news of the war?" The policeman admitted they had little support from France and gave him details of the colony's defences. A German steward served champagne to the guest. Von Spee's blue eyes flashed gleefully as he raised his glass in a toast, "Confusion to our enemies!" Both cruisers took on coal at a leisurely pace. The Tahitians willingly revictualed the warships with livestock and fresh fruit. The Germans paid with British sovereigns taken from Fanning Island. The French flag dipped in salute as they left Bora Bora. In reply von Spee raised the red, white and black German ensign – and heartily wished he could have seen their faces.

The East Asia Squadron began to acquire mystical qualities as, ghost-like, they roved the Far East and paralyzed shipping. Worried merchant-men scanned the lonely horizon for telltale plumes of smoke. Rumours were rife. Inaccurate reports confounded the British Admiralty.

On October 12, von Spee arrived at Easter Island with his three cruisers. He met up with six supply ships and with *Leipzig* and *Dresden*, the latter a newcomer to the squadron. The admiral intended to rest at anchor for a week in this remote spot, training and refitting before he continued his eastward journey. A solitary English cattle rancher on the Chilean island greeted his extraordinary guests in friendly fashion. He was out of touch with the world and unaware of the war. The von Spee family rowed ashore to stroll among the famous monoliths, lonely totems of a vanished civilization. "Nothing beside remains." The ceaseless wind whipped the grass and whistled around the black stones. Their silent faces stared into the empty sea like sailors on an endless watch.

The rendezvous at Easter Island marked *Dresden*'s official arrival in the German East Asia Squadron – and her captain's unwilling debut. In July Captain Fritz von Lüdecke had been ordered to take the new light cruiser *Karlsruhe* from Germany to Captain Kohler of *Dresden*. He was to exchange ships with Kohler and return immediately to Germany with *Dresden* for a much needed refit. Unfortunately for him, war broke out a few days after the ships met in Haiti and exchanged captains. Von Lüdecke was ordered to remain at sea in command of *Dresden*'s crew and to raid allied shipping off the east coast of the Americas.

Captain von Lüdecke had been trained in the Merchant Marine and was not one of Germany's first-line fighting officers. His villainous appearance and his pendulous nose, red and swollen from drink, ill suited the gallant image of a navy captain. He was unhappy suddenly to find himself at war in command of a light cruiser. He sat in his spartan cabin and reluctantly flipped through the manuals.

Von Lüdecke's skills tended more to survival than to fighting. Good luck helped too. Bobbing and weaving around the mid-Atlantic, he somehow eluded several British cruisers. False reports shut down Canadian ports for two weeks even though *Dresden* was cruising thousands of miles to the south. He captured three merchantmen but, rather than sink them, he took pity and let them go free. Each one immediately radioed *Dresden*'s position. In the second week of August he let two more steamers slip through his fingers. Once again they reported his position. At the Rocas Islands a Brazilian lighthouse keeper spotted *Dresden* as she took on coal. On August 14 *Dresden* did sink her first merchantman but released another ship shortly thereafter. Von Lüdecke dropped off the captured crew in Rio de Janeiro, where they immediately reported to the British consul. Throughout this time the cruiser had the good fortune not to meet any British warships. Ironically, while the East Asia Squadron was scrambling to find coal, the ineffectual *Dresden* enjoyed the support of as many as 54 colliers in the Atlantic. She had so much coal that she actually sank a British collier rather than keep the vessel and her cargo.

By the middle of September, Berlin may have suspected that something was amiss with the unwarlike cruiser. Von Lüdecke was ordered to rendezvous with *Leipzig* off the coast of Peru and to submit to Captain Haun's command. After rounding Cape Horn and arriving at Hoste Island, von Lüdecke allowed his sailors some unsupervised free time on the beach at Orange Bay. One of them scrawled on an old notice board the date and the name of his ship. Ten days later British seamen discovered the graffiti. They came from Admiral Cradock's flagship, the armoured cruiser *HMS Good Hope*, on the hunt for the German squadron.

⁂

In 1914, 52-year-old Rear-Admiral Sir Christopher Cradock stood at the peak of his long naval career. He had distinguished himself in 1900 during the Boxer Rebellion in China and later in the rescue of the P&O liner *Delhi* off Morocco. A literary man, he had penned an instructional book for young sailors entitled *Whispers from the Fleet*. The crusty Lord Fisher, Churchill's right hand man in the Admiralty, considered Cradock to be "one of our best officers."

Admiral Cradock already knew the men of *Dresden*. In the early summer of 1914 he had taken a British squadron to Mexico where he rendezvoused with the German cruiser. There he had worked closely with *Dresden* to protect European interests during the revolution. In the same summer Admiral von Spee had displayed the same amicable spirit when he entertained the crew of *Minotaur* in Tsingtao; likewise Captain von Moller had gone hunting on the Pearl River with the British captain of *Teal*. Men of each navy counted friends, even relatives, in the other. Now, in September of 1914, the erstwhile friends had suddenly become sworn enemies.

The British Admiralty gave top priority to destruction of the five German warships. At least three British squadrons and a number of lesser units were ordered to seek them out. Cradock's force in the South Atlantic consisted of the heavy cruisers *Good Hope* and *Monmouth*, the light cruiser *Glasgow*, the auxiliary cruiser *Otranto* and, belatedly, the old battleship *Canopus*. He continually pressed the Admiralty for more ships but his requests were denied. Since *Graf* Spee's squadron was fragmented and its whereabouts unknown, the British had to patrol a vast area spanning two oceans. There were not enough ships to go around and, in any case, Cradock's force was considered a match for the German East Asia Squadron.

Of the heavy cruisers, *Good Hope* was similar in speed and armament to either *Scharnhorst* or *Gneisenau* but the German crews were better trained and their ships were better equipped and armoured. British armour-piercing shells were incapable of penetrating the thick-skinned heavy cruisers. The British guns on the lower deck were poorly situated and subject to flooding in heavy seas. *Monmouth* was somewhat lighter and slower than her sister ship *Good Hope*. In a two-on-two fight, the Germans would enjoy a distinct advantage. The light cruiser *Glasgow* was similar to *Nürnberg*, *Leipzig* or *Dresden*. However, despite the slight advantage in armament afforded by two additional six-inch guns, she would be hopelessly outgunned in a two-on-one. The other two British ships were almost useless: *Otranto*, a former merchantman, was too slow and wielded only four small guns. *Canopus*, though well-armed with massive guns, was a wheezing old relic of an earlier era. With a maximum speed of 16 knots, she was too sluggish and decrepit to be of any use.

The British crews had been mobilized at the outbreak of war. Three months earlier, the sailors had been reservists – clerks, shopkeepers, labourers and fishermen with no naval experience. Among the hastily assembled crew of the admiral's flagship were the four young midshipmen from Canada. Even greener youngsters sailed on the sister ship *Monmouth*: twelve 15-year-old navy cadets from Dartmouth in Devon.

Only *Glasgow*, under the command of Captain John Luce, was manned by a complement of regular sailors. Some of these old hands had recently bought parrots at their South American ports of call. Perhaps they fancied themselves as latter-day Long John Silvers. Sixty colourful birds squawked in cages on the aft deck.

So as not to "waste" ammunition, the British had not yet fired their guns. In contrast, the well-trained German crews regularly competed against each other in gunnery drills. They had been at sea together for two years. The plucky British squadron – outnumbered, outgunned, ill-trained and ill-equipped – sailed straight into a storm.

At the beginning of the war, the British also suffered from ineffective leadership at the highest levels. The overworked Admiralty office was woefully disorganized and prone to miscommunication. In addition, the First Sea Lord, Prince Louis of Battenberg, was fighting his own personal battle against invisible foes in a political whisper campaign. Facing unfounded allegations related to his German birth, Battenberg resigned on October 28, 1914. Churchill replaced him with Admiral of the Fleet Lord Fisher, three days before Cradock faced the German squadron.

In marked contrast to the German General Staff, Churchill insisted on close control of his Navy's day-to-day operations, difficult as that was in the days of cable and wireless. During the weeks leading up to the Battle of Coronel, the Admiralty exchanged several ambiguous messages with Cradock, resulting in confusion and misunderstanding at both ends. In early September Cradock asked the Admiralty for reinforcements. London at first agreed to send him *Defence*, a modern warship stronger than any vessel currently under his command. Then they changed their minds and kept *Defence* in Malta in case von Spee suddenly appeared in the Atlantic. They neglected to tell Cradock. Churchill even hinted that he did not have the courage to seek out the enemy and that his continued requests for more strength were unwarranted. On September 14 he was ordered to search for the Germans on the west coast of South America as far north as Valparaiso.

On their way to Cape Horn, Cradock's squadron stopped in at the Falklands. The aide to the Governor later reminisced that, "He knew what he was up against and asked for a fast cruiser with big guns to be added to his squadron, for he had nothing very powerful and nothing very fast, but the Admiralty said he'd have to go without. So old Cradock said, 'All right, we'll do without,' and he slipped off early one morning." The admiral had witnessed other officers cashiered after accusations of avoiding the enemy. After forty years at sea he had no desire to suffer a similar fate.

Not long after Cradock left the Falklands an extraordinary sailing vessel crossed the South Atlantic in his wake. At the outbreak of war Ernest Shackleton and the crew of *Endurance* had volunteered their services to the Royal Navy but were allowed instead to continue with their Antarctic explorations. Now they were headed for the rugged island of South Georgia – and their own radically different rendezvous with destiny.

On September 22 Cradock's men found the scribbles at Orange Bay, evidence that *Dresden* and her careless crew had recently passed through the area. On October 4 *Good Hope* intercepted a faint wireless message and immediately sent it to London for decoding. A few days later the Admiralty informed Cradock that von Spee had ordered *Dresden* to rendezvous with the rest of the squadron off the west coast of South America, where they planned to raid merchant shipping. The wireless message had bounced an incredible 3,500 miles across the Pacific Ocean before reaching *Good Hope*. Now the hunt began in earnest.

On October 18 *Canopus* finally caught up to Admiral Cradock. The Admiralty had sent her in a belated attempt to reinforce his squadron. Cradock warned the Admiralty that *Canopus* would do more harm than good and that he still needed a fast, heavily armoured cruiser. There was no reply. That same day von Spee and his five warships steamed away from Easter Island and headed for the Juan Fernández Islands west of Valparaiso.

Graf Spee already knew that Cradock's four cruisers were in the area searching for *Leipzig* and *Dresden*. The German consulates in Chile and

Argentina kept him informed on a daily basis. His staff compared guns and rated speeds. With grim satisfaction he realized that, unless he was very unlucky, his squadron could beat the British.

In the lonely harbour of Más-a-Fuera in the Juan Fernández Islands, the German squadron regrouped and took on coal. *Prinz Eitel Friedrich*, the former luxury liner, rejoined them but *Cormoran* had run out of coal and had to intern herself at Guam. Von Spee's cruisers were at the peak of their fighting form. Leaving behind the auxiliary cruiser and the supply ships, the five warships slipped out of the bay.

At that moment Cradock was searching for the Germans near Valparaiso, a few hundred miles east of Más-a-Fuera. He sent *Glasgow* back south to Coronel, a port near the city of Concepción, with despatches for the British consul. In the early morning of October 31, *Glasgow* intercepted wireless transmissions from *Leipzig*. The Germans were cruising only 150 miles away.

Cradock decided the hour was at hand even though he sensed his force was outmatched. He felt the inexorable pull of centuries of Royal Navy tradition, the legend that no British commander had ever run from the enemy. *Canopus* was 250 miles away, out of the action for at least one day. Cradock wouldn't wait for her. He ordered *Glasgow* to rendezvous with the other ships fifty miles west of Coronel at noon the next day, November 1.

At the appointed hour on the fateful day, the four British ships swept north in a broad front spanning 45 miles. *Glasgow*, the closest ship to the coast, spotted a blur of smoke on the eastern horizon and turned toward it.

That afternoon the German ships performed their routine call to battle stations. They donned clean clothes and washed in fresh water to reduce the risk of infection if wounded. Each man wore an identity disk on a red silk ribbon around the neck. In their pockets they carried nose plugs, to reduce the amount of cordite ingested into the lungs, and a rag, to place over the mouth in the event of a smoke attack. They oiled the guns; they checked the torpedoes, lifeboats and medical supplies; they removed debris from the engine room and loose coal from the decks. The drill took only fifteen minutes but the men were not dismissed afterwards. The *Scharnhorst* look-out had spotted on the horizon three columns of smoke, drifting in their direction on the rising southwesterly wind.

At 4:20 in the afternoon, drums rolled as sailors on all five German cruisers ran battle ensigns up the halyards. Fire crews pumped the lifeboats full of water for emergency use. The lookouts identified *Monmouth* and *Glasgow* first. Von Spee swiftly determined his strategy. He planned, for several reasons, to keep his ships between the British and the coastline: to prevent the enemy from reaching neutral Chilean waters; to keep to lee-ward so that smoke from his guns would be cleared away; and to silhouette the British cruisers against the setting sun while his own ships would be hidden against the mountainous grey coastline. He would therefore delay the engagement until sunset. This would also allow time for *Dresden* and *Leipzig* to catch up to the rest of the squadron.

The two squadrons steered a parallel southward course in heavy seas, their big guns just out of range, as Cradock's force attempted to outflank the enemy. By 5:47 the British ships had formed up in line of battle with flags raised. Cradock took pity on the lightly armed *Otranto*, which was having difficulty keeping up, and ordered her out of harm's way. Now it was just three versus five. At 6:04 Cradock realized he would be unable to sweep around the Germans. He turned to attack, intent on forcing the ac-tion while the setting sun still shone in the eyes of the German gunners.

Von Spee ordered his ships to maintain the range at 18,000 yards and to turn away from the attacking British. The wind blew with gale force from the southwest; the cruisers pitched and rolled in deep swells. Waves broke foaming over the bows and surged over the forecastles on the main deck. At 6:45 the setting sun pierced through sheets of rain and cloudy skies and silhouetted the British ships. The moon, almost full, rose over the high Andes. There would be one hour of twilight. Gunners on both sides peered anxiously through wildly waving gunsights. *Dresden* caught up to the rest of the squadron. Von Spee ordered his ships to attack.

The two admirals faced each other across the heaving expanse of grey water. When the ships were 11,000 yards apart, *Scharnhorst* fired the first salvo at *Good Hope*. Her second salvo found its mark. *Gneisenau* opened fire on *Monmouth* and within three minutes set her ablaze. The British ships returned fire but their gunsmoke hung in the air and obscured the view. Their own ships stood out starkly against the western sky but the Germans were just a grey blur on the coastline, ghostly beneath a gibbous moon. Were they under- or over-shooting? The gun crews couldn't see. The lower guns were awash in water. Ammunition carriers lost their footing on the slippery pitching decks.

Leipzig and *Dresden* opened fire on *Glasgow* but the range was too great. As he cleared the decks of *Glasgow* for action, Captain Luce impatiently ordered his men to release the parrots and toss the cages overboard. The disgruntled sailors wished them Godspeed as they circled overhead in a colourful cloud of blue, green and orange. The birds tested the southwesterly gale and searched in vain for the mainland. All sixty returned to the ship. They perched ludicrously on the superstructure and bobbed precariously on stays and signal halyards. There they remained despite efforts by the sailors to scare them away. When the firing began the birds fell to the deck from the shock of the guns. Two were knocked unconscious when they perched on the barrel of a 6-inch gun. Heavy seas swept the pair overboard.

The three light cruisers played cat-and-mouse until darkness made firing difficult. Of the 600 shells hurled at *Glasgow* only five struck the ship and the damage was minimal. Fifty luckless parrots were the only casualties aboard *Glasgow*. *Dresden* never took any hits; neither she nor *Leipzig* suffered any injuries. When the moon broke through a gap in the clouds, Captain Luce saw the other German cruisers bearing down fast upon him. *Glasgow* fled to the northwest and passed the stricken *Monmouth* within hailing distance. Her bow was sinking slowly in heavy seas as sailors waved and even cheered from the stern. Luce left them to their fate, torn between a desire to help and the need to escape. *Otranto* followed at top speed.

Good Hope and *Monmouth* were still firing but they had sustained horrendous damage. At 7:50 a shell slammed into a magazine on *Good Hope*. Hundreds of silken bagged charges of cordite ignited. With a deafening roar the admiral's flagship exploded in an instant. Sailors on *Nürnberg*, six miles away, held their hands to their ears. Von Spee ceased fire and watched in awe as his adversary disappeared in a ball of flame. Later he wrote that she blew up "like gigantic fireworks against the dark evening sky – white flames with green stars reaching higher than the funnels." All hands went down with the ship – nine hundred men including Admiral Cradock and the four lowly midshipmen from Halifax. Hatheway, Palmer, Silver and Malcolm Cann were the first Canadian casualties of the Great War.

The two heavy German cruisers had taken a few punches but no significant damage. Now they switched on their searchlights and directed their full attention to *Monmouth*. *Scharnhorst* and *Gneisenau* fired at the wounded British ship from both sides and destroyed all her guns. She was listing badly but still flew her battle flags as she limped northward and disappeared into a squall.

Von Spee ordered the three light cruisers to search for *Monmouth*. *Leipzig* crossed a field of debris and passed floating British bodies but did not stop to look for survivors. *Nürnberg*, out of position for most of the action, spotted the doomed *Monmouth* at 8:30. Her guns blazed at the British as they tried to run for shore. Unable to escape, *Monmouth* turned to ram *Nürnberg*. The Germans veered away but fired continuously. Safely distant from the action, Captain Luce on *Glasgow* counted 75 flashes as the German guns pounded his comrades. On the bridge of *Nürnberg* Lieutenant Otto von Spee watched in disbelief as their dying adversary, unable to defend herself, still bravely and recklessly flew the battle flag of the Royal Navy. Finally *Monmouth* capsized in a death roll and a few sailors jumped into the water. Captain von Schönberg radioed his admiral at 9:15 to report that *Monmouth* had sunk with all hands. Five hundred and forty men, including the twelve naval cadets from Dartmouth, perished in the depths of the sea.

Under cover of darkness, *Glasgow* and *Otranto* headed south and warned the tardy *Canopus* to flee. *Glasgow* barrelled through the Magellan Strait and made for the Falklands; *Otranto* sailed on through to Montevideo.

On the day after the battle, a clerk in London shuffled through a stack of cables from England's far-flung operations. In the pile he found a message dated November 1 from the British consul in Valparaiso, warning that the German fleet was in the area. Worried that Cradock might be tempted to engage a superior foe in battle, the Admiralty on November 3 finally ordered *Defence* to sail to his aid. However, in Churchill's words, "We were already talking to the void." Britain had suffered her worst naval defeat since the Battle of Lake Erie against the Americans in 1813, one hundred and one years earlier.

One hundred and nine years and eleven days before Coronel, Horatio Nelson had died at the Battle of Trafalgar. Following a British tradition dating from the sixteenth century, Navy captains never fled from the enemy and would rather sink than surrender. Admiral Cradock was the first man since Nelson's time to lead the Royal Navy against an enemy fleet awaiting battle. On his memorial in York Minster these words of bravado are chiselled into marble:

> God forbid that I should do this thing,
> To flee away from them;
> If our time be come, let us die manfully
>   for our Brethren,
> And let us not stain our Honour.

The families of the four midshipmen erected a more humble memorial to their sons in Saint Mark's Anglican Church in Halifax. On December 6, 1917, both church and tablet were destroyed in the great Halifax explosion, a disaster that engulfed the harbour – and the hapless *Niobe*.

The German squadron sailed triumphantly into Valparaiso, Chile, to announce their victory and to receive a hero's welcome from the ecstatic German community. Coupled with the recent exploits of the amazing *Emden*, the Battle of Coronel was a tremendous morale boost to Germany and a crushing blow to British pride. The news flashed round the world by cable. Germans cheered in Batavia, too, in particular Emil and Theodor Helfferich and others who had met the dashing young men of the *Ostasiatische Geschwader*.

Admiral von Spee refused to join in the widespread celebration. Persuaded nevertheless to visit the German Club, he sat moodily in his chair, surrounded by the jubilant throng. At one point a drunken civilian loudly demanded silence and proposed a toast: "Damnation to the British Navy!"

Others rose to their feet, murmuring their assent and watching von Spee, who remained fixed in his seat. Finally he stood and faced the expectant crowd. He glared at the author of the toast, picked up his glass and calmly spoke, "I drink to the memory of a gallant and honourable foe." He drained his glass, threw it away, picked up his cocked hat and strode out of the club.

On the street outside the building, a woman stopped him and offered a bouquet of flowers. Though shocked by the gift of a dozen white lilies, he graciously accepted. He contemplated the unintended irony and thanked her, saying, "They will do very nicely for my grave."

He brooded on his evanescent success and the inevitable response of the wounded British lion. With a deep sense of *Weltschmerz*, a world-weary sorrow, he pulled his squadron out of Valparaiso after one night in port and sailed back to Más-a-Fuera. He wrote to Berlin, "We have at last contributed something to the glory of our arms – although it might not mean much on the whole and in view of the enormous number of the English ships."

Churchill said of von Spee, "He was a cut flower in a vase, fair to see and yet bound to die."

FOURTEEN

SWAN OF THE EAST

SMS Emden, Swan of the East

Captain Karl Friedrich Max von Müller hailed from a vanished era of galleons and caravels. Tall and blond with fine features, forty-one years old, bold and skillful but intensely private, he would have cut a wide swath as a gallant buccaneer of the eighteenth century. Under his command *Emden* earned greater fame and admiration – from both sides – than any other German warship of the Great War.

Von Müller bid *auf Wiedersehen* to the rest of the squadron in Pagan on August 13, 1914. He steered his ship to the southwest, past the Philippines and Celebes and into the Flores Sea. There the Dutch battleship *Tromp* accosted *Emden* and warned von Müller of Holland's strict interpretation of the rules of neutrality. *Emden* could only appear in neutral waters once every three months and during each visit she could only remain for 24 hours. If they attempted to safeguard prizes or to transfer supplies or coal between ships in Dutch waters, they would be in violation of the Hague convention and subject to internment for the duration of the war. This setback was not unexpected but still a bitter disappointment to von Müller, who had hoped to use the ports of the Dutch East Indies as safe havens.

When the battleship disappeared from view, *Emden* set a course for the narrow strait between the islands of Lombok and Bali. Knowing that spies would report the passage of his distinctive three-funnelled German warship, von Müller resorted to a trick which would serve him well in the months to come. From canvas and wood the crew cobbled together a fourth funnel, so that in silhouette *Emden* looked like a typical British light cruiser. The ruse worked. The disguised German ship passed unchallenged through the strait into the emptiness of the Indian Ocean.

For the rest of August and well into September, *Emden* cruised in vain the ocean off the coast of Java and Sumatra. There were no allied ships in these quiet sea lanes. On one occasion she secretly took on coal in Langini, Sumatra, and avoided the heavy British cruiser, *Hampshire*, which had just left. Determined to stir up some action, von Müller took his ship closer to India. On September 8 his luck finally turned when he discovered and captured a neutral Greek boat carrying coal for the British. The cruiser *Emden*, which had been so quick to attack the Russians, now struck the first blow against British shipping.

Off the east coast of India in the following week, *Emden* sank seven merchantmen. She took cargoes of soap and coal as prizes, the soap being even more welcome than the coal. At the first opportunity von Müller steered his ship through a rain squall and ordered all men on deck, naked, for a soapy shower. On September 25 a droll advertisement appeared in the *Empire,* a Calcutta newspaper:

> There is no doubt that the German cruiser *Emden* had knowledge that the *Indus* was carrying 150 cases of North-West Soap Company's celebrated ELYSIUM Soap, and hence the pursuit. The men on the *Emden* and their clothes are now clean and sweet, thanks to ELYSIUM Soap. Try it!

Cartons of cigarettes and crates of spirits were gratefully confiscated. British cargoes sent to the bottom included pencils and paper, low-grade coal, one thousand tons of tea, typewriters, locomotives, Rolls Royce autos and even a thoroughbred stallion on its way to the Calcutta Racing Club. They shot the unfortunate horse before sinking the ship. Von Müller's gentlemanly style of war included the transport of captured crews on a prize ship, under the amiable command of 255-lb Lieutenant Julius Lauterbach, for eventual transfer to a neutral shore. No lifeboats were cast adrift and no lives were lost. Wearing a new coat of grey war paint, the "Swan of the East" had now become, in the words of the British, the "Gentleman-of-War."

The presence of a German marauder in the Indian Ocean was a sudden and serious problem for the British. The Admiralty ordered the cruiser *Hampshire* to destroy her. Near Rangoon von Müller eluded the British warship for the second time and steamed undetected across the Bay of Bengal. On the night of September 22 *Emden* brazenly entered the port of Madras and set the Burmah Oil tanks on fire. After an hour of bombardment she slipped away into the darkness. During the attack the garrison officers were all in town enjoying a party at the Madras Club. They were celebrating the sinking of *Emden* by the Royal Navy, as the local press had enthusiastically but erroneously reported. Much chagrined the officers returned too late to the blazing ruins of the port. Five men had been killed, including seventeen-year-old Merchant Navy Officer Cadet Joseph Fletcher. He became the first and only Merchant Marine casualty of *Emden's* career.

Alarmed that *Emden* was very much alive, the British and now the Japanese redoubled their efforts to find her. While patrolling off Colombo, *Hampshire* narrowly missed the German ship yet again. After six more captures and sinkings in the general area of Ceylon, von Müller collected all the various ships' crews into one prize and sent them away. As they departed, the merchantmen gathered on the deck railing and gave three cheers in salute to the legendary cruiser. In a mere three weeks von Müller and his mates had earned an unusual reputation for their courageous exploits. Not a single person had been harmed intentionally in all of these captures. Every crewman had been treated well and sent homeward as soon as possible. The sailors of *Emden* idolized von Müller. Even in Britain he was appreciated for his fairness and for his gallant struggle against heavy odds and an inevitable end. The *London Daily Chronicle* wrote, "The *Emden* has had a momentous cruise. The ship's company have proved their gallantry. We admire the sportsmanship of their exploits, as much as we heartily wish that the ship may soon be taken."

Emden ducked into the idyllic turquoise lagoons and sandy beaches of the Maldives, then steamed farther south to the remote British island of Diego Garcia in the Chagos Archipelago. There the crew took on coal and overhauled the ship. By flooding the port side compartments with water they were able to scrape barnacles off the exposed starboard side and vice versa, thereby regaining an extra half knot of speed. The British plantation managers on the island watched the operation with curiosity. With cheeky audacity von Müller invited them aboard for a few whisky sodas. It quickly became apparent that they were unaware of the outbreak of war. Much as von Spee had duped the lonely French and English residents of the South Pacific, von Müller and his crew enjoyed the hospitality of the island's friendly but unwitting inhabitants. After purchasing a fresh load of fish and fruit, *Emden* cheerily sailed away. Their grim pursuer, the cruiser *Hampshire*, arrived soon after – but not soon enough.

Outwitting the British warship a fourth time, *Emden* captured and sank seven more merchantmen along with their cargoes of sugar, metal, rubber, copper, tin, coal and cattle. The captured crews clambered aboard *Emden*, eager to see the famous warship firsthand. Excitement quickly turned to shock at the reality of life aboard the lone raider. Cattle, sheep, pigs, chickens and cats crammed the messy decks. Men slept in hammocks under outdoor awnings. The fittings were rusty; coal dust lurked in grimy corners. Spit and polish would have to await the captain's pleasure. In his signature style von Müller moved all the crews onto one of the captured vessels and sent them away. Then he foiled his pursuers by doubling back across the Bay of Bengal. The unsuspecting west coast of Malaya would be the scene of *Emden*'s boldest and most warlike exploit.

Emden arrived at the mouth of Penang harbour early on the morning of October 28. Disguised with the fourth funnel and a British ensign, she slipped undetected past the French destroyer *Mousquet* and the lookouts onshore. She bore down on the sleeping crew of the Russian cruiser *Zhem-*

chug and hoisted the German battle flag. On von Müller's command "*Los!*" two torpedoes rushed from the tubes. The cruiser exploded in flame and sank within minutes. Of 340 Russian sailors aboard, 89 were killed and 123 wounded. The embarrassed Russian Navy later court-martialled the captain for negligence. *Emden* turned about sharply and headed back out to sea where a shocked Captain Théroinne awaited his fate. *Emden's* expert gunners trained their ten 4.1-inch guns on *Mousquet*. The battle was short, gallant, but unequal. Captain Théroinne lost both his legs in a shellburst. He strapped his shattered body to the wheel and sank with his ship as *Emden's* thundering guns sent her to the bottom. Forty-two of his crewmen drowned with him. Von Müller lowered boats and picked up 36 French survivors, three of whom later died of their wounds. The Germans made a clean getaway and put the Frenchmen on the next steamer they met.

By the end of October von Müller and his crew had been at sea for three months, logging 30,000 miles in enemy territory with hostile warships all around them. In the space of seventy days *Emden* had sunk, captured, or plundered 21 merchantmen, destroyed two warships and terrorized Madras. She paralyzed shipping in the whole region and inflicted millions of pounds of damage. Ports in India were blocked with waiting troops. Australia and New Zealand were forced to provide strong escorts for troop convoys. By one account, there were as many as 78 British, Russian, French and Japanese warships on the hunt for *Emden*.

To evade his pursuers, von Müller headed for the Cocos Islands in the middle of the Indian Ocean. There he planned to cut the main cables to Perth in Australia, to Batavia in the Dutch East Indies and to Rodriguez Island in Mauritius. *Emden's* presence so far to the southeast would give the impression that the Germans were heading for Australia. Instead he intended to fool them after the Cocos raid by turning back into the western Indian Ocean. They would buy a little more time for raiding until the ship had to be overhauled again.

Early on the morning of November 9 *Emden* approached Direction Island, a tiny coral outcrop in the Cocos-Keeling group. The wireless operators listened for enemy traffic but the sea lanes were silent. Before dawn the crew raised the fourth funnel to deceive the lookout in the British telegraph station. The captain stopped just outside the reef and ordered the collier *Buresk* to remain out of sight. The landing party lowered themselves on ropes into two boats towed by a steam launch. Lieutenant Kurt Hellmuth von Mücke and 49 heavily armed men stormed ashore.

Pandemonium erupted inside the telegraph station. Admiral Jerram, who well knew his German foe from Tsingtao, had already warned them to prepare for an attack by *Emden*. They should watch for an unmarked cruiser disguised with a fourth funnel. A Chinese worker was the first to notice the strange warship in the early dawn. He awakened the others, including Dr. Ollerhead, who spotted the counterfeit funnel with his binoculars. As von Mücke's crew landed on the beach, the telegraph operator frantically transmitted an SOS over the wireless. The message was jammed, confirming their worst fears.

When the landing party barged through the door they met no resistance. The manager of the station smiled and extended his sardonic congratulations to the Germans. He had just received a Reuters cable with an announcement from Berlin that the Kaiser had awarded the Iron Cross to all the officers of *Emden* and to fifty of the men. Not even Captain von Müller knew yet. He was also smiling because, after the failed transmission, the operator had switched frequencies and successfully broadcast the message, "SOS EMDEN HERE," just before the Germans poured in.

Fifty-five miles to southward, an Australian troop convoy was sailing by on a stealthy voyage to Europe. Like the operators on *Emden*, the crew of *HMAS Sydney* had been silently listening to wireless transmissions. Out of the random crackle they suddenly heard an SOS from Direction Island. Under the command of Captain Glossop, *Sydney* broke off from the convoy and headed north at full speed.

Captain von Müller paced the deck and waited impatiently for the shore party to cut the cables and return to the ship. What was taking them so long? At 9:15 his lookouts spotted an ominous smoke plume and then the white ensign of a large warship. *Emden* sounded the siren to warn the shore party. Von Müller ordered the men to battle stations and prepared to fight for his life.

Sydney was a heavy cruiser, half again as large as her German opponent, more heavily armoured and two knots faster. She was armed with eight longer-range 6-inch guns to *Emden*'s ten 4.1-inch guns. Such a large cruiser would not normally have been doing escort duty but *Emden* was greatly feared.

Twenty-five minutes after spotting *Sydney*, the defiant von Müller opened fire at a range of 10,500 yards. With his lighter ship and his fighting strength reduced by fifty men, he had to seize the advantage. *Emden*'s fourth salvo knocked out *Sydney*'s fire control system and forced the Australian crews to fire the big guns manually. Undeterred, Glossop backed out of *Emden*'s range and began pounding the German ship. *Emden* took a furious beating. Von Müller tried to close the gap but Glossop kept just out of range. Screaming shells demolished funnels and masts. The electrical circuitry died and the torpedo systems failed. Ammunition couldn't reach the guns. Water poured in through gaping holes in the side. Dying men slumped to the deck in agony. At 11:20 von Müller ran his ship aground on the coral reef surrounding North Keeling Island so as, he later wrote, "to reduce it completely to a wreck in order not to make a useless sacrifice of the survivors." *Sydney* fired two more broadsides into the defenceless ship then turned away to chase down the collier *Buresk*.

During the brief lull in the fighting, medics brought *Emden*'s wounded up to the main deck. All the drinking water was gone. Von Müller gave permission for the able-bodied to swim ashore. He ordered the guns destroyed along with all the logs and useful equipment.

Several hours later *Sydney* returned with two lifeboats in tow, carrying the crew of *Buresk*. The Germans had opened the seacocks and scuttled the collier as soon as they spotted the Australian warship. Stopping 4,500 yards short of *Emden*, Glossop signalled the stricken ship to surrender. In response the Germans ran up flags in Morse code which read "No signal book." They had destroyed all their codes but the German battle flag still flew from the topmast, out of reach amid the smouldering wreckage. Glossop opened fire on the mythical raider. Five minutes later a white flag waved from the helpless ship and a sailor struggled aloft to haul down the ensign. Glossop ceased fire and finally put an end to the slaughter. The two salvoes had killed and injured many more, including most of the wounded laid out on deck.

After the SOS from Direction Island there had been no further messages. Glossop suspected that a German landing party had occupied the telegraph station. Impatient to round them up before dusk, he sent a message to von Müller, picked up a few floating survivors and sped off southward to the island, thirty miles away. He left *Emden*'s wounded to suffer the whole night long, unattended and lacking water.

The next morning, von Müller hoisted the German flag upside down to indicate distress, in the hope that a passing steamer might rescue them. *Sydney* reappeared instead and sent two lifeboats to *Emden*. They carried armed men and Dr. Ollerhead from Direction Island – the man who had spotted them the day before. One boat stood off, sailors with rifles cocked, as an officer on the other negotiated with von Müller. The Australians were still wary of the legendary *Emden*. The lifeboats eventually ferried all the survivors to *Sydney*. Captain von Müller was the last to leave.

Captain Karl Friedrich Max von Müller

The *London Daily Telegraph* later wrote: "It is almost in our heart to regret that the *Emden* has been destroyed. Von Müller has been enterprising, cool and daring in making war on our shipping, and has revealed a nice sense of humour. He has, moreover, shown every possible consideration to the crews of his prizes. There is not a survivor who does not speak well of this young German, the officers under him and the crew obedient to his orders. The war at sea will lose something of its piquancy, its humour and its interest now that the *Emden* has gone."

Glossop transferred the intrepid German captain to his old nemesis *Hampshire*, which brought him to Malta as a prisoner-of-war. Von Müller died in 1923 of the effects of malaria, an unwelcome souvenir of his early career in Africa. *Emden's* hulk remained on the North Keeling reef for many years. *Sydney* rejoined the convoy and safely delivered the Australian troops to Europe, into the ravenous maw of the Great War and the pointless carnage at Gallipoli.

The Battle of the Cocos Islands was Australia's first naval action in her history, a proud victory over the dauntless German cruiser. On *Sydney*, four men were killed and eight wounded. Of *Emden's* crew, 134 were killed and 182 taken prisoner, of whom 65 were wounded.

But where were von Mücke and the forty-nine men of his landing party? *Sydney* failed to find any trace of them. They seemed to have vanished.

> *Ein ruheloser Marsch war unser Leben*
> *Und wie des Windes Sausen heimatlos,*
> *Durchstürmten wir die kriegbewegte Erde.*
>
> Our life was like a march without a rest,
> And homeless like the soughing of the wind,
> We stormed across a world disturbed by war.

from "Wallenstein's Death"
by Friedrich von Schiller

FIFTEEN

THE BATTLE OF THE FALKLANDS

German Warships passing Icebergs off Cape Horn

Twelve ships rested at anchor off the bleak and lonely headland of Más-a-Fuera. Admiral von Spee stood on the bridge of *Scharnhorst* and inspected his squadron. Ten days earlier they had stormed out of this bay to fight the British. Their victory had been decisive, but hollow, and the taste of triumph was bittersweet. In his hand the admiral clutched a transcript of a radio message from a secret German station in Chile. Argentina and Brazil had acquiesced to Britain's request to embargo German supply ships. Tsingtao had fallen to the Japanese. Worst of all, *Emden* had been destroyed on November 9 and his favourite captain taken prisoner. In the distance he spied the familiar outlines of *Gneisenau* and *Nürnberg,* where his sons Heinrich and Otto were busy with ship repairs and coaling operations. What did fate hold in store for them?

Von Spee waited impatiently for despatches from Berlin. He had asked for permission to take the squadron back to Germany. The Pacific Ocean no longer held any strategic value; its outer ring bristled with enemies and hostile neutrals; the ships needed overhauling and ammunition; there were few targets, no friendly ports, and coal supply had become a serious problem. By contrast, the presence of the seasoned squadron in Atlantic waters would be a tremendous boon to Germany's war effort. He paced back and forth across the bridge and silently cursed the delay.

On November 16, more than two weeks after Coronel, the admiral finally ordered the squadron to weigh anchor and head south. He scuttled two smaller vessels to streamline his squadron and looked forward with optimism to running the British blockade. Two days later *Leipzig* and *Dresden* returned from a quick trip to Valparaiso with despatches from Berlin. "Make your way home…carry on cruiser warfare." The admiral was pleased. His squadron would sail to Germany.

One ship broke away from the squadron "to carry on cruiser warfare" in the lone tradition of the courageous *Emden*. *Prinz Eitel Friedrich*, the former luxury liner, sank or captured eleven merchantmen in the Pacific and the South Atlantic during the ensuing four months. On March 9, 1915, short of coal and surrounded by the enemy, Captain Thierichens interned his auxiliary cruiser at Newport News, Virginia. Two years later the Americans would use her to ferry troops to France.

The remaining colliers and the five warships – *Scharnhorst, Gneisenau, Nürnberg, Leipzig* and *Dresden* – steamed southward to the Cape. In the Gulf of Peñas, a secluded bay bounded by glaciers and bare rock, the squadron took on more coal. A small party went ashore to cut Christmas trees for the celebration in a month's time. On board *Scharnhorst*, Admiral *Graf* von Spee awarded three hundred Iron Crosses from a grateful Kaiser to his officers and men, including his own sons, for their performance at Coronel.

The squadron set off at a leisurely pace and continued south toward the notorious Cape Horn. Although the Germans could claim mastery of the eastern Pacific, and Britannia ruled the waves elsewhere, a more sinister force commanded the deeps of the Southern Ocean. An ominous swell rocked the ships; *"...the lashed deeps glitter and boil beneath...."* Helmsmen stared into a dark grey wall of cloud and a rolling, foaming, vindictive grey sea, *"...whirlwind and waves upthrown...."* Wind whistled in the stays and rose to hurricane force, shrieking and moaning. A siren lured them to the rocky cape, *"...and on the gale loosening her star-bright robe and shadowy hair poured forth her voice...."* Gusts of wind ripped foam off the angry crests. The waves towered higher and higher until they curled, menacing and mountainous, far above each tiny ship. The helmsmen clung grimly to their wheels as they crawled steeply up each watery cliff and crashed through the top. Propellers spun in the air as tons of water streamed over the bows. Down the far side they careened into a yawning, windless, glass-like trough. Aboard *Dresden* the deck cargo shifted perilously and clogged the scuppers with sacks of coal. A three-foot thick sheet of water sloshed about the deck and threatened to capsize the ship. The captain turned her into the wind and ordered the coal sacks tossed overboard, a meagre offering to an angry sea. Down below, stokers staggered about in the shifting piles of coal, risking their lives to feed the boilers and maintain speed. Five knots was the best they could do. The men on the bridge watched hypnotized as first one, then another, giant Antarctic iceberg loomed ponderously and implacably out of the gloom. Across the frenzied ocean the squadron scattered and disappeared, each ship locked in a lonely struggle for survival.

> As they rounded the cape in total disorder, a raven-haired woman, a phantom, gazed upon them from the famous cliffs, *"...fair as one flower adorning an icy wilderness"* and she called to them, *"...in language whose strange melody might not belong to earth."* But they failed to heed the warning.

On the far side the storm grudgingly abated. The ships exchanged radio messages until, one by one, they found each other and regrouped. Badly shaken but still intact, the squadron headed for refuge in the Beagle Channel. As they steamed away together, the lookouts spotted sails on the horizon. *Drummuir*, a Canadian sailing vessel carrying 2,800 tons of coal, had the misfortune at that moment to cross paths with the German squadron.

She was taken under escort and relieved of her cargo beneath the cliffs of Picton Island. The ships of the squadron, especially *Dresden*, had burned or lost a great deal of coal in the fury of the storm. They replenished their supplies from the scruffy colliers and from the elegant *Drummuir*. Then they sent her to the bottom.

Relieved to have weathered the storm and to be on the Atlantic side of Cape Horn, von Spee allowed his squadron a brief rest. While the other officers went duck hunting, he and his sons continued their natural history forays on the rocky shoreline of Tierra del Fuego. In the weeks since Coronel, a feeling of pride in their epic victory had diluted the sense of foreboding. Von Spee anticipated a rapturous welcome in Germany.

The admiral met with his captains and presented a plan that had been forming in his mind for several days. The undefended Falkland Islands lay between them and home. Why not burn the British storerooms at Port Stanley and take the governor prisoner? Three of the captains demurred, especially Captain Maerker of *Gneisenau*. They claimed the adventure would be more of a political gesture than a military necessity and that it would reveal their presence. Von Spee, never one to avoid a fight, dismissed their cautious objections. An attack on the Falklands complied with Berlin's instructions to raid coastal shipping. If there were one or two warships in the harbour, so much the better. As for a political gesture, what was wrong with that – a blow to British prestige and a morale boost for Germany after the loss of *Emden?* At minimal risk they could disrupt British supply lines in the South Atlantic. Who would be there to greet them, other than a few farmers, their sheep and some gentoo penguins? The captains reluctantly agreed. There would be little to lose as long as Port Stanley remained undefended.

On December 6, a beautiful clear summer day, the squadron steamed out of the Beagle Channel and set a course for Port Stanley. The warships rode low in the water, their holds bulging with coal but their ammunition magazines half empty. The wireless was eerily silent. Unknown to von Spee, the Chileans, along with the Argentines and the Brazilians, had been forced to shut down the German radio stations on their soil. The German intelligence network in South America was crumbling. One of the colliers brought von Spee a comforting message that there were no British warships in the Falklands. The information was correct – at that moment. The admiral had no way of knowing that a mighty armada had risen to challenge him.

❧

Just before the Battle of Coronel, the British Admiralty had belatedly sent Cradock what he needed. A strong force of five ships, including *Defence*, assembled in Montevideo under the command of Admiral Stoddart. On November 4 news of Cradock's defeat shocked the British Navy. A Chilean admiral had informed the British consul-general at Valparaiso, who relayed the message to London. Churchill reacted with characteristic vigour and swiftness. At a secret six-hour-long meeting the Admiralty hammered out the details of a comprehensive plan to defeat von Spee. Vice-Admiral Sir F. Doveton Sturdee, Chief of Staff in London, was given command of a new squadron, including the new dreadnought battlecruisers, *Invincible* and *Inflexible*. His sole objective was to seek out and destroy the German East Asia Squadron. One of his officers later commented on the popular leader, "He is a real admiral [who] doesn't seem to lose his head or get excited."

Vice-Admiral Sir F. Doveton Sturdee

Fisher, the highly capable but choleric First Sea Lord, harboured an intense dislike for the unflappable Sturdee. Despite these personal misgivings he supported Churchill's plan enthusiastically. Upon learning that the two battlecruisers were due to sail on the inauspicious date of Friday the thirteenth, Fisher insisted on a two-day advance in the schedule. When the

Plymouth dockworkers complained of the deadline, Churchill threatened to send them aboard the dreadnoughts to finish the job in battle. He suggested they could return home at some vague future point in time. The ships sailed on November 11th. Those two extra days would be crucial.

Sturdee was ordered to the South Atlantic where he would take over command of Stoddart's operations. Admiral Stoddart remained aboard his flagship *Cornwall*, the same vessel that had sailed to the rescue of Malcolm Cann and the other cadets on the grounded *Niobe* – but which had run aground herself. A British force under Admiral Patey assembled off California. Another British squadron was stationed at the Cape of Good Hope. A large Japanese force patrolled the Pacific between Fiji and the Marquesas. A French squadron cruised off West Africa. Yet another cruiser force watched over the Panama Canal. The Germans would be given no chance to escape.

Glasgow was overhauled in Rio de Janeiro and sent to the Falklands to rendezvous with Sturdee's group. The old *Canopus* wheezed into Port Stanley and beached herself at the harbour entrance where she could defend the port with her 12-inch guns. Mines lurked in the harbour; new guns bristled from strategic points. Signal stations and telephone lines honeycombed the islands. The Falkland Island Volunteers drilled with makeshift weapons and kept a close eye on the sea. After the news of Coronel, everyone in the Falklands was ready to fight, especially Governor Allardyce, Cradock's old friend. Each night his staff buried official papers and code books; each morning they dug them up again. The governor's silverware, wrapped in green baize, was buried along with tablecloths embroidered with the royal insignia. Damp penetrated the cache and stained the tablecloths green, a permanent souvenir of the Battle of the Falklands.

On December 7 Admiral Sturdee steamed into Port Stanley with his two dreadnoughts and five other powerful warships. He planned to take on coal and load up with fresh provisions. Then he would head for Cape Horn and search for *Graf* Spee in the Pacific Ocean. Neither he nor anyone else knew the whereabouts of the German squadron. To save on coal during their layover, he gave permission to *Carnarvon*, *Cornwall* and *Bristol* to douse their fires. It was a fine midsummer evening, their first night in the Falklands. Officers and men strolled up and down the two streets of the little village. Flowers bloomed in the gardens. The war in Europe seemed very remote from the Falklands, though a battle was brewing nearby.

At two o'clock the next morning, December 8, 1914, the lookout on *Gneisenau* peered into the distant northern horizon and spotted the dark outline of the Falkland Islands. Three hours later, in the first glow of dawn, *Gneisenau* and *Nürnberg* turned toward Port Stanley while the three other German warships hovered outside the harbour. The landing parties, including the two younger von Spee's, donned white uniforms and ate a good breakfast. Their orders were to land in the port, destroy the wireless, burn the harbour installations and capture the governor. The morning dawned clear and calm. Small white farmhouses dotted the hillside in a peaceful illusion. The Germans could not have picked a worse day to attack.

At 7:35 a lookout on Sapper Hill spotted two strange ships approaching the harbour and three others waiting in the distance. He immediately rang up the Falkland Island Volunteers and the watch on *Canopus*. The Volunteers lit specially prepared bonfires up and down the coast. *Canopus* raised the signal flags. The lookout on *Glasgow* spotted the flags and signalled the admiral's ship "Enemy in sight." No reply. *Glasgow* fired a gun to alert the watch on *Invincible*. Thus rudely awakened, the bleary-eyed flag lieutenant hastily buttoned his shirt and ran to Admiral Sturdee's cabin.

"*Glasgow* signals enemy in sight, sir!"

The imperturbable admiral stood in the doorway in his singlet and briefs, a white beard of shaving cream surrounding his open mouth. "Well, you had better go and get dressed," he replied. "Full steam in all ships." He calmly finished shaving and ate a hearty breakfast.

All but one of the ships were either shut down for repairs or stuck in various stages of coaling. Only the old armoured cruiser *Kent* was ready to go. She had been scheduled to coal last and carried only enough fuel for a day and a half at full speed. Sturdee ordered her to move out immediately and all other ships to prepare for action within two hours. Stokers worked furiously to feed the boilers and raise the steam pressure. At 8:00 the watch on *Glasgow* identified the two approaching ships as *Gneisenau* and *Nürnberg*. An hour later the admiral gave the venerable *Canopus* permission to fire the first shot.

Eight miles away, Captain Maerker of *Gneisenau* worried about the fires and smoke that he could see on the shore. They had obviously been spotted. As the two ships approached the harbour, the watch on *Gneisenau* identified *Kent*, *Glasgow* and the masts of at least two other warships. Though hidden by clouds of smoke, they looked uncomfortably like the distinctive tripods of British battlecruisers. Maerker ignored the lookout's misgivings. The sudden appearance of one, let alone two, dreadnoughts in the South Atlantic was highly improbable. He knew that his cruiser was more than a match for *Kent* and *Glasgow*. Perhaps the others were just auxiliaries, mere cruise ships reconfigured for war. He wired his admiral for permission to attack.

At 9:15 *Canopus* blindly opened fire with her massive 12-inch guns. A low point of land obstructed her view of the attackers. An observer on the hilltop relayed the result back to the gunners. The second salvo came very close to *Gneisenau* and startled the Germans. The huge shells seemed to be coming from nowhere. The harbour was obviously defended – and strongly. Maerker signalled the bad news to von Spee, who quickly ordered the two ships to break off the attack and rejoin the squadron. The admiral still did not know that two battlecruisers were bottled up in the harbour trying to raise steam – ships that, once at sea, could easily catch and annihilate his entire squadron. Had he known how vulnerable the British were at that moment, he might have ambushed them with a devastating enfilade as they threaded the harbour minefield, one by one. Even so, it would have been a risky and desperate move and it would have been almost impossible to elude the guns of *Canopus*.

By 9:45 all the British ships except *Bristol* were ready. The old *Kent* steamed well ahead of the pack. Sturdee ordered *Kent* and *Glasgow* to give chase while the other ships carefully negotiated the minefield in single file: *Inflexible* first, followed by the flagship *Invincible*, Admiral Stoddart in *Cornwall* and *Carnarvon* in the rear. *Bristol* and *Macedonia* broke off in the other direction to hunt down the two German colliers.

As the six warships emerged from the harbour, the officers of the watch on *Leipzig* confirmed – to their horror and dismay – that two of them were indeed battlecruisers. Von Spee understood in an instant that he was hopelessly outmatched. The two modern dreadnoughts were faster and bigger and their guns were almost twice as large as those on *Scharn-horst* and *Gneisenau*. Ship for ship, the other four British vessels were more than equal to his three light cruisers. Short of ammunition and vastly out-gunned, he knew that his only option was to flee. He looked ruefully at the clock and calculated that the British had at least eight hours of daylight to hunt him down. He thought about the drag on the hulls, fouled after months at sea; he worried about pushing the boilers to the limit; and he regretted his decision to load up with coal. Squinting into the bright clear sky, he cursed his luck and prayed to God for a squall to hide in. How could such a simple plan have gone so horribly wrong? What hubris, what vaulting ambition, what siren call had enticed him to his doom? When *Gneisenau* and *Nürnberg* rejoined the group, he bitterly ordered all five ships to steam southeast at top speed.

Sturdee gave his six ships the stirring order for a general chase. With their 12-inch guns trained forward on the enemy, *Inflexible* and *Invincible* roared along at 26 knots and leaped ahead of the others. Bow waves curled away from the stems; the seas astern mounded high to the aft decks. A bitter wind blew but the sun shone brightly over the sea as the ships raced into battle. Crowds gathered on the hilltops and cheered their sailors on. To allow *Cornwall* and *Carnarvon* time to catch up, the admiral ordered the dreadnoughts to slow down. This prolonged the chase and allowed the men time for an early lunch. Those still in coaling gear washed and changed and sat down to a big meal.

The German captains glumly ordered up meals for their own men, too, not knowing when they might have another chance or, worse, fearing that this might indeed be their last chance. After the meal the captains of the various ships mustered their men on deck and warned them that the fighting would be fierce. At 11:45 the British trailed only 18,500 yards astern. Von Spee ordered the battle flags run up on all ships. Drums rolled, bugles blared and men ran to their battle stations. Each sailor slipped a red silk ribbon over his head and tucked into his shirt the small disc bearing his name. The admiral ordered his ships into battle formation – *Gneisenau* and *Nürnberg* in a column to port, *Scharnhorst* and *Dresden* to starboard, *Leipzig* following astern of the starboard column.

As soon as Sturdee saw the German battle flags, he ordered full speed ahead for all ships. The powerful battlecruisers quickly closed the gap. At 16,000 yards buglers on *Invincible* blew the call to action. Signalmen hoisted the flags to "Open fire" and the battle began.

Inflexible fired the first salvo at the trailing *Leipzig*. At this extreme range and at a speed of 26 knots, the British dreadnought fired in haphazard fashion. For fifteen minutes she scored no hits although shells burst in the water all around *Leipzig*. For one brief moment von Spee imagined the plight of the doomed Admiral Cradock when he bravely turned, against the setting sun, to face the German ships. He thought of Otto on *Nürnberg* and Heinrich on *Gneisenau*. Then he grimly ordered the two armoured cruisers to engage the enemy as long as possible, so that the three light cruisers might escape. One son would fight and the other would flee.

To howls of derision from the British sailors, *Leipzig*, *Nürnberg* and *Dresden* immediately turned southward and pulled away from the two larger cruisers. Having anticipated such a split, Sturdee sent *Cornwall*, *Glasgow* and *Kent* to chase them down. With their powerful 6-inch guns, each of these ships outclassed the Germans and their shorter-range 4.1-inch guns. Even the smallest ship, *Glasgow*, was bigger and more heavily armed than the German light cruisers.

At 1:30 in the afternoon von Spee ordered *Scharnhorst* and *Gneisenau* to turn hard to port. They would attempt to close the gap quickly and to find a chink in the British armour. The British ships veered away on a parallel course and maintained the range at 14,500 yards. *Scharnhorst* signalled "Open fire" even though she lay at the limit of her range and the guns were pointing skyward. Within minutes German sharpshooters scored hits on *Inflexible*.

The British battlecruiser's heavy armour suffered only minimal damage. Their guns could easily reach the German ship and soon the 12-inch shells were wreaking fearful destruction on *Scharnhorst*. The British increased the range to 16,500 yards, just outside the range of the German guns. Von Spee pretended to flee southward, drawing *Inflexible* with him. Then he turned back sharply, reducing the range so that his guns could find their targets again. Despite the superb discipline and marksmanship of the

Scharnhorst gunners, the German shells were too light to inflict any serious damage. Gun smoke hampered the vision of spotters on both sides.

For a few brief moments the men on the warships, both British and German, glanced in amazement at a vision from a bygone era. On the eastern horizon a full-rigged French sailing ship scudded before the freshening breeze, her white hull and bleached sails gleaming in the afternoon sun. Blissfully unaware of the war, her crew had sailed the remote southern oceans for months. They suddenly found themselves on the brink of a ferocious battle at sea. Appalled by the din and the smoke, her captain turned about and fled northward.

Out of sight over the eastern horizon another sailing ship, Endurance, had just left South Georgia on her epic voyage to Antarctica. Long after the Battles of Coronel and the Falklands, Captain Ernest Shackleton would be justly remembered, not only for enduring two harrowing years in polar seas– an incredible story of survival – but for bringing every single one of his men back alive. The German squadron would not be so lucky.

At 3:15 von Spee must have realized his situation was hopeless. He gamely signalled to Captain Maerker on *Gneisenau*, "I am all right so far. Have you hit anything?" Maerker replied, "The smoke prevents all observation." After a short pause von Spee graciously allowed, "You were right after all."

A shell smashed into one of *Scharnhorst's* propellers. She yawed crazily to port, reducing the range to 11,500 yards. The startled British backed off but lowered their gun barrels and began to fire with deadly accuracy. Within minutes *Scharnhorst* lost two of her three funnels. Fires spread rapidly throughout the ship. Shells knocked out each of the guns, one by one. By 4:00 von Spee sensed that his ship had only minutes left to live. In his last signal, as *Scharnhorst* drew the British fire, he ordered *Gneisenau* to "Endeavour to escape if your engines are still intact."

Then *Scharnhorst* turned toward her other attacker, *Invincible*, as if for a torpedo strike. A few salvoes from the British guns stopped her dead. Admiral Sturdee signalled to his adversary to surrender. There was no reply. The German battle flag still flew from the top of the mast. *Scharnhorst* listed to port as the last gun fired. The bow slowly disappeared from view and the screws lifted out of the water. A few men scrambled onto the stern and jumped over the side. At 4:17 *Scharnhorst* rolled over, pitched on her nose and plunged swiftly into the depths.

On *Gneisenau* Lieutenant Heinrich von Spee stared in disbelief as *Scharnhorst* and his father disappeared from the face of the earth. He watched with growing dread as three British ships stormed past the survivors and turned their full attention to his mates and himself. *Carnarvon* had finally caught up to the battlecruisers and joined in the furious bombardment of the lone German cruiser. Captain Maerker could not escape but neither would he surrender. Although the ship took a tremendous beating the gun crews maintained discipline and stubbornly kept firing. They struck *Invincible* three times. Guns roared, shells screamed overhead and hot metal splinters whined across the decks. Shell after shell took their toll on the Germans. Under the deafening barrage, pigs and geese scurried and slid among the bodies and the smouldering wreckage.

At 4:47 the three British ships ceased fire when the Germans struck their battle flags. In reality, Captain Maerker had lost his third and last ensign in the gunfire and had no intention of surrendering. His remaining guns blazed away. In response to an order to surrender, a German salvo struck *Invincible* amidships. The British reluctantly resumed the unequal fight and reduced *Gneisenau* to a smoking ruin. At 5:45, lacking steam in the boilers, out of ammunition and suffering six hundred casualties, Captain Maerker gave the order to scuttle the ship. She listed and shuddered as the torpedo tubes filled with water. Three hundred men jumped overboard as the ship went down with her defiant captain. A German sailor waved a flag from the stern until *Gneisenau* sank out of sight.

The British ships lowered the rescue boats. When *Carnarvon* responded too slowly, Sturdee lost his composure for the first and only time and angrily signalled, "Lower all your boats at once." In the frigid Antarctic seas, the survivors from *Scharnhorst* had already succumbed to exposure, as did many of the men from *Gneisenau*. In the words of a midshipman aboard *Carnarvon*, "It was shocking to see the look on their faces as they drifted away and we could do nothing to save them. A great many were drowned…. We could see them floating past, a horrible sight."

While *Scharnhorst* and *Gneisenau* were still locked in a losing battle, the three German light cruisers raced for the straits to the southwest. *Dresden* led the trio, with *Nürnberg* to port and *Leipzig* to starboard. *Glasgow*, *Cornwall* and *Kent* followed in hot pursuit. The faster British ships gradually closed the gap until the range narrowed to 12,000 yards. Captain Luce on *Glasgow* relished his chance to avenge Coronel. At 2:45 in the afternoon he gave the order to fire.

The feisty captains of *Leipzig* and *Nürnberg* realized there was no hope of escape. They turned broadside and returned fire. As they did so, they watched in dismay as *Dresden*, commanded by Captain von Lüdecke, the former merchant mariner, plowed straight ahead at top speed.

Captain Luce had to make a difficult decision. The afternoon was wearing away and a patchy grey haze obscured the western horizon. *Dresden* was almost as fast as *Glasgow*. He might lose her in fog or in darkness. If he chose to pursue her, there was a chance that *Leipzig* and *Nürnberg* might outrun *Kent* and *Cornwall,* who were somewhat slower than *Glasgow*. To lose all three German ships would be a disaster and a huge embarrassment. Reluctantly he let *Dresden* escape and concentrated his fire on the other two ships.

Leipzig and *Glasgow* exchanged salvos from afar but every time *Leipzig* turned broadside to fire, the range decreased between the two ships. Thirty seconds elapsed between the flash of the guns and the fall of the shot, a time that passed in agonizing slowness to spotters with binoculars. *Cornwall* caught up to *Glasgow* and joined in the bombardment of *Leipzig*. *Kent* chased after *Nürnberg*. Both sides battered each other relentlessly. Amid the noise and the smoke, the officers on the bridge of *Leipzig* watched *Dresden* disappear into a heavy bank of cloud. Perhaps Captain Haun allowed himself a brief moment of doubt, a twinge of regret, as he turned to face his foe.

Fifteen minutes later, *Leipzig* took a hit below the waterline and her speed diminished to 20 knots. The British closed in. Aboard *Leipzig* determined gunners pummelled both *Cornwall* and *Glasgow* as the range decreased. Their hopes rose as darkness approached but ammunition was running low.

Then the British switched to inflammable lyddite explosives. Fires ignited on *Leipzig* and raged out of control. The ammunition ran out. Captain Haun fired torpedoes at both ships but missed. The British trained a searchlight on *Leipzig* and called on the burning ship to surrender. The stricken vessel sent no signal but the battle flag, ringed with flames, still flew from the mast. The two British ships continued to fire at the helpless Germans. According to the improbable account of a surviving German officer, "Several of the dying asked whether the flag was still flying and were comforted by the assurance that it would be kept flying till the ship sank." At 7:20 Captain Haun ordered the men to abandon ship. With difficulty they lowered the lifeboats from the listing vessel. A shell hit one of them as *Glasgow*, under the vengeful Captain Luce, kept shooting. Two huge explosions tore *Leipzig* apart. She keeled over and sank an hour later under the glare of British searchlights. Only eighteen men survived.

In the other race, *Kent* gained steadily on *Nürnberg*. The British stokers worked furiously to drive the steam pressure to dangerous new highs. They chopped up ladders, lockers and chicken coops and threw the wood into the blazing furnace. The straining boilers thrust the ship two knots over the limit. The Germans did the same but, with a full load of coal and a hull roughened by months at sea, they just could not pull ahead. By late afternoon *Kent* raised the gun barrels skyward and began to fire. The Germans responded with full force.

The two ships blasted each other amid a terrifying din. Shells whined in the air and crashed into *Kent*. A cordite charge landed in the ammunition hoist and dropped down the passage to the startled crew. A fresh load of shells lay on the hoist beneath the flaming cordite. Sergeant Charles Mayes picked up the burning charge with his bare hands, threw it clear of the other shells, closed the watertight doors to the magazine and flooded the compartment with a fire hose. Without his presence of mind *Kent* would have blown sky-high and vanished like *Good Hope* at Coronel.

Within minutes the more powerful British 6-inch guns began to take an awful toll. At 5:35 two boilers burst on *Nürnberg*. She was doomed. Within half an hour the masts and funnels had collapsed and only two guns were still firing. By 7:00 the last guns fell silent and a furnace of flame surrounded the conning tower. To prevent further carnage Captain von Schönberg struck the battle flag. They lowered a damaged lifeboat but it sank immediately. Bobbing heads and faint cries filled the sea and slowly faded away in the frigid Antarctic waters. Only two of *Kent*'s lifeboats survived the ferocious gunfight unscathed. Twenty frantic minutes passed before the others were patched. At 7:27, just as the remaining rescue boats hit the water, *Nürnberg* rolled abruptly to starboard and sank. Ten hours after the first shot, the Battle of the Falklands had ended.

No one survived from *Scharnhorst*. The British rescued about two hundred men from *Gneisenau,* although many of them died that night of their wounds and exposure. Eighteen survived from the crew of *Leipzig* and a mere seven from *Nürnberg*. Of the 2,500 sailors who had breakfasted on the German ships that morning only 182 – and the crew of *Dresden* – remained alive. The British lost six men.

Neither Otto nor Heinrich von Spee survived. The Iron Crosses disappeared with them into the depths along with the carefully preserved botanical specimens, the Christmas trees and thousands of red silk ribbons, each carefully inscribed with a man's name.

> The Queen of the Southern Ocean *"wept and clasped her hands… and she unveiled her bosom."* She embraced the sailors in her palace beneath the waves, where *"the green and glancing shadows of the sea did play o'er its marmoreal depth."*

In the space of a month the German East Asia Squadron had sailed from a smashing victory to crushing defeat. At Coronel and Cocos-Keeling and the Falklands, almost four thousand sailors had lost their lives. In thousands of homes across Germany and Britain, wives and parents mourned the loss at sea of their loved ones and left the celebration of glorious victories to others. They were not alone in their grief – before the Great War ended in 1918, ten million people would die.

As the battlecruisers steamed back to the Falklands that night, some of the survivors sat down to dinner with the victors. One British officer observed, "We were all good friends after the fight and both agreed that we did not want to fight at all, but had to." Admiral Sturdee wrote to the *London Gazette*, "I deeply regret the needless sacrifice of so many lives by an enemy who displayed such bravery, skill and endurance; after the ships were defeated and sinking and in no position to make any further defence, they did not surrender." Lord Fisher refused permission to publish the letter.

One ship remained to taunt the British: *Dresden*, a reluctant addition to the East Asia Squadron, and her captain, the unwilling warrior von Lüdecke. Would she become a folk hero to the Germans? Lord Fisher was furious at Sturdee for allowing her to escape. After the war the resentful Sea Lord allowed that, "No one in history was ever kicked on to a pedestal of fame like Sturdee. If he had been allowed to pack all the shirts he wanted to take…[he] would have been looking for von Spee still!"

※

Nova Scotians never forgot the loss of their sons in battle. On August 24, 1928, the *Yarmouth Telegram* advertised a film: "The greatest naval picture ever produced anywhere: a pictorial reenactment of two naval battles, battles which shall live for all time in the memory of Britishers the world over, the battles of Coronel and the Falkland Islands showing at the Majestic Theatre in Yarmouth. The picture is amazing in its realism. It has been produced with a prodigality of material and minuteness of detail made possible only through the cooperation of the British Admiralty. Thirty-eight ships from dreadnoughts to dockyard tugs were used. Admirals Fisher, Sturdee, Cradock and von Spee, who were the central figures in the stirring naval drama, are worthily represented here by actors who have the dignity which the great event calls for."

※

Exactly twenty-five years after the Battle of the Falklands, at the beginning of another world war, the German pocket battleship *Graf Spee* cruised the South Atlantic and Indian Oceans under the command of Captain Hans Langsdorff. He sank nine Allied ships, totalling 50,000 tons, and treated the captured crews with a courtesy worthy of Captain von Müller of *Emden*. At dawn on December 13, 1939, *Graf Spee* fought a pitched battle with three British cruisers and escaped to the safe harbour of neutral Montevideo. Langsdorff negotiated a 72-hour layover with the Uruguayans and prepared to face the cordon of Allied warships waiting for him outside territorial waters. He envisioned a glorious battle in the tradition of their namesake admiral but in this ambition he was thwarted. Unwilling to suffer a humiliating defeat in a battle at sea, Hitler ordered the captain to scuttle his ship in the harbour. On December 17, 1,500 miles north of the old admiral's watery grave, *Graf Spee* was scuttled and the crew interned. Alone in his cabin, Captain Langsdorff shot himself.

SIXTEEN

SHIPS OF THE DESERT

Ayesha leaving Direction Island

A gibbous moon shone high over the Indian Ocean. The morning star gleamed brightly in the east. In the quiet hour before dawn, the moon and the pale blue sky illuminated the backs of sailors as they clambered down ropes from a warship. Each man dropped into a dinghy with a muffled thud. Water slapped against the steel hull as rough arms held the vessels apart. The low rumble of the ship's engines mingled with the hiss of the steam launch. After the last man sat down and set his rifle between his knees, Lieutenant Kurt Hellmuth von Mücke tapped the helmsman on the shoulder and ordered him to cast off. The palm trees of Direction Island beckoned in the distance. He looked up to Captain von Müller on the bridge of *Emden* and touched a finger to his white pith helmet in farewell. In his left hand he gripped his sword. Unknown to either man, this day, November 9, 1914, would be the warship's last.

Von Mücke and forty-nine heavily armed men stormed ashore, bent on destruction of the British telegraph station on Direction Island. Their mission started well enough. Mr. Farrant, the station manager, had greeted them with a wry smile and grandly announced that the Kaiser had awarded them Iron Crosses. The serious young lieutenant looked nonplussed but quickly turned to the problem at hand. They demolished all the equipment in the telegraph office and began to haul down the wireless mast beside the tennis court. Farrant stood guard by the net. He shouted and waved his arms wildly at the Germans. Destroying the office was "a damned nuisance" but damaging his tennis court was unacceptable. Von Mücke thought that the Englishman was challenging him to a game. Feeling somewhat overdressed in sword and pith helmet, he politely declined. In a sporting gesture he ordered his men to drop the mast carefully. Of greater concern was their inability to find the three marine cables. The operation bogged down and they lost precious time. They had only managed to locate and cut the cable to Perth when *Emden*'s siren surprised them.

The Germans ran back to the jetty and cast off in haste. The steam launch towed the two dinghies astern and chugged ahead at full throttle. Von Mücke stood anxiously in the bow and watched *Emden* hoist her battle flag and pull away fast. The lieutenant stared at the disappearing warship and shook his head in disbelief. There was no way they could catch her. *Emden* fired the first broadside. Her distant opponent replied with a salvo of five shells. Von Mücke grimly signalled the helmsman to turn about and head back to Direction Island.

To fend off an assault from the unknown warship, the Germans positioned their four Maxim machine guns on the beach overlooking the jetty. They ran their ensign up the flagpole and placed the twenty-nine protesting Englishmen under guard. Then they turned their attention to the battle at sea. Von Mücke stood on the station rooftop to get a view above the coconut palms. Within a very short time it became clear that *Emden* was doomed. With each distant salvo the Englishmen cheered like spectators at a football match. The Germans became more and more glum. One of them asked for pen and paper so that he might write to his mother. The English took pity on the well-mannered Germans, who now faced certain defeat and imprisonment. They chatted amiably and offered sandwiches, cigarettes and cold beer.

Von Mücke's eyes narrowed as he strained to observe the two combatants, locked in unequal battle on the northern horizon. He and his men were marooned on a remote enemy island with nothing but the clothes they wore and the weapons they carried. Their ship was being annihilated and their comrades killed, including perhaps the captain he idolized. In a few short hours their assailant would arrive to hunt them down. Between them and safety lay thousands of miles of ocean, patrolled by the greatest naval power in the world. Beyond the ocean lay Africa, the Middle East and India – hostile lands, inhospitable and, to him, unknown. His options were clear: to fight a hopeless ground battle against a vastly superior force, to surrender and spend the rest of the war in prison, or to flee and face the hazards of a long journey home. The 33-year-old lieutenant – outgoing and audacious, as tall, slim and handsome as an old-fashioned storybook hero – knew instinctively what he should do.

He had to act fast. Within a few short hours they would have to find a boat and provision it with water, food and equipment. They had to leave quickly, so that morning would find them out of sight of the island. The motor launch and the two dinghies were too small for the journey. What they needed was an ocean-going vessel. By amazing good fortune the solution to their predicament lay at anchor in the lagoon – an elegant three-masted schooner. The Germans had planned to scuttle her but luckily they had run out of time. Her name was *Ayesha*, named after the favourite wife of the prophet Mohammed. She was 90 feet long, 97 tons, painted white and she held berths for five. In the past she had carried copra from Cocos-Keeling to Batavia two or three times a year. Although not particularly old, she now rested in genteel retirement, decaying slowly in the shallow lagoon. The sails had lain in lockers for years and were mildewed though serviceable. The wooden hull looked rotten but *Ayesha* was their only hope. Von Mücke commandeered her without hesitation.

The station personnel parted with half their provisions and enough drinking water to last a month. As the Germans busily loaded the flimsy craft, the Englishmen drank beer on the jetty, offered advice on winds and currents and debated the best route to Europe. What jolly good sport!

Von Mücke loudly announced his intention to sail to German East Africa. No stranger to subterfuge, *Emden's* wily first lieutenant had been the first to propose the ruse of a fourth funnel and the tactics of criss-crossing the ocean.

The steam launch towed *Ayesha* carefully through the reef and past the surf line, leaving the coral beach and the coconut palms in her wake. The Englishmen waved to the intrepid crew and shouted three hurrahs. Beyond the reef the Kaiser's newest and smallest warship set sail with fifty men aboard. Her white hull and billowing sails glowed in the setting sun and the German ensign fluttered from the mast. For a few quiet minutes, as the "pirate" ship faded into twilight, the Englishmen watched this golden vision from *Treasure Island.* Then they set about repairing the station. Using carefully hidden spare parts they resumed communications with Singapore that evening and restored the Perth connection a day later. There was no damage to the tennis court.

Von Mücke set a westerly course until the stars came out and the island disappeared into darkness. Another landing party had just arrived at the telegraph station, this time a group of Australian sailors from *Sydney,* the cruiser that had destroyed *Emden* a few hours earlier. Farrant told the disappointed officer that the Germans had left for East Africa on a sailboat.

Relieved to have made a clean escape, von Mücke abandoned his ruse of sailing to Africa and ordered a sharp turn to starboard. By the light of a kerosene lamp he inspected a page-size map of the Indian Ocean and set a course for Padang on the coast of Sumatra, eight hundred nautical miles to the northeast. The wooden masts creaked in a comforting old-fashioned way as the sails pulled them along in the starlight. At midnight the moon rose above the horizon and shone off the starboard bow.

Men lay everywhere – squeezed into berths, jammed into the hold and draped over the deck. They had plenty of food but soon discovered to their dismay that the leaky bilge had fouled the drinking water. In the days to come they replenished the supply by collecting water during cloudbursts.

The officers had sailed a schooner once before, as young cadets, but the seamen had no experience whatsoever. One generation after *Elisabeth* sailed past the thundering cone of Krakatau, the ancient lore of wood and canvas had wasted away. When the wind freshened before each blow they slowly and carefully shortened sail. But one afternoon a storm caught them unawares. Sails flapped and snapped in the sudden squall. Men aloft struggled to reef them amid wildly careening spars and booms. The mizzen topsail landed on the gaff arm and ripped apart. Huge waves threatened to wash them all overboard. In the hold the frail planking bulged and dripped with each pounding from the angry sea just inches away. Dark clouds blackened the sky and turned day into night. Thunder rumbled without pause. Ragged lightning bolts crashed down all around them. In the middle of the night the wind settled down but the vessel wallowed dangerously in the heavy swell. St. Elmo's fire danced a foot above each masthead. Their luck held. Despite her fragile sails and the rotten hull, Mohammed's "wife" survived the fierce beating. A famous lady in her own right, she defied the sea goddess and saved their lives.

Day followed day in the baking tropical sun, days punctuated only by storms and the respite afforded by nightfall. A week passed, then another. Often becalmed and adrift in the southeasterly current, *Ayesha* never sailed faster than eight knots and averaged only two. At last they spotted the Mentawai Islands off the west coast of Sumatra and sailed through Selat Bungalaut, the "Seaflower Strait." With no more than the small map, a compass, a faulty chronometer and the stars to guide them, the astonishingly skilful navigators had steered straight to their destination. The Dutch destroyer *Lynx* shadowed them until they arrived in Emmahaven harbour at Padang on November 27, exhausted but fit after eighteen days at sea. Upon their arrival, the captain of *Lynx* confirmed their worst fears about *Emden* but reassured them that von Müller and more than half of their comrades, though imprisoned, were still alive.

The Dutch authorities tried to intern *Ayesha* as a prize of war but von Mücke stoutly insisted she was a warship and thus entitled to leave. He pointed to their rifles and the four Maxim machine guns bristling on the deck. The Dutch eventually agreed but warned him to leave within 24 hours and not to return for three months. Johann Schild, the German consul in Padang, arranged for provisions and assistance during their short stay. Von Mücke slipped him a piece of paper with the latitude, longitude and approximate date of a secret rendezvous on the high seas. He asked the consul to pass the note to a friendly steamer captain.

Shaved, well-fed and refreshed, the men squeezed back into the schooner the next day, along with ten live pigs. At dusk they sailed into the setting sun. Late at night two voices hailed them from a rowboat. Two brawny men pulled strongly on the oars and caught up to *Ayesha* as she drifted in a light wind. They were German sailors from one of the steamers and they wanted to join the crew from the famous *Emden*. Von Mücke welcomed them aboard.

Bedevilled by fickle winds they tacked slowly back and forth along the coast of Sumatra, through the Mentawai Islands and into the open Indian Ocean. At the rendezvous point they drifted under close-reefed sails, scanned the horizon impatiently and waited for an unknown steamer to arrive. Each plume of smoke prompted anxious debate – friendly, neutral or foe? The days dragged on and stretched into a week. Perhaps the steamer, if there was one, had missed them and travelled on. How much longer should they wait? December 8 came and went like any other. On the other side of the globe four shattered German ships sank to the sea floor. Only *Dresden* and *Prinz Eitel Friedrich* still roamed at large. The men of the "warship" *Ayesha* were now, unwittingly, one of the last fighting remnants of the East Asia Squadron.

In thick fog and heavy rain on December 14, a steamer loomed out of the murk. To his astonishment, Captain Minkwitz of the German collier *Choising* found the schooner exactly at the coordinates scribbled on his piece of paper. Across the rolling swells he shouted to the bearded, half-naked crew to wait for better conditions in the morning. But the weather deteriorated rapidly. That night a gale struck them with malevolent force, the worst onslaught since the storm a month earlier. The wind ripped the sails to shreds. Helpless before the driving sea, *Ayesha* drifted in darkness toward the treacherous reefs off Pagai Island.

Ayesha tussled with the sea goddess but her good luck held and she dodged the reefs. After two more days the storm abated and allowed the sailors to transfer to *Choising*. They lowered the ensign and removed everything of value, including the weapons, the steering wheel, the figurehead and the surviving pigs. Then they drilled holes in the hull and abandoned ship. The crew stood by the deck railing and watched *Ayesha* settle into the water stern first. The bow plunged abruptly downward, the iron ballast rolled forward and she sank like a rock with her rudder in the air. *Choising* dipped her flag in salute and the men gave her three heartfelt cheers. She had carried them safely for 37 days across 1,700 miles of ocean.

The collier, a fire-damaged old rustbucket, could barely manage a speed of eight knots. Salt water sloshed around the holds in an ongoing effort to contain a smouldering coal fire. She would be easy pickings for a British patrol. Von Mücke leafed through a stack of recent newspapers and pondered his options. Tsingtao had fallen…now all of Asia was either neutral or in the hands of the allies. German East Africa under siege… there would be no safe haven anywhere on that huge continent either. He searched in vain for news of the German Navy. Perhaps, he thought, it might be possible to reconnect with the rest of the East Asia Squadron. It was a wild idea for, the last he heard, they had just defeated the British off the coast of Chile. He folded the papers, climbed the stairs to the bridge and asked the captain for news of the squadron.

Captain Minkwitz hesitated, then turned and looked out to sea as he spoke. Von Mücke listened in stunned silence. All the main ships were gone and more than 2,400 German sailors had died. The lieutenant stepped outside onto the windy deck, clutched the railing and stared into the ocean's unforgiving, empty grey vastness. He thought of his lost comrades and felt very much alone.

Fifty-one men looked up to him for leadership and guidance. Upon his shoulders rested the legacy of the lost squadron and the challenge of their own survival. They had lasted this far but what next? He recalled a short news item about the Middle East – Turkey and Britain were now at war. He knew that the Turks had formed a loose alliance with the Arabs and had built railroads, with German help, deep into the Arabian Desert. A far-fetched idea took root in his mind. If Turkey was now a German ally, it might be possible for his crew to sail into the Red Sea, cross the Arabian Desert to the Baghdad railroad and then take a train to Constantinople. This risky venture seemed to be their only viable option. The Red Sea was not too far away. Crossing the desert would allow them to avoid capture aboard the sluggish collier. But what about the Arabs? The various tribes were fractious and disunited. What kind of welcome would they offer a small band of Germans?

Following the demise of the German squadron, the collier *Choising* could serve no better purpose than to bring the men of *Emden* home. But first she had to negotiate the busy shipping lanes around Ceylon and India and to pass under the vigilant eye of British patrols in the Gulf of Aden and the Red Sea. Captain Minkwitz searched for a disguise in Lloyd's Register of English ships sold to foreign countries. He found the name *Shenir*, a steamer registered in Genoa. This was convenient because Italy was more or less neutral at that time. But they needed an Italian flag. With pots of blue and yellow paint a sailor with artistic talent dyed a green curtain to the correct shade. He stitched it to panels of red and white bunting and painted a coat of arms in the centre. The flag and the new name served them well for no one accosted them and the real *Shenir* never appeared.

On January 8 they safely reached Al Hudaydah on the eastern shore of the Red Sea. Two officers from *"Shenir"* jumped at the chance to join the adventure. At the same time von Mücke was pleased to leave one trouble-maker behind. The *Emden* landing party, now swollen to fifty-three, waved farewell to Captain Minkwitz and rowed to the beach in four lifeboats.

Hostile Arabs with levelled rifles confronted the intruders on the bare muddy shore. The German sailors had entered a strange new world and von Mücke feared he might have made a terrible mistake. Perhaps these Yemeni tribesmen knew nothing of Turks and Germans or, worse, they might even be enemies. After some initial unfriendliness, confusion and miscommunication in various languages, it became apparent that Al Hudaydah indeed lay in the hands of the Turks and that these Arabs were their allies. With the help of a gold sovereign – and the threat of the machine guns – he persuaded the Yemenis to be German allies too. By the time they walked into the city they had attracted a retinue of eight hundred Arabs, dancing, singing and shooting their ancient rifles.

They remained in the area for two frustrating months. The nearest railhead lay at Al Ula, more than a thousand miles distant across a hostile desert. To travel on the Red Sea was equally difficult because French and

British gunboats patrolled the waters. Von Mücke began to regret his decision to leave the relative safety of *"Shenir."* Their quarters in the Turkish garrison were reasonably comfortable but many men fell ill with typhus, dysentery or malaria. The Turkish authorities, for their own obscure reasons, tried to prevent the Germans from leaving. On one occasion they did attempt to cross the desert with a caravan of mules, donkeys and horses – but no camels. After ten days in the trackless desert they made it only as far as Sana'a, a march of one hundred miles. Plagued with illness among his men and lacking reliable supplies of food and water, von Mücke abandoned the hopeless venture.

Before leaving the citadel of Sana'a he rode around it in growing amazement. It had been built to withstand attacks from both Turks and Arabs. The fortified outer perimeter enclosed three compounds – Arab, Turkish and Jewish – each one separated from the other by high walls. Within the compounds each sturdy brick dwelling protected a family from its neighbours – a stronghold behind a wall inside a fort – an image of mankind's barbaric past or a disconcerting vision of the future.

When they arrived back in Al Hudaydah he procured two *sambuqs*, forty-foot long Arab dhows rigged with triangular lateen sails. On March 14 the Germans returned at last to their familiar element and sailed north along the coast of the Red Sea. Lice and cockroaches infested the boats; many of the men were still sick. They shed their pith helmets and wrapped their heads in the native fashion. Thus disguised they weaved through a maze of shallow reefs and avoided enemy patrols. One night a *sambuq* struck a reef in heavy weather and sank. In desperation the men on the remaining boat lit a fire on the wooden deck. The survivors swam through the waves toward the flickering light and dragged the sick behind them. They recovered all the weapons, including the machine guns, but lost all the medical supplies. Attracted by the light, another Arab *sambuq* approached out of the darkness. If the Germans hoped for rescue they were quickly disappointed. When the Arabs saw the white faces they turned away in disdain. They were men of the hostile Idrissi tribe, in revolt against the Turks and their allies. Neither persuasion nor bribery could induce them to return.

The lone *sambuq* was extremely overcrowded and many of the men were ill. Despite these difficulties they covered the three hundred miles from Al Hudaydah in only four days. Von Mücke took a chance and landed at Al Qunfudhah. To his relief the local Turks welcomed him and provided them with a larger boat. They sailed on for a further five days to Al Lith, at the northern end of the protective archipelago of reefs. Here they decided to attempt another crossing of the desert. After much hard bargaining with the Sheik of Al Lith they hired a caravan of camels and made ready to march to Jiddah, a distance of one hundred miles up the coast.

On March 27 typhus claimed the life of Seaman Keil, their first casualty in the four and a half months since the loss of *Emden*. A party of men rowed a short distance offshore and gave him the dignity of a military burial at sea, complete with a rifle salute of three volleys.

The next evening a caravan of ninety camels set forth under the light of a full moon. Each of the sailors perched on his mount in wonderment and swayed in his saddle to the unaccustomed motion. The stars of a clear Arabian night twinkled overhead. The bright moon cast mysterious dark shadows across the dunes.

Moonlight March through Ras al Aswad

The novelty quickly wore off. They spent fourteen to eighteen hours a day in their creaking saddles, mainly in the relative coolness and safety of night. Widely scattered oases offered a chance for rest and refreshment although the water was vile. To reach it they lowered leather bags into pits about fifteen metres deep. Contaminated with dead animals, the brackish, evil-smelling brown fluid swarmed with insects. Dinner was more palatable – rice and mutton cooked over fires of scrub wood. In the daytime they slept under straw mats, stretched over thorn bushes to give protection from the sun. Several times daily the Arab guides offered their prayers to God. They faced north toward the holy city of Mecca, beyond the hills just a few miles away.

Tethered from nose to tail, the camels plodded along slowly in the darkness. The naval ensign from *Emden* dangled from a pole strapped to the saddle of a "ship of the desert." The sailors held their rifles at the ready as they passed through Ras al Aswad, the Father of the Wolf, a dangerous and lawless wasteland where bandits preyed on the unwary. The safety of Jiddah lay within reach, just a day's march away.

Without warning, a dozen mounted Arabs reared out of the night. They vanished just as abruptly. Moments later, bullets whizzed around the sailors. The men leaped off their camels and took cover behind sand dunes. Orange muzzle flashes blazed all around. Bullets thumped into the sand and wounded the camels. Sporadic firing continued all night long. When the sun rose the Germans saw hundreds of armed men creeping about the hills. As they looked around at their own position they realized that most of their Turkish and Arab escorts had disappeared.

Von Mücke took stock of his weaponry. Their armament consisted of four Maxim machine guns, 16 modern rifles, 10 old Turkish rifles and 24 pistols, most of which had travelled all the way from Direction Island. To remain cowering behind the dunes would be suicide. He desperately need-ed a show of strength. Under covering fire from the machine guns a party of men fixed bayonets. With blood-curdling yells they charged their closest adversaries and killed ten. The feint worked and the firing stopped. They reassembled on the surviving camels and trotted toward the sea, where they hoped the open country would offer a better field of vision.

After ten minutes on the march they ran into another ambush. Sea-man Rademacher was shot and killed. Von Mücke sent one of the remain-ing guides under a white flag to parley with the enemy while he organized his men into a defensive position. Behind a barrier of kneeling camels they built four walls out of sand and saddles, buried the water contain-ers and mounted machine guns in the four corners. The terrified Arab ran back to announce that the parley had failed. Shots crackled from the hills. Bullets ricocheted off rocks and zinged past their heads. The machine guns protected them – for the moment. As the afternoon wore on, neither side gained the advantage. The only respite from fighting came at night as anxious sentries searched the gloom for stealthy figures. Sublieutenant Schmidt died of his wounds and was buried beside Rademacher. In the short interval between sunset and moonrise von Mücke sent an Arab guide to Jiddah to alert the Turkish garrison. The frightened man vanished into the dark.

The Arabs attacked in force the next morning but a strong volley from the machine guns forced them to retreat. They fired from the dunes all day long without letup. The Germans used the dead camels for shields but they decomposed quickly in the hot sun. Entrails burst out of the swollen hides. Under cover of night they dragged the heavy, smelly beasts far away. A third man, Stoker Lanig, died of his wounds. Two more Arab messengers left for Jiddah.

On the third day the sun burned white-hot in a clear sky. Thirty vultures circled overhead. The temperature in the full glare at ground level soared well over 50°C (120°F). Saddles smouldered. Rifle barrels were too hot to touch. Thousands of black scarab beetles infested the earthworks. Tumbling and somersaulting, they rolled balls of camel dung up and down the dusty sides. Fine powdery sand coated the men and their weapons. It infiltrated every crack and pore and raised the fear of tetanus infection among the wounded. Both sides continued shooting. At night the Arabs ceased fire but other marauders arrived – jackals and hyenas feasting on the dead camels.

By the fourth morning the camp was in critical condition and almost out of water. The fighting had stopped although muffled sounds of distant rifle fire punctuated the eerie quiet. At noon a man waving a white flag approached the perimeter. Von Mücke bluffed about the strength of their position and refused his demands. The Arabs tried another parley later in the afternoon but still the Germans refused to surrender.

A profound silence settled over the dunes. The attackers had disappeared. In disbelief the weary survivors poked their heads over the sandy battlements. They spotted movement on the far horizon, a mirage in the shimmering heat. One by one the men all turned and watched in wonder as the magical vision came closer, a glorious image from the Arabian Nights of old. A party of seventy men, all brilliantly dressed, galloped toward them on camels. They sang, beat drums and shouted. At the head of the column rode a man in a splendid turban. In his hand he held a magnificent dark red banner, emblazoned in gold with verses from the Koran. Abdullah, son of the Emir of Mecca, had charged to their rescue.

Amazed at the sight and overjoyed to be alive, the men drank their fill of fresh water and tended to their wounds. Abdullah told them that the attackers were paid by the British but that his father was a Turkish ally. After a brief service in honour of their three dead comrades the sailors packed their weapons, mounted their camels and set off once more toward Jiddah. As they wearily filed away von Mücke heard shouting in the rear. He turned in his saddle to see their former attackers swarming out of their hiding places. They were picking through the abandoned gear and looting with impunity. It appeared as if they had struck some kind of deal with Abdullah. Von Mücke looked warily at his supposed rescuer, who calmly assured him there was nothing to fear. A nagging doubt festered in von Mücke's suspicious mind. After months in the desert he knew that things were not always what they seemed, that it was sometimes difficult to distinguish the truth from the lies. He kept his hand on his pistol just in case.

The Turkish garrison at Jiddah greeted them with pomp and celebration. Among the soldiers lining the street were the caravan escorts who had fled at the first sign of trouble. Von Mücke learned that his party had killed forty of the Arab attackers and wounded thirty-six. The Turks were impressed by the legendary *Emden* crew – and by their four Maxims, weapons more powerful than anything in their own arsenal. The German lieutenant's suspicions grew darker when they advised him to keep going overland. This time, they assured him, it would be safer. He was now convinced that the Turks and the Emir had orchestrated the attack at Ras al Aswad – to further their own byzantine political aims and to capture the Maxims. In the face of determined resistance they had abandoned the attempt. Two could play this subtle game. Von Mücke made elaborate and ostentatious plans for another camel caravan – and negotiated secretly for a *sambuq*.

They wasted no time. Four nights later, on April 8, the sailors crept down to the beach in darkness and set sail once again on the Red Sea.

Disguised in native dress, they squeaked through the British blockade of Jiddah. Safely past the initial dangers, the sailors settled into a familiar naval routine, punctuated by the strange, haunting call to prayer, "*Allahu akhbar!*" On the first morning the Arab pilots faced eastward to Mecca during prayers. As they continued their rapid northward progress the pilots faced south. Two weeks earlier the camel drivers had faced north. Like human compass needles, they pointed unerringly to the magnetic pole, the lodestone of their Islamic faith.

Twenty uneventful days after leaving Jiddah, the Germans arrived at Al Wajh near the northern end of the Red Sea. They assembled another caravan of camels and began the hundred-mile march to the town of Al Ula at the southern terminus of the Hijaz railroad. They hoped for better luck on this, their third, attempt to cross the desert. The mountains were refreshingly cool, allowing them to march by day and to sleep by night. Water was plentiful and drinkable. With success seemingly within reach they took no chances. Each night they dug trenches, mounted machine guns on the perimeter and posted sentries. Halfway to Al Ula they crossed into the domain of a rival sheik. Their Arab escorts grew increasingly nervous and sent for reinforcements. More and more Arabs joined the remarkable caravan until they reached a total strength of four hundred men. The sailors were surrounded by a vast armada of noisy camels, truly like ships in the desert. Ferocious men rode high in the saddles, men with eagle eyes, aquiline noses and long Arab flintlocks. Von Mücke and a small escort galloped ahead.

Hundreds of camels trudged across the parched valleys and hills above Al Ula. Waves of sand and rock rolled away to the distant horizon, curved like the edge of the ocean. A black plume of smoke rose above the shifting dunes, as from a ship sailing to their rescue. One man halted his camel on the crest of a hill and pulled out a pair of navy binoculars. The smoke billowed from the stack of a train under steam. He called to the others and pointed the way. They prodded their camels to trot, then gallop, as the flintlocks and pistols fired and hundreds of voices sang and shouted down the hill and across the dusty plain.

Von Mücke rode into Al Ula just ahead of his crew on May 7, almost six months since the landing party had disembarked from *Emden*. A journalist, Emil Ludwig, looked up at the bearded lieutenant astride his white camel and asked him, "A bath – or Rhine wine?"

"Rhine wine!" he cried. He dismounted, shook hands with excited German and Turkish officials and slapped the side of the waiting locomotive with satisfaction. A few hours later the rest of the armada thundered into the valley in tumultuous disarray, a desert extravaganza on a biblical scale. Von Mücke rode out one last time on his camel to greet them – his colourful, suntanned, shaggy-haired crew in their turbans and tattered uniforms. Tears of joy welled in their eyes as they shouted in exultation.

The sailors were given good food, champagne, baths, new clothes and a ride home at twenty miles per hour on red-cushioned seats. Whooping with excitement and firing their rifles, their Arab friends raced alongside the locomotive. Crowds and bands appeared at each way station to greet the dazed celebrities. For the previous three months their saga had transfixed the world. Friends and enemies alike speculated in the press on their whereabouts and waited in suspense for their return.

As the train chugged and clacked its way northward, the sailors stared silently out the windows at the Holy Land – a sweeping vista of rock, sand and desert. They passed Amman and Dar'a where, later in the war, Lawrence of Arabia would attack this same railroad. In Damascus they saw from a distance the Grand Umayyad Mosque, where Saint John the Baptist was buried and where, in the seventh century in perfect harmony, Muslims prayed on Friday and Christians on Sunday. At Aleppo they received their first letters from home, new uniforms and a special consignment from the Kaiser – an Iron Cross for each man. Even for the toughened sailors it was a poignant moment as they fingered the medals and remembered their lost comrades in the squadron. They recalled their warship's last day and the sardonic congratulations of the Englishman on Direction Island – the man who told them that the Kaiser had just awarded Iron Crosses to the men of *Emden*. They thought of *Emden*'s gallant career and her terrible destruction; the elegant schooner *Ayesha* and the scruffy collier *Choising*; the brutal marches to Sana'a and Jiddah; the Father of the Wolf and the son of the Emir of Mecca; *sambuqs* on the Red Sea and camels in the desert by moonlight.

On Whitsunday, May 23, 1915, the train pulled triumphantly into Haydar Pasha, facing Constantinople across the Bosporus. Wearing their new uniforms and Iron Crosses, parading the tattered ensign they had brought the whole way, the sailors stood to attention in front of Admiral Wilhelm Souchon of the Mediterranean Fleet. Von Mücke raised the hilt of his new sword to his lips, lowered the point in salute and announced, with a slight catch in his voice, "Beg to report, landing party from *SMS Emden* numbering five officers, seven petty officers and thirty-seven men, present and correct, sir!"

In honour of the homecoming heroes, the German brewery in Constantinople laid on a lavish *Bierabend*, an evening beer party in a local pleasure garden. Late that night, still basking in the adulation, the sailors finally retired to the luxury of clean beds. As they drifted off to sleep in the humid silence, the warm protective glow slowly faded, exposing the fear and the horror, the sorrow and the guilt of the previous seven months. Unlike their mates they had survived and they were free. Of some three thousand men in the German East Asia Squadron only a few hundred were still alive. Most of these survivors spent the rest of the war in camps for internees and prisoners. The *Emden* landing party was the only German naval unit in the Great War to suffer the loss of a ship and to return from overseas to fight again.

For a brief period of time they were not the only free-roaming survivors. Two months after this unique achievement six other men of the German East Asia Squadron rode across the same desert. Captain von Moller had abandoned his gunboat on the Pearl estuary near Hong Kong on August 4, almost a year earlier. He set out with five men and travelled overland through China, narrowly escaped internment in the Dutch East Indies and sailed for eighty days in a small boat clear across the Indian Ocean to Arabia. They reached the walled city of Sana'a and from there followed the same route as the *Emden* party. In Al Lith they hired camels and Arab escorts to guide them through the notorious Ras al Aswad. On the very outskirts of Jiddah, hundreds of vengeful Arabs fell upon the small band. They killed all six of the sailors, took their weapons and left their mutilated bodies to rot in the sun.

Upon their return to Germany, the men of the *Emden* landing party were all reassigned to warships. Many of them died in battle. Von Mücke never quite recovered from his "finest hour." He quarrelled with his superiors and ended his naval career with a string of lacklustre appointments. Although he achieved considerable success by writing books and lecturing, he failed in his attempts to form a right-wing political party. When Hitler seized power in 1933, von Mücke applied for permission to emigrate. The Nazis refused, preferring to muzzle him within his own country. He became, in effect, an internal exile. His *Emden* colleagues were promoted to senior naval positions during World War II while he remained a virtual recluse, implacably opposed to the Nazis but permitted to live in peace for the sake of his past heroism. He died a lonely man in 1957 at the age of 73.

⚜

In *The Seven Pillars of Wisdom*, T. E. Lawrence described a desert battle near the end of the war in which "...the German detachments [fought exceptionally well]; and here, for the first time, I grew proud of the enemy who had killed my brothers. They were two thousand miles from home, without hope and without guides, in conditions mad enough to break the bravest nerves. Yet their sections held together, in firm rank, sheering through the wrack of Turk and Arab like armoured ships, high-faced and silent. When attacked they halted, took position, fired to order. There was no haste, no crying, no hesitation. They were glorious." In this battle – also for the first time – Lawrence ordered his men to take no prisoners.

Captain T. E. Lawrence worked in the British Intelligence Department in Egypt at the time von Mücke and his crew rode the Hijaz railroad to Haydar Pasha. In 1916 he journeyed to Hijaz and from then on worked to unite the Arab tribes. Throughout 1917 and 1918 he attacked the Turks and blew up railroads in the desert. This culminated in the attack on Dar'a between Amman and Damascus in which his Arab force destroyed the three rail lines converging on the city. Shortly afterward this led to General Allenby's successful march into Damascus, the failed attempt at Arab unity and Lawrence's disillusionment with the strictures of armies and governments. Later he wrote:

"I was sitting alone in my room, working and thinking out as firm a way as the turbulent memories of the day allowed, when the Muedh-dhins began to send their call of last prayer through the moist night over the illuminations of the feasting city. One, with a ringing voice of special sweetness, cried into my window from a near mosque. I found myself involuntarily distinguishing his words: 'God alone is great: I testify there are no gods, but God: and Mohammed his Prophet. Come to prayer: come to security. God alone is great: there is no god – but God.'

"At the close he dropped his voice two tones, almost to speaking level, and softly added: 'And He is very good to us this day, O people of Damascus.' The clamour hushed, as everyone seemed to obey the call to prayer on this their first night of perfect freedom. While my fancy, in the overwhelming pause, showed me my loneliness and lack of reason in their movement: since only for me, of all the hearers, was the event sorrowful and the phrase meaningless."

SEVENTEEN

THE FLIGHT OF
DRESDEN

Dresden under Fire at Más-a-Tierra

On December 8, 1914, the British sank four of the five German warships in the Battle of the Falklands. Only *Dresden* escaped, much to the chagrin of her British pursuers – and the doomed German sailors on the other ships. Admiral *Graf* von Spee had tried to ensure the survival of his three light cruisers by ordering them to flee. *Leipzig* and *Nürnberg* trailed the faster *Dresden* as three large and powerful British warships steadily closed the gap. When the first British shells burst around *Leipzig*, she and *Nürnberg* turned to face the enemy. The sailors on the two ships watched in dismay as *Dresden*'s stern disappeared into a fogbank and left them to their grim fate. Only twenty-five men survived from the two light cruisers.

Admiral Sturdee's hastily assembled task force had almost totally destroyed the crack German squadron. But gratitude, like the slippery

Dresden, would elude him. Lord Fisher of the Admiralty was furious with Sturdee for not finishing the job. Churchill was angry too. They both unfairly blamed Captain Luce of *Glasgow* for allowing *Dresden* to escape while he focused his fire on the remaining two ships. Sturdee actually did make a serious effort to find the missing cruiser. He searched for several days with three large warships – ships that would have been more useful in the dangerous sea lanes of the North Atlantic.

The British worried needlessly about *Dresden* and her captain, von Lüdecke. Unlike the fighting captains of the other German ships he had no stomach for war, no interest in heroics and no wish to harm anybody or to sink any ships. In his heart he was still a merchant mariner. He never volunteered for combat in the first place – he was simply the man who had delivered the refurbished *Karlsruhe* to the navy and who then found himself trapped on *Dresden* at the outbreak of war.

After the Falklands battle, von Lüdecke sent frantic signals to the rest of the squadron. When he received no answer he feared the worst. *Dresden* vanished into Tierra del Fuego and hid in the maze of channels and islands at the tip of South America. When the bunkers ran low on coal, a party went ashore to cut timber for the boilers. A Chilean destroyer discovered the woodchoppers on December 11 and warned them not to return for three months. This was a rude surprise for the Germans. A month earlier the Chileans had been more tolerant but now they felt compelled to cast their lot with the British. Ignoring the warning, von Lüdecke loaded up with 750 tons of coal at Punta Arenas a few days later. The Chileans alerted the British consul. Two British cruisers charged in from Port Stanley the next day but *Dresden* had already slipped the noose. Shortly afterward the whole squadron arrived, including two Japanese ships and one Australian. They scoured the narrow passages for days but found no sign of *Dresden*, no plume of smoke, no wood chips, no scribbles on notice boards. Christmas and the New Year approached. The Admiralty ordered Sturdee and the two dreadnoughts home, where the powerful ships would be more useful. Fisher was still angry with him.

Dresden hid in a channel that did not even exist on British charts. Coded wireless messages still trickled through the tightening cordon. Berlin twice ordered her home but von Lüdecke pretended not to hear.

He had no desire to dash across the Atlantic and risk a fight. Instead he thought he might float around the empty reaches of the Pacific and head for the neutral Dutch East Indies. This was a possibility that worried Lord Fisher, who wrote in a memo, "If the *Dresden* gets to the Bay of Bengal by means of colliers arranged with Berlin, we shall owe a lot to Sturdee." The last thing he needed was another *Emden*. He had little to fear. *Dresden* sank only one ship – a British sailing vessel. She was bound for Australia with 2,400 tons of barley and had the misfortune to cross paths with the hidden cruiser. Sinking the barley boat was *Dresden*'s only warlike act since the Battle of Coronel.

Six British ships continued to search for *Dresden* well into the new year. The cruiser *Kent* accidentally stumbled across her in fog on March 8 but she managed to squirt free and disappear into the Pacific off Chile. As a result she lost contact with the collier that had been travelling with her. Her days were numbered by the lumps of coal in her hold. On March 14, 1915, a brief but fateful wireless signal between the two ships revealed *Dresden*'s position. *Kent*, *Orama* and her old nemesis, *Glasgow*, finally pinned her down at Más-a-Tierra in the Juan Fernández Islands. Von Lüdecke had run out of coal and places to hide. He had just informed the Chilean governor that he wished to intern his ship and the crew. Now he waited anxiously for the protection of a Chilean warship.

The British had other plans. Captain Luce of *Glasgow* noted that the anchored ship was flying her flag and had overstayed the 24-hour limit. He bitterly recalled the loss of *Good Hope* and *Monmouth* at Coronel, his own lucky escape from *Dresden*'s bombardment and the furious battle with her sister ships off the Falklands. During the painstaking search of the past three months, he had suffered criticism from London for letting *Dresden* escape. Luce made up his mind and *Glasgow* opened fire. *Dresden* fired back but after two salvoes von Lüdecke quickly hoisted the white flag. In those few brief minutes eight men had been killed and sixteen wounded. He sent Lieutenant Wilhelm Canaris in a dinghy to parley with Captain Luce while his men set demolition charges to scuttle the ship. The Germans abandoned her and rowed madly to shore just before a huge explosion sent *Dresden* to the bottom. Although some sailors later escaped and found their way home, most spent the rest of the war in tedious intern-ment on Quiriquina Island.

The *Deutsch-Ostasiatische Kreuzergeschwader* had ceased to exist. Ad-miral *Graf* Maximilian von Spee, his ships, his two sons and thousands of sailors faded into ghostly obscurity – *requiescat in pace.*

Dresden's Escape from the Falklands

Lieutenant Canaris escaped from Quiriquina Island in August, 1915. Un-der cover of darkness he rowed to the mainland in a small leaky boat. He exchanged the boat for a horse and trekked across the Andes to Argentina. The German Embassy in Buenos Aires gave him a Chilean passport and a ticket to Rotterdam on a Dutch steamer. In October the frail, diminu-tive, courageous young man finally returned to Germany. Kaiser Wilhelm welcomed him as a hero on the scale of Hellmuth von Mücke of *Emden*, promoted him to captain and awarded him the Iron Cross. He rejoined the fight and eventually commanded a U-boat in the Mediterranean.

After the war he rose to the rank of Admiral and directed the German Intelligence arm, the *Abwehr*, in Hitler's Third Reich. In the years leading up to World War II he tried to talk Hitler out of his mad ambitions but soon realized his efforts were hopeless. In 1938, under the cover of coun-ter-espionage operations, he began to foment resistance movements in the armed forces. Atrocities committed during the conquest of Poland turned him further against the Nazis. After the invasion of the Soviet Union he increased his efforts to topple the regime. He tried to mitigate Heydrich's crimes of genocide in Russia; he passed information to the Allies; he fed Hitler false reports about Italy's will to fight; he saved the lives of some captured French officers; and he rescued Jews from concentration camps. The Gestapo grew suspicious and watched him constantly. Hitler fired him from his post in February, 1944. Three days after the July 20 assassination attempt on the *Führer,* the Gestapo arrested him, broke into his safe and uncovered his ties with the Resistance.

Canaris spent the winter of 1944 in the Flossenburg concentration camp awaiting his execution. The man who fought the British at Coronel, who fled the slaughter at the Falklands, who escaped from Chile to fight again, and who proudly served his country while plotting against its brutal leadership, had reached the bitter end. He wrote, "I die for my fatherland. I have a clear conscience. I only did my duty to my country when I tried to oppose the criminal folly of Hitler." On Hitler's personal order, and by the hand of a judge who still unthinkingly "followed orders," the SS hanged Canaris on April 9, 1945, just a few weeks before the German surrender.

At *Pater* Heuken's mountain retreat the Sunday morning service had ended. I had been reading war stories in a corner of the cabin while they talked of Christian forgiveness and of turning the other cheek. I supposed that God makes an exception for soldiers. Young people clattered in the kitchen and set lunch dishes on the table. I closed my book and thought about the men who fled and those who refused to surrender.

Most historians and authors criticized *Dresden's* captain for avoiding a fight. Some of them were quite sarcastic and harsh in their judgments. Captain von Lüdecke of the Merchant Marine, with his "bulbous" red nose and his allegedly "villainous" appearance, was obviously no hero. To save his life and his ship he abandoned his colleagues on *Leipzig* and *Nürnberg*. While the other ships went down with flags flying, he disappeared into a fogbank and scurried away to the safety of Tierra del Fuego. A five-minute fight convinced him to abandon ship. He spent the rest of the war in comfortable internment in Chile as silt and seaweed slowly covered *Dresden* and her sister ships.

Naval tactics in the Great War were two-dimensional and brutally simple. At the Battle of Trafalgar Nelson could split the French and Spanish line, but the age of cannonball, sword and sail had long since vanished. Future captains would have to contend with a complex array of submarines, aircraft and Exocet missiles. But in 1914 faster ships, bigger guns and more of both ensured victory. *Glasgow*, *Cornwall* and *Kent* were just as fast and more heavily armed than their three German opponents. Defeat seemed to von Lüdecke like a foregone conclusion and he knew that his disciplined Navy compatriots would fight to the death. Why would he want to be part of such a disaster? His instinct for survival overcame the urge to help his friends and to avoid "staining" his honour.

In their zeal to emulate the Royal Navy, German officers adopted the long and noble British tradition of never surrendering in the face of the enemy. To do so would be cowardly and dishonourable, as the anonymous poet stated on Cradock's memorial in York Minster. Honour was more important than life or common sense.

Graf Spee had ordered his three light cruisers to flee. He sacrificed his ship and his own life in order that they might escape. The two slower warships, *Leipzig* and *Nürnberg*, eventually had no other option but to turn and fight. They fought hard and courageously, almost to the last man, and refused to surrender even when resistance was clearly futile. The fastest ship, *Dresden*, followed orders and escaped intact, enabling her captain, in theory, to pick a more equal fight on a better day.

Hellmuth von Mücke and the landing party of *Emden* fled in *Ayesha* rather than face their Australian attackers. They returned home as heroes to admiring Germans and Britons alike. Unlike the men of *Dresden*, they were powerless to rescue their comrades aboard *Emden* and thus avoided the sting of censure.

After the Battle of the Falklands, Captain Luce of *Glasgow* suffered the wrath of Churchill and Fisher for allowing one of three ships to escape. However he endured no such criticism for surviving the Battle of Coronel. Unable to assist *Good Hope* or *Monmouth*, he fled only after a determined fight against unbeatable odds.

What were these men fighting for in this so-called "Great War?" Were the Germans and the British defending their women and children, their homes and their freedom, or protecting their politicians and their royal dynasties? In 1914 the war was hugely popular on both sides. A strong surge of patriotism gripped ordinary people, naïve though they may have been in hindsight. A structured, submissive era was ending; mankind teetered on the verge of global slaughter. Only decades later did it become clear that Europe had stumbled into the Great War amid a confusing welter of royal jealousies and political entanglements. National honour blinkered men's vision. The war was unjustified, wasteful and horrific on a colossal scale. Millions of people died and many more suffered the scars. Millions of others lost their loved ones. The Great War spawned yet another war even worse than the first.

Who followed the right course – *Graf* Spee, Admiral Cradock and thousands of brave men, who loyally and unquestioningly fought for their country, who preferred a glorious death to an honourable surrender – or Captain von Lüdecke, who avoided a fight, survived a senseless war and brought his men safely home to their parents and wives and sweethearts? In 1914 the question would have been viewed as ludicrous and the answer clear. In a more realistic and cynical era, and with the advantage of hindsight, the answer is less obvious.

As the American poet, Carl Sandburg, said, "Sometime they'll give a war and nobody will come." The Great War ended two weeks after German sailors mutinied in Kiel. Although the war was already drawing to a bloody close, this event hastened its end. "Imagine all the people," John Lennon once sang, "living life in peace." Unimaginable as it may be, if all the sailors, of all the navies – and all the soldiers, of all the armies – had laid down their arms and refused to fight, the war would have ended much sooner. Instead of questioning their blundering leaders, they saluted.

The free-thinking Wilhelm Canaris, a hero to Kaiser Wilhelm, was vilified as a traitor by many Germans in the immediate aftermath of World War II. Like any ordinary soldier he had sworn an oath to defend his fatherland and the *Führer*. He should have stood by his friends, obeyed orders and fought to the death. But unlike most of his compatriots he questioned his country's objectives and took action to stop the slaughter. Years later he became a hero again in the light of his lonely, courageous, but failed attempts to end the tyranny of the Third Reich. In the end he had no qualms about disobeying orders or targeting his leaders. A true patriot, he would never have carried a placard reading, "My country, right or wrong." Perhaps his experience aboard *Dresden* imbued him with uncommon sense and shaped the future course of his life. If Canaris had received more support or enjoyed better luck, the course of history would indeed have changed.

❦

The priest and I sat on the patio steps in the afternoon sun and watched the students fill up a van with backpacks, guitars, leftover food and plastic water bottles. They laughed and jostled each other like my troop of Boy Scouts, loading a truck for a camping trip. I told *Pater* Heuken that I planned to take the boys to Pelabuhan Ratu. We would camp on the beach and watch the surf pounding in from the Indian Ocean.

"The Queen's Harbour?" He looked at me doubtfully. People had drowned there, most recently the husband of a teacher at the International School. "Don't let them wear green bathing suits, *ja?* The Queen likes green," he chuckled. "Better yet, don't go swimming."

Adja had said the same thing. I thought of the colourful story of Senopati and the sea goddess, of the sailors who guard her palace of pearls and rubies beneath the waves. Perhaps the men of the German East Asia Squadron, the "gentlemen-of-war" in white uniforms, stood guard too. No doubt they flirted with the palace maids.

I described to my Jesuit mentor the puppet-master's performance and his more recent tale of the stone soldiers who refused to surrender. The priest nodded and smiled as he rose from the steps. I asked facetiously if Helfferich had built the cenotaph in memory of the men of *Dresden*.

"I don't think so," he laughed. "He didn't know them anyway."

But Helfferich certainly knew *Graf* Spee and the rest of his doomed squadron. After the war he and Theodor intended at first to build a memorial on North Keeling Island – beside the wreck of *Emden* in the Indian Ocean. Then they realized that nobody would ever see it. Emil wanted it to inspire the German community in Batavia. In a way, it still does.

When I thanked *Pater* Heuken for the books, he suggested that I read about Karl Helfferich. While Emil helped the interned German sailors in Batavia and enjoyed weekends at Artja with Dina, his controversial eldest brother directed the war from Berlin. Like Canaris, Karl Helfferich could have changed the course of history too. In postwar Germany he was a popular right-wing leader when Hitler was being tried for treason.

"What happened to Karl?" I asked.

"You'll see."

The van was packed and our time ran out. I waved at the departing students, so friendly and gentle. Next week they might be shouting at soldiers and the troops might be shooting at them. Indonesia, so green and peaceful on the surface, seethed like the grand volcanic craters that rim the archipelago. The German graveyard perched on the flank of one of those volcanoes – like Indonesia in miniature – a meeting of cultures, a hodge-podge of religions. A dark and disorderly spirit world lurked beneath the green trees, the whitewashed monuments and the tidy crosses. Helfferich's inscription hinted at a violent past. Stone soldiers rose from the soil. Voices whispered in the leaves.

Pater Heuken leaned out of the window and called to me cheerily as the van drove away, "Don't swim in the Queen's Harbour!"

PART 4

ARTJA

EIGHTEEN

THE QUEEN'S HARBOUR

Adja's Hut at Artja

The Bluebird bus rumbled down the highway to Pelabuhan Ratu. The horn had died on the first blind corner and now the driver looked worried. In Indonesia the horn is second only to the steering wheel in importance, even more useful than the brakes. I was relieved because the driver had to slow down and I could stop nagging him. Other trucks and buses rushed past in both directions, tailgating and honking, each Muslim driver secure in the knowledge that God had already determined the date of his death.

Forty Boy Scouts filled the seats behind me. The younger ones bounced around like puppies and shouted to each other in high-pitched voices. The oh-so-cool older ones lounged in the back. They wore their caps backwards, strummed their guitars and muttered in low tones about girls, rock bands and power tools. The bus hurtled toward the south coast of Java with this motley troop from a dozen nations – Americans from Alaska to Texas, a

Canadian Eagle Scout, a Japanese bugler – boys from all the continents of the world. Each of their trusting parents had signed a piece of paper allowing me to take their children on a wild ride to the Queen's Harbour, to the sandy beach and pounding surf of the huge Southern Ocean.

We entered the broad valley between Gunung Pangrango and Gunung Salak. The beach was still two hours away to the south and the driver had slowed down. I leaned back in my seat and relaxed.

❧

A week earlier I had visited the German graveyard to put the finishing touches to a description of the "Artja Domas Trail." The path meandered along a scenic plantation road and crossed four streams as it snaked in and out of ravines on the flank of the volcano. The serpent-eagle shadowed my steps as she turned slow circles in the clear blue sky. I had seen her so often I assumed she must have a home among the old trees. On outstretched wings she wheeled higher and higher until she shrank to a tiny speck and vanished over the distant ridge.

A lone man trotted down the rough path in front of me. Two netbags full of bright orange carrots dangled from a pole balanced across his sinewy shoulders. His thigh muscles bulged under a pair of ragged shorts as he struggled beneath the heavy load. He grunted at me, nodded awkwardly and then he too faded into the distance. His peculiar scuttling gait propelled him rapidly down the hill, where he passed a group of tea-pickers and hailed them on the fly. I looked for the woman in the green sarong but she wasn't there.

The trail ended in the dappled shade of trees near Adja's hut. Large fronds of bananas and ginger plants drooped over the tidy garden and the well-swept yard. A roof of red clay tiles covered four simple walls of plaited bamboo sheets, smudged black from the soot of kerosene lamps. Red dirt and green mould stained the footings, where rain poured off the roof and splashed onto the muddy ground. The shutter of a small window creaked on the back wall and allowed a light breeze to waft through the smoky interior. A low murmur of voices drifted from the front porch. Chickens clucked and scattered at my approach. I poked my head around the corner and saw Adja, Mohamad and another man sitting on a bench against the wall.

"*Aduh, Pak*! Where did you come from?" asked Adja in surprise.

I smiled at Adja's bewildered grey face and apologized for my intrusion. An old woman tottered out of the hut. She touched the wooden doorpost, blinked her pale watery eyes in the sunlight and turned her head sideways as if to see better. Beside her, a double bed fitted snugly into the inner corner of the porch. Adja introduced me to his wife, Imas, whom I had not met before. From the bottom of my daypack I retrieved a small bag of sugar, saved for just such an occasion. She seemed pleased with the gift and shuffled back inside to brew a pot of coffee. I pulled out a pack of *kreteks* and offered them to the three men. Adja and Mohamad accepted with pleasure. I had not seen Mohamad since the *Volkstrauertag* ceremony.

The stranger politely refused and I realized to my surprise that he was a Baduy tribesman. Like the men I had seen on the streets of Jakarta, he wore black shorts, a white homespun shirt and a black jacket with no buttons or pockets. Around his head he had wrapped a batik scarf, coloured in black and indigo-blue. Snowy-white eyebrows shaded his eyes and a tuft of curly white hair sprouted through the top of his headdress. His face with its high gaunt cheekbones looked older and more wrinkled than any I had ever seen, gnarled like an ancient *waringin* tree. Small piercing eyes glowed darkly between slanted eyelids. He seemed to be reading my mind.

I had read about the Baduy and had listened to Robby Ko's stories. He sometimes visited the reclusive tribe in their homeland of West Java. Five thousand people inhabit a broad area among the Kendeng hills. Like the concentric bands on a spinning wheel, they have settled into three groups based on the strength of their religious beliefs. Those unwilling to hang on to the traditional lifestyle have gradually drifted into the wide outer ring. They surround a smaller group, the so-called Outer Baduy, who cling precariously to the old ways among quaint huts in a protected forest. A bamboo bridge across the Ciujung, the Last River, separates them from a few hundred people in the core community – the three villages of the austere, secretive Inner Baduy tribe. At the headwaters of the Last River lies the Forbidden Forest, within which they jealously guard their innermost sanctuary, Artja Domas.

The Outer Baduy wear dark clothing and act as intermediaries with the rest of the world. Adja's guest was obviously one of these, probably a *dukun* – a healer or soothsayer. The Inner Baduy wear white clothing and safeguard their culture by refusing to mix with outsiders. Their religion is essentially Hindu with a hint of animism and a smattering of Islam. Their lives are governed by a thousand taboos – no glasses, no plates, no cutlery, no furniture, no alcohol, no kerosene, nothing from the outside. They grow their own coffee and sweeten it with sugar from the sap of the *aren* palm. They use the leaf of the same palm to roll home-grown tobacco into cigarettes. The Baduy are a gentle folk but stubbornly independent. Modern Indonesians leave them alone because they fear their magical powers. *Dukuns* wander the city streets and earn spare change by foretelling the future, healing disease or casting spells on one's enemies.

Adja introduced his guest to me as Yakmin. When Imas emerged from the hut and offered four glasses of coffee, the old man graciously accepted. As the *dukun* sipped from his glass, Adja worked up the courage to ask him a favour. He pointed to his half-blind wife. Yakmin stood up and peered into her cloudy eyes. He riffled through the contents of his rough bark handbag and pulled out a small vial. He removed the lid, smeared the sticky ointment on the end of his finger and dabbed her eyelids as he mumbled a brief incantation. Adja looked up to me for help. I pulled a crumpled Rupiah note from my pocket and passed it to the *dukun* when he had finished. He took it without comment, drank the last drop of coffee and spoke a few words to Mohamad and Adja. Then he faced the mountain and briskly walked away.

We watched him disappear into the trees. The *dukun* carried himself with assurance and with surprising agility for such an old man. When he was well out of earshot, Adja whispered to me that he was 170 years old and that he was here to pay his respects to the graves of his ancestors. He said they were buried in the old Artja Domas.

I wondered what he meant by "old" but before I could ask him, Adja apologized for the old man's brusque departure. The Baduy shy away from foreigners, he said. They believe in racial and cultural purity. Even Indonesians are forbidden to enter the sanctuary of the Inner Baduy.

Adja looked me in the eye, smiled and stood a little taller. "He is a *dukun* but I am a *dalang*. Let me tell you how we deal with foreigners. Would you like to hear how the Dutch came to Java?"

Mohamad cleared his throat, stood up and bowed self-consciously as he offered his apologies for leaving. He invited me to visit him some day in his airy gazebo overlooking the rice paddies. He could tell me his own stories of the foreigners – the Germans, the Japanese, the Gurkhas – and how he fought the Dutch.

I thanked Mohamad for the invitation and watched him descend the trail to the village. Adja tapped the bench where the *dukun* had sat. I took my seat, leaned against the bamboo wall of the hut and watched in amusement as Adja wound himself up. He hopped around the yard in his baggy old pants and shooed away the chickens. When the stage was clear he stepped gingerly back and forth, first to the left, then to the right. Slowly and deliberately he waved his arms and hands about his head, like a shadow puppet with short grey hair and big ears.

"You remember *Nyai* Roro Kidul, the Goddess of the Southern Ocean. Her father, the King of Pajajaran, banished her for refusing to accept an arranged marriage. She had two sisters. When the Muslim army destroyed Pajajaran, one of those sisters fled with the eight hundred soldiers into the hills. When they all turned to stone, the princess fled higher up the mountain to Artja Manik, where she met an *ajar*, a holy man named Sukarsi. He looked like a Baduy *dukun* but dressed in white instead of black. She fell under his magic spell and married him.

"Soon she told him, 'I am with child.' Nine months later she gave birth to a daughter, *Sang* Putri, who grew into a woman of dazzling beauty. The Muslim Pangeran of Jayakarta heard of this extraordinary princess and summoned her to his palace. He lavished attention upon her, plied her with food and wine, gave her luxurious clothing and ushered her into a fabulous bedchamber. One evening he entered her room and compelled the reluctant princess to make love to him. With greedy delight he settled himself between her unwilling knees.

"Suddenly he roared in pain and leaped out of bed!" Adja danced around the yard and clutched himself in agony. His eyes bulged. "Fire burst from her womb! Flames licked his legs and singed his manhood! He panted with rage, jumped around the room and beat himself furiously until the flames flickered out. The next morning he banished her to an island in the Java Sea."

Adja's wife poked her head out of the door and rapped her knuckles on the wall. She clucked in reproach and noisily retreated, leaving Adja on stage with the frightened chickens. His arms hung limply by his side and he continued in a more sober tone.

"After a while the Pangeran got an idea. He offered the 'flaming' princess to the Sultan of Cirebon, hoping to curry favour with his eastern neighbour. But the Sultan met the same horrible fate and passed the princess on to Sultan Agung in Solo, the most powerful ruler on Java. This sultan suffered the same misfortune as the others and he angrily returned the princess to the Pangeran. Once more he exiled her to the island called Pulau Putri.

"*Sang* Putri lived on the island in sorrowful isolation for three long years. Eventually the Pangeran sold the difficult woman to a roving Dutchman for the price of three cannons. He sent one cannon to Banten and the others to his singed friends in Cirebon and Solo. You can still see them if you go there. Maybe he was making amends or maybe just a sly little joke."

"Who was the Dutchman?" I asked.

"Sukmul – he was born in Java, the son of *Sang* Retna, the most beautiful of the twelve Javanese wives of a great Dutch captain. But she had offended her husband. He confined her to the kitchen and never slept with her. She was desperate for children, so much so that one day an amazing thing happened – she gave birth to a seashell! Within the shell lay twin boys whom she named Kasender and Sukmul. Kasender later joined forces with Senopati, a hero of Java and the lover of *Nyai* Roro Kidul. They had many adventures with a golden bird, Garuda, and a flying horse, Sembrani.

"Sukmul became a sea captain like his father. After giving the Pangeran three cannons for *Sang* Putri he brought the maiden to his ancestral home in Holland. Their wedding night approached. He had heard the rumours about the 'flaming' princess. Sukmul was concerned but excited, too, for he loved a challenge. That night she lured him onto the bed and embraced him passionately. 'Make love to me,' she said. And so he did...no flames! In time she bore him a son named Mur Djangkung.

"Djangkung became a great warrior for the Dutch. When he asked his mother about his ancestors, she told him that his maternal grandmother came not from the West but from Pajajaran. She was a princess of a kingdom destroyed by the Muslims. Djangkung swore revenge upon the Pangeran of Jayakarta, the man who had sold his mother for the price of three cannons. With a fleet of fifteen ships he set sail for Java.

"After arriving in the harbour of Sunda Kelapa, he called on the Pangeran and offered him gifts. In great secrecy he built a fortress, Kota Tahi, and armed it with cannons. Djangkung bombarded the town but he couldn't defeat the Pangeran's huge army. So he tried a trick. He loaded the cannons with coins and blasted them all over the city. The Pangeran's men crawled out of their hiding places to gather up the windfall. Djangkung switched to real cannonballs and destroyed them all. The Pangeran fled to the mountains where he became a hermit and a rebel, a thorn in the side of the new Dutch rulers. To his dying day he regretted ever having set eyes upon the 'flaming' princess, *Sang* Putri.

"And that is how the Dutch came to Java." The old *dalang* bowed deeply.

I thanked him for the amusing story of the "flaming" princess, a popular theme in Javanese legend – a method by which women controlled the royal succession. The colonial justification was ingenious too. I gleaned the underlying history from *Pater* Heuken's book on Jakarta. Djangkung was actually Jan Coen, the first governor of the Dutch East Indies. His mother was not a princess of Pajajaran and his father was probably not born in a seashell. He was certainly not the great-nephew of the sea goddess. However Kota Tahi, literally "Shit City," was very real. The Dutch used a terrible weapon to subdue the natives....

In 1610 the Dutch bought a piece of land in Jayakarta from the Sultan of Banten. They built a warehouse on the east bank of the Ciliwung River and then a fort. A few years later the English built a small trading post on the west bank. The Sultan grew uneasy over the growing Dutch military presence. In 1618 he attacked the Dutch fort with the help of English ships. But the Bantenese quarrelled among themselves and withdrew. The defenders celebrated by renaming their fort Batavia in honour of the Batavians, ancestors of the Dutch. On May 30, 1619, the newly appointed Dutch Governor-General Jan Pieterszoon Coen fought the resurgent English and Bantenese forces. In the process he attacked and completely destroyed the surrounding city of Jayakarta. He firmly established Dutch control over a vast colonial treasure, a rule which would survive more than three centuries.

But the early years were difficult for the young Dutch colony. In 1628 Sultan Agung of central Java stormed in from Mataram with an army of 80,000 men. He laid siege to Fort Hollandia, where Sergeant Hans Madelijn led the beleaguered Dutch garrison. According to a book written by Johann Neuhof in 1666, Madelijn hailed from the Rhine Palatinate, the homeland also of the wide-ranging Helfferich family. When his men ran out of ammunition the resourceful sergeant got a desperate idea. He ordered them to empty latrine buckets on the enemy as they tried to climb the walls. The attackers ran away in disgust and shouted, "*O seytang orang Hollanda de bakkalay samma tay*! You Dutch devils fight with shit!" These are probably the first Malay words ever recorded in a German book. The natives renamed Hollandia "Kota Tahi." The old fort now lies buried under the modern but seedy Glodok Shopping Centre, a fate some may deem appropriate.

Adja had another story to tell about cannons – those fearsome weapons of the West, now revered by childless Indonesian women....

"There is a cannon in Solo called *Nyai* Setomi," he began. "Some say it is one of the three cannons of Sukmul but others tell a different story. In the magic years before the Muslim invasion and the Dutch conquest, the Hindu King of Pajajaran woke up in a sweat one night from a bad dream. He saw a huge new weapon and he heard a terrible sound like the rolling of thunder. The next morning he ordered his prime minister, *Kyai* Setomo, to search his kingdom for the fearsome thing. He threatened him with death if he failed.

"The prime minister was obviously not very happy. He went home to his wife, *Nyai* Setomi, and discussed this hopeless mission with her. They closed their house to all visitors and meditated from dawn until dusk. After several days the king grew impatient and sent soldiers to the home of his prime minister. They knocked on the door and got no reply. They broke into the house but there was nobody home – just two huge cannon barrels! *Nyai* Setomi and *Kyai* Setomo had been transformed by the power of their meditation. The soldiers rushed to tell the king. When he arrived at the house and stared at the extraordinary sight, the king recognized the cannons as the weapons of his nightmare.

"The great Sultan Agung of Mataram soon heard about the cannons and demanded that they be brought to his palace in Solo. *Nyai* Setomi meekly acquiesced and she rests to this day in Solo, sad and lonely. She weeps tears into a bowl. But *Kyai* Setomo refused to leave his homeland. He escaped in the night and rolled all the way to the gate of Sunda Kelapa. What a sight that must have been – a cannon barrel rumbling down the old road from Pakuan! He spent the night outside the locked city gate. In the morning the astonished residents found a huge cannon on their doorstep. He must be a sacred omen, they decided. To protect him from the heat they covered him with a large paper umbrella. They called him Si Jagur, Mr. Robust.

"Today Si Jagur lies in the courtyard of the Wayang Museum in old Jakarta. Childless women used to visit it on Thursdays and make offerings of flowers. Then they sat on top of the barrel and prayed for a baby. Have you ever seen it?" He raised one quizzical eyebrow and poked his thumb between two fingers.

"Yes," I answered as I laughed at his gesture. The cannon was actually Portuguese and had an interesting history. In 1641 the Dutch conquered the Portuguese trading post in Malacca and brought sixteen large cannons back with them to Batavia. They placed one of them on a bastion of the fort controlling the harbour. It bears the Latin inscription *"Ex me ipsa renata sum –* Out of myself I was reborn," suggesting that it was recast from an even older cannon. A clenched fist protrudes from the breechblock. The thumb pokes between the second and third fingers in the old Malay gesture for sex. Make love, not war – like the Dutch sea captain and the "flaming" princess.

Si Jagur

Adja dropped his arms and sighed. He shuffled over to the bench and sat down beside me, his shoulders hunched with exaggerated weariness. He reached into his pocket for a *kretek* and lit it with silent satisfaction. In the distance I could just make out the white monument through the large *waringin* trees. He could sit on this bench on moonlit nights, watching the stone soldiers and listening to the voices. Perhaps he lay there in the bed on the porch with his eyes and ears open, as Imas slept beside him.

He took a strong pull on his cigarette. "I wonder how the *dukun* got here. The Baduy can fly, you know. They don't need cars or airplanes. All those modern things are taboo anyway. Maybe he just walked. You remember that the last King of Pajajaran disappeared in a cloud of smoke?" I nodded as Adja exhaled a round blue puff. "Well, the Baduy believe he turned into a bird called a *beo* and flew across the mountains looking for a new home. When he saw the beautiful woods of the Kendeng hills, he landed by a river and dipped his beak into the water. Poof! He turned into a man and claimed the hills for his people. He called the place Cibeo. It's one of the three villages of the Inner Baduy, on the edge of the Forbidden Forest."

"Maybe he just came by bus," I suggested.

"*Aduh*, where's the magic in that? The bus! I'll tell you something else. Phantom tigers fly over the forbidden forest. They keep the Baduy safe."

We sat quietly for a while and gazed at the old trees beyond his hut. I asked Adja if he knew the location of Helfferich's cottage. I had seen a photo in his memoir, *Ein Leben*. The cottage was trim and white with mullioned windows, rose bushes in the front and dark brooding trees in the background. It used to overlook the river valley a short walk from the monument. Perhaps its foundations lay under Adja's hut. The old man shook his head. He had never seen it.

I stood up and called inside the hut to his wife. She shuffled out the door and sat down on the edge of the bed. I said goodbye and hoped that her eyes improved. I looked at Adja, the grizzled old man with the big ears and the snaggly teeth, and thanked him for the stories. He sat on the bench stoop-shouldered with his legs crossed, a skinny elbow perched on his knee. He waved his cigarette and flashed a yellow grin.

Past the gnarled trees and through the gap in the stone fence, I hiked down the well-beaten footpath to the graveyard, the final stop on the "Artja Domas Trail." I saw the tall cenotaph and the familiar plaque in memory of the *Tapferen*, the brave ones of the German squadron – the von Spee family, the jaunty men of *Emden*, the sailors on camelback, even Wilhelm Canaris. Friedrich Steinfeld, the U-boat captain, and his nine mates rested under the line of Iron Crosses. Green mould tinged the white tombstones. The skulls on Ganesha leered at me.

A dark shadow lurked at the edge of my vision. I peered into the gloomy hollows of twisted grey stems and saw the *dukun* squatting beneath the ancient tree. Like smoke from a fire he rose and vanished into the forest.

The bus stopped at the edge of the Indian Ocean and we pitched camp. Tents and cooking shelters sprang up in a grassy field behind the beach. We took care to avoid palm trees, so that neither the coconuts nor the shallow-rooted trunks would fall on us during the night. I watched a huge coconut crab creep up a tree trunk. Its single giant pincer looked like a green scimitar. By mid-afternoon the camp was in order and the cooks began to light fires. I took some boys on a hike to Gua Lalay, a bat cave beside the ocean.

Near the cave we meandered through a field of tall sawgrass and a dense grove of scrubby trees. We brushed the leaves off our faces and swatted the cobwebs. One boy ran into a giant *Nephila* spider and yelped in shock. Its black-and-yellow body was as big as a thumb and its legs spanned the boy's frightened face. We looked around uneasily and saw hundreds of golden orb weavers. The swarm of leggy predators dangled from a vast untidy web that spanned the canopies of several large trees. We detoured at a respectful distance.

When we reached the cave entrance an odious smell wafted from the hole. We sat outside in more pleasant surroundings and waited for the bats to emerge. Swallows and swiftlets disappeared as the first bats fluttered out of the hole. Deep underground a warm seething mass of primordial creatures unfurled their leathery wings and dropped from their rocky perches. A black cloud whirled out of the cave. We heard a pattering sound like approaching rain and realized too late what it meant. As we raced for cover the cloud soared overhead and bombed us with batshit.

The sun reddened and sank below the grey horizon. We hiked back to camp and rinsed our heads under the tap. The boys returned to their friends and joined in the supper preparations. Spider and bat stories grew fantastic in the retelling. After cleanup and campfire the boys crawled into their tents and sleeping bags. Flashlight beams flickered on the tent walls amid spasms of muffled laughter. I walked down to the darkened beach, took off my boots and rambled barefoot through the surf. Lights twinkled from a line of bamboo fishing platforms stretched far along the coast. A few boats chugged out to sea for the night. As each skipper left the "Queen's Harbour," he would throw a plate of rice over the side to ensure a safe return the next morning. A full moon followed the sun's path and left a shining trail on the restless sea. The trail pointed in the direction of the Cocos-Keeling Islands, where the cruiser *Emden* had come to grief and where the schooner *Ayesha* had embarked on her epic voyage.

The legendary home of the Queen of the Southern Ocean lay somewhere out there beneath the waves. I wondered what her "palace of rubies" might look like in the dark void of the Java Trench, beneath the crushing weight of seven thousand metres of water. She was obviously a force to be reckoned with. What was it she had said to Senopati? "If you should ever need me, stand straight with your feet together and your arms crossed on your breast, looking up toward the southern sky. Soon I shall arrive with my armies of sea spirits, all fully armed." I remembered how Adja had stood and I tried it myself. With my feet pressed together and my arms crossed, I faced the crashing surf and the moon trail over the dark southern ocean. I felt like an Indian chief in an old Hollywood western. No one could see me, fortunately, and nothing much happened. The warm wind blew and the surf rumbled ashore.

The Queen's earthly abode lay just a short distance along the beach from our camp. I could see the lights glimmering dimly from the windows of a highrise building, the famous Samudra Beach Hotel. Singularly out of place on this idyllic coast, the bleak Soviet-style hotel was built by President Sukarno in the early sixties with money from Japanese war reparations. Yellowing rectangular outbuildings and giant ventilation ducts greet visitors upon arrival. An outcrop of black volcanic basalt towers near the entrance like the remains of a ruined castle. According to local legend, Sukarno chose this particular site after days of meditation with a *dukun* beneath a *ketapang* tree on the beach. He thrust his Javanese *kris* into the sand but it kept falling over. When the *kris* stayed upright for two days, he knew that he had found the right place. But *Nyai* Roro Kidul came to him that night in a vision, a *wangsit*. She would allow him to build his hotel on one condition – that he reserve Room 308 for her in perpetuity.

This was remarkably fortunate for the high-priced hotel, because Room 308 is a magnet for Indonesian and foreign tourists alike. Giddy with anticipation, visitors pass through the plain doorway as if entering a graveyard at night. Though tiny, the room is outrageously green and gaudy – green floor tiles, green wallpaper, green satin bedsheets, green and gold-tasselled curtains, green bulbs in a fancy chandelier. Paintings of the sea goddess adorn each wall, surrounded by flowers and the plumes of peacocks. A sea serpent carries the raven-haired beauty, wild-eyed and dangerous, through storm-tossed waves. Elsewhere she looks shy and serene, no more threatening than a pretty *jamu* lady selling home-made tonics or a young tea-picker in the green hills. Sukarno gazes down on this dream room from his own lurid and mystical portrait. A golden *kris* dangles from his waist. In the far corner by the door, beside a closet packed with green gowns, hangs a handwritten scroll of names. All the kings and queens of Java are listed, from Senopati to the last king of Pajajaran, along with the precise – amazingly precise – dates of their reigns. Other icons of worship lie scattered about the room. An Indonesian flag stands watch by the portrait of Sukarno. High above the bed, an "*Allah*" in Arabic script reminds visitors to leave a contribution in the green *kotak amal,* a Muslim donation box. Green is also the colour of Islam. Incense burns on a platform beneath one particularly winsome depiction of the sea goddess. Guests are encouraged to kneel on the prayer rug and to pay their respects to God, the Queen, Sukarno, the flag – or to all of them.

I returned to my tent and listened to the rush of the waves just a few feet away. In the morning a murmur of voices and the clatter of pots awakened me. After breakfast we toured the fish market and bought a few red snappers for supper. The boats must have returned safely because the market was packed with tuna, mackerel, prawns, cuttlefish, squid and many other creatures. Young hammerhead sharks sprawled lifeless on the slimy concrete floor. We shuddered to imagine the sight of a big one in the surf. The great hammerhead grows to twenty feet and patrols shallow tropical coastlines on the hunt for stingrays. Sometimes it attacks people.

Hundreds of fishing boats packed the harbour. They ranged in size from tiny outrigger canoes to huge tuna longliners with upswept wooden hulls like the Bugis schooners. Some were jammed together at the water's edge, in a kind of marine limbo between the active fleet and the lifeless hulks stacked high above the tideline. Small boats motored in and out all day long, their hulls newly painted in red and blue for the upcoming festival, *pesta nelayan.* In April the weather changes and the fishing improves. Just to be sure, the fishermen would soon slaughter a cow, wrap its head in a white sheet and drop it in the middle of the ocean to please the sea goddess.

After lunch the boys stripped down to their bathing suits and descended on the beach. The sun was hot and the water looked cool and inviting. Local boys were splashing in the surf all up and down the shore.

We posted a lifeguard with a megaphone. One of the other men and I waded through the surf and stood with our heads above water just beyond the line of breakers. We told the boys they could swim between us and the beach. They should listen for the megaphone and use the buddy system. All forty boys quickly streamed into the water. Compared to the natives of Pelabuhan Ratu they looked like creatures from northern lakes, alien and out of their depth. I noticed that several of them wore green bathing suits.

For a long time I bobbed up and down in the swell. My feet bounced lightly off the sandy bottom. I watched in approval as the lifeguard called "Buddies!" every few minutes. A few boys swam out to visit me but I shooed them back toward shore. Swimming in the surf was a great idea. There was no better way to spend a hot Saturday afternoon.

Something unpleasant brushed against my ankles and sucked sand grains out from under my feet. I shook my legs but the thing kept pulling me deeper. The bottom dropped away as I struggled to keep my head above water. With a sudden sense of panic I stared at the shore. The local boys had left the sea and were squatting on the beach, watching. Our boys were still swimming in the surf but moving away from shore, fast. Rip tide! I yelled as loudly as I could but my cries drowned in the roar of the ocean. The rip sounded like a rushing river, louder than the pounding of the surf, deep and malevolent. I waved my arms but nobody saw me.

The fingers of sea spirits closed around my ankles and pulled me out to sea. I fought back. My toes clung to the slippery shifting sands and I stroked hard toward shore. Shouting men ran along the beach. They jumped into the ocean with surfboards and plucked boys out of the torrent. I reached shallower water and grabbed one little fellow as he floated by. The waves boiled past a rocky headland where the rest of the boys dragged themselves out. Cut and bleeding, some crying, they crawled across the barnacle-encrusted stones to safety. In a final act of spite, the current flung one of the rescuers around the headland. I ran out to the point and watched in relief as the rip died away and he paddled his surfboard back to shore.

We counted heads. All present. After campfire that evening I saw the flashlights dancing in the tents and listened to the sounds of laughter. I thanked the Good Lord, whoever he or she may be, for our good fortune.

We broke camp the next morning and loaded up the truck. I walked down to the beach one last time and listened to the booming surf. The wind blew hard off the ocean. Sea foam and ghost crabs skittered across the brown sand. Farewell, Queen of the South Sea. She had taught me a lesson.

I felt relieved. Within a few hours – God willing, *insyallah*, on the busy highway – I would deliver these boys safely back to their parents. No more worries, no more rip tides. After a few days of rest I might dream up another adventure in the jungle, another encounter with Indonesia's exotic and unpredictable culture – *dukuns* and stone soldiers, flying Baduy and phantom tigers, cannons and princesses, *beos* and serpent-eagles.

Flocks of terns swept up and down the windy shoreline and dived for fish in the roiling waters. No seagulls flew. I thought it strange that those wanderers over the wide oceans of the world rarely landed in Indonesia. Gulls live in India, the Philippines and Australia but not in between. Why not, I wondered? Seagulls are quintessential travellers and opportunists.

A stuffed seagull inspired Emil Helfferich as a young boy to travel to distant lands. Gulls followed him almost all the way to the Far East and greeted him on his return trips to Europe. In 1914 Emil and Dina sailed back to Batavia just before the outbreak of war. For the duration of the conflict they were confined to the Dutch Indies like wind-tossed birds or marooned sailors. One dark night, buffeted by the winds of war and flung to the far end of the earth, one such lonely wanderer landed on Helfferich's doorstep.

NINETEEN

MAROONED SAILORS

Interned German Ships and Sailors, Batavia, 1914-18

The telephone jangled in the quiet of late evening. Emil sprang out of bed and answered the call.

"Helfferich?" a Dutch voice asked.

"*Ja,*" replied Emil warily.

"I've just sent a drunken German sailor to your house. He'll be there in a few minutes." The caller hung up abruptly.

Still in pyjamas, Emil tiptoed downstairs so as not to disturb Dina. He waited behind the front door and peered anxiously through the lace curtain. There were no street lights and the veranda was dark; he couldn't see a thing. Heavy feet crunched on the gravel path and stamped unsteadily up the marble steps. Helfferich flicked on the veranda light, opened the door and stepped outside. Both men squinted at each other in the sudden brightness. Helfferich recognized the tangled blond hair and the dark flickering eyes.

"Is that you, Jess?" he asked.

"Of course it's me, goddammit!" he yelled, "and I want to know where I'm spending the night!" His herculean form towered over Helfferich as he clenched and unclenched each meaty fist. The knuckles looked raw and bloody. Sweat poured from his face; his mouth was twisted with drink and fury.

"You know the answer. They won't take you any longer at Sukasari. You'll have to spend the night at the police station."

"Goddammit! I've been slaving all day – for a stinking shopkeeper for Chrissake! I'll be damned if I'm going back to the police station!" He reached into his pocket and flung a handful of copper coins around the veranda. "They just kicked me out anyway," he added.

A police car pulled up and the doors swung open. A Dutch officer and two constables leaped out and ran toward the house. Seaman August Jess turned to face them and folded his arms across his brawny chest. His biceps bulged menacingly. "Well, well, goddamn you all, what have we got here?"

Helfferich feared there would be a terrible fight. He ran down the steps in his pyjamas and stood between the policemen and the sailor. "He's all right, officer. I can look after him. You can leave," he told them, "Thanks for coming." The constables weren't convinced but they returned to the car and drove away in relief. When all was quiet again, he smiled hopefully at Jess and asked, "Well? What now, my boy?"

"I'm not your goddam boy!" Jess shouted.

"All right, all right, I'm sorry. Keep the noise down."

"And don't say 'all right' either, mister!"

All he needed was a bed for the night. He couldn't go to the police station because he'd just been there and had a fight with a Belgian sailor. The Belgian had started to sing his national anthem and so, Jess figured, he would sing the German anthem too. That's when the fight started. No, he wouldn't go back there tonight. Gradually he calmed down. He muttered to himself and began to pick up the coins.

"Jess, I'll give you some money for the sailor's hostel. Come to my office tomorrow morning at ten and we'll talk about finding you a job."

The sailor took the money with a grunt, shook hands and staggered back down the street. Jess failed to show up the next morning. Helfferich called the police station and spoke to the chief. Yes, the sailor was there all right – behind bars. He had stumbled into the Versteeg Restaurant late at night, tipped over a few tables and smashed some dishes. The police finally wrestled him to the ground and put him under arrest.

Helfferich visited the young sailor in jail a few days later. Jess was a changed man, modest and pleasant, embarrassed and sorry for the trouble he had caused. He promised to behave and to stay off the bottle. The two men chatted for a while about their homeland. Jess had grown up in Altona and knew the streets of St. Pauli as well as anyone. Helfferich offered him a job at his palm oil factory in Surabaya and then applied to the police chief for his early release. As they shook hands in farewell, he warned Jess to stay sober and to work hard. Helfferich was pleased to have found him a job far away.

On August 3, 1914, the day that Germany declared war on France, the flag of the fatherland fell from the roof of the German Club in Batavia. Flown in honour of the birthday of the Dutch Queen Mother, the flag snapped in a stiff gust of wind and ripped the pole from its moorings. Like a dead bird, the flag and the pole flopped to the ground. Britain declared war on Germany the next day.

Emil Helfferich had just returned to Batavia on *Rumphius*, the last German boat to leave Singapore unchallenged. After a sleepless night listening to the radio, he disembarked in Tanjung Priok, where Dina and his brother were waiting for him on the pier. Theodor shook his head sadly. Germany had plunged into war.

In the following weeks, German steamships fled the French and British colonies in Asia and arrived in the harbour at Tanjung Priok. Holland declared herself neutral and allowed ships of all nations to find refuge in the sprawling Dutch East Indies. Although warships were subject to strict rules and had to leave Dutch waters within 24 hours, commercial shipping was permitted more relaxed treatment. Cargo carriers and passenger ships from North German Lloyd, Bremer Hansa, Hapag and the German-Australia Steamship Company sailed to safety in Batavia.

Within a short period of time, 21 German ships and 500 sailors interned themselves. Following the departure of Admiral von Spee's squadron from Asian waters, German merchant shipping had no protection on the high seas.

Financing the ships' internment was a major headache not only for the owners but also for the consuls, such as Georg Rademacher in Surabaya, and for local German businessmen, like the Helfferich brothers in Batavia. Each line set up its own pay regulations. Where these rules differed from each other, they caused much hard feeling among the various ships' crews. In time they settled the pay disputes but not the more difficult problem of handling marooned sailors.

Although the Dutch allowed the officers and men to disembark, many were reluctant to do so. "Why should I go ashore?" one might ask. "I can see land just fine from my ship." But time dragged on. Sweltering below decks in rusting ships, they grumbled, argued and fell sick in the tropical climate. Fistfights erupted among the sailors. A man on *Offenbach* was beaten to death by his mates. The captains suffered just as badly: Roscher of *Manila* died of fever; Rens of *Freiburg* died a lingering death as his body and limbs twisted grotesquely; Weiss of *Offenbach* shot himself; Ketwisch of *Imkenturm* slit his own belly. The captain of *Iserlohn* tied a weighted line to his waist and jumped overboard at dawn.

Other men found release in less violent ways. Some found love adventures in cheap hostels or took menial work in the harbour. One captain, with a wife and children at home in Germany, married a young Javanese woman and disappeared.

Concerned for the welfare of their sailors, the German community formed a Support Committee and nominated Emil Helfferich as the chairman. At Sukasari on the Puncak road, not far from the Cikopo tea plantation, the committee rented a large rest house and made it ready for fifty seamen. They set up other similar houses throughout the East Indies. Helfferich expected a big rush but he was soon disappointed. Only a few sailors took advantage of the cool mountain air. Those who did refused to work in the garden. "Why should I work?" they complained. "That's what the coolies are for." Whoever left Sukasari or deserted ship, or those who couldn't afford shelter in hostels, ended up in the police station.

August Jess was one of those sailors, as was a man named Möhring. Möhring appeared in Helfferich's office just before noon one day. He too was strong and broad-shouldered with an honest face and wavy blond hair. He was looking for work but his name rang a warning bell with Helfferich. "Are you from the *Offenbach*, Möhring?"

"*Ja,*" replied the well-dressed young man.

Helfferich recognized his name as one of the men who had been charged with killing a shipmate in a drunken brawl. "Where have you come from?" he asked.

"From prison. They released me six months early for good behaviour. Here are my papers." He showed Helfferich the forms. "Sir, I need work. I promise you I won't drink anymore," he pleaded.

Helfferich felt he was serious. Jobs were hard to find at that time, especially for Germans, let alone ex-convicts. Fortunately, the director of the Prison Administration in Batavia had phoned Helfferich a few days earlier with a request. He told him he was looking for a European supervisor to guard native prisoners in Sumatra.

Helfferich smiled at the irony. "Would you like to go back to jail?" he asked Möhring.

The job suited him and the prison director agreed. The convicted murderer and former inmate left immediately for another prison to supervise people much like himself.

A creative approach came naturally to Helfferich, especially in wartime Batavia. Though cut off from home, blockaded and blacklisted by the English and disheartened by the sudden demise of the German East Asia Squadron, Helfferich assumed it was his duty to boost the morale of his countrymen. He relished the chance to take charge, to become a pillar of his community. In addition to his service at the head of the Support Committee, in early 1915 he founded the *Deutsche Bund*, the German Society, and the *Deutsche Wacht,* a monthly newspaper. He wrote books, poems and articles, and encouraged the literary efforts of others. He even supported the German Opera group, which had been stranded in Batavia at the outbreak of war.

His brother Theodor supported the German community in his own subdued style – as manager of the Batavia branch of Behn, Meyer & Company and as the chief *Vertrauensmann* for the German Navy in the Dutch East Indies. He carried on secret activities in support of the Navy, even though by December, 1914, the job had lost most of its significance. He dutifully collected and transmitted intelligence long after the East Asia Squadron had ceased to exist.

Helfferich toyed with the idea of signing up to fight but realized the attempt would be futile. An army doctor had examined him in a smoky Neustadt beer hall in 1903 and had released him on account of poor hearing and shortsightedness. To travel the perilous route back to Germany was almost hopeless anyway. Although some young Germans did try to leave the Dutch East Indies, most returned in frustration. The Dutch authorities issued cards to identify the various nationalities but this only resulted in a thriving black market for false papers. Swiss was the favoured citizenship for German-speakers. Swedish, Danish, Italian and Rumanian identity cards were also popular. One young German bought the papers of an Italian tightrope walker from a middleman at a very high price. He walked up to the counter at the office of a shipping agent and confidently asked for a ticket to Genoa. The official asked him for his name.

"Gabriele Stefano," the German replied in a carefully modulated voice. He pushed his papers across the counter and tried his best to look lithe and athletic.

The official eyed him curiously. "That's remarkable," he replied. "The man standing beside you is also called Gabriele Stefano."

The German looked in horror at the swarthy man beside him and realized that he did indeed look like an Italian tightrope walker. The circus performer had obtained a new pass from the Italian consulate. The ersatz Stefano fled in haste and booked passage on another ship.

Helfferich contented himself with a less dramatic life in Batavia although he did use subterfuge when necessary. He played at espionage much as he had played at war almost twenty years earlier. He and his Hamburg partners were struggling to create a new bank to cater to the needs of German businesses in the East Indies. They exchanged messages in secret code and invisible ink. On one occasion a Dutch sailor dropped off a present from "*Herr* Helfferich's girlfriend in Rotterdam." The gift was a pair of opera glasses in a fine leather case. Helfferich found two tightly wrapped films stitched inside the lining. They contained instructions for founding the *Ostindischen Produktenbank*, a fledgling banking venture which ultimately survived and prospered.

The war in Europe often seemed very far away and almost unreal. The interned German steamships rocked idly at anchor as merchant vessels from most other nations sailed in and out with impunity. One day in May, 1916, an unusual flurry of excitement rippled through the harbour. Half-destroyed by shellfire, the German ship *Marie* broke through the British blockade and arrived from East Africa to safe haven in Batavia. Helfferich immediately and proudly took Captain Sörensen and crew under his wing. Soon afterward the brave captain and three of his men continued their long homeward journey in a sailboat. In the middle of the night they cast off in the small craft, christened *Dina* in honour of the woman who had sheltered them. But the adventure was doomed to failure. The Philippine Constabulary captured the sailboat in Manila and sent the four men to an internment camp in the United States.

Captain Sörensen in "Dina"

Aside from ships and sailors and secret messages, Helfferich worked hard to keep the Straits and Sunda Syndicate afloat. As soon as war broke out, the English pressured the Dutch to dismiss German employees and to refuse to do business with German firms. No German products could be sold or shipped without the approval of the British Consul in Batavia. Helfferich received a curt telegram from his head office in Hamburg: "Don't rely upon any remittance from here." Bank after bank in Batavia declined to finance his Syndicate. In the end, only two establishments maintained ties with German companies: the Java Bank and the shipping firm, KPM. Both firms were critical to the survival of English companies in the Far East and were thus immune to outside pressure. In addition, Helfferich enjoyed a longstanding friendship with the director of the Java Bank. Dina herself opened many doors into the Dutch world.

The Java Bank enabled the Straits and Sunda Syndicate and all of its plantations and factories to survive. With financing from the Java Bank, Rademacher and the Helfferich brothers reincorporated Behn Meyer's Java assets under the laws of the Dutch East Indies. This allowed Behn Meyer to continue to do business with Helfferich's Syndicate and protected them from the British. The war itself brought some unusual opportunities. The sudden demand for tropical goods allowed German export firms to sell everything in their warehouses. Import firms took advantage of the dwindling supply of European goods. Prices skyrocketed.

But the war dragged on and on. Life became increasingly difficult for Emil Helfferich and his Syndicate. Rumours spread of a plot by Helfferich and two of his employees to overthrow the government. A drought destroyed the tea harvest of an entire year. His tea expert switched citizenship and left to work on a Dutch plantation. The British stranglehold on shipping led to a surge in freight rates. Later when the harvest improved, tea, rubber and coffee lay stacked to the rafters in German warehouses. Debts climbed in proportion to the declining quality and value of the unsold goods. The ugly memory of the 1907 pepper crisis loomed large in his imagination.

Then a saviour appeared in the form of a Japanese businessman named Yamamoto. He managed a plantation for his firm in East Java, spoke fluent German and had read Helfferich's financial articles with great interest.

When he approached the Straits and Sunda Syndicate with a proposal to form a partnership, he was, at first, gently rebuffed. After all, their countries were at war with each other. It was not even possible for the Syndicate to sell the Japanese any of their huge surplus of tea.

Yamamoto discovered a solution. He would buy an entire plantation from the Syndicate, including the surplus tea. Dutch property rules allowed the sale of a plantation without contravening the "blacklist." This loophole allowed Helfferich to sell the Semplak estate near Buitenzorg along with one and a half million pounds of tea. Although the estate had seen good times, including the party in 1913 for the East Asia Squadron, it had less romantic appeal to Helfferich than the lofty highlands of Cikopo. He had no intention of selling his "Special Property" on Gunung Pangrango. Yamamoto asked him to continue to manage the Semplak plantation, including the sale of all of its produce. The Syndicate made a huge profit and erased all of its debt. Thus began a fruitful lifelong association between Helfferich and the businessmen of Japan.

In the middle of the crisis, just before Yamamoto's proposal saved him from ruin, Emil received bad news. On a sunny morning in late May, 1917, he and Dina were visiting the Cikopo plantation. They were guests of the supervisor, Egloffstein, in the spacious two-storey villa near the tea factory. Theodor's motorcar pulled into the driveway unexpectedly. His brother looked even paler and more sombre than usual. More German ships sunk? The defeat of the fatherland? No, he had just received a telegram about their father, Friedrich. On May 17 in Neustadt the old man had died in his sleep. Theodor had not seen his father in the ten years since Friedrich had persuaded Emil to take him to the Far East. Emil glumly recalled his own last visit, just before war broke out, when he had hugged his father as if they would never meet again.

Several months later, a second blow struck Emil – malaria. The disease that attacked him as a young man in Teluk Betung lurked in the cells of his body and erupted from time to time in chills and high fever. In 1915 a combined onslaught of malaria and typhoid had nearly killed him. This time his doctor recommended a long spell of recuperation in the cool dry mountains of East Java. Emil demurred. He was too busy trying to hold his company together. Would it be possible to stay somewhere closer to Batavia, at Cikopo perhaps? He could rest in a house at the healthy elevation of one thousand metres above sea level. The doctor agreed.

Helfferich telephoned Egloffstein and asked him to prepare the field house for his arrival. The small white cottage stood high on the ridge above the river valley, near four old fig trees. Seven years earlier, as he and Dina stood on the stone bridge by the tea factory, he had pointed up the valley to the distant grove at Artja. At that time the manager was planning to build a house on the ridge to keep an eye on workers in the upper levels. Emil had promised to take her to the cottage some day, to enjoy a peaceful refuge from the heat and bustle of Batavia. Now she would have to take him.

They left Batavia early one morning and called on Egloffstein and his Javanese wife, Sassih, at the plantation villa. They continued by horse buggy up the rough stone road to Artja, passed under a twisted arch of fig trees and approached the white cottage. Red and white rose bushes greeted them in the front yard. Tree ferns waved over a thatched roof. They opened a pair of narrow French doors and walked inside. A bedroom and kitchen lay to the right. In the sitting room on the left, a pair of large mullioned windows overlooked the valley and the hazy Java Sea. Beneath the windows stood a small desk, painted white like the rattan chairs, the bamboo walls, and everything else in the cottage. The sun gleamed through the window and a cool breeze wafted through the open door. Dina pulled a pen and a blank pad of paper from her bag and laid them on the desktop for Emil.

Far above them a cloud covered the summit of Gunung Pangrango. At Hotel Sindanglaya on the other side of the mountain, Emil had recuperated in 1903 from his first serious bout of malaria. During that long-ago convalescence he had climbed to the peak of Pangrango's sister, Gunung Gede. This time he had no interest in such heroics.

Emil spent several weeks resting in the cottage. He wrote poetry at the desk while Dina sketched outside. A telephone connected him to the outside world and to his struggling business. The fever roughened his skin and forced him for the first time in his life to stop shaving. Dina suffered his untidy face with bemusement. The stubble was rough and black. He looked like a mossy man of the jungle, an *orang hutan*, as if the creeping roots and vines of Artja had embraced him. She hoped he would shave it off when his health improved. But as he approached his fortieth birthday Emil squinted into the mirror with his thick glasses and saw, for a brief and startling instant, the kindly bewhiskered face of his father. The beard remained and grew into a thick bushy *Rauschebart*. Along with his receding hairline and an expanding waistline the beard suited the image of a successful businessman. He wore it until the end of his life in remembrance of the man he had loved and admired.

The rest at Artja and the ministrations of his *Lebensgefährtin* cured him of his ills. The malaria vanished and never returned. Helfferich went back to work in Batavia.

Late one afternoon, on his way home from the office, he caught sight of three men striding down the sidewalk. One of them looked familiar. He was tall, strongly built and he rolled with a sailor's gait. Helfferich's heart sank. "August Jess, is that you?" he called.

The tall sailor swaggered over to him and doffed his cap. "Yes...good God, sir – you've changed!"

Helfferich stroked his full black beard. "It's my new style – like a sailor. I've heard good reports about you. You've been working at the Surabaya factory for a year now, haven't you?"

"Yes, but I've just quit, sir, sorry to say. A year was long enough in one place and I've saved 200 guilders. Time to move on."

Helfferich tried to hide his disappointment. To keep him out of trouble he would have to help him find another job. The other two men looked impatient. "Why don't you come to my office tomorrow and we can talk?"

"Fine, sir. I'll see you then." The three men barrelled down the street.

Jess showed up late the next morning, looking hung over and sheepish. Helfferich eyed him critically and asked, "Jess, you don't look so good today. What have you been up to?"

"You couldn't even imagine," he whined. "I tell you one thing – I'm never going to drink again."

Helfferich thought he might have heard that line before. He felt irritated, as if a mosquito were trapped in his bed netting. All the man's pocket money was gone. He took Jess down to the sailor's hostel and found him some work. Then he enjoyed another long spell of peace until a friend brought him bad news. August Jess was laid up in hospital with a crushed skull…

Sailors from the Dutch Navy boarded in the hostel too. One Sunday afternoon several of them were loitering on the veranda. They were hard, sturdy, square-shouldered blokes and they swigged huge gulps of beer from quart bottles. A few Germans slouched nearby, among them August Jess. Talk turned to the war…muttered insults…strong opinions…loud voices.…

"You Germans started this war and you're going to lose it."

"Ya, well, you Dutch are toadies of the English and you won't fight." Jess swaggered up to the Dutchmen, raised his huge fist and blustered, "This is how we Germans settle it. Fight me, you bastards!"

The sailors spluttered in rage and lunged at him. Beer bottles crashed to the floor.

"Oh-ho! All at once, eh? That's no good." Jess clapped the strongest one on the shoulder. "Come on, Jan, give me your best shot!"

The Dutchman was ready. They pounded each other and staggered around the veranda. The others surrounded them, yelling and cheering as the two fighters kicked and punched furiously. Crashing and thumping and cursing, they disappeared into the shrubbery. The bushes stopped shaking and all went quiet. Exhausted and bleeding, Jess wobbled out of the garden. The Dutchmen found their champion unconscious in the dirt. They rushed back and tackled Jess, pinned him to the ground and smashed his head open with beer bottles. The Germans pulled their limp hero to safety and hauled him off to hospital. He stayed there for weeks until he could walk again. Then once more he disappeared from view.

Helfferich contemplated the senseless fight. The strong feelings were no surprise. Despite Holland's officially neutral position, private opinion ran firmly against the Germans – with good reason, as Helfferich well knew. They were the *"buitenlandsche vijand,"* the foreign enemy. Germans did indeed bear the major responsibility for starting the war and Germany loomed menacingly large across the fragile Dutch border. In earlier centuries that threat had not existed. As the Dutch fought with the sea and explored the world, amassing vast wealth and colonies in the process, they looked down upon their poor and disunited neighbours. But in 1871 Bismarck had organized Germany into a huge nation built on hard work, order and discipline. The small, proud, independent nation of Holland grew suspicious. Great Britain, a traditional rival in politics and commerce, warmed up to Holland. In the Far East the Dutch inevitably tilted toward the English. The East Indies were surrounded by thriving British interests in India, Ceylon, Burma, Singapore, Hong Kong, Australia and New Zealand. English investments in the archipelago were massive, much more so than Germany's, and Dutch products found a huge market in Britain. For Emil Helfferich, a German patriot and a lifelong friend of the Dutch, it was a major disappointment but a sad fact of life that their countries and sailors should fight.

No sooner had Jess vanished than Möhring reappeared on Helfferich's doorstep. At first he didn't recognize the pleasant young sailor. "Möhring! What are you doing here? I thought you were in Sumatra, working in the prison."

Möhring hesitated. "Yes, that's right. I came from the prison."

"From inside or outside?" Helfferich probed.

"From the inside…I'm really sorry. I can explain."

Möhring had killed a second man. The Dutch had posted him to Ombilin in South Sumatra as a guard in a prison for natives. One day a riot erupted among the inmates, during which Möhring shot and killed the instigator. The police arrested him for his excessive zeal and sent him to jail for manslaughter. Once again the court reduced his sentence for good behaviour. By nature he was a good man and he was lucky too. Helfferich found him another job in Batavia as a tram conductor. They shook hands when they parted and Möhring promised he would never lay a hand on another man as long as he lived.

As the war limped into its fourth year, conditions for the interned sailors deteriorated badly. Unrest rumbled through the rusty ships. Years of idleness and drink took their toll. Venereal diseases ravaged the men. Sailors left their ships and wandered around Java. So many inmates crammed the cells of the Batavia police station that the Dutch built a new barracks for them in the suburb of Tanah Abang. The police transferred seventy of the hardest cases to the new quarters and asked Helfferich to visit them often. He made sure they bathed regularly, used mosquito nets and had enough food. Twice a week he brought in potatoes, sausages and one bottle of beer each. When trouble flared in the cells, the police chief would ask Helfferich to drop by and lecture them.

After one such occasion, Helfferich was working alone in his office on a Saturday afternoon. The sound of heavy footsteps intruded on the peace and quiet. Three drunken sailors barged through the door. He knew them well: Drechsler, a cheeky little rogue; Hohenstein, a heavyweight boxer; and Leonmann, a discharged colonial soldier and slightly crazy agitator. They were out on a pass from the old police station and had been toasting the Kaiser's health since early morning. Hohenstein rolled up his sleeves and displayed his muscular forearms.

"What are you doing here?" Helfferich demanded.

"We want to talk to you," blurted Drechsler.

"All three of you? All at once? I'm sorry, I can't do that. It has to be one at a time. I'll talk to one of you now and the other two can wait outside."

Hohenstein and Leonmann lurched back outside and slammed the door shut. Drechsler wobbled in front of the desk, an impudent smile plastered on his face.

"So what do you want, Drechsler?" Helfferich asked again.

"I told you…we want to talk to you…about our financial situation," the sailor replied, slurring his words.

"What do you mean your 'financial situation?' We've talked about it enough already. You get paid the same as everyone else. There's nothing more to say. Is that it? Nothing else?"

Drechsler stood his ground in obstinate silence. His mouth twitched in anger.

"All right, Drechsler, that's enough. You can go."

"No, goddammit!" he shouted.

Helfferich reached impulsively for the phone. In fury Drechsler pounded the glass top of the desk and swept the phone to the floor. His two pals heard the commotion and burst through the door. Three clenched fists hovered in front of Helfferich's nose.

He tried to stay calm. He folded his arms and looked each of them straight in the eye. "You think this is how you get what you want? Do you think I'm afraid of you?"

"Are you going to talk with us or not?" Drechsler demanded.

"First pick up the phone."

Leonmann bent over unsteadily and replaced the phone on the desktop. Helfferich could see that Hohenstein was by far the strongest of the trio. He put his hand on the boxer's shoulder and spoke to him confidentially, "I'll listen to you, Hohenstein, but you can see that your two friends are drunk. Get them out of here. Then you and I can talk together."

Hohenstein grabbed his two friends and hustled them out the door. They came to blows on the street but the boxer punched them senseless. He packed their beaten bodies into a pony cart and sent them off to the police station. Hohenstein returned an hour later, his shirt spattered with blood.

"All right," Helfferich continued, "Now we can talk. But look at you. You're not sober either and you're covered in blood. Get yourself cleaned up and come to my house in the morning. I'll help you – I promise." The boxer left peacefully and showed up on Helfferich's front porch early Sunday morning. He gave him enough money to travel to East Java and never heard from him again.

The sailors had good hearts, wild as they were. Helfferich grew fond of the rascals, even as he loaned them money and bailed them out of prison. There were sad times, too, when he spoke over the graves of those who had fallen victim to disease. Caps in hand, the seamen stood silently by the simple wooden coffins, their sober weather-beaten faces turned to him in humility.

Helfferich once had to bury a Turkish sailor from a German ship. Sick with tuberculosis, the hapless man bounced back and forth between the German and Turkish consulates. Helfferich stopped the bureaucratic juggling and admitted the dying man to hospital. He invited the Turkish consul to visit his countryman but the busy man replied that, unfortunately, he had no time. Two weeks later the sailor died and Helfferich phoned the consul again, this time to invite him to the funeral. The consul once more expressed his regrets. After the burial the next morning, Helfferich received an urgent phone call.

"So, where has my countryman been buried?" the consul asked.

"In the European cemetery," Helfferich replied with a grimace. Too late, he realized the cultural *faux pas*.

The telephone exploded in his ear. A few hours later the furious consul drove up in a limousine and confronted him. "I have just been to see the Dutch resident. He has assured me that our man will be removed from the Christian graveyard immediately and, like a good Muslim, will be reburied in the holy ground of a native cemetery. You Germans will bear the cost." The Turkish consul stomped out the door. Helfferich wearily shook his head. There had been little interest in his humble soul while the poor sailor was still alive.

Emil's best friend, Georg Rademacher, endured similar trials in his position as the German consul in Surabaya. One morning his secretary told him that a sailor named Eberhard had died in hospital the previous night and would be buried that afternoon. Rademacher vaguely remembered him, a modest, quiet, law-abiding young man. He made plans to attend the funeral, wrote a short speech about Eberhard and left the office for the morgue. He politely declined to view the body and quickly signed the papers. The casket was closed and transported to the cemetery. Rademacher delivered the eulogy as Eberhard's comrades mournfully shovelled three spadefuls of earth into the grave. *Requiescat in pace*.

One hour later the efficient Rademacher returned to his desk. He heard a loud knock at the door. "Come in!" he shouted. The door burst open. His hair stood on end and he gasped as if he had seen a ghost.

"*Herr* Rademacher! It's me – Eberhard!"

They had buried a different Eberhard. Georg swapped such stories with Emil on his friend's frequent trips to Surabaya. Combining business with pleasure, both Emil and Dina had many reasons to visit. Georg had remarried in 1910, three years after the tragic death from typhoid of his first wife and child. In 1911 his wife gave birth to a healthy girl named Elsi, who soon found a special place in the hearts of *Onkel* Emil and *Tante*

Dina. Throughout the war years the childless couple visited Surabaya often to play with Elsi, their "sunshine," and to reminisce with Georg about the "old" days in Teluk Betung. Years later Emil arranged a meeting between Elsi, the Rademacher's only child, and his nephew, Rolf, the son of his older brother Philipp. Their romance flourished with the discrete support of *Tante Dina* and they married in 1933.

⁂

On November 11, 1918, the Great War ended. Helfferich agonized over the terrible waste and the destruction of his beloved fatherland. A few months earlier, during Germany's spring offensive, his patriotic fervour had overcome his pacifist leanings. But now the war was over and Germany lay in ruins. In his newspaper, *Deutsche Wacht*, he penned a motivational piece to his countrymen – a wistful, sentimental, mournful appeal to rebuild the fatherland.

Christmas was a sad time for the German community in Batavia. Even though the war was over, Germans were not yet allowed to return home. The interned ships remained in port, pending negotiations with the victors. Helfferich resolved to boost the flagging morale of his friends. He threw a big Christmas party in the popular Versteeg Restaurant, where August Jess had once run *amok*. He organized the sailors into shifts and worked them day and night, welding sculptures out of iron, carving wood, drawing, painting and building. The *pièces de résistance* were 34 models of the interned ships. Sailors packed the restaurant. On the lawn outside, the marooned operatic troupe performed one of their well-rehearsed numbers. Helfferich spotted Drechsler and his roguish friends, now stiff and starched in their clean white uniforms. Soon, thank goodness, they would be going home.

One blustery afternoon Helfferich stood at his office window and watched palm trees flailing about in the monsoon. Lightning cracked nearby and sheets of rain swept through the grey streets. He wondered what would become of his sailor chums in this turbulent world. Above the din of the storm he heard a hesitant knock at the door. Möhring walked in, dripping wet. Helfferich saw him now and then on the streets of Batavia – Möhring, the blond tram conductor, waving at him from a streetcar.

"I've been fired!" the young man cried.

"What for?" Helfferich asked.

"I nearly killed a man."

"Good God! Not a third!"

"Yes…an Arab. He had a fake ticket so I shoved him out the door. But it's all right. He's coming around, I think."

The twice-convicted murderer apologized for causing so much trouble. Helfferich warned him to lie low when the police came looking for him. Within a few months a ship would arrive to take him away. Möhring thanked him for all his help and trudged away in the pouring rain. Helfferich watched through the window as his broad back and blond hair disappeared down the flooded street.

After the armistice the English claimed all German vessels in the Dutch East Indies. Almost a year later, in October, 1919, a ship finally arrived in Batavia to take the sailors home. On the eve of their departure they gathered at the German Club to say farewell to the men and women who had supported them loyally for five long years, especially the Helfferich brothers and Dina. Helfferich prepared a florid speech and a long melancholy poem in which he described his own bitter experience and offered the young men hope for the future. He himself had returned to Germany with empty pockets and had learned to rely on his own wits – and so too would they. The fatherland had nothing to give them….

> …Und später, als ich dann 'drüben' gewesen,
> Gefegt mit des Lebens eisernem Besen,
> Und erfahren, dass man nicht immer erlebt,
> Was man sich wünscht und sehnlichst erstrebt,
> Dass guter Wille und emsiger Fleiss
> Noch lange nicht sichern des Sieges Preis;
> Kurz, als der schöne Traum vernichtet,
> Den jeder gute Mensch sich dichtet,
> Und ich dann kummerschwer beladen

Rückkehrte zu den Heimatsgestaden,
Den Blick umflort und auf Nichts gerichtet,
Da hab' ich mich wieder hinaufgeflüchtet,
Hinauf nach dem alten Lieblingsort
Und schaute hinab in den Hamburger Port
Und lauschte den tausendstimmigen Tönen,
Und fand im Lauschen und im Schauen
Das eine wieder – das Selbstvertrauen!...

And later, when I lived overseas,
The iron broom of life swept me aside.
I learned that one does not always get
What one wants and so fervently wishes,
That good will and hard work
Will not always guarantee success,
That one's dream can be destroyed,
Even the poem that lies in one's heart.
Burdened with grief, I returned to my homeland
Without any plans.
I found refuge in my favourite old place –
I looked all around the Hamburg port,
Listened to a thousand sounds,
And found, in listening and watching,
That something else returned – a belief in oneself.

Seventy inmates of the Tanah Abang police station came to Helfferich's office to say goodbye. They all crowded into his office. Drechsler was there and Leonmann too. Helfferich looked into their eager eyes and shook their hard muscular hands. He loved them all, these rough, simple, stout-hearted fellows.

One sailor was notably absent. Convicted of yet another offence, August Jess had been imprisoned on the quarantine island of Onrust. Liquor was hard to find on the island but somehow he managed to scrounge a bottle. In a drunken rage he seized a heavy iron bar and stormed through the barracks. He flattened walls and terrorized the inmates. The Dutch lieutenant and his ten assistants waited until he collapsed in a stupor then they locked him up for another six months. Helfferich eventually received a letter from Semarang prison on the north coast of Java. "I, August Jess of Altona, am sitting here in prison. It will be quite a while before I can return to my fatherland. Please send me 10 guilders." On his way home a few months later, Jess dropped in to Helfferich's office. He was the last German sailor to leave the Dutch East Indies. They shook hands and part-ed sadly like two old friends who had seen tough times. Helfferich never saw him again.

In the spring of 1920 Emil and Dina boarded the Dutch ship *Tabanan* bound for Amsterdam. The months and years had drifted by. Dina was fifty now and this was their first voyage outside the archipelago since 1914. Among other minor deprivations, Emil had waited six years for a profes-sional haircut. The European barbers in Batavia refused to serve Germans. Too proud to get his hair clipped on the street, he had persuaded Dina to keep it trim. On board ship Emil at last found a willing Dutch barber. He sat down in the chair with an audible sigh of pleasure. The barber stared in dismay at his dark beard and ragged hair. He asked, "Sir, have you been living a long time in the wilderness?"

German passengers were not allowed to disembark on the trip home. When the ship passed through Suez and entered the wide Mediterranean, Emil stood at the bow and breathed once more the bracing cool air of Europe. Seagulls soared and swooped over the waves. He and Dina played with the Dutch children on board and sang:

> *Varen, varen over de baren,*
> *Varen, varen over de zee!*

> Sailing, sailing over the waves,
> Sailing, sailing over the sea!

TWENTY

KARL HELFFERICH

Hotel Atlantic, Hamburg, 1920

Sailors flung hawsers over the side of *Tabanan*. The horn sounded as the Dutch steamship inched closer to the quay. Stevedores grabbed the ropes, twisted them around worn iron bollards and dragged the ship to a final groaning halt against the wooden pier. Homecoming passengers waved hats and handkerchiefs to the Amsterdam crowd. A frail five-year-old boy cried as his parents retrieved him from the arms of Emil Helfferich. Little Jan van Dapperen loved the playful, bearded German *Onkel* and couldn't bear to say goodbye. No more "*Varen, varen over de baren.*"

In Amsterdam's elegant Hotel de l'Europe, Emil and Dina dined on dainty *hors d'oeuvres* and pastries. Well-dressed patrons bustled to and fro in the bright sunshine of March, 1920. A few tens of miles to the south lay the pockmarked battlefields, now ploughed and green with the first buds of spring. In a Dutch hotel the Great War seemed as remote and unreal as it had in distant Batavia.

The train to Hamburg chugged past gently turning windmills and fields of fresh tulips. In the far distance lay the castle at Doorn, where Kaiser Wilhelm II lived in exile and chopped wood for exercise. The train crossed the German border and clunked to a halt in Osnabrück. Steam whooshed from the boiler and mingled with the acrid smell of coal. Dark shabby coats and grey faces waited sullenly on the lightless platform. As the train pulled away on the last leg of its journey, Emil stared out the window in disbelief at the bleakness of his impoverished fatherland. Beyond the Elbe and the muddy fields to the north lay the hills and valleys of Bahrenfeld, where he and Georg Rademacher had joined the artillery and played at war. He wondered how many of his old friends were still alive.

In Hamburg Emil attended to business, then drove south by motorcar with Dina to Neustadt. French soldiers checked their papers at the bridge over the Rhine near Mannheim, where armies had fought back and forth for centuries. They crossed the bridge and drove into the Pfalz hills, now under French occupation. A short while later the car stopped at the doorstep of the old family home in Neustadt, where Emil fell into the outstretched arms of his widowed mother.

Augusta Helfferich described how his father had died three years earlier. He had already suffered a mild stroke and knew that his condition was serious. One evening after supper they were sitting as usual in the living room. His father read the newspaper, drank a cup of tea and smoked a good cigar. Then he folded the paper and climbed upstairs to bed. As he lay under the sheets he began to cough and grow restless. Augusta hurried up the stairs and placed a pillow under his head. She told him she would call the doctor but he squeezed her hand and pulled her down beside him. No, he said, this was the end. He kissed her, told her he loved her, thanked her for everything she had done in their lives together and asked her to say goodbye to their children. Then he fell asleep and never woke up. He died in peace, a man who told his children to "do good and never harm anyone."

Emil took three ladies – Dina, his mother and his sister Emilie – on a two-week driving vacation through Heidelberg and the east bank of the Rhine. His mother needed respite from the sight of French soldiers. After they passed the checkpoint at the bridge, Augusta told him that the French had arrested two of his brothers at the end of the war. She had asked a French officer how long her sons would be imprisoned and the man replied, "Fifteen years, *madame*." She almost fainted. Fortunately they were quickly released amid the confusion and turmoil of the postwar occupation.

Helfferich saw for himself the political turbulence swirling around Germany in the early years of the Weimar Republic. The German Expatriate Society invited him to talk about his overseas experience at their monthly meeting in Hamburg. The chairman warned him to expect trouble because, no matter how carefully he chose his words, someone was bound to object. Three weeks earlier, communists at a similar meeting had angrily denounced the guest speaker. When the time came for Helfferich's speech the hall of the Convent Gardens filled to capacity with 1,500 people. In the front row sat a group of disorderly young men in shabby clothes. Hecklers shouted at Helfferich as he walked to the lectern. They continued more loudly when he started to talk. He spoke of the moral obligation of Germans to work hard to rebuild their country and to bridge the differences between opposing groups. His conciliatory words praised the resilient spirit of working men and women. He appealed to his audience to lift themselves out of the desolation of defeat; not to blame each other but to help one another and to believe in themselves. The more he said, the quieter the young men became. He delivered a left-leaning speech filled with inspiration, benign platitudes and genuine emotion. In conclusion Helfferich described the troubles of the German sailors in the Dutch East Indies and he quoted from the poem he had written upon their departure. The applause was heartfelt and polite but one man leaped out of his seat. "Discussion! Discussion!" demanded the wild-eyed man with the tangled hair. The chairman and the rest of the audience ignored him and left the hall. Helfferich confronted the young agitator and apologized for his deafness, which made it difficult for him to field questions from the audience. He mollified the heckler but the newspapers were more critical. The next morning Helfferich read unfavourable reviews in the Hamburg press. They labeled him "the red Helfferich" and accused him of delivering a weak-kneed speech in favour of communism.

He was "red" only by virtue of the stark contrast between himself and his famous eldest brother. Karl Helfferich was now a rising star in the

right-wing DNVP, the *Deutsch-Nationalen Volkspartei* or German National
People's Party. Not long after Emil addressed the Expatriate Society, Karl
delivered a speech in Hamburg to 8,000 adoring members of the DNVP.
He started out badly, fiddled with his glasses, looked down at his notes
and mumbled incoherently. His head was barely visible above the lectern.
Emil felt embarrassed for him. Then as if magically transformed, he stood
up tall, pulled off his reading glasses and raised his voice to a clear and
strident pitch. He pointed his large nose defiantly in the air and pounded
the lectern with his fist. With sharp blows and angry shouts he hammered
away at the audience. Over and over he ranted about the humiliation of
Versailles, the burden of war reparations and the failures of the new democracy. In the end he switched to a more compassionate tone and concluded
with an inspirational plea to overcome all these difficulties and to build a
better country in the future. The applause was thunderous and ecstatic; an
enthusiastic roar engulfed Emil and swept him from his seat.

The next morning the two brothers met on the balcony of Karl's room
at the Hotel Atlantic. The sun shone without warmth in a leaden sky. A
few motorcars splashed through puddles in the street below. An old couple
pushed a wheelbarrow through a crowd of glum faces. Emil looked warily
into his brother's steely eyes. He saw the prominent forehead and the arrogant nose, the short hair, thin moustache and the hard edges of his mouth,
creased in a permanent scowl. Karl had been through a lot. During the war
he had risen to the highest levels of government and then plummeted all
the way back down. He was now rising again as a populist of the extreme
right.

"Father would have enjoyed the speech yesterday," said Karl.

Emil smiled at his brother's immodesty. "Yes…and he would have
marvelled too."

"Marvelled?" asked Karl suspiciously.

"Yes, he would have marvelled that you've changed so much," Emil
waffled, "and that would have made him happy." Like the rest of his family, Karl had at one time espoused liberal ideas but he was an elitist at
heart. He disdained ordinary people, whom he considered ignorant and
emotional. After a disastrous war and a turbulent career he had abandoned
his liberal ideas and become an embittered nationalist. Along the way he

discovered the unpleasant reality that he needed the support of common people. Without them he could never fulfill his dream of leading the right-wing movement. Now when he spoke in public, he professed sincere concern for the downtrodden and vowed to lift them out of their misery.

Karl smiled thinly but his eyes glinted grey and cold. "You're a good diplomat, Emil. Why don't you come to dinner tonight? My DNVP friends will be there. You might be interested in joining the party."

Emil declined politely. He would have to return to Batavia soon, he said. He left unsaid a more personal reason – Karl strongly disapproved of his relationship with Dina. Much as Emil loved his eldest brother he had no illusions about him and could never work with him. His knowledge, diligence and stubborn persistence would overwhelm Emil, just as Karl wore down his political enemies. He had no sense of humour, no *joie de vivre*, and he would never compromise on any issue. Emil wondered where this political quest would take him.

Karl Helfferich

As a Director of the Deutsche Bank, Karl Helfferich had made a strong impression on the ministers of the Kaiser's government. In early 1915 they appointed him Secretary of the Treasury and placed him in charge of the Loan Department. In one of his first official pronouncements he said, "We hold fast to the hope of presenting our opponents at the conclusion of peace with the bill for this war that has been forced upon us." He would ultimately find it difficult to transform this deluded hope into reality, much as he found it difficult to control the German economy. Despite his formidable economic reputation, based partly on his 1903 book, *Das Geld* or *Money*, his administration was responsible for the wartime inflation of German currency.

In 1916 the Kaiser promoted him to Vice-Chancellor and Secretary of the Interior, one of the highest ranking positions in the cabinet. In addition to his many larger responsibilities, he played a leading role in the construction of a merchant class of submarines, precursors of the U-boats which travelled the long sea route to Southeast Asia in 1944. These unusual state-of-the-art vessels were designed to smuggle certain critical raw materials from the neutral United States through the Allied blockade. The submarines *Deutschland* and *Bremen* were christened in early 1916. Although *Bremen* disappeared with all hands on her first voyage, *Deutschland* under Captain König returned twice from the USA with valuable cargoes of tin, nickel, chrome, vanadium and rubber. The shipments were organized in New York by Adolf Schönberg, a colleague of Emil Helfferich and a former director of Behn Meyer in the Straits Settlements. He had escaped internment in Singapore during the Sikh rebellion on February 15, 1915, and eventually arrived in America. The sale of German dyes, chemicals and pharmaceuticals paid for the construction of the two vessels many times over. Six more merchant submarines were built from the profits until the severance of diplomatic relations with the USA prematurely ended the program. Karl Helfferich deemed the venture a spectacular success.

Submarines played a crucial role in those severed relations and in the subsequent entry of the United States into the war. Despite Helfferich's strong initial opposition, a majority in the cabinet supported a policy of unrestricted submarine warfare – the sinking of merchant ships without warning. At a cabinet meeting on August 16, 1916, Helfferich stated, "The reactions of the U-boat war from the political and economic standpoint must not be underestimated. Everybody is perfectly convinced that a break with the United States and a war with the United States would be unavoidable.... America will desire to win the war as quickly as possible and will summon all its energies for putting this wish into execution....I see nothing but catastrophe following the application of the U-boat weapon at this time."

At another meeting on January 9, 1917, the cabinet nevertheless decided to unleash a policy of unrestricted submarine warfare. Helfferich was notably absent. Kurt Rietzler, secretary to Chancellor von Bethmann-

Hollweg, recorded his impression of the fateful meeting, "[It was] a leap in the dark. We all have the feeling that this question hangs over us like a doom. If history follows the laws of tragedy, then Germany should be destroyed by this fatal mistake, which embodies all its earlier tragic mistakes." Under strong political pressure Helfferich subsequently reversed his stand and became a reluctant defender of the program. He chose not to resign, a decision which he felt to be the worst intellectual sacrifice of his career.

Infuriated by Germany's announced policy of unrestricted submarine warfare, the United States broke off diplomatic relations in February. Unable to persuade the Germans to reverse their policy, the Americans declared war on April 6, 1917. As Karl Helfferich had predicted, the results for Germany were catastrophic.

Helfferich's star plummeted along with Germany's fortunes. At odds with the military and most of the cabinet, he was forced out of power in the fall of 1917. In July, 1918, the Foreign Office dispatched him to Moscow. For two months he performed his futile ambassadorial duty amid the chaos of revolutionary Russia. By the end of the war he was bitter and unemployed. He tried twice to volunteer at the office of the Berlin military commander. Although Helfferich wore the uniform of a major in the artillery reserve, the officer sent him away both times. At a dinner party on October 25, 1918, he declared that "every German should allow himself to be shot dead before we surrender…Better that my *Pfälzer* homeland also go up in flames."

After the war he wrote a three-volume memoir entitled *Der Weltkrieg* or *The World War*. He claimed that the impulse to record his experience was "the will to [discover] the truth." Several decades later, Emil would feel compelled to write a similar memoir of events leading up to World War II. He would subtitle the book *Ein Beitrag zur Wahrheitsfindung* or *A Contribution to the Search for Truth*.

While Karl poured his anger and frustration into writing, another politician, Matthias Erzberger, was rising to prominence as Vice-Chancellor and Finance Minister of the Weimar Republic. Erzberger represented everything that Helfferich despised. He signed the Treaty of Versailles and supported the fledgling democratic movement. Worse, he occupied

Helfferich's old job and was partly responsible for his political demise. The hatchet-faced Helfferich hated the soft, gentle Erzberger with a burning passion. Using pamphlets and public statements, Helfferich ruthlessly attacked his competence, honesty and intelligence. Eventually Erzberger had no choice but to sue for libel. In a brutally unfair trial, Helfferich turned the tables on his adversary and eloquently convinced the judges that most of the accusations against Erzberger were justified. The judges fined Helfferich a nominal sum for slander and made him pay for the cost of the trial. Erzberger viewed this as a political defeat and on March 16, 1920, he promptly resigned his cabinet position.

More than a year later, on August 26, 1921, two young ex-Navy officers accosted Erzberger on a walk in the Black Forest and shot him eight times at close range. He died instantly. In a comment partly intended for Helfferich, the *Frankfurter Zeitung* reported that "he was a sacrifice to the poisoned atmosphere which was created by the people who have engaged in such unprincipled and brutal rabble-rousing."

After the Erzberger trial Karl Helfferich became the darling of the DNVP. The Nationalists supported the Imperial heritage, a constitutional monarchy and capitalism. They rejected war reparations, the republican revolution and socialism. Although neither he nor the party was particularly racist, Helfferich did find it useful to state in a speech that "today the great Asiatic peril, together with Bolshevism, knocks at the German gate, as in the days of the barbarian invasions." His ideal was "the feared and respected German Empire." Socialists loathed him, although the distinguished Rudolf Breitscheid once commented, "I must say, to my regret, that the presence of Dr. Helfferich [in the Reichstag] is extraordinarily welcome to me; because to see here such a classic example of unrepentant reaction is extraordinarily bracing and stimulating for every left-wing politician."

Helfferich continued to launch energetic and personal attacks against liberal politicians. On June 23, 1922, he made a violent and provocative speech in the Reichstag against the foreign minister, Walter Rathenau. Like Helfferich's other opponents, Rathenau was committed to the Weimar Republic and to the necessity to pay war reparations. The next morning three right-wing extremists shot Rathenau as he sat in his open limousine on the way to work. Against the advice of party members, Helfferich drove to the

Reichstag that same afternoon. Cries of "Murderer!" rained down upon him as he strode into the hall. No one ever established a direct link between Helfferich and the two murders but no one could deny that assassins had killed two of his foremost opponents in the space of a year. Helfferich's own life was now in danger. The safety and wellbeing of his family were also at risk. Left-wing thugs broke into the house of his brother Philipp in Neustadt, under the mistaken impression that Karl was inside.

Divisive politics and ruinous inflation were tearing the country apart. The scourge of inflation, which began under Helfferich's wartime administration, spiralled out of control in the postwar years. Inflation was fuelled by internal borrowing, the unrestricted printing of money and taxation to meet the onerous reparation payments. Germans watched their life savings vanish. Grainy film images showed ordinary people carting money in wheelbarrows to buy groceries. Helfferich pondered the problem in 1923 while he relaxed in Switzerland on a summer vacation. In the clear mountain air he developed a fresh plan to stabilize the mark and thus to subdue inflation. The cabinet invited him to present his recommendations upon his return to Germany. They were willing to try anything, even a proposal from the reactionary right. The government successfully implemented the plan in October, 1923, and Helfferich rapidly became famous as the *Erfinder der Rentenmark*, the founder of the Rentenmark. As a result of his novel idea, based on land values, Germany enjoyed a spectacular five-year economic recovery. Only the global crash of 1929 brought it to a sudden halt.

With the taming of inflation, Helfferich's popularity rose dramatically throughout Germany, not only among the sympathetic right wing but also among ordinary people, the same people whom he had once despised. DNVP campaign leaflets proclaimed, "Helfferich's money put your household planning back on a sound basis. Helfferich's Party can also give your people a strong, reliable leadership." The DNVP organized a huge Party Congress in Hamburg to coincide with the birthday of Bismarck, the revered founder of a united Germany. On April 1, 1924, the assembled delegates gave Karl Helfferich a tumultuous reception. After his speech thousands of people leaped to their feet and chanted over and over again, "*Heil* Helfferich! *Heil* Helfferich! *Heil* Helfferich!" The mood was electric, the moment an eerie foretaste of the future. Overcome with emotion, Helfferich raised his arms for silence. "If you must shout '*Heil!*'" he said, "then don't shout '*Heil* Helfferich,' but '*Heil* to our German *Volk* and *Vaterland!*'"

Riding on the glow of such unaccustomed adulation, Germany's pre-eminent right-wing politician boarded a train to Italy to spend the Easter holiday with his family. His destination lay near Stresa on the south shore of Lago Maggiore, where his new wife's family owned an elegant villa. In 1920, at the age of forty-eight, the longtime bachelor had married well. Annette von Müffling was one of the six daughters of the famous Georg von Siemens, a founder of the Deutsche Bank. Now they had a two-year-old son, Friedrich, who found a surprisingly warm place in his father's heart. Karl Helfferich had finally begun to soften up. They were joined at the villa by his mother, Augusta, and by his brother, Theodor, who had recently returned to Europe from Batavia.

During the previous winter Karl had spent several months at the villa restoring his unsteady health. His lungs had never fully recovered from the riding accident as a young man. While recuperating at Lago Maggiore, he had taken the opportunity to travel farther south to Rome where he met with Italy's new fascist leader, Benito Mussolini. In April, 1924, Helfferich enjoyed the strong support of his party and planned a follow-up visit with Mussolini later in the year. In the meantime he enjoyed the spring sunshine at Villa Siemens and caught up on the latest news.

Adolf Hitler, a right-wing agitator seventeen years younger than Helfferich, was back in the papers. He was standing trial for his part in the failed Munich "Beer Hall Putsch" of November 9, 1923. The newspapers printed Hitler's views along with transcripts of the trial proceedings. Helfferich felt considerable sympathy for the passionate and eloquent young man. He thought that people should not be too quick to judge him until all the evidence was in. Perhaps he should meet with Hitler, too, as well as with Mussolini.

⁂

"As a people made up of the most extraordinary mixing and mingling of races…the Germans are more intangible, more ample, more contradictory, more unknown, more incalculable, more surprising and even more terrifying than other peoples are to themselves….It is characteristic of the Germans that the question "What is a German?" never dies out among them….The German soul has passages and galleries in it; there are caves, hiding places and dungeons therein; its disorder has much of the charm of the mysterious; the German is well acquainted with the bypaths to chaos."

Friedrich Nietzsche (1844-1900)

TWENTY ONE

THE TRAINS OF
BELLINZONA

Clouds over Teluk Betung

The parting words of the Chinese fortune-teller had come to pass. *"Belakangan Tuan besar sekali*! Later you will become a great man!" Emil Helfferich had prospered in the thirteen years since 1907. After the pepper crisis he had crawled out of the pit of despair and had become, in his own words, a *"Valutamensch,"* a man of substance. At meetings of German societies in the spring of 1920, he was introduced with respect as *Herr Direktor* Helfferich of the Straits and Sunda Syndicate. The investors and partners admired him. Not only had he guided the Syndicate through the difficult war years, with no support from the homeland, but he had actually increased the value of their investments. His personal wealth had increased too. He donated funds to German scientists and he presented sacks of coffee and tea to the shopkeepers of Neustadt. In the belief that a little money can indeed buy happiness, he showered gifts upon his nieces and nephews. At last he had achieved his cherished goal of success and recognition.

Spring passed into summer and the Indies beckoned. Plantations, palm oil factories and thousands of workers needed Helfferich's attention. Emil hugged his widowed mother goodbye and promised to return to Neustadt before too many more years flew by. He and Dina repacked their steamer trunks and sailed to Batavia.

A wave of optimism engulfed the Dutch East Indies. In the words of Governor-General Fock, the country was "a land of unlimited possibilities." The war had nurtured a feeling of freedom among its inhabitants. Europeans and indigenous people alike had learned to fend for themselves as neutrals in a hostile world. Responding to pressure for self-government, the Dutch instituted the *Volksraad* in 1918, a People's Council composed for the first time of both Europeans and "natives." Its limited powers spurred the drive for greater autonomy. Tens of thousands of restless young men and women attended the new Dutch-language school system, *Hollandsche Inlandsche Scholen*, perhaps the single most important colonial institution in the Indies of the twentieth century.

Sukarno, the future founding father of Indonesia, attended one such school in Surabaya during the war. There the young man met and boarded with *Haji* Umar Said Cokroaminoto, the pre-eminent leader of the fledgling nationalist movement. Cokroaminoto had founded *Sarekat Islam* in 1912. Within a few short years this so-called Islamic Union had attracted several hundred thousand members, becoming the first political group to win wide support among ordinary people. The organization promoted Islamic teaching and community self-help, mixed with a large and popular dose of anti-Chinese rhetoric. The man in the street envied and detested the supposed wealth and power of the Chinese minority, the "Jews of the Orient." They spoke a different language, worshipped Buddha, and were often skilled and aggressive in business. No matter how many centuries they had lived in the Indies, the Chinese were treated as perpetual immigrants on the fringe of Malay society. Cokroaminoto tapped into a reservoir of racial ill will that was, of course, a persistent scourge of the wider world and not unique to the Indies. He also appealed to the traditional Javanese belief that a charismatic leader would arise to guide the nation. Neither he nor Sukarno, in a later era, would be too shy to assume the role.

In addition to *Sarekat Islam*, the Dutch had to contend with several other new and unsettling political movements. In 1908 a group of Javanese doctors in Batavia had formed *Budi Utomo*, the first real political organization in the country. Their most significant achievement was a farsighted proposal to unify the country by adopting the Malay language. Malay was and still is the *lingua franca* of the archipelago and forms the basis of modern *Bahasa Indonesia*. Javanese, though spoken by tens of millions of ordinary people on Java, was regarded elsewhere in the country as the language of the ruling elite.

In 1910 a Eurasian named Douwes Dekker, known as Setiabudi, founded the Indies Party and lobbied the government for parliamentary rule. He was a descendant of the famous Dutchman of the same name, but known as Multatuli, the author of the widely acclaimed anti-colonial novel *Max Havelaar*, first published in 1860. Exiled to Holland for his views, the younger Dekker continued to promote the name and concept of an independent Indonesia.

In 1912 in Yogyakarta, midway between the Hindu temple of Prambanan and the Buddhist shrine of Borobudur, devout Muslims formed the Islamic party Muhammadiyah. Despite the party's Javanese origins, its principal adherents were the Minangkabau tribe of central Sumatra, among whom Mohammad Hatta, the future first Vice-President of Indonesia, was the most famous.

In 1914 yet another party arose, a distant wing of the international socialist movement. Within ten years this group secured the backing of Moscow and renamed themselves the PKI, the Communist Party of Indonesia. During the turmoil of the Vietnam War, General Suharto and his allies used the PKI threat to justify the toppling of Sukarno's regime. As many as half a million Indonesians died in the ensuing bloodbath from 1965-66, "the year of living dangerously."

In 1920, amid this postwar excitement and unrest, the economy of the Indies surged forward. The lifting of trade restrictions in 1919 released pent up demand for tropical goods. The Dutch administration built offices, schools, hospitals and harbours. They encouraged industry, banking, mining and oil exploration. The police department recruited boatloads of former German soldiers, such as those who had been captured at Tsingtao and imprisoned in Japan during the war. Immigration boomed. German and Austrian doctors, engineers, geologists and scientists arrived with their wives and children. Some of them slept in garages or cheap new housing. Emil Helfferich returned to a country in the grip of a massive but unsustainable economic boom. He had seen it before – the swing of the pendulum, the swish of the heedless "broom of life." He carefully positioned the Syndicate so that the company actually profited when the inevitable downturn occurred a year later.

Many of the new immigrants lost their livelihood and went home during the "*malaise*" of 1921. Two of the people closest to Emil decided to quit their jobs and join the exodus. The first to leave was his forty-one-year-old brother, Theodor, after fourteen uninterrupted years in the East Indies. The war had exhausted him. As the Navy *Vertrauensmann,* he was distressed by Germany's defeat and saddened by the loss of his comrades in the East Asia Squadron. His chronic lung disease flared up and he pined for the more salubrious climate of northern Italy. His health deteriorated to the point where Emil worried over his ability to survive the long voyage home. On the eve of his departure, he and Dina wished him farewell over dinner with friends. Recalling their years together and the blessings bestowed by their parents, Emil wrote a sentimental poem for the occasion:

> *Du kehrest, mein Bruder, zur Heimat zurück,*
> *Du findest die Heimat nicht wieder,*
> *Zersprungen ist unser deutsches Glück,*
> *Verklungen sind unsere Lieder.*

> *Und am Rhein, am Rhein, am deutschen Rhein*
> *Da stehen fremde Soldaten,*
> *Und willst Du in unsere Pfalz hinein,*
> *Passierest Du ihre Paraden...*

Doch im Hause wohnt uns're Mutter, so gut,
Die harret Deiner seit Jahren,
Es hielt ihre Liebe in treuer Hut
Den Sohn in der Welt voll Gefahren.

Sie zählet die Tage und Stunden gar
Und kennt in ihrem Leben
Nur noch den einzigen Wunsch fürwahr,
Dass Du zurück wirst gegeben.

Und trittst Du zu ihr ins Kämmerlein
Und beugst Dich zu ihr nieder,
Dann, Bruder, grüss' mir das Mütterlein,
Dann hast Du die Heimat wieder.

You're returning, my brother, back home,
But you'll find that it isn't the same.
The joy we once knew has been shattered,
Our songs have all faded away.

By the Rhine, the Rhine, the German Rhine
The foreign soldiers stand guard.
And if you should wish to visit our Pfalz,
You will pass by their men on parade.

But in the old home lives our mother,
She has waited for you for years.
She has loyally loved and cared for you,
Her son in a dangerous world.

She is counting the days and the hours
For she knows that in her old age
She has only one wish to fulfill
That you should come home again.

So on the day that you enter her room,
And bow down before her once more,
Then, brother, kiss Mother for me,
And be happy once more in your home.

Shortly after his brother's departure, his best friend, Georg Rademacher, left too, taking his wife and ten-year-old daughter, Elsi, with him. The loss hit Emil hard. They had travelled life's road together for a quarter of a century, ever since they met as recruits in the Holstein Artillery. As shipmates on *Prinz Heinrich* they sailed into Penang harbour at dawn. They were partners under a thatched roof in Teluk Betung, successful pepper traders one day, destitute the next and wealthy in middle age. They had celebrated a wedding and suffered through the loss of Georg's first wife and child. Then they had celebrated a second wedding and the birth of Elsi, their "sunshine." But in 1922 Georg, like Emil, had become a "*Valutamensch.*" His crippled fatherland tugged at him and cried out for help.

More than ever before, Emil relied upon the love, support and common sense of his *Lebensgefährtin*. Although they never married and she never relinquished her strong opinions, Dina had long since abandoned any thought of an independent life as an artist. She devoted herself entirely to their home, to their friends and to Emil's dramatically successful career.

By 1924 the Straits and Sunda Syndicate had reached a peak of prosperity. They controlled 21,000 hectares on Sumatra, Java and Bali. Twenty-nine plantations produced tea, rubber, quinine, palm oil, sugar, copra, rice and coffee. In one year they harvested almost four million pounds of tea and one million pounds of quinine, much of which came from the Cikopo plantation. The total annual value of the produce was 9.5 million guilders, worth roughly 40 million US dollars today, from which the Syndicate reaped a 10% profit. Helfferich and his investors had become wealthy beyond their dreams.

At the low point of his wartime troubles, Helfferich had been saved by a clever proposal to sell the Semplak plantation to a Japanese company. That event sparked a long and successful relationship between Helfferich and the Japanese. Very few Japanese came to Java before 1914 but commerce between Japan and the East Indies increased substantially during the war. Branch offices of large Japanese corporations rapidly took over the country's sugar production and, at the same time, imported cheap Japanese goods. More ominously, small Japanese photo shops became secret meeting places for spies collecting intelligence on Dutch defences. Many Europeans mistrusted the aggressive newcomers but Helfferich embraced them. Even as a young boy he hung a Japanese parasol above his desk. Alone among his colleagues he made an effort to overcome the linguistic and cultural barriers which separated them. He befriended an accomplished and diligent businessman named Arimura, along with his wife and two children. This personal connection was crucial. Through Arimura the gregarious Helfferich came to know many other Japanese, to forge strong commercial links and to travel to Japan.

In the spring of 1924 Raita Fujiyama, president of Dai-Nippon Seito, invited Helfferich and *Frau* Uhlenbeck to Tokyo to discuss plans for modernizing the Japanese plantations in Lampung. Before he sailed to Japan, Helfferich visited their operation in Sumatra to see the problems firsthand. After completing his inspection he returned to Teluk Betung and wandered around the familiar streets at dusk. He felt a twinge of nostalgia for the humble town – his first real home in the Indies, the place where his dream began. He missed Captain Kamdami, now retired, and the unsteady old riverboat, *Sri Tadjau.* In the early morning hours of April 24, he boarded a new coastal steamer for the trip across the Sunda Strait. At daybreak the boat weighed anchor and sailed across a gentle sea into a cerulean blue dawn. Two wispy clouds glowed pink above the rising sun. The lonely pair drifted across the empty sky until they turned white and vanished before Helfferich's eyes. The dormant shell of Krakatau crouched on the grey horizon. Later that day, in Batavia, he received an urgent telegram from Europe.

‹❦›

By the shore of Lago Maggiore in northern Italy, Karl Helfferich rested in the comfortable Siemens villa with his family. Their week-long Easter holiday was coming to an end. Karl had to leave Annette and Friedrich behind with his brother and return to work in Germany. On Thursday, April 24, he was scheduled to address a party rally in Hanau, near Frankfurt. His mother, Augusta, planned to travel with him as far as Mannheim then transfer to another train and head home to Neustadt.

On the afternoon of April 23, Karl kissed his wife goodbye on the marble steps of the villa. He picked up his baby boy and gave him one last hug. Theodor drove Karl and Augusta to the station in Stresa, where they boarded the train to Milan. The whistle shrieked as the steam locomotive chugged away from the station. Augusta turned and waved out the window at Theodor's frail figure. *"Auf Wiedersehen!"*

Karl sat beside his mother and worked on his speech. He gazed at sailboats on the lake and the fading light on the far hills. They changed trains in Milan but learned to their disappointment that the northbound Basel express would be delayed for several hours. Karl would be late for the party rally. They boarded the train just before midnight and settled into their comfortable berths for the long trip through the mountains.

The train rocked them to sleep as it rumbled through the night. They hurtled north along the dark tracks toward the Swiss Alps and the St. Gotthard tunnel. The engineer pushed the train hard to make up for lost time. Ahead of them in the blackness the southbound Basel-Milan express had just passed through the tunnel. Unaware that the northbound train had been delayed, a railroad operator near Bellinzona switched the southbound express onto its usual track. At 2:30 in the morning the two trains raced toward each other on the same rails and careened fast around a sharp bend. In wide-eyed horror each engineer spotted the rapidly approaching headlight of the other train. They pulled desperately on the brakes. Sparks flew from the screaming wheels. With a thunderous crash the locomotives collided. The impact tossed them high into the air and killed the crews in one terrible instant. The cars screeched and crumpled and tumbled off the rails. Steam hissed from pipes in the momentary silence. A man and a woman clawed their way out of the smouldering wreckage as noxious gases fouled the night air. Their car groaned and teetered on its end. The dazed pair jumped to the ground and fled in terror. A massive explosion knocked them down. They staggered to their feet and stared helplessly at the ghastly inferno. Flames engulfed the car from which they had just escaped. Silhouetted black against the orange glare were five men and women, including Karl and Augusta Helfferich. In vain they banged their fists on the windows and screamed for help. Their bodies twisted and turned in agony.

The mortal remains of Augusta Helfferich were laid to rest beside those of her husband. Karl was buried in an impressive ceremony in Mannheim. Lavish memorial services were held in Berlin and Neustadt. The exiled Kaiser Wilhelm II sent a wreath from Doorn.

The Nationalists of the DNVP had lost a brilliant and passionate leader. No one of Karl Helfferich's stature arose to replace him. In 1929 Hitler and his Nazis swallowed the party whole. Like a steel locomotive, massive and powerful, oiled and gleaming in the gathering darkness, Germany hurtled to its doom.

Milan to Basel Express, 1924

Emil was shattered. The accident seemed unreal, too awful to believe. Seared into his mind forever was the image of the two clouds. He had watched them disappear over the bay of Lampung at the same moment that his mother and brother had died in Bellinzona. How could he lose a mother in such a gruesome way? And his eldest brother, so different from him and yet so close? There were no simple answers for Emil, no faith to turn to, no comforting passages from a holy book. Dina held him tightly and cradled his head on her shoulder.

He could not postpone the trip to Japan. With heavy hearts a week later, they boarded the first of three ships, bound for the real Far East for the first time in their lives. After a month of travel through Hong Kong and Shanghai they steamed into the harbour of Kobe. A busy round of meetings and social engagements greeted them on arrival and masked the pain of grief.

Emil gave speeches and toured factories. Together they visited traditional homes, temples and gardens. Their Japanese hosts broke tradition by inviting Dina to a formal Geisha party. In Tokyo they witnessed the devastation caused by the great earthquake of 1923 and they paid their respects at the foremost memorial to Japan's war dead, the Yasukuni shrine. During World War II *kamikaze* pilots, loyal *samurai* of Emperor Hirohito, would call to each other as they climbed into their aircraft, "See you at Yasukuni!" In later years the shrine became notorious as the final resting place of convicted war criminals.

But when Dina caught a glimpse of the future emperor she lost her petticoat....

Crown Prince Hirohito had recently married nineteen-year-old Princess Nagako. Such joyful news so soon after the earthquake generated a frenzy of public adulation and catapulted the young regent into the limelight. One day the prince travelled by ceremonial cavalcade from his palace in Tokyo to the grand palace of his mentally incompetent father, the Taisho Emperor. Emil borrowed a car so that he and Dina might get a better view of the royal procession. He hoped that the driver would take them to a building overlooking the route, so that they might watch the spectacle from the comfort of an upper window. No, the driver said, shaking his head: that would be "too difficult." No one could stand above the emperor; neither could one climb trees or lamp posts. They drove through the crush of people until the car bogged down on the square in front of the palace. On foot they waded through the milling throng. Emil's head floated above the crowd like a Western ship in an Asian sea. Hundreds of thousands of people, perhaps a million, lined the parade route. Flags and banners fluttered everywhere. Everyone looked well-scrubbed and their clothes appeared to be new. Emil and Dina finally reached the edge of the motorway. White-gloved policemen asked them to kneel so as not to obstruct the view of the people behind.

They kneeled for a long time and waited patiently for the royal procession. Two small detachments of mounted soldiers in modern European-style uniforms escorted a plain Mercedes-Benz limousine. Darkened windows concealed Hirohito and his bride. In a moment they were gone. What a disappointment! No pomp and pageantry, no *samurais* and swords, no chrysanthemum carriage. The crowd rose as one and flowed behind the parade in a turbulent stream. Emil and Dina drifted helplessly in the current. She gripped his hand as people pressed in hard. Someone stepped on the hem of her long skirt and Dina felt something give. In Dutch she cried, "I've lost my slip!" Emil turned and surveyed the sea of bobbing heads. Behind them in the crowd, a young man waved her white silk petticoat like a flag above his head. Emil elbowed his way toward him. He bowed politely and pointed to the undergarment. The man bowed in reply and returned the slip to the embarrassed couple. Hours later, exhausted but intact, they trudged through the hotel door.

They left Japan a few days later. Instead of sailing back to Batavia, the two travellers embarked on a long-planned round-the-world tour in the opposite direction – via Canada and Germany. The summer weather would be pleasant and the scenery spectacular. As the ocean liner pulled away from the dock, the horn sounded and hundreds of coloured paper streamers fluttered down upon the cheering crowds. *Sayonara*! Emil and Dina remained on deck and peered into the distance for a last view of Mount Fuji. There is a saying that whoever sees the sacred mountain on departure will return. In vain they scanned the hazy horizon. For one brief moment the clouds parted and revealed the summit crater. The curtain closed and the mountain disappeared from view. Would they both return?

The Canadian Pacific ocean liner *Empress of Australia* was formerly the German *Tirpitz* of the Hamburg-America line. Traces of her German heritage still survived on plaques and printed notices. At a separate table at dinner, Emil and Dina sat with the only other German on board. The remaining passengers hailed from Canada, America or England. After almost six years of peace, the world still treated Germans as pariahs. Helfferich knew the feeling. When ships passed through English harbours such as Singapore, loudspeakers barked, "Germans and Austrians not allowed ashore!" Dur-

ing the week-long voyage across the Pacific, Helfferich had time to rumi-
nate on the contrasts among Germany's erstwhile enemies: the friendliness
of the Japanese and the vindictiveness of the rest.

Canada failed to live up to Helfferich's expectations. He saw no Indians; the food was expensive; he had to shine his own shoes and, thanks
to Prohibition, he couldn't buy a drink anywhere between Vancouver and
Montreal. Only one thing impressed him – the magnificent, soaring, gla-
cier-clad Rocky Mountains. They rode through the Rockies in an open
sightseeing car at the back of the train until the soot from the smokestack
drove them inside. For days and miles the train clickety-clacked across the
endless prairie and the black spruce muskeg. The contrast between crowded Japan and the empty Canadian wilderness was overwhelming. As Dina
slumbered beside him in the dark of night, Emil lay awake in bed, gently
rocking, and listened to the mournful whistle of the train. He dreamed of
a train roaring through the Italian Alps, of his mother and brother sleeping
peacefully in their berths.

In civilized French-speaking Montreal he was delighted at last to order
a bottle of burgundy with dinner. They hired a car and drove up and down
Mount Royal for a view of the city. On the way back to the hotel he spotted a new war memorial and asked the driver to stop. Two German guns
flanked the monument. Helfferich recognized the damaged artillery pieces
as similar to those he had fired and dragged through the fields around
Bahrenfeld. He removed his hat and bowed his head in respect.

"Where are you from?" asked the curious driver.

"Germany," Helfferich replied.

He was the only German on the crowded English ship from Montreal to Cherbourg. The immigration officer pulled him out of the queue
when they arrived in France. Dina waited patiently beside him. After he
cleared all the other passengers, the officer stamped his passport and breez-
ily waved him through.

By train and by car they travelled from Cherbourg through Paris and
then on to the Pfalz. Ruined castles stood among the hills where he played
as a boy; green fields of ripening grapes passed on either side; the tall church
steeple of Neustadt beckoned over the last rise. At the old family home his
sister and brothers welcomed him in tears. He drove immediately to the

cemetery and kneeled in silence by the still fresh grave of his mother. "*Gelt,
Emil, bleibst brav!* Be good!" she had warned him years ago when he left
home.

Emil Helfferich had seen the world. He had sailed the oceans round,
lived in foreign lands, weathered the ups and downs, lost and made fortunes. But even in such a vast and exciting world there was, indeed, no
place like home. Despite his success overseas, he longed for fresh challenges and recognition in Germany. For the first time in his life, Helfferich had
seen enough of other countries and other people. He bristled at Germany's
prolonged humiliation and vowed to mend his war-torn country. The fatherland tugged at his heart and begged him to return.

TWENTY TWO

FAREWELL TO ARTJA

Helfferich's Memorial at Artja 1926

In the melancholy summer of 1924 doubts and dark thoughts rolled around Helfferich's mind, shifting and pitching like a ship's cargo in stormy seas. The chains loosened and threatened to snap. He felt an irresistible urge to come home. But where exactly *was* home? Neustadt was too small and provincial, Berlin too political. Hamburg was the obvious choice: the city of Helfferich's youth, his first job, his year in the army, the home of his best friends and many of his business colleagues. Seagulls and ships called to him from the busy harbour. Dina found a small house on a hill overlooking the Elbe. Glass surrounded the veranda and sunshine streamed into the rooms. She fell in love with this cheery sunhouse, her *zonnehuisje*. On a whim they bought it. They purchased some furniture, settled in for the summer and let the sun's warmth creep into their hearts.

Karl Helfferich's financial program survived his untimely death. Inflation gradually subsided from its peak in 1923. For the first time in years ordinary Germans looked forward to prosperity. Convicted of treason, Adolf Hitler spent most of 1924 safely behind bars in Bavaria's Landsberg prison. In growing indignation he dictated to Rudolf Hess the first volume of his venomous treatise, *Mein Kampf*. His comrades in the Munich Beer Hall Putsch dispersed to their homes or to exile. Badly wounded, Hermann Goering fled with his wife to Austria, then to Italy. Heinrich Himmler returned sullenly to his chicken farm. An aimless and penniless Joseph Goebbels lounged around his parents' home and read about the decline of the west. In the summer of 1924, inflation and the Nazis were beaten.

Unaware of the impact these men would soon have on his life, Emil Helfferich sat at his desk facing the Elbe and wrote ponderous articles about business in the Far East. He prepared a speech for the German Chamber of Commerce. In Berlin's sumptuous Hotel Esplanade, Georg Rademacher sat in formal evening dress and listened to his old friend expound upon Germany's new role in the world. "We Germans must continue the struggle," he intoned, "not against the world but with it…not to destroy the world but to build." Memorials to the Great War, like the two cannons in Montreal, lay scattered around the world. In the harbour of Port Stanley stood a grandiose white pillar, crowned by a British sailing ship perched imperiously on a globe. It commemorated Sturdee's destruction of "the German squadron under Vice Admiral *Graf* von Spee thereby saving this colony from capture by the enemy." None of these foreign monuments would be likely to induce pride in the heart of a German patriot. But in Helfferich's view these memorials were not so much signs of defeat as enduring symbols of Germany's far-reaching power.

Emil fretted about the future. He blamed his malaria for the vivid dreams that awakened him at night and for the strange visions that shimmered in ballroom chandeliers when he delivered his speeches. Uncertain which direction his life should take, he left with Dina for a one-month holiday in Italy. He found his brother, Theodor, pale and weak but strong in will. They reminisced about an earlier crossroads in Emil's life – the pepper debacle of 1908, when a healthy Theodor had cajoled his unemployed brother back to good health. After several weeks of Italian wine and uncharacteristic lassitude, Emil's puzzling anxieties seemed to melt away.

Back in Hamburg he temporarily set aside his ambitious plans for Germany and for the Straits and Sunda Syndicate. On a mild autumn afternoon Emil sat on the veranda, pen and paper in hand, and dabbled in sentimental poetry. Dina coughed in the upstairs bedroom. A summer cold lingered in her chest. She brushed it off as a minor affliction but he brooded over her odd malaise. People walked by the house on the street below. He stared at the passing faces, blinked and abruptly leaped out of his chair. Mother! His mouth twitched as if to call to her and he broke into a cold sweat. He loosened his grip on the veranda railing, sheepishly removed his thick glasses and wiped them with a handkerchief. Emil lowered himself back into the chair, tapped his pen on the paper and wrote a few lines about a boy's love for his mother. He made up his mind. They would wind up their affairs in Batavia and then they would come home.

On their way to Genoa in November Emil and Dina stopped in the small town of Bellinzona and met the railroad stationmaster. He escorted them to the curve in the tracks where the two trains had collided just seven months earlier. Under the lowering skies of late autumn, by the withered grasses and leafless trees, Emil pictured the horror and the inferno that had so recently consumed his mother and eldest brother. In the same grey month in other far corners of the world, by the cannons of Mount Royal and the pillar of Port Stanley, men and women stood in silence and remembered. Wreaths of poppies adorned granite cenotaphs in memory of the greatest war in human history, a conflagration infinitely more horrific than the crash at Bellinzona.

In Genoa they boarded a Dutch passenger liner, *Princess Juliana*. Nicknamed the "rocking goat," the notorious princess rolled unsteadily even in fair weather. Like the old Sumatran river steamer *Sri Tadjau*, the "earthen vase princess," her upper deck swayed in huge giddy arcs from one side to the other and from stem to stern. The voyage was the worst of their lives. A tremendous storm battered the ship in the Mediterranean. Bad weather dogged them through the Red Sea and on into the Indian Ocean. Dina was sick all the time and her cough grew worse. She never left the cabin for weeks and found relief only in the calm waters of the Java Sea.

Old friends and household servants welcomed the travel-worn couple at the Tanjung Priok docks in Batavia. Back at last in the tropics and in her own comfortable home after eight months away, Dina felt rejuvenated and her cough went away. But Emil sometimes found her asleep on the veranda in the middle of the day. She looked unwell, she still felt tired and once she actually fainted. Emil eventually persuaded his reluctant *Lebensgefährtin* to see a doctor. The diagnosis struck him with the force of a mortal blow – breast cancer.

Three surgeons operated on Dina in the Cikini hospital near their home in Weltevreden. Although the operation was successful a Dutch doctor insisted she had to undergo modern radiation therapy in Europe. Wrapped in bandages and accompanied by a nurse, Dina boarded *Tabanan*, the same ship that had carried them to Europe after the war. As the boat pulled away from the quay she lay in a deck chair by the railing and clutched a poem that Emil had written for her that morning. She looked down at his distant, sad, bewhiskered face and waved.

Dark angel wings beat overhead and blotted the sunshine from Emil's life. He couldn't believe he might lose the woman he loved. Pressure of work forced him to stay in Batavia but he wrote her a letter every day. When the mail packet arrived in Amsterdam Dina read one heartfelt message after another. She replied in kind, one letter a day. In between letters she read the newspapers. In 1925 there appeared in print a series of short articles of little apparent significance.

> Adolf Hitler had been released from Landsberg prison by sympathetic judges in December 1924, barely one year into a five-year sentence. A Munich publisher made the final edits to *Mein Kampf,* soon to be released for all to read – a paean to social Darwinism and a vicious diatribe against Jews…. Hermann Goering moved to Sweden and entered a mental hospital…. A newly recharged Joseph Goebbels greeted Hitler's release with an article published on New Year's Day, 1925: "We greet thee, leader and hero, and there is an enormous joy and anticipation in us with the knowledge that thou art again in our midst." Two months later Hitler refounded the Nazi party and Heinrich Himmler signed up. By the end of 1925 the party would grow to 27,000 members.

In good times Dina had battled the demons of depression but in adversity she faced her malignant enemy with buoyant optimism. With her cancer in remission, she returned to Batavia in June of 1925 to her overjoyed partner. He showed her the stack of letters that had kept him sane, one every day for months. After she recovered from the journey Emil and Dina left the city and drove up to Artja for a holiday. Just as he had once recovered his health in the mountain cottage, so too would she recuperate from her recent ordeals. They brought their cook, *Babu* Maria, and they all enjoyed the adventure of a ride in their Hudson motorcar. The jaunty sedan had been almost new when they last drove into the mountains on Easter weekend, 1923 – with a duke and a baron.

⁕

Batavia's small German community stirred with the excitement of an aristocratic visit. In 1923 *Herzog* Adolf Friedrich von Mecklenburg arrived in the Dutch East Indies to promote German business interests. As head of the *Deutsche Bund*, Helfferich planned the itinerary for his distinguished visitor. He offered the duke a tour of the Cikopo tea plantation and an added bonus – a hike through the cool wooded hills of Artja, high above muggy Batavia.

They left the city early on Good Friday in two gleaming cars – Helfferich's new Hudson and a Nash for the duke. Emil turned to Dina and recited a verse he had composed for the occasion:

> *Hinter uns die Schreibkontore*
> *Und Batavias staub'ge Luft,*
> *Vor uns stolz Bergempore,*
> *Rein im blauen Himmelsdurft!*

> Behind us now the office small
> And Batavia's dusty air,
> Before us mountains proud and tall,
> Shining pure in heavens fair!

Dina smiled and patted his hand. She stared through the windscreen at the crowded lane ahead. In Batavia, as in modern Jakarta, there was no freedom of the open road. A two-wheeled pony cart trotted in front; a bus pressed close behind, rattling and wheezing as young men hung from the open doors. Vendors shuffled along with heavy loads slung on bamboo poles across their shoulders. Old white-capped *hajis* loitered in the shade. Children played in the sun and shoppers brushed both sides of the car. Women sold fruit, betel nuts and drinks by the side of the road while others fried bananas and rice in brightly painted *warungs*. In the slow-moving cars the passengers perspired. At the outskirts of the city the cars broke through the crush. The drivers stepped on the gas and careened southward to Buitenzorg at thirty miles per hour.

Rice fields stretched as far as the eye could see. In the *kampungs* among the paddies, tall trees laden with mango, jackfruit, rambutan and durian shaded the red-tiled roofs. Ahead of the cars two lofty peaks towered over the plain: Salak on the right and the vast bulk of Pangrango on the left. In the morning sun, the light reflected pale green from the ridges and a darker hue from the ragged gullies, like the buttressed roots of giant trees.

The rubber tires crunched to a halt in the gravel lane of a small cottage in Buitenzorg. In the garden an old man whittled a block of wood. His name was Steuerwald, a traditional German clockmaker and a staunch monarchist of the old school. He greeted his aristocratic guest with pleasure and he spoke proudly of the wooden sled he had shipped to Germany for the war hero, *Feldmarschall* Hindenburg. But what had happened to the old Germany, he wondered? What was wrong with the young people? Would the Kaiser return from his wood-chopping exile in Holland?

Hundreds of clocks and carvings adorned the tables and shelves of his cottage. The clockmaker gave the duke a traditional wooden "Traben Troll," a mythical creature of German fairytale forests. As the distinguished visitor turned to leave, a hen clucked loudly behind him and laid an egg. The duke picked it up, cracked the shell expertly and downed the yolk in one gulp. Laughing and waving, they climbed back in the cars and disappeared down the lane.

The cars turned off the Puncak motorway at Cigadog and bumped their way uphill to the Cikopo tea plantation. In the village of Pasir Muncang people strolled along the roadside in their best clothes. Shears in hand, barbers stood at the ready beside the plantation pay office. Good Friday was not only a national holiday and the holy day of the Muslim week, but also a payday and the customary occasion for a haircut.

Beyond the village the cars turned left into a narrow lane lined with young pines. A handsome white riding horse grazed on the lawn beneath an ancient fig tree. The lane opened onto a garden of red and blue flowers and ended at the plantation villa, built in the old Dutch style with a steep roof and shuttered windows. On the front veranda an imposing old soldier held the high ground. He was the Chief Superintendent of the Cikopo plantation, Baron August von und zu Egloffstein. He stood rigidly erect in shiny black boots, leather gaiters, riding breeches and a well-tailored white tunic. Trim and athletic, he looked younger than his sixty-four years, but his tanned and weathered face bore the traces of hardship and a lifetime in the tropics. Beneath the prominent nose a grey moustache camouflaged a scar across his upper lip, a souvenir of his army service in the rebellious province of Aceh. His eyes were remarkable – the piercing look of a hunter, full of fire and vigour but tinged with sadness.

Helfferich introduced the baron to the duke. They had old family connections and greeted each other warmly. After showing his guests to their rooms, Egloffstein escorted Helfferich to the study. The baron pointed to a pair of austere wooden armchairs and sat down wearily. Consumed with worry over the arrangements for his exalted guest, he had slept poorly. He had checked and rechecked the bedrooms, called for drinks and ordered lunch for everyone. Emil noticed that Dina had already disappeared into the kitchen to help the new cook. Egloffstein's Javanese wife, Sassih, no longer lived with him. Emil looked into the anxious blue eyes of his old friend, and thought of the man he had hired in 1911 to run the plantation.

August von und zu Egloffstein was born into the German aristocracy in 1859. As a cadet in military school he ran up bad debts and left Germany in disgrace. He fled to Holland and signed up as a common soldier in the KNIL, the Royal Dutch Indies Army. He shipped out to Batavia in 1878, the year Emil Helfferich was born.

The nineteen-year-old soldier arrived in the Indies penniless and alone. His early years in the Batavia barracks were miserable. On weekend passes he visited a brothel just beyond the barrack gate. The KNIL ran the establishment in an attempt to control the spread of venereal diseases. Where his boisterous mates saw only brown-skinned prostitutes, the lonely young baron saw Javanese beauties. One woman in particular caught his attention. With a delicate slender face and a finely upturned nose, she embodied the classic features of Hindu legend. She might have danced in the Kraton of the Sultan of Yogyakarta. Young August was entranced. He proposed marriage to Sassih and she willingly accepted. They promised each other a lifetime of loyal support and devotion.

In August, 1883, the blast from Krakatau reverberated through Batavia and the soldiers' barracks. Egloffstein joined the first rescue mission to the stricken coast of the Sunda Strait. He fed the survivors, pulled down wreckage, buried the bodies and poured carbolic acid into festering swamps. Soon afterward the army sent him to Aceh on the northern tip of Sumatra, where for sixty years the natives had fought bitterly against Dutch subjugation. He grappled hand-to-hand in desperate jungle battles and suffered severe wounds. Sassih waited behind the lines during the fighting and nursed him when he returned.

After twenty-four years of exemplary military service, the Dutch awarded him the Sword of Honour and the Knight's Cross of the Willems Order. Honourably discharged as a commissioned officer, he joined the Forest Service in Sumatra. For several years he tended trees until he put his experience to better use as the Commandant of Police in Asahan.

His job was to enforce the law. One day he took custody of three convicted murderers, whom the courts had sentenced to death by hanging. On the day of the execution, police guards marched the prisoners to the scaffold. They tied sacks over the men's heads, bound their legs and tightened the nooses around their necks. An awesome silence hung over the courtyard. No one moved. At Egloffstein's command the trap doors swung open and the doomed men plunged through the floor. Their legs twitched and they moaned but the scrawny little men were too light. Egloffstein coolly ordered the guards to grab their feet and pull. The struggling ceased and the job was done.

His formidable reputation attracted the attention of Theodor Herrings, the "King of Asahan," the pre-eminent landowner and businessman
of North Sumatra. Egloffstein regularly caught and punished the miscre-
ants on his tobacco plantations. In 1910, when Herrings advised his friend
Helfferich to buy the Cikopo plantation, he also recommended Egloffstein
for the position of Chief Superintendent.

Helfferich hired him a year later to manage the plantation. When they
first met, the baron had spoken Dutch. He was no longer comfortable in
his native language and the years of isolation had forced a certain shyness
and nervousness upon him. During the war his fluency in German slowly
returned. Although social chitchat was difficult for him, he could recite Faust
by memory and he knew reams of military history. Most of his ancestors were
soldiers and one them had fought for Napoleon. To Helfferich the baron
was a living book. Despite the uncomfortable armchairs he enjoyed sitting
in the spartan study, lit by a kerosene lamp and lined with history books and
weapons, and listening to stories of German soldiers in foreign lands. The old
baron never wished to see his homeland again. "What would I do there?" he
asked, "I would be just like a prisoner who is released after thirty years in jail
and who immediately turns around shouting, 'Take me back!'"

Helfferich wondered if he, too, would feel like a prisoner when he returned
to Germany. He banished the thought from his mind, stood up from the
wooden chair and joined the others for lunch. Following an afternoon tour
of the tea factory they entertained the duke with a simple plantation dinner and retired early to bed.

Just after dawn the next morning, Helfferich, the duke and the baron
drove to a tea station high on the mountainside about ten kilometres from
Artja. Resplendent in traditional *Lederhosen*, feathered caps and sturdy
boots, they toasted the day's adventure with coffee from the baron's ther-
mos. Village children gathered around and stared at the shiny cars and the
tall Europeans in strange clothes. When his guests were ready, the baron
picked up his walking stick and led them on a traditional German *Spaziergang* in exotic Java. The stone road to Artja curved smoothly around gullies
and ridges at a steady elevation of one thousand metres. With each bend
in the road the view changed from the volcano overhead to the distant red

roofs in the valley below. Green rolling waves of tea covered the broad ridges as far as they could see, dotted here and there with the hats of tea pickers and the bright red leaves of poinsettia. Cinnamon trees grew in pink-leaved profusion on the steeper hillsides of the Cisukabirus River. Three rustic stone bridges spanned the wooded tributaries above the rice paddies, beyond which the trail meandered northward to the trees of Artja.

At the white cottage among the grove of *waringin* trees they stopped for a rest. Egloffstein carefully retrieved from his pack some photographs he had taken a decade earlier. Helfferich noticed that his hands trembled as he displayed the pictures. The stark black-and-white images showed mounds of old, rounded, mossy stones lying scattered beneath the trees. Crudely carved faces, shoulders and arms poked out of the dense foliage. A keen historian and an old warrior himself, the baron declared they were the last eight hundred soldiers of the Pajajaran Empire. Their graveyard was called Artja Domas, "the place of eight hundred statues." In the old days barren women had come to the soldiers of Artja to seek fertility. The shapes were so ambiguous that one could imagine rough stone phalluses and voluptuous hips. The pilgrims' quest evolved into a belief that a heavy stone block, if carried around the sacred ground three times, would grant the bearer one wish. Egloffstein claimed to know a humble Chinese labourer who, having once performed this curious rite, had died a rich and influential man. But by 1923 the stones had almost all disappeared. Workers had cleared them to plant tea bushes and either sold them to collectors or used them for paving stones. "Nothing in life is eternal," announced the last *raja* of Pajajaran before he, too, vanished in a puff of smoke.

The hikers picked up their walking sticks and ambled down the cobblestone road to the villa. At dinner time the old soldier seemed tired and distracted. When Helfferich and the duke swapped stories, he listened politely but told none of his own. The baron looked wistfully at Dina and remembered his long life with Sassih, his own beloved.

During their years at Cikopo, Sassih worked diligently in the background. She did all the cooking, kept the villa spotless and handled all the minor annoyances and grievances that came his way. He was her *Tuan,* her master. Looking after him had always been the central aim of her life. The baron loved her and had eyes for no others.

By 1917 the fifty-eight-year-old Egloffstein found the work at Cikopo increasingly difficult. He worried so much about the plantation that he collapsed from the strain and asked to retire. Helfferich gave him a pension from the Straits and Sunda Syndicate and helped him settle into a small house at Bandar Peteh on the road between Buitenzorg and Cikopo. He could still ride his horse and he could catch up on his reading, especially military history. Sassih hired a cook and looked forward to their well-earned retirement together.

One day she fell ill. Egloffstein called a doctor but neither of them could diagnose the problem. Her condition rapidly deteriorated and became critical. He watched her helplessly as she thrashed about and the fever rose. In despair for her life he summoned her family from central Java. While he slept in another room they sat by the bed and kept a patient vigil through the long nights.

The fever broke. Colour returned to her cheeks. She regained her strength and began to eat again. Her husband thanked her relatives, who quietly returned home. In gratitude he looked down on her delicate thin face. With callused hands he carefully bathed and fed her. He soothed her with gentle words, as she had so often done for him when he was sick or wounded. They had lived together for forty-two years and, God willing, they would share many more.

Sassih recovered within a few weeks. With help from the cook she entertained friends and relatives who came to offer congratulations on her miraculous recovery. But old age can be troublesome. The strain of illness takes its toll on caregivers too. No sooner had she regained her own health than her husband fell sick, overcome by dizziness and violent spasms of vomiting. Word reached Helfferich, who sent a car to bring him to hospital in Batavia. After two weeks of rest he felt much better and returned home to his anxious wife.

Soon afterward he fell ill again and the pattern repeated itself. When he suffered yet a third bout of the debilitating illness, his doctor began to worry that this was no ordinary tropical disease. He consulted with his colleagues and concluded that the symptoms indicated poisoning by arsenic. In confidence the doctor phoned Helfferich with the diagnosis. Upon hearing the unwelcome news, he drove immediately to the modest Batavia hotel where his old friend was recuperating. Egloffstein sat upright in bed and spluttered in disbelief. It couldn't be true. It was just not possible. Helfferich assured him that the doctor was certain. The old soldier gazed out the window and thought carefully about the implications. A rebel from Aceh, perhaps? A convict on parole? A poacher? He had many potential enemies but how could they poison him? A steely glint flickered in his blue eyes and he turned to face Helfferich. "Someone must have paid the cook to poison me," he said.

Helfferich drove to the little house in Bandar Peteh and told Sassih that the cook had poisoned her husband. She angrily summoned the young woman and berated her in shrill rapid-fire Javanese. The cook burst into tears and pleaded her innocence. She begged them to believe that she would never do such a thing. Sassih watched the performance impassively. The desperate woman was obviously lying to save face and to save her job. Within the hour the cook left the house with her belongings in hand and a few of Helfferich's guilders in her purse. He offered his condolences to Sassih. With mixed feelings of relief and sadness, Helfferich drove back to Batavia.

The baron's joy in returning home to his wife was tempered by the disturbing thought that the cook had poisoned him. In all his years of battle and suffering, of wounds and illnesses, of struggles with rebels, poachers and criminals, never had such a wicked thing happened to him. He persuaded himself that it wasn't arsenic after all, just another mysterious tropical infection. His life soon returned to its former happy state. They hired a new cook. Each morning he shared breakfast with the love of his life, pulled a book from the shelf and read contentedly in his comfortable chair.

Two months later the nausea returned. The doctor advised him to undergo thorough testing in a laboratory. Several days later the lab delivered its report in a sealed package. The conclusion was clear: Egloffstein had been poisoned by arsenic-laced coffee. The doctor alerted Helfferich and the police.

A fan turned quietly in the high ceiling of a hotel room in Batavia. Helfferich stared silently out the window with his hands clasped behind his back. Crumpled in bed lay the baron, a shattered man. Tears welled in his eyes as he asked over and over, "Why?"

A Dutch police inspector accompanied Helfferich on the grim ride to Bandar Peteh. Sassih greeted the two solemn men at the door.

"He's not dead, is he?" she pleaded.

"No," Helfferich replied, "He's getting better. Someone poisoned him." The two men towered over her and stared in silent accusation.

Sassih cupped her hands to her mouth, fell to her knees and began to wail. She flung her arms around Helfferich's legs, looked up at him wide-eyed and shrieked, *"Tidak! Tidak!* No! I am his wife! I could never poison him! He has always been good to me!" She sobbed violently and threw herself down on the floor. Helfferich turned away in disgust.

The inspector ordered her to leave the house immediately. He would report the matter to the Justice Department but, so long as she went peacefully, her husband refused to press charges. The sobbing stopped. She dragged herself off the floor and wiped her eyes. She quietly walked away and returned in a short while with a bag of belongings. Her face was as cold and flat as stone, her eyes fixed on a distant point. Without saying a word, Helfferich handed her an envelope of cash from her husband. He stepped aside as Sassih walked out the door and out of their lives.

Weeks later the Dutch inspector dropped in to Helfferich's office. He had interviewed Egloffstein, the cooks and a notary in Buitenzorg, among others. Helfferich gestured toward a padded leather chair and offered him a glass of *genever* gin. He gratefully accepted and sat down to explain what he had learned.

Two years earlier, Egloffstein had drawn up a will with this notary in Buitenzorg. Sassih was the sole beneficiary. The estate was not large by Dutch standards, about 20,000 guilders or so, but to poor people it was a fortune. Although the will was confidential, the notary's scribe couldn't resist blurting the secret to Sassih. In her own turn, Sassih proudly revealed her good fortune to her family. Her prestige rose dramatically and there was no further mention of her youthful profession. She became the "Sultana" of her extended family.

When she fell gravely ill and nearly died, the family gathered around her. They stoically accepted her fate but prayed fervently for her recovery. Behind the stolid faces lurked a frightening thought. If she were to die, what would become of the money? Neither she nor anyone in her family would inherit a single guilder. Despite her miraculous cure the fear remained. They talked among themselves. She was no longer young – in fact she looked quite aged and worn. The fever had almost taken her. A second time she might not be so lucky and then the family would have nothing.

A deputation of relatives travelled again from central Java to Bandar Peteh. They politely greeted the silver-haired baron and announced that they had arrived to celebrate his wife's recovery. While he puttered in the garden they spoke earnestly to Sassih.

"Surely you understand," a cousin said. "For you to inherit the money your husband must die before you do. Of course he is a good man, in fact a very good man, and he has always been kind to you. But, God knows, he is an old man now. You can see him slowing down by the day. His useful life is behind him. How much longer can he possibly live? Whether he dies sooner or later, what does it really matter?"

Sassih reluctantly nodded her head. It was her traditional duty to look after her family by ensuring that the money would eventually rest in their hands, even if she died first. But to ask her husband to change his will was inconceivable. That would be *malu*, shameful and disrespectful.

A toothless old uncle spoke up. He had fished the Java Sea all his life. To stun the fish he sprinkled arsenic powder on the reefs. He could give her some – one spoonful in a cup of coffee would do the trick. It had to be given day after day over a long period of time. Once wasn't enough – slowly, slowly, one spoonful at a time. No, he wouldn't taste it, the old man said. He knew from experience.

After sharing a lifetime of joy and sorrow, tending to his every need, Sassih prepared for him each day a cup of poison. Smiling like a princess of the Ramayana, she offered her husband a cup of hot coffee and patiently watched him drink the last drop. Through all those years she had offered her husband not romantic love but loyal service. As twilight settled over their lives together she had to organize a fitting end to her term of service. She knew her family was right. Why should his money go to strangers in a foreign land? He was her husband, her own.

Egloffstein never did regain his former robust health. The loss of his wife was worse than death. Helfferich watched with growing concern as he spiralled into depression. When Egloffstein recovered his mobility Helfferich offered him his old job back. He hoped that the Cikopo tea plantation would keep him busy and get him out of his lonely house in Bandar Peteh. But it soon became obvious that the work was too much for him. After the duke's Easter visit in 1923 Helfferich assigned a younger man, Schmidtmann, to assist him and to learn the plantation routine. When Emil and Dina arrived at the villa in 1925 the old soldier had already retired for the last time. Schmidtmann, his wife and their young children greeted them from the veranda. Red and blue flowers bloomed in the garden but the white horse was gone.

⁂

Emil and Dina stepped down the winding stone staircase from the villa to a pair of gateposts at the bottom. They turned onto the road and strolled across the stone bridge to the tea factory on the other side of the Cisukabirus River. Two years earlier Helfferich had enthused to the duke about the number of hectares under cultivation, the number of workers, the total production of tea and quinine, and, most importantly, the annual profit. Today he was content just to tour the spotless marble floor, to listen to the hum of well-oiled machines and to chat with the shy young workers. Afterwards they paused on the bridge, as they had done years before, and looked up to the distant grove of tall trees. Grey clouds obscured the summit of Pangrango and rolled down the mountain toward them. They walked briskly back up the stone steps, said goodbye to the Schmidtmann's and drove up the final steep and bumpy stretch to Artja.

Rain clouds billowed down the mountainside and thunder rolled over the distant ridges. Bamboo windmills creaked and whirred in the first rush of air. When the car pulled up to the cottage, the young houseboy, Mot, ran out to meet them. He and *Babu* Maria grabbed the luggage and the food. The first flash of lightning cracked on the hillside. Violent gusts shook the boughs overhead. Huge raindrops drummed loudly on the roof and sheets of water poured off the eaves in a silver curtain.

Mot organized their belongings while Dina helped *Babu* Maria sort out the food. Amid the din of the storm they shouted to hear each other.

Emil donned a sweater to ward off the chill and he lit a kerosene lamp. Settling himself into a comfortable wicker chair, he pulled out the guestbook. He leafed through the pages and paused at the more memorable inscriptions. Many of the lines he had penned himself:

> Seit langer Zeit zum erstenmal
> Hat uns dein Zauber Artja wieder!
> Versunken ist der Erde Qual,
> Wie Segen fällt es auf uns nieder.

> Du kleines Haus am Rosenhag,
> Wo Farne wie Fontänen springen,
> Wo Taubengirrn und Vogelschlag
> Aus Ficus und Waringin klingen,

> Wo durch des Mindi grün Gefieder
> Des Höhen windes Odem weht,
> Und mächtig wie der Welt Gebieter
> Der Berge Riese schweigend steht!

> Was füllt die Augen uns mit Sonne?
> Was macht die Sinne uns so klar?
> Was gibt uns neue Lebenswonne?
> Dein Zauber, heil'ger Platz Artja!

> So long ago since first you cast
> Your spell upon us, Artja fair!
> Our earthly woes have gone at last
> And blessings float upon the air.

> O little house among the flowers,
> Where ferns like fountains touch the breeze,
> Where birds sing long in leafy bowers
> Of ancient figs, waringin trees.

Through plumage green of boughs unfurled
The wind blows high above the land,
Majestic masters of the world
The giant mountains silent stand!

What is it fills our eyes with light?
What makes our sense so clear and keen?
What fills our hearts with hope so bright?
Your magic, Artja, heaven's green!

His verse could not be compared to Goethe, he wryly admitted, but he liked this hymn to Artja. It captured his sentimental yearnings. Outside the cabin the storm rumbled unabated. In the fading light the trees looked like ghosts waving behind a grey screen. Emil reached for a fountain pen and shook it gingerly. Ever since that long-ago dawn off Penang he had never quite trusted the newfangled contraptions. He turned to a fresh page and began to write:

Was wünsch' ich weiter als ein Bambushaus,
Mit Palmenmatten Flur und Wände,
Und davor einen grossen Rosenstauss,
Und dann den Blick ins Weite ohne Ende!

Weitab von allem, was da stürmt und tobt,
Weitab von allem, was da schilt und dobt:
Rein wieder Mensch im Sinne der Natur,
Doch, ach für zwei ganz kurze Tage nur!

What more could I wish than a bamboo floor,
With mats of palm on roof and side,
A scent of roses by the door
And endless vistas far and wide!

Far from the world of wind and wave,
Far from those who rant and rave:

Warm and pure in earth's embrace,
Alas, God grants but two days' grace!

He turned to Dina and recited his latest literary effort. Her eyebrows lifted gently as she searched for something encouraging to say. The rain eased off while they ate dinner. Thunder rumbled far to the north where Batavia bore the brunt of the storm. Sheet lightning flickered in the dark sky. They blew out the lamps and settled into their spartan cots, falling asleep to the gentle sound of dripping rain.

Emil awoke before dawn to the first hesitant chirping of birds. He threw back the covers and stood up stiffly, shivering in the chill mountain air. He rubbed his arms to stay warm and shuffled down the wet flag-stones to the bathhouse. Venus shone brightly in the pale eastern sky. In the *mandi* he stripped down quickly and doused himself with buckets of cold water. Now thoroughly awake, he dressed, tiptoed out of the quiet cabin and tramped through the tea to the edge of the forest.

The dark volcanic outline of Gunung Pangrango cut cleanly through the sky and glowed in the first rays of sunshine. A band of monkeys chattered and rustled in the forest canopy. Birds sang in the dawn chorus and an eagle soared overhead. Emil was completely alone. There was no place on earth he would rather be. As a young man he had struggled against malaria to climb Gunung Gede. On its summit he had gazed at Pangrango, his "veiled opportunity," towering above the clouds across the chasm. During the ensuing decades in the Indies, he had transformed this vision into reality. Two years earlier he had proudly escorted a German duke on a tour of Cikopo, his "flagship" plantation – and hiked along this same trail. In his mind's eye he glimpsed the baron and the duke in leather shorts and feathered hats. Emil walked back down the path and stood among the four ancient *waringin* trees. He gazed at the distant Java Sea, still covered in a bank of white clouds. He thought of the soldiers of Pajajaran and the sailors of the German East Asia Squadron. An idea took root in his mind.

He wandered over to the cottage, now gleaming white in the morning sun. Red and white roses bloomed above an exuberant row of pink bego-nias. Drops of rain from the storm glistened on the petals. Dina greeted

him at the door with a pot of coffee and a smile undimmed by her recent distress. Emil looked into the loving eyes of his *Lebensgefährtin* and
thanked God she was alive. They remained a few more days in the mountains and then drove back to Batavia.

Later in the year they embarked on another road trip in the Hudson, this
time to Yogyakarta, the ancient city at the heart of Java. By the light of a full
moon they visited Borobudur, the largest Buddhist temple in the world. They
ascended a steep flight of stairs to the highest level and wandered among the
seventy-three bell-shaped stupas, each one containing a seated Buddha. Silver
moonlight bathed the distant rice paddies in a magical glow and silhouetted
the jagged contours of Gunung Merapi, the "Mountain of Fire."

Built in the ninth century, destroyed by earthquakes, buried in mud
and rediscovered a thousand years later, Borobudur rose again in majesty from its earthly moorings. Archeologists guided its slow resurrection.
Helfferich chanced to meet one of them on the veranda of a small hotel
at the base of the temple. Dr. Stein-Callenfels lay on a *chaise longue* in his
pyjamas in the middle of the day. A rough old man with a long, bushy,
grey beard, he looked like a giant from another world. His feet were bare.
An uncut yellow nail on his big toe twisted and curved over the end of the
chair. On the floor beside him lay an empty bottle of *genever* gin. He reminded the disappointed Helfferich of the two men in Teluk Betung years
ago, the ones who lay in their chairs on the hotel veranda day after day,
"waiting for news." The old archeologist succumbed to the magic spell of
Borobudur and died several years later, consumed by drink and demons.

In the year before Dina moved in with Emil, she had lived and painted
in her uncle's house in the valley between Borobudur and the equally ancient Hindu temple of Prambanan. Her best work, "The Fortune-Teller,"
dated from this period. In addition to her uncle's home she had one other
place to visit in this special part of Java. Emil drove her there without com-
plaint. They scrubbed and weeded a small plot and placed flowers on the
grave of Karel Uhlenbeck, Dina's first and only husband.

They drove on to Prambanan. In a chamber deep inside a tall spire
the elephant god Ganesha brooded on a stone throne. Helfferich, a good
tourist and an ardent collector, admired the sculpture and decided that

he needed a Ganesha in his own home. And a Buddha too. In a roadside Yogyakarta studio he ordered replicas made of the two icons and had them shipped to Batavia.

Back in their home in Weltevreden, Helfferich positioned the two stone statues on either side of the path leading up to the front door. To the right sat a smiling Buddha in the lotus position; to the left squatted a menacing Ganesha. An antique Buddha head perched on a pedestal at the head of the path. It reminded him of the one he had given to his late father and which now sat in their sunhouse by the Elbe.

Helfferich stood by the gateposts at the bottom of the path and admired his new lawn ornaments. He folded his arms and stared at the disembodied head. Sunshine glinted off the freshly painted idols. With a thrill of inspiration he pictured a pillar among the trees of Artja. He ran inside the house to tell Dina.

On their last trip to Europe, Emil had spoken to Theodor about building a memorial to the East Asia Squadron. Theodor suggested that a fitting site would be North Keeling Island, where *Emden* had fought her last battle. Emil agreed at first but then they realized that no one would ever visit such a remote spot. Now he could write to Theodor and recommend a much better location close to Batavia – an ancient sanctuary with a distant view of the sea. Among the stone soldiers of Artja, in the timeless style of a Buddhist temple, they would build a lasting monument to German sailors.

In early 1926 Helfferich learned that the cruiser *Hamburg* would arrive in Batavia in October – the first visit of a German warship to the Indies since 1914. It would be a fitting opportunity to remember the sailors who perished in that ill-fated year. Over the next few months he supervised the work of an architect, a gardener, stonemasons and dozens of labourers. The stone came from a quarry in Cirebon, the statues from Yogyakarta. Among the four trees of Artja he composed a likeness of his front lawn in Weltevreden, with Ganesha on the left, Buddha on the right and in the centre a multi-tiered pillar crowned with a tiny stupa. By October the stage was set.

In the dim light of dawn on Thursday, October 14, 1926, a group of men and women gathered on the dock at Tanjung Priok. Not since the arrival of *Scharnhorst* and *Gneisenau* more than twelve years earlier had there been such excitement in the German community. Not even the duke's 1923 visit could compare. A smoke plume appeared on the horizon, then the distinctive three funnels of a light cruiser. *Hamburg* was a sister ship to *Leipzig*, one of the four cruisers to go down with flying colours in the Falklands. She had survived the Battle of Jutland and the end of the war. Now she sailed with a crew of young cadets as a training ship of the resurgent German Navy. A twenty-one gun salute reverberated across the harbour. The Dutch coastal battery thundered in reply. Flags fluttered from halyards and everyone cheered.

Early the next morning a detachment of 230 sailors boarded the express train to Buitenzorg. As guests of the local German community they toured the Botanical Gardens, watched a Javanese dance, marched with their band around the city and then hungrily descended on the lunch tables. Free beer slaked their tropical thirst. After lunch they returned to the train station in a more exuberant mood. Bored already with parades and ethnic dances, the cadets looked forward to a one-night pass and a more lively exploration of Batavia's native culture. They jostled each other on the platform as the train approached. One young man lost his balance. To the horror of his stunned comrades he fell beneath the wheels of the locomotive.

There was no pass for the sailors that evening. They buried *Obermatrose* Thiel with full Dutch and German military honours in Batavia the next day. But the program had to continue. A more sombre group of men arrived back in the Buitenzorg train station early on Sunday morning, October 17. A line of twenty-one cars left the station and drove up the Puncak motorway to the Cikopo tea plantation. The new superintendent, Schmidtmann, greeted the unusual naval convoy and showed the drivers where to park. Sailors, officers and civilians alike walked half an hour up the rough stone road. Just before the old grove of trees, they passed under an elaborate arch of flowers and woven palm strips that announced in grand letters, "*Willkommen auf Artja!*" Beneath the *waringin* trees a large white cloth draped the monument.

Herr Helfferich and *Frau* Uhlenbeck greeted each person at the top of the trail. They shook hands with fifty-six sailors, an equal number of friends from the city, eight junior officers and Captain Otto Groos, the commander of *Hamburg* – a man whose honours included a Doctorate of Philosophy. Mindful of her guests' hearty appetites, Dina escorted them to tables laden with food and drink. The vigorous hike up the flank of a volcano, the overarching trees, a distant view of the sea, the sunshine, cool air and food combined to make a spectacular impression.

The crack of a pistol announced the ceremony. Dressed in tropical white uniforms the sailors lined up in loose ranks and faced the veiled monument. Helfferich sported black pants and a white jacket, not unlike the one he wore in 1899 on the day he sailed into Penang. He stood beside Buddha, adjusted his glasses and fidgeted with his notes. When all was quiet he opened with thanks to God and three cheers for Queen Wilhelmina. He spoke at length about the visit of *Hamburg*, the ship's namesake city, the beloved fatherland, the East Asia Squadron and finally, his brother Theodor, the former Naval *Vertrauensmann* for the Indies. He thanked all those who had helped, read a telegram of greetings from his absent brother and then ceremoniously unveiled the cenotaph:

DEM TAPFEREN
DEUTSCH-OSTASIATISCHEN
GESCHWADER
1914

ERRICHTET
VON
EMIL UND THEODOR HELFFERICH
1926

Helfferich asked for a minute of silence. The sailors removed their caps and bowed their heads. Birds sang in the trees and a breeze rustled the leaves. Helfferich looked at the faraway sea and tried to control his emotions. A feeling of pride and exhilaration stirred within him as he took a deep breath....

Wir kannten Euch! Zum fernen Palmenstrand
Bracht' Euer Wimpel stets ein Stückchen Heimatland.
Wir kannten ihn, Graf Spee, den ries'gen Admiral,
Die tapfern Kapitäne, die Offiziere all'.

Und uns're blauen Jungs im weissen Tropenkleid,
Die Augen hell und klar und Herz und Sinn so weit.
Noch hör' ich ihren Schritt durch uns're Strassen hallen,
Das stolze Flaggenlied aus rauhen Kehlen schallen,

Und seh' an Bord zum abendlichen Feste
Batavia's Bürger dann als Eu're Gäste. –
Das war einmal. – Dann kam die schwere Zeit.
Wir alle wussten es: Ihr war't dem Tod geweiht.

Vom übermächt'gen Feind gejagt, gehetzt, umstellt,
Galt's wie die Nibelungen zu sterben als ein Held!
Und als im blut'gen Ringen mit Monmouth und Good Hope
Der junge Lorbeer sich um Eure Stirnen wob,

Da waret Ihr bereit; es kam der harte Schlag,
Dort bei den Falklandsinseln der Flotte letzter Tag. –
Erschüttert denken wir der Edlen, Guten,
Die tief jetzt ruhen in des Meeres Fluten.

We knew you! You brought to our tropical strand,
Your flag – a piece of the fatherland.
We knew him, *Graf* Spee, the Admiral tall,
The captains brave and officers all,

And all our young sailors in uniforms white,
Their eyes shining clear and their hearts burning bright.
I can still hear their steps resounding on roads,
The anthem sung proudly from a hundred rough throats.

And see on board ship in their evening best
Batavia's finest, who came as your guests –
That was once – but later, hard times drew nigh.
We dreaded your fate – you were destined to die.

Hunted and chased by implacable foes
Like Wagnerian heroes you struck the first blows.
Monmouth and *Good Hope* sank in circles of gore,
Like rings of red wreaths round your foreheads you wore.

You were ready to fight in the final fray
In the sea by the Falklands, the squadron's last day.
Saddened, we think of the ones who were brave,
Who now rest beneath the deep ocean waves.

Emil Helfferich in 1927

He concluded his speech with a heartfelt benediction:

> "May the waves that drift today over their grave carry the news of our commemoration. May this memorial that we have built in their honour stand forever. May this holy ground become a place of pilgrimage for all Germans in the world who love their fatherland. May the stones speak of a faith that will never fade."

In the three days that followed there were more parties, more speeches, more anthems, more misty-eyed toasts to the fatherland, past glories and future Dutch-German cooperation than the dazed sailors could ever remember. When *Hamburg* weighed anchor, the ship's band played the Dutch and German anthems one last time. In the years to come she would no longer train cadets but served instead as a floating barracks for U-boat crews, some of whom sailed the long sea route to Java. The lofty sentiments of Dutch-German cooperation were dashed in 1940 when Hitler's army invaded Holland. In 1944 *Hamburg's* career came to a sudden end. Tethered to the dock in the harbour of her namesake city, below the very eyes of Emil Helfferich as he huddled in his home on the Elbe, *Hamburg* sank under the furious bombardment of Allied planes.

Back in Batavia, Helfferich sent telegrams describing the Artja ceremony to Theodor and to *Gräfin* Spee in Kiel, the woman who lost her husband and two sons in the Falklands. After posting the messages he sat with Dina on the veranda of their home and poured himself a whisky and soda. Cicadas hummed in the trees as evening settled swiftly on the city. The ceremony at Artja marked the beginning of the end of his life in the Indies. When he removed the white drapery from the cenotaph he had symbolically unveiled a memorial not only to the sailors but to himself and to his "Eastern bride" – the fulfilment of his dreams. The plantations in Java and Sumatra produced vast amounts of tea, coffee, rubber and quinine. In Batavia the German community read his biweekly newspaper, the *Deutsche Wacht*. They joined the *Deutsche Bund*, the club he founded, and congregated at the *Deutsche Haus,* the cultural centre that he had recently opened. His brother and all of his old friends had gone home. The last of his colleagues from the early days, Albert Paulmann, had left the Indies soon after Dina's return from Amsterdam. Helfferich's unflappable partner had once drifted around a pirate-infested sea with 40,000 guilders in silver bars. But the adventure and the romance had long since faded. He knew, like Helfferich, that it was time to move on.

On the last day of 1927 Emil and Dina watched the sun set behind the cottage at Artja. The crescent moon followed the same path and vanished below the trees and the ragged edge of Gunung Salak. Dina read by lamplight while Emil cobbled together a torch from wood and rags. He had a romantic notion to herald the New Year in a mystical, medieval way. Just before midnight he struck a match to the kerosene-soaked rags and paraded by torchlight to the monument. His bemused partner followed the shifting shadows by his feet. Around them loomed the dark silhouettes of the fig trees and, far above, the outline of Gunung Pangrango. The stars shone brightly in a clear sky. Ganesha and Buddha swayed in the dusky shadows beyond the light. Emil waved the torch in front of the inscriptions on the pillar and read the words out loud. Then he rested the torch on the base and sat down on the steps with Dina. Hand in hand they watched the lights in the valley stretching far away to Batavia. They reminisced about the good times…standing among the stupas of Borobudur by moonlight and watching the silver light gleaming on the paddies and the Mountain of Fire…leaning on a ship's railing and gazing at the shining sea trail of the moon…evanescent moon trails like rainbows and dreams. The conversation trailed off into silence. Emil picked up the sputtering torch and they wandered back to the cottage.

Seventeen days later they returned to Artja to celebrate Emil's fiftieth birthday. A few friends made the long trek from Batavia to bring flowers and to wish him well, but otherwise they were alone. They watched the sun rise and walked in the woods. Dina sketched outside while Emil wrote poems at his desk. He looked sadly out the window. His heart told him that there was no place on earth he would rather be, but reason urged him to return to Germany. They might visit Artja once or twice more and then they would sail away forever. They had a booking in six months' time on *Rendsburg*, the freighter that would take them home.

Helfferich handed over leadership of the *Deutsche Bund* and the Straits and Sunda Syndicate to his successors. He and Dina took one last motorcar trip around Java. They travelled as far as Bali, where one sparkling day they drove along the sandy beach at the incredible speed of fifty miles per hour, laughing and shouting as the salt spray flew over the roof. In east Java they stayed overnight at Sarangan, a resort built by two Germans stranded in the Indies during the war. They visited Borobudur one last time and then Emil sailed to Sumatra to check on his plantations. In Teluk Betung his old house had disappeared and no one remained from his early days. Only one old man remembered him. Dressed all in white like Tunku Tiga, he gave Helfferich a rattan walking stick marked with elfin inscriptions. The old *haji* suggested it would protect him from sea monsters.

They moved out of their home in Weltevreden and packed their belongings into fifty-seven wooden crates, each one emblazoned with broad red stripes. Buddha and Ganesha remained on the front lawn. The rest they gave away to their servants. They wanted no part of a public auction, the usual melancholy end to life overseas. In their final days they stayed in the finest suite of the Hotel des Indes, in Helfferich's opinion the largest and best hotel in Southeast Asia. He happened to be a director on the board of the hotel, a position that ensured excellent service. For their farewell dinner the kitchen staff prepared a one metre-high chocolate and sugar model of the ship that would take them away.

In black tie and ball gowns, the German community came to dinner to wish them goodbye. Helfferich delivered a farewell speech that was more strident than usual. Five years earlier, before his round-the-world tour, he had exhorted his fellow Germans to work hard and cooperate to "ensure that these troubles lead to a new life, that goodness endures and that a mature, strong and noble German nation arises. Then the vanquished will become victors – victors over ourselves." On this final occasion he lectured more ominously, "Germany stands now in struggle, a struggle for its freedom, a struggle for a humane existence. Perhaps the struggle will be decided without bloodshed. Whatever happens, whether we fight with our minds or with weapons or both, it is our duty to remain strong and healthy in morals and in body. It is our duty to work hard in the service of the fatherland!"

This shift in attitude had occurred slowly. His speech echoed the 1897 sentiments of his mentor, Witthoefft, who had formed the German Association in Singapore in part "as a means to further our business interests where forceful persuasion is required." In 1915 Helfferich discussed the war and his own *Deutsche Bund* in Batavia with an article in *Deutsche Wacht*: "An invisible wave infused and fired our blood, and our hearts beat as one.... Even those who were estranged from the old country...felt like magic the old blood stirring in their veins. And the more the world stormed against German ways and German standing, the more united we became. The urge which led to the foundation of the *Deutsche Bund* had been present as a latent power during the long peaceful years of work. The war released this power and translated it into action. This impulse is deeply rooted in us Germans throughout the world.... Every step an Englishman advances in this world brings him nearer home, whereas...we were strangers everywhere." In another article he ascribed the causes of the war to "Britain's rise to the leading position in world trade...a feeling of British superiority...the increase of German competition in world markets...'Made in Germany' became a stigma...a planned all-British Customs Union indicated the end of free trade."

During the war Helfferich had railed against the confiscation in Singapore of German homes, private possessions and companies, including all of Behn Meyer's assets. He was upset to hear of friends languishing in Australian internment camps. After the war he suffered petty humiliations aboard foreign ships and in foreign countries. He witnessed Germany's postwar disarray and destruction. The loss of his brother and parents – and Dina's illness – had taken a toll too. If called upon, he would indeed be ready "to work hard in the service of the fatherland."

⚜

In the Reichstag elections of May, 1928, the Nazi party won twelve seats. The rabble-rousing demagogue Joseph Goebbels occupied one of those seats. In another sat Hermann Goering, recently discharged from a Swedish asylum for the criminally insane and still recovering from an addiction to morphine. Heinrich Himmler had joined the SS, Hitler's personal bodyguard, and would assume its leadership within months.

One year earlier, German judges had lifted the ban which prevented Hitler from speaking in public. They let slip the basilisk, the king of serpents, upon the masses. Like the mythical reptile, with a lethal stare that turned a man to stone, his eyes glowed with a fanatical inner light that transfixed his audience. On August 21, 1927 he staged the Nazi party's first rally at Nuremberg. More than twenty thousand brown-shirted SA men stood to attention and listened to the charismatic voice of their *Führer*. A band of Hitler Youth joined in the celebration. Seventy thousand men and women now claimed membership in the Nazi party.

⚜

On a July morning in 1928 Emil and Dina drove for the last time in the Hudson to the dock at Tanjung Priok. Their two Airedale retrievers, Minka and Stromer, sat on the back seat and poked their heads out the window. Tails wagging, they trotted up the gangplank with their masters, the only passengers aboard *Rendsburg*. She was a freighter of the Hapag line, a slow boat to Europe, bound for Hamburg. Helfferich wanted to feel like a sailor on a real working ship. After the exciting but exhausting round of parties and farewells, he looked forward to a relaxing homeward voyage. He would assist the captain with the ship's accounts while Dina helped wash the laundry. This was obviously his idea.

The horn blew as the freighter pulled away from the dock. Dozens of handkerchiefs fluttered in the hands of well-wishers. Emil Helfferich smiled bravely and waved to the crowd. He felt that a ring had closed around his life, a career that had begun one morning in 1899 off Penang when his golden ring slipped into the waves. A ring encircled his finest achievements in the Indies – his "Eastern bride," all that was good and wholesome. Beyond lay the unknown. In the receding distance he spied the peaks of the two giants, Gede and Pangrango.

> *Was winkst du mir, mein Berg Gedeh?*
> *Schon schliesst sich über mir die See.*

> My mountain Gede, why do you wave at me?
> Over me slowly closes the sea.

This poem and many others appeared at that precise moment on the doorsteps of hundreds of Helfferich's friends in Batavia. Dina had collected all the poems he had ever written. She had this opus printed and bound, with instructions to distribute the books after the ship left the dock. His friends could now read that, "I rode into the glow of the dawn...I must show you the magic of life's splendour...Love, I shall whisper to thee in poems...Never again will grief enter my heart...."

Rendsburg sailed through the Sunda Strait, past the lighthouse at Anyer, the dock at Teluk Betung and the long-dead sea monsters vanquished by Tunku Tiga. The black islands of old Krakatau, three-cornered like a pirate's hat, lurked in the centre of the strait. One year earlier, bubbles welled up from the deep between the islands and roiled the choppy surface. Fountains of water gushed from the sea. Pumice and ash exploded out of the ocean and flames flickered on the water. On January 26, 1928, one week after Helfferich's fiftieth birthday, the baleful child of Krakatau rose for the first time above the waves.

The freighter stopped in Padang on the west coast of Sumatra to take on cargo. Just four months before her arrival, a German warship had paid a courtesy call in the same harbour. The new *Emden* was the first ship of the German Navy to be christened after the war and the second, after *Hamburg*, to visit the Dutch East Indies. Unlike her famous namesake she had only two funnels, not three, and she had no need of a false fourth. The new German consul, Paul Schneewind, welcomed the crew to a party and dance, where Johann Schild brought the history of *Emden* to life. Schild had been the German consul in Padang for 27 years and now filled the post of consul for Austria. In 1914 he had arranged the secret rendezvous between the collier *Choising* and the schooner *Ayesha*, manned by Lieutenant von Mücke's stalwart band. After the speech and the dance *Emden* sailed away to the south. She laid a wreath on the wreck of the old *Emden*, beached forlornly on the island of North Keeling.

When *Rendsburg* arrived in Padang a few months later, Paul Schneewind invited *Herr* Helfferich and *Frau* Uhlenbeck into his home. He gave them two sacks of Sumatran coffee as a parting gift and introduced them to his wife and four children. Schneewind's eldest son, eleven-year-old Fritz, stepped forward and told them all about the visit of *Emden*. He wanted to go to school in Germany and join the navy.

"That's what I wanted to do, too, when I was your age," Helfferich replied. He tapped his thick eyeglasses. "But my eyesight wasn't good enough. I had to join the army instead. Maybe you'll have better luck." The young boy would indeed join the navy and emulate the heroes of *Emden*. One day he would pilot a "Monsoon" U-boat into history.

Helfferich's departure from Padang, a city famous for hot peppers and spicy *sambal*, was a fitting end to a career which began as a humble pepper trader in nearby Lampung. Like his fictional counterpart, Lord Jim, he had lived and worked by "the sea with its labouring waves for ever rising, sinking and vanishing to rise again." In the exposed ocean off the northern tip of Sumatra, the Queen of the South Sea, *Nyai* Roro Kidul, bid them farewell. A monsoon storm struck the ship hard. Enormous green waves crashed over the deck. Salt spray lashed the windscreen on the bridge. Helfferich gripped the railing on the upper deck and rode giddily up the flank of each wave and down, down into the gaping trough. Pants and jacket flapping, his beard flying in the wind, he shouted aloud in pure childlike joy.

On August 7, in the sultry calm of the Red Sea, Emil and Dina toasted each other on the twenty-fifth anniversary of their chance encounter on *Australien*. Through the Suez Canal they sailed, past Crete and Gibraltar and on to the English Channel. On a hot summer day *Rendsburg* entered the narrow North Sea Canal at Ijmuiden and docked at Amsterdam to unload cargo. Like a truant schoolboy, Georg Rademacher drove down from Hamburg and ran aboard to join Emil and Dina on deck. For a few brief minutes the two grey-haired men leaned side by side on the railing of "*Prinz Heinrich*" and watched the bustling harbour of "Penang" below them. Helfferich patted the new, more reliable fountain pen in his pocket. At dawn several days later, he whimsically donned a batik sarong and stood beside the ship's captain on the bridge. They steamed up the Elbe and came to a final stop at the dock in Hamburg, the city where his dream began. Their new home lay on the hillside above.

The fifty-seven red-striped crates overwhelmed Dina's "sunhouse." For several weeks the newcomers stayed with Georg Rademacher and his wife

while they debated what to do. With timely good luck they found a perfect house just down the street from the Rademachers. A large red brick
mansion with beautiful gardens crowned a hill overlooking the river. Dina
christened their new home "Artja an der Elbe."

PASSAGES

The Eagle and the Serpent

In 1999 I left Indonesia with mixed emotions. Emil Helfferich would have understood the dilemma – the loss of friends, the excitement of departure, the tug of the homeland, the sadness of leaving one place forever and the fear of disappointment in another. They say that one can never really go home but we were both fiftyish and had lived full lives in Southeast Asia. Though eager to move on, we left behind secure jobs and a supportive community. However, I failed to match his penchant for souvenir collection and I fell far short of his record fifty-seven red-striped crates. His treasures now reside in Neustadt for all to see.

Amid the turmoil of the post-Suharto era, I witnessed a weak democracy replace a brutal dictatorship. Old afflictions resurfaced and spread – religious fundamentalism, crime and rampant corruption. Tanks and taxi bandits cruised the streets of Jakarta. This was a part of the Indonesian scene that I would not miss. But there was a more wistful side that I was loath to leave behind. Indonesians have a word for the feeling – *rindu alam*, a yearning for nature as it used to be. In the Puncak hills above Jakarta one can dine in a restaurant of the same name and come to appreciate the meaning. Modern Indonesia streams by the window – cars, trucks and buses squeezing through an endless corridor of ramshackle roadside shops. Far above, beyond the crowd and the cacophony, an ancient forest rises gracefully to the summits of the giants, Gede and Pangrango.

Like Helfferich, I too found solace on the slopes of these enchanted mountains, high in the cool clean air, far from the noise and the bustle. Before leaving the country I hiked the "Artja Domas Trail" one last time with a large group – *Pater* Heuken, Robby Ko, Nanno Nommensen and other friends. After crossing streams and wending our way through miles of tea plantation and jungle, we rested in the shade of the old *waringin* trees at Artja. Adja welcomed us to his tidy cemetery and hovered shyly in the shadows. The middle-aged members of our group sported walking sticks and old character hats. I thought of Easter Sunday, 1923, when Helfferich, the baron and the duke – in feathered hats and *Lederhosen* – had hiked the same trail and stood in the same spot.

One journey was ending and another beginning. My *Jakarta Hike and Bike Trail Guide* was now in print and I had retired as Scoutmaster. The cenotaph reminded me of *Pater* Heuken's insistence that I write a book. "Start with Helfferich," he had said, when he showed me *Ein Leben* and the 1903 painting of Dina. Robby Ko, on the other hand, had advised me not "to bring it to the open" because it was "NOT TACTFUL" to the Germans. He changed his mind, of course. His enthusiasm for natural history and the legends of Artja Domas overwhelmed any concern he might have had for German feelings. We planned a future trip together to the homeland of the reclusive Baduy tribe, to learn more about their curious rituals and their sanctuary in the Forbidden Forest.

As we relaxed in the dappled shade among the white monuments I warmed to the idea of writing a book. Much later it became obvious that the German Squadron and Helfferich's first fifty years would easily fill the pages of one volume. The ten graves from World War II demanded a separate book – the Asian U-boat saga, the interwoven tales of the Papadimitriou and Nommensen families and the darker, more sombre years of Helfferich's

life in Nazi Germany. Spun by an unseen hand, a web of uncanny connections intrigued and ensnared me – Marco Polo and the monsoon submarines, the U-boats that flew all three Axis flags, the men who survived
and the men who died, the whimsical German Republic of Nias, cannibals
and missionaries in Sumatra, a Dutch refugee camp guarded by German
submariners and Indian Sikhs, a pair of eerily similar Dutch and Japanese
prisoner ships, a railroad across Sumatra and a bridge to Artja Domas.

Shadows lengthened and the time came to leave. I said goodbye to Adja
and shook his hand for the first and last time. We left the graveyard and
started walking home down the cobblestone road. The day was fine and
a light breeze fanned the blades of windmills in the rice paddies. I remembered the rain squall after the *Volkstrauertag* ceremony, when I had
stumbled down the slippery path with a banana leaf on my head. On that
turbulent afternoon I had followed a woman in a green sarong down the
mountain. Adja was pulling my leg, surely, when he said she was the sea
goddess. I turned around to wave but he was already gone.

In 1928 Emil Helfferich and Dina Uhlenbeck-Ermeling left the Dutch
East Indies forever. They sailed past the coast of Java and Sumatra into
a gathering storm and an uncertain future. The cinder-black child of
Krakatau rose from the sea, hissing and gurgling in the ship's wake. The
surf pounded the shore in an endless rhythm, resonant with the cadence
of the *gamelan* – the crash of the drum, the tinkle of the *gambang* and
the echo of the gong. In a wild monsoon gale the sea goddess bid them
farewell....

> *"...she rose, and on the gale*
> *Loosening her star-bright robe and shadowy hair*
> *Poured forth her voice; the caverns of the vale*
> *That opened to the ocean, caught it there,*
> *And filled with silver sounds the overflowing air."*

The sea goddess, *Nyai* Roro Kidul, crested the waves with her army of sea spirits, all fully armed. Her hair flew in the wind and she turned to speak.

"Such is this conflict - when mankind doth strive
With its oppressors in a strife of blood...
The Snake and Eagle meet - the world's foundations tremble!"

"This shalt thou know, and more, if thou dost dare
With me and with this Serpent, o'er the deep,
A voyage divine and strange, companionship to keep."

She bid them heed *"the dark tale which history doth unfold"* and then she vanished beneath the waves.

⁂

On the slope of the mountain at Artja, women in colourful sarongs and wide-brimmed hats picked tea leaves off the bushes. Sinewy men carried firewood and vegetables down to the market and drove buffaloes through the mud of rice paddies. Among the bushes surrounding the plantation villa, Schmidtmann's children played tag. A five-year-old boy, Mohamad Syarib, watched the European children from the shade of an enormous fig tree. His father was German, a retired plantation foreman, and his mother was Sundanese. He was sad because the children wouldn't play with him. His mother was depressed because his father refused to convert to Islam and had gone home to Germany without them. She took solace in her religion and taught Mohamad verses from the Koran. She hoped that one day he would go on the *haj*, a goal that she herself had long since abandoned.

Higher up on the ridge another Sundanese mother suckled her infant boy, Adja. She and her husband found occasional release from the drudgery of farm chores by watching shadow puppet shows – all-night performances of the Ramayana epic accompanied by a *gamelan* orchestra. She stroked her baby's head and dreamed of the day he would be a famous *dalang*, a puppet-master in the Sultan's court.

The white cottage stood empty on the hillside. Schmidtmann used it when he toured the upper levels of the plantation. His workers tended the red and white roses but let the grass grow wild. A green patina of age crept slowly over the white monuments. Only a few people ever came to visit. In 1928 there were no U-boat sailors and no Iron Crosses – only spirits in the trees and the mute remains of eight hundred stone soldiers.

The four trees towered above the deserted graveyard. The trunks were ancient and immense, gnarled and twisted like the spindly arms and legs of grey goblins. A serpent-eagle rested in the highest branches and surveyed the scene below. Her yellow eye caught a slight movement, a shifting shadow. A long sinuous shape slithered through the weeds beyond the pillar. Golden rings adorned the muscular grey body of a young king cobra, the Hindu manifestation of Siva, the god of beasts and the father of Ganesha. The snake passed the warlike elephant god and approached the Buddha, raising its hood as it reared off the ground. The serpent tested the air with its flickering tongue and scanned its surroundings with slitted eyes. Its fearsome gaze and its venomous bite paralyzed its victims and turned them to stone.

The eagle watched the serpent glide past the black stone wall and disappear into the bushes beneath the old trees. The cobra was too big and too dangerous to pursue. She faced the mountain, took wing and soared away.

Waringin Tree at Artja

MAPS

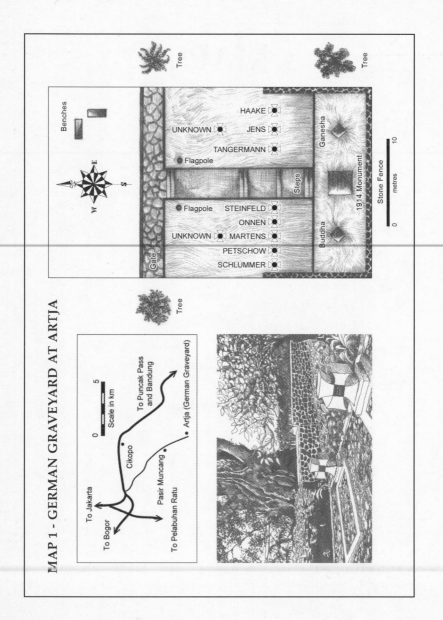

MAP 1 - GERMAN GRAVEYARD AT ARTJA

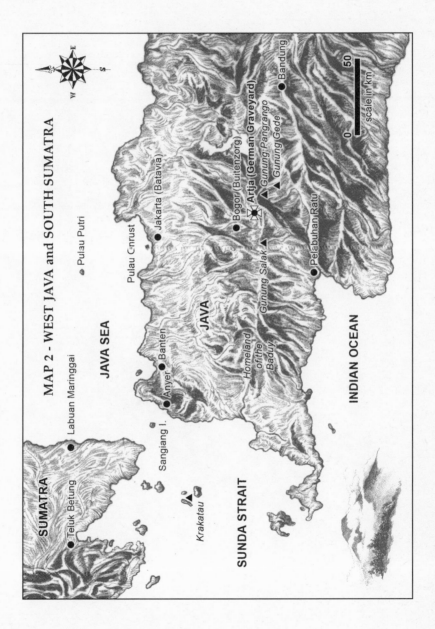

MAP 2 - WEST JAVA and SOUTH SUMATRA

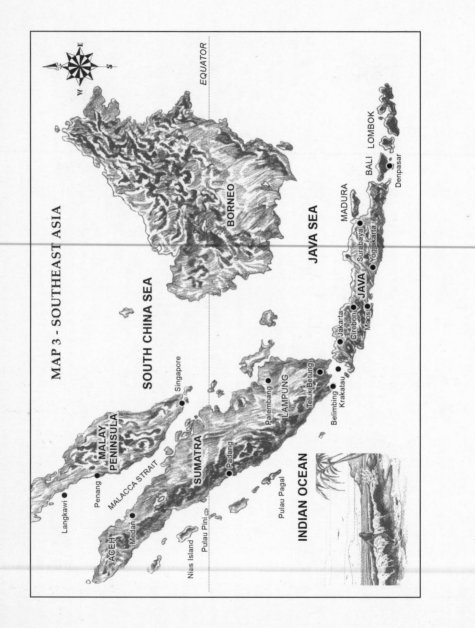

MAP 3 - SOUTHEAST ASIA

EQUATOR

N
W   E
S

BORNEO

SOUTH CHINA SEA

JAVA SEA

MADURA

Surabaya
Yogjakarta

BALI   LOMBOK

Denpasar

JAVA

Jakarta
Cirebon
Meos

MALAY
PENINSULA

Singapore

Langkawi

Penang

MALACCA STRAIT

SUMATRA

LAMPUNG

Palembang

Teluk Betung

Belimbing

Krakatau

Padang

ACEH

Medan

Pulau Pini

Nias Island

Pulau Pagal

INDIAN OCEAN

MAP 4 - THE OLD WORLD

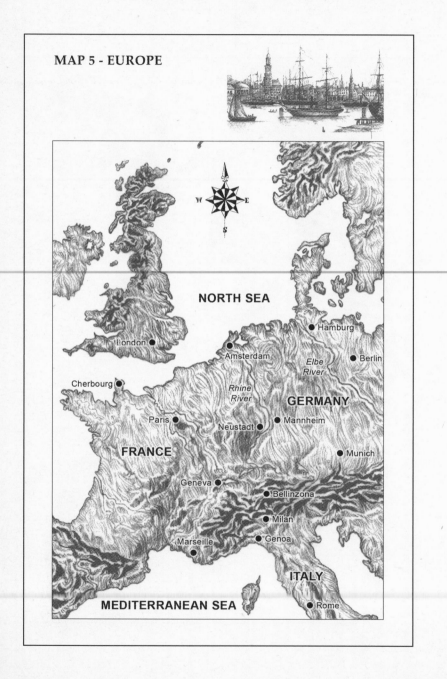

MAP 5 - EUROPE

NORTH SEA

● Hamburg

London ●

● Amsterdam

Elbe River

● Berlin

Cherbourg ●

Rhine River

GERMANY

Paris ●

Neustadt ●

● Mannheim

FRANCE

● Munich

Geneva ●

● Bellinzona

● Milan

Marseille ●

● Genoa

ITALY

MEDITERRANEAN SEA

● Rome

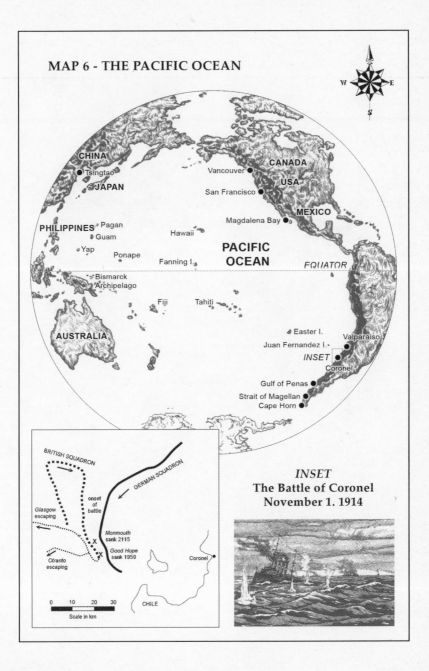

MAP 6 - THE PACIFIC OCEAN

CHINA
Tsingtao
JAPAN

Vancouver
San Francisco

CANADA
USA

Magdalena Bay

MEXICO

PHILIPPINES
Pagan
Guam
Yap
Ponape

Hawaii

Fanning I.

PACIFIC
OCEAN

EQUATOR

Bismarck
Archipelago

Fiji   Tahiti

AUSTRALIA

Easter I.
Juan Fernandez I.

Valparaiso

INSET

Coronel

Gulf of Penas

Strait of Magellan
Cape Horn

INSET
**The Battle of Coronel
November 1. 1914**

BRITISH SQUADRON

GERMAN SQUADRON

onset
of
battle

Glasgow
escaping

Monmouth
sank 2115

Good Hope
sank 1950

Otranto
escaping

Coronel

CHILE

0   10   20   30
Scale in km

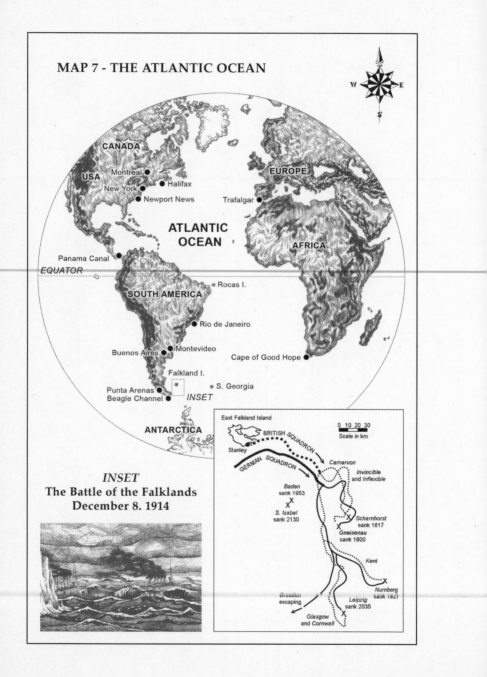

MAP 7 - THE ATLANTIC OCEAN

CANADA

USA
Montreal
New York
Halifax
Newport News

EUROPE

Trafalgar

ATLANTIC OCEAN

AFRICA

Panama Canal

EQUATOR

Rocas I.

SOUTH AMERICA

Rio de Janeiro

Buenos Aires
Montevideo

Cape of Good Hope

Falkland I.

Punta Arenas
Beagle Channel
INSET
S. Georgia

ANTARCTICA

INSET
The Battle of the Falklands
December 8. 1914

East Falkland Island

Stanley

BRITISH SQUADRON

GERMAN SQUADRON

Carnarvon

Invincible
and Inflexible

0 10 20 30
Scale in km

Baden
sank 1953

S. Isabel
sank 2130

Scharnhorst
sank 1617

Gneisenau
sank 1800

Kent

Nurnberg
sank 1927

Dresden
escaping

Leipzig
sank 2035

Glasgow
and Cornwall

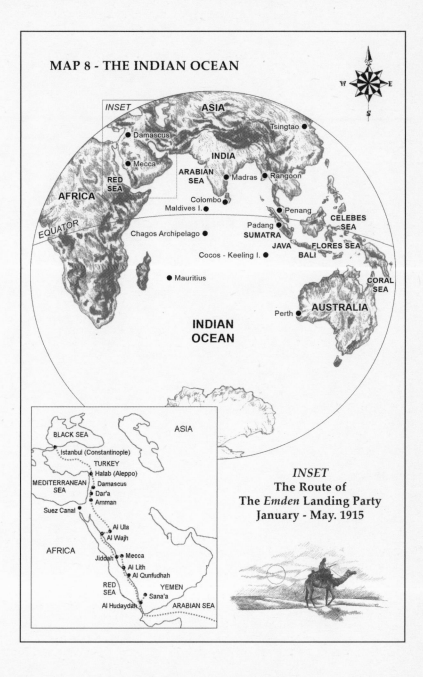

MAP 8 - THE INDIAN OCEAN

ASIA

Tsingtao

INSET

Damascus

INDIA

Mecca

ARABIAN
SEA

Madras

Rangoon

RED
SEA

AFRICA

Colombo

Penang

Maldives I.

CELEBES
SEA

EQUATOR

Chagos Archipelago

Padang

SUMATRA

Cocos - Keeling I.

JAVA

FLORES SEA

BALI

Mauritius

CORAL
SEA

INDIAN
OCEAN

Perth

AUSTRALIA

BLACK SEA

ASIA

Istanbul (Constantinople)

TURKEY

Halab (Aleppo)

MEDITERRANEAN
SEA

Damascus

Dar'a

Amman

Suez Canal

Al Ula

Al Wajh

AFRICA

Mecca

Jiddah

Al Lith

Al Qunfudhah

RED
SEA

YEMEN

Sana'a

Al Hudaydah

ARABIAN SEA

INSET
The Route of
The *Emden* Landing Party
January - May. 1915

SOURCES

Affandi, Soleh. *Tungku Tiga – A Tale from Sumatra*. PT Rosda Jayaputra, Jakarta, 1991.

Bennett, Geoff. *The Jakarta Hike and Bike Trail Guide*. Jakarta, 1998.

Bennett, Geoffrey (no relation to author). *Coronel and the Falklands*. B.T. Batsford Ltd, London, 1962.

Carnegie Endowment for International Peace. *Official German Documents Relating to the World War, Vol II*. Oxford University Press, New York, 1923.

Conrad, Joseph. *Lord Jim*. Dodd, Mead & Co, NY, no date (first edition printed in London, 1900).

Deutsche Wacht. *Besuch des Schulkreuzers "Hamburg" in Niederländisch Indien*. Batavia, October, 1926.

Deutsche Wacht. *Obituary for Theodor Helfferich*. Batavia, 1931.

Dixon, T.B. *The Enemy Fought Splendidly*. Blandford Press, Poole, Dorset, 1983.

Djoewisno, M.S. *Potret Kehidupan Masyarakat Baduy*. Khas Studio, Jakarta, 1987. (In Indonesian)

Dylan, Bob. Lyrics to *"Blowin' in the Wind."* Copyright 1962 Warner Bros. Inc. Renewed 1990 Special Rider Music.

Erdmann, Karl Dietrich, ed. *Rietzler, Kurt: Tagebücher, Aufsätze, Dokumente*. Göttingen, 1972.

Frederick, William H. and Robert L. Worden, eds. *Indonesia – a country study*. Federal Research Division, Library of Congress, 1992.

Gisevius, Hans Bernd. *To the Bitter End*. Houghton Mifflin Company, The Riverside Press, Boston, 1947.

Gobius, A. A.. *Gids voor Buitenzorg en omstreken*. Kolff, Batavia, 1905.

Harris, Keith. *Cibodas to Cibeureum, Mt. Gede Pangrango National Park*. Grafimatra, Jakarta, 1994.

Helfferich, Emil. *Erlebtes*. Hanseatische Verlagsanstalt, Hamburg, 1938.

Helfferich, Emil. *Ein Leben*. Volume I. Hans Dulk, Hamburg, 1948.

Helfferich, Emil. *Südostasiatische Geschichten*. C.L. Mettcker & Söhne, Jever/Oldenburg, 1966.

Helfferich, Emil. *Zur Geschichte der Firme Behn, Meyer & Co.* Volume II. Hans Christian Verlag, Hamburg, 1967.

Helfferich, Emil. *Behn, Meyer & Co. and Arnold Otto Meyer*. Volumes I and II. Translated from the 1967 edition by Heidi Hartmann and Douglas Earp. Hans Christians Verlag, Hamburg, 1981.

Heuken, Adolf. *Historical Sites of Jakarta*. 6th Edition. Yayasan Cipta Loka Caraka, Jakarta, 2000.

Hoyt, Edwin P. *Defeat at the Falklands*. Robert Hale, London, 1981.

Irving, John. *Coronel and the Falklands*. A.M. Philpot Ltd, London, 1927.

Keats, John. *Keats – Poetical Works*. Edited by H.W. Garrod, Oxford University Press, London, 1966.

Kipling, Rudyard. *Rudyard Kipling's Verse*. Definitive Edition, Hodder and Stoughton Ltd, London, 1969.

Kipling Rudyard. "The Crab that Played with the Sea" in *Just So Stories*, MacMillan Children's Books, London, 1984.

Knappert, Jan. *Myths and Legends of Indonesia*. Heinemann Educational Books (Asia) Ltd, 1977.

Knappert, Jan. *Pacific Mythology – An Encyclopedia of Myth and Legend*. Diamond Books, London, 1995.

Lange, Thomas & Jo Forty. *Beers*. PRC Publishing Ltd, London, 1998.

Lawrence, T.E. *The Seven Pillars of Wisdom*. G.H. Doran, New York, 1926.

Lee Khoon Choy. *Indonesia between Myth and Reality*. Nile & Mackenzie Ltd., London, 1976.

Lennon, John. Lyrics to "*Imagine*". Lenono Music/BMG Music Publishing Ltd, 1971.

Lochner, R.K. *The Last Gentleman-of-War*. Translated by Thea and Harry Lindauer. Naval Institute Press, Annapolis, Maryland, 1988.

Milner, Marc "The Original Rainbow Warrior" in *Legion Magazine*, Ottawa, May/June 2004.

Das Ostasieninstitut der Fachhochschule Ludwigshafen. *Die Helfferich-Sammlung der Stadt Neustadt an der Weinstrasse*. CD-ROM, 2002.

Pitt, Barrie. *Revenge at Sea*. Stein & Day, NY, 1964.

Pramoedya Ananta Toer. *Internet article on Sukarno*, 1999.

Ricklefs, M.C. *Jogjakarta under Sultan Mangkubumi, 1749-1792: a history of the division of Java*. Oxford University Press, London, 1974.

Sandburg, Carl. *The People, Yes*. Harcourt Brace & Co, Florida, 1936.

Satjadibrata, V.R. *Artja Domas*. From Dongeng-dongeng Sasakala (Stories of ancient Java, including the tale of the stone soldiers), no date.

Sekapur Sirih Foundation and the Japan Foundation. *Baduy Culture Exhibition*. Jakarta, September, 1998.

Selosoemardjan. *Social Changes in Jogjakarta*. Cornell University Press, 1962.

Shelley, Percy Bysshe. *Shelley – Poetical Works*. Edited by Thomas Hutchinson, Oxford University Press, London, 1967.

Smithies, Michael. *Yogyakarta*. Oxford University Press, 1986.

Sukarno. *An Autobiography as told to Cindy Adams*. The Bobbs-Merrill Company, 1965.

Tempo. *Badui*. Written by Riza Sofyat, Jakarta, 25 Aug 1990.

Thurston, Arthur. *Midshipman Cann*. ISBN 0-921596-03-0. Yarmouth, Canada. 1991.

Van der Vat, Dan. *The Last Corsair – The Story of the Emden*. Hodder and Stoughton, London, 1983.

Voice of Nature. *The Baduy Face the Twentieth Century*. Written by Nurhadi Rangkuti, Jakarta, 1987.

Von Hohenzollern, Prince Franz Joseph. *Emden*. Herbert Jenkins Ltd, London, no date (circa 1920).

Von Mücke, Hellmuth. *The "Ayesha."* Edited by J.G. Lockhart. Philip Allan & Co., London, 1930.

Williamson, John G. *Karl Helfferich 1872-1924 – Economist, Financier, Politician*. Princeton University Press, 1971.

Willumsen, Peter. *Krakatau – Events and Geology*. Printing sponsored by the Indonesian Petroleum Association, Jakarta, 1997.

352   THE PEPPER TRADER

Winchester, Simon. *Krakatoa*. HarperCollins Publishers, NY, 2003.
Wright, Bruce. *Midshipman Hatheway*. In *The Atlantic Advocate*, Halifax, July 1968.
Zimmer, Helen, tr. *Beyond Good and Evil*. Modern Library Edition no. 244, no date.

Additional oral and written contributions from Robby Ko, Adolf Heuken, Alex Papadimitriou, Nanno Nommensen, Jörg Helfferich, Bevan Slater, Ed McKinnon, Adja, Suparman, Mohamad Syarib (1997-2005).

SOURCES FOR EACH CHAPTER

CHAPTER 1 – PUPPET-MASTER
  Helfferich (1948) – New Year 1928 from the chapter *Die letzten Jahre draussen*
CHAPTER 2 – THE SERPENT-EAGLE
  Heuken (2000) – Jakarta history
CHAPTER 3 – A DAY OF REMEMBRANCE
  None
CHAPTER 4 – QUEEN OF THE SOUTHERN OCEAN
  Helfferich (1948) – 1926 ceremony from the chapter *Die letzten Jahre draussen*
  Knappert (1977) – *Ratu* Kidul and Senopati
  Knappert (1995) – details of the Sea Goddess, *Ratu* Kidul
  Ricklefs (1974) – excerpts from *Sěrat Sakondar*
  Selosoemardjan (1962) – predictions by *Ratu* Kidul
  Smithies (1986) – historical facts regarding Senopati and Sultan Agung
CHAPTER 5 – A VOYAGE DIVINE AND STRANGE
  Shelley (1967) – excerpts from "The Revolt of Islam"
CHAPTER 6 – THE RHINE AND THE ELBE
  Helfferich (1948) – Emil's life from childhood to Penang
  Williamson (1971) – history of Neustadt

CHAPTER 7 – SUMATRA PEPPER TRADER
> Affandi (1991) – Tungku Tiga
> Conrad (1900) – quotations from *Lord Jim*
> Harris (1994) – the natural history of Gunung Gede
> Helfferich (1938) – Helfferich's stories from Teluk Betung
> Helfferich (1948) – Helfferich's life and business in Teluk Betung from the chapter *Romantik im Osten*
> Helfferich (1966) – Mr. and Mrs. Wood, Po Tjong
> Helfferich (1981) – 1901 economic conditions
> Willumsen (1997) – Krakatau
> Winchester (2003) – Krakatau

CHAPTER 8 – A SHIPBOARD ROMANCE
> Helfferich (1948) – Jeanne and Dina – from the chapter *Die Grosse Gnade*

CHAPTER 9 – HARMONIE IN BATAVIA
> Conrad (1900) – quotations from *Lord Jim*
> Helfferich (1938) – Bali massacre, from chapter 3: *Bilder aus Insulinde*, taken from a book by van Weede
> Helfferich (1948) – his life in Batavia from 1903-1907 from the chapter *Batavia*
> Kipling (1969) – quotation from "Departmental Ditties, 1885"
> Kipling (1984) – quotation from "The Crab that played with the Sea"
> Winchester (2003) – Krakatau

CHAPTER 10 – THE CHINESE FORTUNE-TELLER
> Deutsche Wacht (1931) – Theodor's career up to 1907
> Helfferich (1948) – Paulmann's disappearance from the chapter *Batavia*; other stories from the chapter *Die Grosse Pfeffertransaktion*
> Helfferich (1981) – Behn Meyer history 1908
> Shelley (1967) – quotations from "The Revolt of Islam" and "Ozymandias"

CHAPTER 11 – TEA AT CIKOPO
> Conrad (1900) – quotations from *Lord Jim*
> Helfferich (1948) – from the chapters *Die Rehabilitierung, Die Neue Aufgabe*, and *Straits und Sunda Syndikat*
> Helfferich (1981) – rubber industry and details of Behn, Meyer history
> Williamson (1971) – early career of Karl Helfferich

CHAPTER 12 – STONE SOLDIERS

    Dylan (1990) – lyrics to "Blowin' in the Wind"

    Gobius (1905) – myth of the stone soldiers

    Heuken (2000) – Pajajaran history

    Keats (1966) – quotations from "Ode on a Grecian Urn"

    Satjadibrata (no date) – myth of the stone soldiers

CHAPTER 13 – THE BATTLE OF CORONEL

    Bennett (1962) – German East Asia Squadron, Battle of Coronel

    Dixon (1983) – coaling operations at sea

    Helfferich (1948) – visits to Batavia of German ships from the chapter *Batavia*

    Helfferich (1981) – prewar history of Germans and Behn, Meyer in Singapore

    Hoyt (1981) – Tsingtao history, German East Asia Squadron, Battle of Coronel

    Irving (1927) – Battle of Coronel

    Lange (1998) – Tsingtao beer

    Milner (2004) – *Rainbow*

    Pitt (1964) – Battle of Coronel

    Thurston (1991) – Canadian midshipmen

    Van der Vat (1983) – German East Asia Squadron

    Winchester (2003) – Krakatau and *Elisabeth*

    Wright (1968) – Canadian midshipmen

CHAPTER 14 – SWAN OF THE EAST

    Hoyt (1981) – *Emden* career

    Lochner (1988) – *Emden* career

    Van der Vat (1983) – *Emden* career, quote from Schiller

    Von Hohenzollern (no date) – *Emden* career

CHAPTER 15 – THE BATTLE OF THE FALKLANDS

    Bennett (1962) – Falklands

    Dixon (1983) – Falklands and *Dresden*

    Hoyt (1981) – Falklands

    Irving (1927) – Falklands

    Pitt (1964) – Falklands

    Shelley (1967) – quotations from "The Revolt of Islam"

    Thurston (1991) – Canadian midshipmen, Falklands war preparations

CHAPTER 16 – SHIPS OF THE DESERT
    Hoyt (1981) – *Ayesha* and the landing crew of *Emden*
    Lawrence (1926) – quotation from "The Seven Pillars of Wisdom"
    Von Mücke (1930) – *Ayesha* and the landing crew of *Emden*
    Van der Vat (1983) – *Ayesha* and the landing crew of *Emden*

CHAPTER 17 – THE FLIGHT OF *DRESDEN*
    Bennett (1962) – *Dresden*
    Dixon (1983) – *Dresden*
    Gisevius (1947) – Canaris
    Hoyt (1981) – *Dresden*
    Irving (1927) – *Dresden*
    Lennon (1971) – lyrics from "Imagine"
    Pitt (1964) – *Dresden*
    Sandburg (1936) – quotation from *The People, Yes*

CHAPTER 18 – THE QUEEN'S HARBOUR
    Djoewisno (1987) – Baduy facts
    Heuken (2000) – the cannon Si Jagur, Jan Coen, Kota Tahi
    Lee (1976) – description of the Baduy and Yakmin; story of the cannon Si Jagur
    Ricklefs (1974) – story of Sang Putri, Sukmul, Djangkoeng, Kota Tahi
    Sekapur Sirih Foundation and the Japan Foundation (1998) – Baduy quotation
    Tempo (1990) – Baduy facts
    Voice of Nature (1987) – Baduy facts

CHAPTER 19 – MAROONED SAILORS
    Helfferich (1948) – Helfferich's life in Batavia during WWI – from the chapter *Der Erste Weltkrieg 1914/1920*
    Helfferich (1966) – stories of the German sailors - from the chapter *Seeleute*
    Helfferich (1981) – wartime economic conditions in Batavia

CHAPTER 20 – KARL HELFFERICH
    Carnegie Endowment for International Peace (1923) – quotation from Karl Helfferich regarding submarine warfare
    Erdmann (1972) – quotation from Kurt Rietzler
    Helfferich (1948) – Helfferich's trip to Europe after WWI – from the chapter *Die Nachkriegszeit 1920/1924*

Helfferich (1981) – Schönberg and the submarine *Deutschland*

Williamson (1971) – Karl Helfferich's career during WWI and afterward

Zimmer (no date) – quotation from Friedrich Nietzsche

CHAPTER 21 – THE TRAINS OF BELLINZONA

Frederick and Worden (1992) – 20th century Indonesian political history

Helfferich (1948) – Helfferich's postwar life in Batavia - from the chapter *Die Nachkriegszeit 1920/1924* and *Die erste Japanreise*

Pramoedya (1999) – Sukarno and Cokroaminoto

(1971) – Karl Helfferich's death

CHAPTER 22 – FAREWELL TO ARTJA

Deutsche Wacht (1926) – visit of *Hamburg* to Batavia, dedication ceremony at Artja

Helfferich (1938) – Egloffstein, the visit of the Duke, and Artja - from the chapter *Eine Osterfahrt mit Herzog Adolf Friedrich*

Helfferich (1948) – Emil and Dina's last years in Batavia from the chapters *Die Nachkriegszeit, Der Schatten, Die letzten Jahre draussen,* and *Heimkehr und Weltwirtschaftskrise.*

Helfferich (1966) – Egloffstein and Sassih

PASSAGES

Bennett (1998) – the "Artja Domas Trail"

Shelley (1967) – excerpts from "The Revolt of Islam"

MAPS

Bennett (1962) – Battle of the Falklands

Pitt (1964) – Battle of Coronel

ACKNOWLEDGEMENTS

This project would never have been completed without the help of the following people, listed here in approximate alphabetical order.

Adja and his wife **Imas** looked after the German cemetery at Artja until Adja's death in 2002. They never failed to greet me on my frequent visits and to chat beneath the huge fig trees.

Lorraine Bennett read the book in its formative stages and offered valuable advice on content and style.

Gary and Charlene Butler alerted me to the memorial in Port Stanley

Rory Clancy, with his love of walking and an Irish gift for story-telling, took an early interest in the Artja Domas trail.

The late **Dr. James Clements**, of Ibis Publishing, edited the manuscript for stylistic and other errors. His support and enthusiasm will be greatly missed.

Berdina DeRidder of Cadboro Bay Book Company, Victoria, provided support and useful advice from a bookseller's perspective.

Karel Doruyter not only produced the cover and all the illustrations but became an unflagging supporter of this project and a stalwart friend.

John Dyck, **Tim Kelly** and **Richard Lorentz** tackled the ticklish business of reading a friend's book and suggested a number of useful changes to the manuscript.

Chris Gibson-Robinson, a former editor, read an early edition of this book and offered valuable advice on splitting the book into two parts as well as comments on characters and style.

358   THE PEPPER TRADER

Roger Gould described for me his personal account of a pilgrimage to Mecca.

Mark Hanusz, the publisher of Equinox, agreed to take on this project with all of its risks and unknowns.

Gretel Harmston visited the Helfferich family in Neustadt and persuaded Jörg Helfferich **to** contribute books and information about Emil's life.

Michael Harrison, publisher, offered several useful comments after reading the initial chapters.

Colonel Bruno Hasenpusch and other staff members of the **German Embassy in Jakarta** provided a raft of documents and enthusiastic support.

Don Hasman showed me his collection of Baduy photographs and shared with me his extensive knowledge of the Baduy tribe.

Jörg Helfferich, the great-nephew of Emil Helfferich, is custodian of the family archives. He sent me a CD of the Helfferich Collection, allowed me to borrow several privately printed books and contributed personal insights into the lives of Emil and Dina.

Gus van Heusden and **Marijke Moerman** translated Dutch books and documents, some from an old version of the Dutch language.

Patrick Hunt, a retired submarine commander, edited the U-boat stories for correct terminology.

Hans-Joachim Krug, the author of *Reluctant Allies*, gave me an eye-witness account of his voyage on *U-219* and his subsequent adventures on Java.

Maria Lawrence, an artist in Victoria and a member of the Island Illustrators group, introduced me to Karel Doruyter and persuaded him to produce illustrations for the book.

Barbie Lemanski and **Barbara MacNeill** provided moral support as well as access to the Heritage Library in Jakarta.

Ed McKinnon, a devotee of Indonesian archeology and prehistory, provided articles and background information on the Hindu era and the old stones.

Nanno Nommensen, a retired soldier and the former superintendent of Dutch War Graves in Indonesia, opened my eyes to the World War II story of *Junyo Maru* and the history of the Nommensen family in the Dutch East Indies.

Alex Papadimitriou, the Greek-German-Japanese sailor who "refused to surrender," provided a huge amount of fascinating personal history and became a central character in the story. My wife and I spent many rewarding hours talking to Alex and his wife **Caecile** in her antique shop and in their well-appointed home.

Ken Pattern, a Canadian artist and long-time resident of Jakarta, supported the "Archie Domas" project from an early stage and recommended Equinox as a publisher.

Jamie Rosequist read an early edition of the book and offered advice on writing style. A published poet in her own right, she helped me refine the English translations of some of Helfferich's poems.

Andrea von Samson-Himmelstjerna sent me copies of old articles published in *Welt am Sonntag*.

The staff of **Samudra Beach Hotel**, Pelabuhan Ratu, allowed me access to the Queen's bedchamber and regaled me with stories of the sea goddess.

Margareta and **Beat Schnueriger** obtained documents from the German Embassy, helped with translations, took photos and shared with me their own keen interest in the story of Artja.

Manfred Schwencke and **Lee Nam Kwang** of Behn, Meyer & Co contributed books and background information on Behn Meyer's history in Singapore. **Francis** and **Jessie Zhan** introduced me to Mr. Lee.

Bevan Slater, a retired Canadian naval officer, alerted me to the tale of the Canadian midshipmen at Coronel and sent me documents from obscure sources in Nova Scotia.

Enrico Soekarno drafted the eight maps.

Mohamad Syarib and **Suparman**, from the village of Pasir Muncang near Artja, contributed much in the way of oral history.

Herbert Tärre wrote letters detailing his experience in the Dutch army during the Indonesian revolution. A mutual friend, **Lee Slind**, introduced me to Herbert.

René Trautnitz, Cultural and Press Affairs of the German Embassy in Jakarta, was instrumental in obtaining funding for the publication of this book.

Herwig Zahorka, a Bogor resident, shared with me the documents he found in his own enthusiastic pursuit of the story of Artja.

To the many other friends and family members who have asked, "Is your book finished yet?" – thank you for your unflagging interest and encouragement. In addition I would like to offer my thanks to a few special people who helped me with this book...

Pater **Adolf Heuken** – author, publisher and priest – provided many references, read the book at least twice and suggested many useful changes. I am grateful for the hours we spent together, discussing German and Indonesian history in the den of his stately old home and in the hills surrounding Artja.

Dr. Robby Ko provided the spark, the impetus and the enthusiasm from the very beginning. It has been a pleasure to share adventures on Java with Robby, whether hiking in the mountains, camping with Boy Scouts, spelunking in caves, visiting the Baduy tribe or talking for hours in the gazebo of his lovely home in the Puncak hills.

I am particularly grateful to my son **Andrew**, who read and critiqued several drafts of the manuscript over the years, and to my wife **Wendy**, who not only provided the traditional loyal support of a spouse throughout a project which must have seemed endless, but who spent hours and days reading, editing and discussing.

In conclusion, I beg the forgiveness of those people who appear as characters in this book. They have all been good sports, polite and good-humoured, even as I dressed them and put words in their mouths. *Terima kasih banyak.*

BIOGRAPHIES

GEOFFREY BENNETT, Born in Ottawa, Canada, Geoff Bennett has lived in six Canadian cities as well as Denver, Houston, Paris, Jakarta, Singapore and Bangkok. He studied engineering at the Royal Military College of Canada and geophysics at the University of British Columbia. For over thirty years he has worked as an exploration geophysicist, half of that time in Jakarta, Indonesia. At present he lives in Victoria, Canada, and works for Pearl Energy in Singapore. Exploration is both a profession and a hobby for Mr. Bennett. In addition to five papers on geophysics, he has published *The Jakarta Hike & Bike Trail Guide* as well as several articles on birding, Scouting, canoeing and mountaineering.

KAREL DORUYTER, Born in Rotterdam, Holland, Karel Doruyter immigrated with his sister and parents to Canada in 1953 and settled in the interior of British Columbia. His interest in art began at an early age and he held his first exhibition in 1959. At UBC he studied fine arts, philosophy and social psychology. He worked in Canada and Australia as a draughtsman, graphic artist, manpower planner and industrial psychologist. In Australia he developed an interest in boat building and design, which led to a sailing voyage across the Pacific and a subsequent business chartering expeditions to the Queen Charlotte Islands. He continued to pursue his long-time interest in painting and drawing and made it his career in the early 1990's. Exploring the BC coast and working with native artists influenced both his subject matter and style. He has displayed his artwork in many exhibitions and has illustrated four books as well as numerous magazine articles. He currently resides in Victoria in a home overlooking the sea.

INDEX

SHIPS

PLACES

GENERAL

also from **EQUINOX PUBLISHING**

NON-FICTION

NEW

**SRIRO'S DESK REFERENCE
OF INDONESIAN LAW 2006**
Andrew I. Sriro
979-3780-20-7
2006, softcover, 592 pages

NEW

**THE SECOND FRONT:
Inside Asia's Most Dangerous
Terrorist Network**
Ken Conboy
979-3780-09-6
2006, softcover, 256 pages

NEW

**WARS WITHIN:
The Story of *TEMPO*,
an Independent Magazine in
Soeharto's Indonesia**
Janet Steele
979-3780-08-8
2005, softcover, 368 pages

**SIDELINES:
Thought Pieces from
TEMPO Magazine**
Goenawan Mohamad
979-3780-07-X
2005, softcover, 260 pages

**AN ENDLESS JOURNEY:
Reflections of an
Indonesian Journalist**
Herawati Diah
979-3780-06-1
2005, softcover, 304 pages

**BULE GILA:
Tales of a Dutch Barman
in Jakarta**
Bartele Santema
979-3780-04-5
2005, softcover, 160 pages

**2005
Kiriyama Prize
Notable Book
Award
in Nonfiction**

**THE INVISIBLE PALACE:
The True Story of a
Journalist's Murder in Java**
José Manuel Tesoro
979-97964-7-4
2004, softcover, 328 pages

**INTEL: Inside Indonesia's
Intelligence Service**
Ken Conboy
979-97964-4-X
2004, softcover, 264 pages

**KOPASSUS: Inside Indonesia's
Special Forces**
Ken Conboy
979-95898-8-6
2003, softcover, 352 pages

TIMOR: A Nation Reborn
Bill Nicol
979-95898-6-X
2002, softcover, 352 pages

**GUS DUR:
The Authorized Biography of
Abdurrahman Wahid**
Greg Barton
979-95898-5-1
2002, softcover, 436 pages

**NO REGRETS: Reflections
of a Presidential Spokesman**
Wimar Witoelar
979-95898-4-3
2002, softcover, 200 pages

FICTION

NEW

SAMAN
Ayu Utami
979-378011-8
2005, softcover, 184 pages

THE SPICE GARDEN
Michael Vatikiotis
979-97964-2-3
2004, softcover, 256 pages

**THE KING, THE WITCH AND
THE PRIEST**
Pramoedya Ananta Toer
979-95898-3-5
2001, softcover, 128 pages

IT'S NOT AN ALL NIGHT FAIR
Pramoedya Ananta Toer
979-95898-2-7
2001, softcover, 120 pages